EROTIKON

EROTIKON

ESSAYS ON EROS, ANCIENT AND MODERN

Edited by Shadi Bartsch & Thomas Bartscherer

The University of Chicago Press | Chicago and London

Shadi Bartsch is a professor of classics and in the Committee on the History of Culture and the Committee on the Ancient Mediterranean World at the University of Chicago. *Thomas Bartscherer* is a doctoral candidate in the Committee on Social Thought at the University of Chicago.

The University of Chicago Press, Chicago 60637
The University of Chicago Press, Ltd., London
© 2005 by The University of Chicago
All rights reserved. Published 2005
Printed in the United States of America

14 13 12 11 10 09 08 07 06 05   1 2 3 4 5

ISBN: 0-226-03838-6 (cloth)

Library of Congress Cataloging-in-Publication Data

Erotikon : essays on eros, ancient and modern / edited by
   Shadi Bartsch & Thomas Bartscherer.
      p.   cm.
   Includes bibliographical references and index.
   ISBN 0-226-03838-6 (hardcover : alk. paper)
   1. Love.   I. Bartsch, Shadi, 1966–   II. Bartscherer, Thomas.

   BD436.E77 2005
   128'.46—dc22

                        2004022687

♾ The paper used in this publication meets the minimum requirements of the American National Standard for Information Sciences—Permanence of Paper for Printed Library Materials, ANSI Z39.48-1992.

Contents

WHAT SILENT LOVE HATH WRIT:
AN INTRODUCTION TO «EROTIKON»

SHADI BARTSCH & THOMAS BARTSCHERER

"The twenty-eighth English rendering of the *Odyssey* can hardly be a literary event." This sentiment, which opens the introduction to one curious translation of Homer's *Odyssey*, could well apply to a new anthology on eros.[1] From its earliest records, Western culture has been replete with the stories and images of eros, and there has been no shortage of teachings and treatises dedicated to the topic. *Erotikon* belongs to that long, illustrious, often scandalous tradition while simultaneously standing in its immense shadow. What role the book plays will ultimately depend on the roughly two dozen contributions that constitute it, but some preliminary remarks may help to clarify our intentions.

Erotikon draws together innovative and influential scholars and artists from many domains, including classics and art history, poetry and philosophy, theology and film. We have sought out thinkers with bold transdisciplinary agendas, writers who reach a large and diverse audience. Plato's *Symposium* is a conspicuous analogy and in some ways a precedent for our enterprise: gather a handful of contemporary luminaries, announce eros as the topic, and let the conversation begin. The colorful cast of that dialogue finds a distant echo in *Erotikon's* varied lineup. As in the *Symposium*, monologue predominates here, although each essay is followed by a direct response. And our contributors are no less contentious, no more unified in opinion, than those ancient symposiasts. The analogy is imperfect, of course, not least because the *Symposium* is the design and execution of a single mind. While Plato achieves polyvocality through

1. The translation, published under the assumed name T. E. Shaw, was in fact the work of T. E. Lawrence. His extraordinary prose rendering is still in print, now in a volume edited by Bernard Knox. We cite from the translator's note to the first edition: Homer *Odyssey*, v.

compelling artifice, we have relied on impresario zeal. Still, the key similarity bears emphasis. In lavishing his most elaborate polyphony on the dialogue dedicated to eros, Plato suggests that this topic, more than any other, inspires and demands variety; likewise, *Erotikon* proceeds from the belief that to think deeply about eros requires that one pay heed to many voices and a plurality of expressive modes. Consequently, this collection not only cuts across disciplines and historical periods but also attends to manifestations of eros in a broad array of genres and media. Moreover, the contributions themselves vary widely in tone and genre, encompassing formal essays, less formal responses, lyric poetry, and an epilogue in fiction. The book's mode of exploration has been, in a word, polymorphous; our goal, what the poet Hopkins called "pied beauty."

Although the figures treated in *Erotikon* span two millennia, the contributors are contemporary writers, and so the more recent past forms the immediate background for these essays. A cursory overview of that historical background might well begin with the publication of Sigmund Freud's *The Interpretation of Dreams* in 1900. Freud's psychoanalysis, a melding of hard science and hermeneutics, became the dominant analytical paradigm for approaching eros throughout much of the twentieth century. His theory placed biological sexual instincts firmly at the root of erotic phenomena; other manifestations of eros came to be understood via a theory of sublimation. Through the work of French theorists in the second half of the century, most notably Jacques Lacan, Freud's influence was modified, amplified, and extended. With the publication of the first volume of *The History of Sexuality* in 1976, Michel Foucault began to transform the agenda for thinking about eros, focusing attention on the historically contingent character of erotic phenomena and, more specifically, on the social and political powers at play in the constitution and comprehension of sexual experience. During the last three decades, the questions and methods articulated by Foucault have guided a great deal of the scholarly inquiry into erotic life undertaken in the humanities and social sciences.[2]

2. There are, of course, many other significant trends and players in twentieth-century efforts to bring reason and theory to bear on the erotic. To name just few salient examples: the anthropology of Bronislaw Malinowski (*Sex and Repression in Savage Society*; *The Sexual Life of Savages*) and Margaret Mead (*Coming of Age in Samoa*; *From the South Seas*); the sociological approaches of Alfred Kinsey (*Sexual Behavior in the Human Male*; *Sexual Behavior in the Human Female*) and, in a very different mode, Niklas Luhmann (*Love as Passion*); feminist theory (e.g., Simone de Beauvoir's *The Second Sex*); theology (e.g., Paul Tillich); literary and philosophical undertakings like those of Denis de Rougemont (*Love in the Western World*), Georges Bataille (*Erotism*; *The Tears of Eros*), and

These theoretical developments over the last hundred years are mirrored in the visual and literary art of the period. The work of surrealist painters and of filmmakers like Luis Buñuel and Alfred Hitchcock has deep affinities with psychoanalytic theory. Twentieth-century artists challenged restraints on their freedom to depict erotic content, and their work grew increasingly less inhibited. In literature, censorship trials marked the progress of liberation, from James Joyce's *Ulysses* through D. H. Lawrence's *Lady Chatterley's Lover* and Henry Miller's *Tropic of Cancer* to William Burroughs's *Naked Lunch*. Visual art followed a similar trajectory, passing, say, from Pablo Picasso's 1907 canvas *Les Demoiselles d'Avignon* through Yves Klein's *Anthropometries* of 1960–61 to Robert Mapplethorpe's photography in the late 1970s and early 1980s. Toward the end of the century, attention shifted to the social construction of gender, and a self-reflexive, historicist mode, an archival fascination with the history of representations of sexuality, came to the fore in art, paralleling the theoretical work of Foucault and his successors. As with much in twentieth-century art, Marcel Duchamp was prescient, destabilizing gender categories with his female alter ego, Rrose Sélavy, and reconstructing traditional motifs, pastiche-wise, with a mustached *Mona Lisa* in *L.H.O.O.Q.* His two greatest pieces, meanwhile, *The Bride Stripped Bare by Her Bachelors, Even* and *Being Given*, incorporate between them a set of themes—voyeurism, narcissism, the machinery of desire, delay, profanation, exploitation, appropriation, difference, iconoclasm, irony—that reads like a program of the twentieth-century artistic engagement with eros.[3]

Some hundred years after *The Interpretation of Dreams* and *Les demoiselles d'Avignon* and a quarter-century after *The History of Sexuality*, *Erotikon* aims to catalyze the debate on eros in the twenty-first century. Both psychoanalytic and historicist theses are at play in the contributions, but neither group is axiomatic for the volume and divergent views are also canvassed. Past writings on eros are explored not only as historical curiosities or potential influences on subsequent times, but also as manifestations of thought still worth grappling with today. This might well suggest that *Erotikon*'s subject is perennial, the love

---

Octavio Paz (*The Double Flame*; *An Erotic Beyond: Sade*); and more recent developments that have emerged in the wake of Foucault, such as gender studies and queer theory.

3. Here again, myriad other names and works could be mentioned. Among them, Thomas Mann's *Death in Venice* (1913), the journals of Anaïs Nin (1966 ff.), and Vladimir Nabokov's *Lolita* (1955); photographers Alfred Stieglitz, Edward Weston, and Garry Winogrand; painters Egon Schiele, Gustav Klimt, and Georgia O'Keeffe; Andy Warhol's prints and films; and cinema directors Alain Renais, Pier Paolo Pasolini, and Bernardo Bertolucci.

that Shakespeare likens to the sun: "For as the sun is daily new and old/so is my love still telling what is told." Yet we also find much that is unexpected, even startling, in the following contributions. To cite just a few examples, these pages offer the outline of a steadfastly Christian theology suffused with the Augustinian understanding of love, which nevertheless proposes abolishing the notion of sin in favor of a revived conception of tragedy; a reading of Nietzsche that posits eros as the key to his diagnosis of nihilism; a cyber-savvy, modern-day Psyche, as curious as ever about her elusive Amor; a Freud who *doesn't have* a theory of eros; a Roland Barthes who defends old-fashioned novelistic pathos and celebrates *caritas*; and speculations on the sexual life of the Virgin Mary.

This sampling of views on eros maps out the contested ground of the concept. The general territory is familiar enough. At some basic level, there is the simple fact of the sexual nature that human beings share with much of the rest of the animate world. Superimposed on that is the richly varied terrain of human erotic experience shaped by culture and the overlapping but not coterminous realm of affectionate attachments. And at the outer reaches is a lingering desire for something more, something beyond the satisfactions of embodied mortal life. Differing accounts of eros often part company on the crucial question of the nature of that desire for more: Is it illusory? Even delusory? Or is it the manifestation of the human longing for the divine? Or an inarticulable blind spot in our nature? Or something else altogether? Unanimous responses to these and related questions are, no surprise, not to be found in *Erotikon*, but the differing voices contribute to a common conversation. Issues raised by one author recur in other essays; similar motifs surface in different contexts; sometimes goals or strategies are shared; often the points of reference coincide. Thus, while the essay-response pairs are straightforwardly in dialogue, a more subtle, underlying or overarching conversation is sustained across the volume. In the balance of this introduction, we adumbrate a few major themes of that broader discussion and sketch in some background.

AMBIVALENCE

One theme that emerges forcefully from *Erotikon* is a profound ambivalence toward the subject, an ambivalence that has deep roots in the Western tradition. Sappho, composing her poetry some time in the seventh century BC, expresses this succinctly when she calls eros "bittersweet." According to Greek myth, the ten-year Trojan war, the backdrop for so much of what has come down to us from antiquity, is triggered by the abduction of Helen by the love-stricken Paris. Similarly, the Romans attribute the origin of the Carthaginian wars to the curse spurned Dido casts on her departing lover, Aeneas. Violence is manifold in ancient Greek depictions of eros; and in tragedy, overweening desire can bring about the destruction of whole families. Sappho underscores the dangerous and destructive power of eros when she calls it *lusimeles*, an epithet that is used also of death and the Furies: "Eros, once again, the loosener of limbs, whirls me round."[4]

Yet for all the destructiveness of eros, the ancients also recognized its sweet, even salutary side. Throughout her fragmented corpus, Sappho sings not only of love's pain but also of its splendor and beauty. And in classical Athens, the erotic relationship between an adolescent and his older lover readied the former for entry into civic life, thus acknowledging and facilitating the role of erotic desire in the life of the city. In Plato, meanwhile, eros attains supreme importance both pedagogically and philosophically. The *Symposium* and the *Phaedrus* depict eros as the catalyst in the edifying relationship between teacher and student and as the key category in the Socratic account of the desire to know. According to Plato's Socrates, the very impulse to philosophy is erotic.

The essays collected in *Erotikon* reflect, and reflect upon, this ambivalence. The title of David Tracy's contribution sets the tone: "The Divided Consciousness of Augustine on Eros." Tracy examines the contradictory manifestations of eros in Augustine's thought and shows how, for this key figure in the transmission of ancient thought to later times, the deceptive and destructive force of eros as *cupiditas* can only be overcome if it is transformed by the gift of divine agape to become Christian *caritas*. But Tracy goes on to cast doubt on the success of this optimistic synthesis, arguing that in later writings Augustine depicts a human will so distorted that it makes self-delusion in erotic experience inevitable: we are *curvati in nos ipsos* (curved in upon ourselves).

Many thinkers have, in fact, been skeptics when it comes to eros, as Martha Nussbaum indicates in her essay on Proust. Yet Nussbaum also reminds us of the other side of the coin by raising the question of whether a life that forgoes eros "would be impoverished, a life without radiance, a life possibly lacking in the strongest sources of social beneficence" (p. 226). Nussbaum places Proust's response to this dilemma within a tradition stretching back to Plato, in which the common theme is ascent. According to Nussbaum, writers in this tradition seek to retain the creative power of eros while purifying it of dangerous excess through a therapeutic ascent such as that described by Socrates in Plato's *Symposium*. For Proust in particular, redemption comes through the agency of art.

4. Lobel and Page, *Poetarum lesbiorum fragmenta*, fr. 130.

Not only is the artist's heartache transfigured into joy through the making of art, but the work, as a selfless gift to the audience and as the medium through which separate minds can meet, also promises a triumph over narcissism. In words that Nussbaum quotes from Proust, "Through art alone are we able to emerge from ourselves, to know what another person sees" (p. 235). Yet ultimately Nussbaum argues that even this version of the ascent model reveals a fundamental narcissism at its core. To love "people as fictions" means to fail to open oneself to the full potential of human love.

While Tracy and Nussbaum evaluate strategies for the moderation and reformation of eros, Susan Mitchell's poetry—represented in this volume by the poem entitled "Erotikon"—makes what Mark Strand has called a "lavish and clear...case for the wisdom of excess." In the subtitle, "a commentary on *Amor and Psyche*," Mitchell alludes to the ancient tale of how winged Eros becomes enamored of the mortal girl Psyche, takes her for his mate, but to conceal his identity only visits her under the cover of darkness. One night Psyche, overcome by curiosity, lights a lamp, but the instant of illumination provokes Eros to fly off in anger. Eventually the two are reunited and the child of their union is *Voluptas* (Pleasure). Mitchell runs riot with these motifs in a lyric voice fittingly called voluptuous. "I feel the need for something that does not exist," she writes near the start of the poem, and proceeds to sing a rollicking ballad of desire and fulfillment and ever more desire. Eros here looks not so much like a force that can be purified, redeemed, or even modified, but rather more like the very power that moves us, or the current of life.

One might well expect that in this context an essay on Roland Barthes—author of *The Pleasure of the Text*, theorist of literary jouissance—might also explore the wisdom of erotic excess. As Philippe Roger observes, "Over the course of two long decades, it is always at the service of Eros Pantocrator that [Barthes] portrays himself" (pp. 248–49). But on Roger's unorthodox reading, we see Barthes in his late writings arguing for a decidedly desexualized, sober, even nonerotic love as the supreme value in literature. The novelist-hero for Barthes is in the end neither narcissist nor voyeur, and his novel is to be "written under the double invocation of *Pietas* and *Caritas*, the accomplishment of rites owed the dead, and the 'transcendence of egotism'" (p. 254). Roger thus presents a Barthes who responds to the egotistical, even narcissistic, hazards of eros by positing a new understanding of the novelist's mission and by offering at the end of his life an "apology of caritas." (Juxtaposed with Tracy's essay, the Augustinian resonance here is striking.) Responding to Roger, Eric Marty goes so far as to say that for Barthes this new conception of love, embodied in the novel, represented the only way to move from the negating tendencies of modern critical theory toward "an ethical language and writing" (p. 260).

The persistent ambivalence toward eros, both in the tradition and in the present volume, is matched by a similarly sustained desire to settle the matter. One strategy for overcoming this ambivalence is simply to cleave eros in two, as Pausanius does in Plato's *Symposium*, thereby keeping the noble eros safely segregated from the base; keeping, in effect, "darkness on one side, light on the other. As if opposites really did exist," to borrow Mitchell's words (p. 16). This tendency is prominent in Augustine's later works, where the author comes near to embracing a "Manichaean radical dualism between the spirit of Light and the matter of Darkness," as Valentina Izmirlieva observes in her response to Tracy (p. 110). Tracy himself, meanwhile, argues that Augustine's earlier, more optimistic writings promise a resolution not in the form of an ultimate cleavage but rather through a synthesis made possible by "the pure gift of divine agape" (p. 91). In Ingrid Rowland's essay, we see how the heirs of Augustine in the Renaissance turned to pagan motifs, and to the erotic poetry of the Hebrew Bible, to depict a world in which "sex and piety could coexist in perfect contentment" (p. 147).

Yet beside these various efforts at resolution stand innumerable cultural artifacts from the whole span of Western history which suggest that the tension is irresolvable, that ambivalence is built into the erotic phenomenon. Sappho's epithet, "bittersweet," fits perfectly the eros of the *Hypnerotomachia poliphili*, a novel published in 1499 and discussed by Rowland in her essay. As Anthony Grafton observes in his reply, the novel depicts a world in which all lovers end up in "rueful contemplation of the refined tortures that love inflicts on his votaries" (pp. 164–65). Such ineluctable ambivalence is implicit in the "tragic sensibility" of Martin Luther to which Tracy refers, and in the "tragic" vision of eros in Hitchcock's *Vertigo* as presented by Tom Gunning. Responding to Gunning, Robert Pippin emphasizes the particularly modern features of Hitchcock's treatment of this perennial issue. "There is something about eros," writes Pippin, "that cannot be accommodated easily within Christian or liberal-egalitarian humanism" (p. 280).

PARADOX

That eros bodies forth an irresolvable ambivalence is the conclusion reached by the poet and classicist Anne Carson in her book on the topic: "Whether apprehended as a dilemma of sensation, action, or value, eros prints as the same contradictory fact: love and hate converge within erotic desire."[5] Here ambivalence shades into paradox, and while the distinction between the two is not clear-cut, we may identify the latter as another major theme running through the essays in *Erotikon*. In fact, paradox often emerges from these discussions as the key category, the exactest center of eros. Again, the outlines are clear in antiquity, where eros was frequently the locus of paradox: both young *and* old; linked to both death *and* life, pleasure *and* pain; the child of lack *and* plenty. The *Symposium* is once again exemplary, for as Glenn Most demonstrates in his essay, the eros of Plato's dialogue is shot through with paradox: it is a divinity and a social practice, the subject of medical science and folk wisdom, the site of a vulgar aesthetics and a metaphysical one. The *Symposium's* series of conflicting speeches is finally interrupted by the epiphanic arrival of a walking paradox: Alcibiades, a beautiful young man who, against all custom, depicts himself as the ardent lover of ugly old Socrates.

In *Erotikon* paradox proliferates, often playing a pivotal role in argument and imagery. Tracy insists that both the optimistic and the pessimistic Augustinian teachings on eros must be acknowledged, and he concludes with an unapologetically paradoxical vision of an erotic and tragic Christianity. Pippin identifies an erotic paradox at the core of Nietzsche's account of modern nihilism, expressed most succinctly in the epigraph to the essay, taken from Nietzsche's *Gay Science*: "Not ist nötig." Need is what is needed. The dilemma is, as Pippin suggests, difficult to address philosophically, and it is one that comes to expression more frequently in poetry (as in Mitchell's "Erotikon," for example: "My desire . . . is for new desires, new appetites/to hunger and surprise me" [p. 27]). Nussbaum explores the paradoxical character of desire in Proust's artistic enterprise, arguing that even though we find in Proust's oeuvre "a love that embraces the entire world with even-handed joy," it is still the lover's failure to wholly possess the beloved that continues to goad desire. The fact that Albertine lives and laughs independent of Marcel leaves him restless, his desire for possession unfulfilled. Only when she is unconscious can he have her—"In a way, her sleep realized to a certain extent the possibility of love"—yet in that moment she is no longer Albertine but becomes instead merely, "a creature that breathes . . . nothing else besides" (quoted on p. 230). Marcel's "possession" of Albertine is just as illusory as Scottie's possession of Madeleine in *Vertigo*. In his essay on the film, Gunning juxtaposes Hitchcock's tragic evocation of perpetual lack with the comic overabundance of an obscure 1943 film titled *The*

---

5. Carson, *Eros the Bittersweet*, 9.

Geography of the Body, which itself alludes to Plato's *Symposium*. Gunning thereby weaves into his essay on a mid-twentieth-century film the Platonic question of whether eros implies want or abundance or somehow—paradoxically—both.

Paradox registers in very concrete terms when eros fuses together pleasure and pain, as in Gian Lorenzo Bernini's *Saint Teresa* sculpture. Rowland's essay calls attention to how Bernini's depiction of the saint illustrates an analogy between religious rapture and sexual ecstasy: both manifest the paradoxical simultaneity of pleasure and pain. Bernini had as precedents the testaments of Teresa of Avila herself, in which she describes the visitations of an angel of God, who would pierce her heart with a flame-tipped golden spear. "The pain was so sharp," writes Teresa, "that it made me utter several moans; and so excessive was the sweetness caused me by this intense pain that one can never wish to lose it, nor will one's soul be content with anything less" (p. 151). When the visitor is not divine but human, however, this coincidence of pleasure and pain can obtrude on ethical life in potentially troubling ways, a point David Halperin makes in his contribution. He argues that giving pleasure and causing pain come so perilously close to one another in and through sex because the object of sexual desire is obscure and elusive, perhaps even unobtainable. In Halperin's words, the lover is in effect telling his or her beloved, "I want you, but you are not what I want" (p. 55). The flesh becomes an obstacle and, in the worst case, leads to "the horrific and pointless ransacking of the body in search of the qualities that make it erotically desirable," which Halperin calls "the dark side of Platonism" (p. 56).

"The ugly underside of idolatry" are the words used in J. M. Coetzee's epilogue, "Eros and Psyche," to articulate a parallel insight about the disturbing aspect of erotic paradox. In this story, Elizabeth Costello, a straight-talking novelist on the threshold of old age, spares no details in her meditation on sexuality, mortal and immortal. Coetzee's novel *Disgrace*, published in 1999, renders a similarly unflinching portrayal of Eros the Ungovernable. The opening line of the novel—"For a man of his age, fifty-two, divorced, he has, to his mind, solved the problem of sex rather well"—is thick with an irony one would almost call tragic were it not for the undertone of banality.[6] The words are echoed later in the book when the protagonist, David Laurie, defends himself against charges of sexual harassment: "I was not myself. I was no longer a fifty-year-old divorcé at a loose end. I became a servant of Eros" (52). In Laurie's case, thinking he has a solution means failing even to see the problem. With

6. Coetzee, *Disgrace*, 1.

Elizabeth Costello, Coetzee returns to the "problem of sex" through the lens of a more thoughtful character. No solution, no resolution is offered here either, but there is perhaps a faint glimmer of wisdom—at the very least, at the last, Costello manifests an awareness of what happens when Psyche's lamp is lit.

The theme is unmistakable. Repeatedly in the contributions gathered in *Erotikon*, to speak of eros means to invoke paradox. It may be a divine thing, or maybe a daemon, or maybe just something all too human, but in any case, eros is perpetually liminal, an unsolvable problem; like darkness it is all around and yet remains unseen; like Dionysus it is "living always, always dying." If the archer Cupid is a figure for eros, paradox is the tension in his bow.

EXPRESSING EROS

However can such an elusive phenomenon come to expression? The question is one of genre, but it goes beyond that. Slavoj Žižek offers this radical formulation: "Is . . . love itself not the supreme example of the 'enigmatic term'? It refers by definition to an unknowable X, to the je ne sais quoi which makes me fall in love—the moment I can enumerate reasons why I love you, your properties which made me fall in love with you, one can be sure that this is not love" (p. 215). Granting Žižek's point, it would seem to be simply impossible to speak of love. Yet for millennia there has been no end to trying. Artists have often attempted to render images, verbal and visual, that capture the enigma of love. Hitchcock's *Vertigo* illustrates Žižek's claim brilliantly, for who is less able to enumerate his reasons, or more surely caught in love's thrall, than the protagonist, Scottie? The film suggests that nothing is a more potent metaphor for the state of the mind contemplating paradox, or the state of the soul falling in love, than vertigo. As Gunning puts it, "In a manner of expression perhaps unique to the visual fascination and almost physical effect of cinema, the film figures the power of eros precisely as vertigo" (p. 266). How is this "enigmatic term" explored and expressed across a variety of cultural artifacts? How do cinematic depictions differ from those in lyric poetry or sculpture or fiction or philosophy? Such questions are implicit throughout *Erotikon* and are explicitly addressed in several contributions. Peter Brooks, for example, responding to Nussbaum's essay on Proust, draws a clear distinction between "moral philosophy and narrative fiction," while Pippin argues that, in Nietzsche's treatment of the erotic, such distinctions between philosophy and literature become exceedingly difficult to maintain. In Halperin's "Love's Irony," this complex of issues is central. He argues that the intrinsically paradoxical character of the erotic phenomenon means that ultimately, "The only way to write well about love is to write about it ironically" (p. 57). Consequently, it is Plato's mastery of the ironic mode that allows him to write so lucidly, so compellingly, about the enigma of eros. Moreover, Halperin goes on to posit a profound correspondence between the structure of erotic desire and the very nature of literature itself.

The contributions from Mitchell and Coetzee highlight another aspect of the intersection of eros and literature. The erotic is often symbolized by the touch, both in physical and in spiritual terms: "love is touching souls," according to a popular lyric, and as such it is the paradigm of communication. Love permits, or seems to permit, knowledge of the other, whoever or whatever the other might be. Both the poet and the novelist in *Erotikon* explore how creative writing parallels this possibility, how the writer, through art, presumes to get inside the being of another. In Mitchell's poetic commentary, mythological figures (like Psyche), everyday objects (like wings), and abstractions (like darkness) come to life as characters who assume various, shifting identities in an imaginary hypertext. The poem relates that a character called Tango (Latin for "I touch"), navigating through the hypertext, "clicked on Women Who Disobey and from there she went to Author where a woman's voice kept saying, *the Author is always a woman when he's writing.* And a man's voice confessed, *now I know what it's like to be a woman.*" And what of the author Elizabeth Costello, portrayed by Coetzee in "Eros and Psyche," a woman written into existence by a man? Costello, herself a novelist, wrestles in her own way with the question of how far one can go in the direction of touching, of knowing, the existence of another. She argues in a lecture recounted elsewhere that if she has the ability through her art to "think [her] way into the existence of a being who never existed," she ought also to be able to think her way into the existence of animals.[7] In "Eros and Psyche," it is in fact the poet Mitchell's ruminations on the intercourse of god (Eros) and human (Psyche), or what Costello calls "congress across a gap in being," that occasions the novelist's reflections. Both Mitchell and Coetzee train our attention on the enigmatic promise held forth by both love and literature. For when fiction succeeds, the reader crosses a similar "gap in being," and the circuit is completed. In a sense, this is the moment at the core of the myth upon which Mitchell and Coetzee, coming from opposite directions, converge. It is, again, the moment of curiosity when the light goes on . . . and eros disappears.

7. Coetzee, *Elizabeth Costello*, 80.

TEMPORALITY

"Love," writes Octavio Paz in his book-length essay *The Double Flame*, "does not save us from time, it opens it a crack, so that in a flash love's contradictory nature is manifest: that vivacity which endlessly destroys itself and is reborn, which is always both now and never."[8] Perhaps no subject gives rise to such linguistic and logical contortions as does erotic temporality. In Plato, as Most illustrates, eros is said to mediate between the eternal and the temporal by facilitating the time-bound lover's participation in the eternal. Halperin, in his response, echoes the words of Paz: "Love imparts to creatures who are going to die an intuition of eternal reality" (p. 55). Nothing twists time like eros. Who in love has not at some point had an inkling of what Blake means by "eternity in an instant"? The phenomenon welds together the most intense immediacy and the longing for forever. In love, time flies, slips past, circles around again. Plato was by no means the last to evoke mystery at the nexus of eros and temporality, as the history of lyric love poetry amply attests. It is found in Sappho's recurring instantaneousness, in the infinite delay of the Provençal troubadours, in the love poems of Donne and Marvell, and in so many of Shakespeare's sonnets. It is clearly on the mind of Mark Strand, who chose for *Erotikon* two poems—Walt Whitman's "To a Stranger" and Wislawa Szymborzka's "Love at First Sight"—that play on the theme; and in her "Erotikon," Mitchell notes drolly that sexual ecstasy simply baffles the linguistic parsing of time: "there aren't enough tenses for all this to happen in" (p. 21). Prompted by Mitchell's poem, Coetzee's Costello recognizes in the various mythological tales about sex between gods and humans an image of the mystery of erotic temporality. The theme is conspicuous in Hitchcock's *Vertigo* as well, where the sequential unfolding of the seduction plot is suffused with an uncanny temporality that Gunning calls "deep time" and Pippin refers to as "mythic time."

FREUD

While art often endeavors to portray the uncanniness of eros, it is in part the work of theory to bring as much of the mystery as possible within the domain of reason. No one was more industrious on this score than Freud, and as might be expected, his thought exerts a substantial gravitational pull on *Erotikon*. We have here not so much a common thematics but rather a body of thought that serves as a frequent point of reference. In the following pages, some of the most formidable contemporary interpreters of Freud undertake a profound

8. Paz, *Double Flame*, 134–35.

and path-breaking engagement with psychoanalytic theory on the question of eros. With bracing candor, Jonathan Lear calls upon his readers to acknowledge that "for all practical purposes, we don't yet have" a psychoanalytic conception of eros (p. 200). He proposes that Freud's theory of eros serves to conceal and obfuscate exceptions to the pleasure principle, which should instead be put down to a disruption of the mind's activity by the mind itself—what Lear calls "break." Lear is challenged in turn by Žižek, and their exchange over Freud and Lacan on love and death manifests a smoldering debate in that region where philosophy and psychoanalysis intersect. Like Lear and Žižek, James Porter also takes on the much-disputed question of Freud's invocation of eros and thanatos as the "two primal instincts," whose mutually opposing actions chart the course of life. While Porter too has Lacan in mind, his main point of reference in this essay is Lucretius, and he develops a fresh and provocative line on love and death in Freud. Porter's essay transforms not the pleasure principle but the death instinct, and here it is the latter that has been misunderstood. The fascination with death, he writes, "is an attempt to locate meaning in life" (p. 137). Richard Wollheim weighs in with a contrapuntal response to Porter, while Eric Santner in his response to Pippin offers something of a Freudian meta-analysis of Pippin's reading of Nietzsche.

HISTORICITY

As the subtitle of the book indicates, *Erotikon* deliberately spans a long period of time and thereby raises questions about the historicity of its subject. How do conceptions of eros alter over time? What remains the same and what changes when we move from a Greek to a Roman context, or from a pagan to Christian one? What has eros been in the past, and what might its future be? For many authors—past and present—a broad, transtemporal conception of eros is fundamental to understanding human life. Freud, for example, reckoned a general congruence between what Plato called "eros" and what he himself refers to as the "love-force or libido." As we have noted, many scholars in more recent years have sought to document the historicity of eros. In this volume, both Most and Lear take up the question of the putative connections between Freudian libido and Platonic eros. Most also argues that what is commonly called "Platonic love" today has very little to do with what we find in the dialogues, where there is a sublimation and redirection, rather than an extirpation, of sexual desire.

Shadi Bartsch contextualizes eros still more, emphasizing the contingent and historically specific character of her subjects and, indeed, seeking to puncture any sense that Greek and Roman attitudes toward the connection of philosophical and erotic practices can be treated together as the same ancient phenomenon. She unearths first-century Roman social practices around the profession of philosopher in the context of this culture's ambivalent reception of the Platonic pederastic tradition and thereby finds an explanation for the curious phenomenon of a particular Roman career slur: the philosopher likes to be buggered. We are far from the *Symposium* here, in a culture where sexuality and philosophy are rarely seen hand in hand. Catharine Edwards, in her response, calls attention to the role played by Epicureanism in shaping the Roman Stoic response to Greek philosophy, and she teases out an undercurrent of eroticism in Seneca's writing on philosophy that highlights additional nuances in the reception of the Greek tradition. Surveying the Roman scene at a much later point in history, Rowland speculates on how Renaissance and Baroque architects negotiated a complex relationship with the classical pagan heritage to design an architecture simultaneously in the service of the Christian faith and suffused with erotic energy.

At the heart of many contributions to *Erotikon* lies the question of the future of eros. One easily discerns in Tracy the aspiration to reintroduce eros into contemporary Christian theology, and in Nussbaum an engaged defense of its place in any viable moral philosophy for our time. Lear seeks to expose the shortcomings of Freud's psychoanalytic theory of eros for the express purpose of working toward a better theory in the future. And a similar aim, though more muted, comes across in what Wollheim refers to as the "covert" optimism of Porter's essay. In other contributions, it is the twilight of eros that provides the occasion for reflection on its future. "We don't give parties like that any more," muses the speaker in one of the two poems by Strand reproduced here. This short lyric, which is one section of the book-length poem *Dark Harbor*, offers a wry and rueful account of erotic passion recalled in later, more phlegmatic years. Yet Strand, clearly alive to the paradox, also chooses to include Stanley Kunitz's poem "Touch Me," written when the poet was near ninety years of age, in which the resilience of eros is felt even very late in life. "What makes the engine go?" asks the poet, a question he might well take up with Elizabeth Costello, if he could get in touch with her. The answer toward which both of them turn is simple. In Kunitz's words: "Desire, desire, desire." Though in quite a different register, a similar query animates Pippin's essay on Nietzsche. As Pippin notes, it is a question that is "addressed more regularly by modern romantic and confessional poetry than by philosophy" (p. 188). He argues that for Nietzsche, modern nihilism is best understood as the waning or failure of desire, "the flickering out of some erotic flame," understood in a broad, civilizational sense (p. 177). Nietzsche's diagnosis of nihilism does not turn primarily on matters of belief or of will, according to Pippin, and so merely getting the facts straight or resolutely positing values will not sufficiently respond to the crisis. In place of such interpretations, Pippin sketches out Nietzsche's erotic etiology of nihilism and evaluates his account of why eros flags and how it might be sustained. Nietzsche's vision is fixed firmly on the future—"some day I wish to be only a yes-sayer," he writes in *The Gay Science*—yet as Pippin shows, this vision has proven elusive for Nietzsche's interpreters because his teaching on eros is often expressed in densely imagistic language. To understand the "erotic Nietzsche," Pippin suggests, one must read with an ear attuned to the poetry in his idiom.

"Isn't it an awful thing! Our poets have composed hymns in honor of just about any god you can think of, but has a single one of them given one moment's thought to the god of love, ancient and powerful as he is?"[9] So exclaims Phaedrus in the account given in Plato's *Symposium*. He goes on to complain that in fact no one has yet offered a worthy hymn to eros, leaving this great god neglected and unsung. It is in response to this alleged neglect that the symposiasts offer their speeches. Yet it is difficult not to read Phaedrus's remark ironically, since any reader familiar with the Greek literary tradition, which Plato knew well, will realize that eros is surely not ignored by the ancient poets. Might Plato be suggesting that the presence, even surfeit, of eros in our arts and letters does not necessarily signify an adequate understanding of it? We may think we know, or have come to know, what eros is—an ancient and powerful deity, or the devil's work, or the love of God, or the one thing needful, or the "word known to all men," or the sexual instinct, or a sociohistorical construct, or the "supreme example of the 'enigmatic term'"—but a real discussion about it begins only when we recognize with Phaedrus that no one has yet offered an adequate hymn to eros.

9. Plato, *Symposium*, trans. Nehamas and Woodruff, 177a–b.

EROTIKON (A COMMENTARY ON «AMOR AND PSYCHE»)

SUSAN MITCHELL

1

Some things are still going on, even though it's late, it's dark. Gravity, for example, the pull the earth exerts on the moon and the moon on the ocean. Listening to the tides sweep through the darkness (higher over there, a little lower here), I come to a moment when the ocean lets out a sigh like a train pulling into a station. Its doors slide open, but no one climbs aboard the astral glare of ante meridian.

Giddyap, says the ocean, sometimes

I feel the need for something that does not exist. This wanting is like speed entering a tunnel. *Philia,* said Augustine, keeps everything moving from one place to another. *Orexia,* said Aristotle, because he liked the sound of the word. I want depth in what does not exist and inside depth, the sound of water running. It is a process, too, the nonexistent, and further in, like that lattice of veins behind the eye, a seeing. Or, if not a seeing, what silvers glass into seeing. Darkness on one side, light on the other. As if opposites really did exist, *dúm-duh* and *duh-dúm.* Jetting across the longitudes, it is possible, said Aristotle

to discover the place where darkness begins
to be darkness: night stalled
beside the plane like a cold front, its towers

Reprinted, with permission, from *Erotikon* (New York: HarperCollins, 2000).

city blocks palliated and sheered off, battleships

and tenebrous bergs of ice

the shadow of a shade, said Aeschylus, the palpable
obscure, said Milton, and several mention
sables, but there aren't enough
words for night. Why is that? There aren't

enough words for the dark. Show me, said Erebus,
darkness penetrable and darkness penile,

the darkness called skyscraper

but surprise, we are passing through, so not solid, the darkness, though pala-
tial; and twilight, behind us now, how briefly it endured our passage through
veils of diaphanous. What I want, I said, is a darkness not yet limited to twelve
hours or twenty-four. Swarthy, dusky—they don't do it for me, they wash off
like makeup. Bituminous? The tongue is barely stained. What I want is a darkness that can run lap after lap, it doesn't give out, it lives on junk food and
nerves, on dives and divas, on tango and

Up, sideways, and beyond—these, said Varro, are the three motions of the moon.
Oooooooo, we said, *hic jacet* with herbage and tussock, with verdure and clumps
of cosmopolite the moon
          ossuary
          bone pot

Give us a hollow sound.
                 Marble?
                     Not good enough.
Mausoleum?
          Keep going.
             I tombi?
With fimbriae, with galloons?
                  With ivy, with rigamarole
and cupids cold to the touch.

What a goof you are. A grand slam of sound is what's needed, with echoes ambulating the curvatures, with arabesques hexachording the anharmonic, as if the plane had tilted and stewardesses with trays of tea and vodka—a slosh of sound in the grand basins of the ear. Listen,

sometimes I get worked up, I have to look at the moon rising between huge chiffonny sails and ships rigged like clouds. So there is a gap in what you are reading, a diapause where I began to elongate and drifting slowly, broke apart. Between the *bes* and *ques* of *arabesques* is a scissors of light, a rip down the word you were just sounding like a theorbo. Hey, would

you do me a favor? Keep reading, but imagine you have stopped. Can you do that? Keep reading, but imagine you are looking at the moon. To help you focus, a soprano is singing *as possibility it is dazzling* while a bass recapitulates *where I began to drift.* Oooooooo, we said, the bivalve attention, *l'attention hermaphrodite.* So many genitals to arouse, all those tabs and keys to press and the sun honeying the saxophone and clarinets, shining up a brass meander of light down which the hereat and thereabout

now bare as retreat, as low tide—
yes, let afternoon be its own pavilion, let indigence
surround, the sumptuous disappearances intoned
through loudspeakers, the less and—

instead of slosh and overbrim
I would look through books in search of some *cwm,*
some *psykter,* words for the eye alone, all
sound squeezed out of them, the listening
ablated: Would it be a real wind or a purely
visual wind filling the valves
of the afternoon, a horn
sounding its memorials, its distances

for the eye only? And the afternoon,
would it be a real afternoon? Or open on one side
like a bathhouse, a cabana, and that place where she kisses him,

that place in the story where so many put their mouths,
is it all listened up, sucked back
into the ear, heard to death?

Just as the fairest leopard is made with his spots, and fire maketh the gold
to shine and the straw to smother, something pushes through, intoning the
off-key, streaking its fuschias like a bad lipstick smear across the ordinary, all
its radios whiffing, porning the glee in elegy

And shall I come sweet Sex to thee
bound truelovewise?
O take fast hold, said Sex to me,
of the moneybox, and night was our koine
with its bleats and glottic stops
its suctions and seductions.

All night we laved a fierce lallation.

Wake now, my love, I said to Sex.
Be not overly
subtle with periods and semicolons.
O take fast hold of quim and quid.
By morning I was catamount.
Sex was microcephalic.

The way night comes again and again, it could be happening on a screen. The
way the two bop off each other, night and day, one of them fragmenting. Then
the pieces coming together again. This is a kind of wordlessness. Bubbles out
of the mouth of a fish is another example. The wordlessness a temptation and
a discomfort. And also none of these.

It was around that time that I began to collect. At first, things that never
happened. Then distinctions that seemed out of control. And also different
kinds of steam. Steam rising up out of a manhole. Or the sibyl sitting over a
hole in the ground, like a potty, breathing in steam. Also dictionaries. I started
with heaps: sand, gravel, grit, stonedust, sweepings. And what washes up on
beaches; corks and pumice, thorns, balls of tar barnacled, roundabout and
wormtube, runnel, the easily broken. From these I went on to dictionaries

of the erotic. The way a lover would examine his beloved, checking her parts, the saliva on her tongue with its little suds and bubbles. Sputum. Spit.

Or those furrows water wears into stone, the ciphered, the incised: the finger as stylus, the finger reading a language climbed like steps—*clit clitcb clitoris*—or stilled as murex, as conch.

At specified times I would go over the gaps and lacunae, the pauses ancient as the backs of giant tortoises. I savored the silences as if they were fabrics, the silks and serifs codified, the serrations and suspirations as if a wind blew through the pages, stirring up ripples and minnows of sound

the wings, the pellicules   pennants in the sea

and pop-up dictionaries, the definitions expanding, with windows that opened and doors through which gleaming, yet indefinite

In one dictionary words were in constant motion, changing as I read them, the way skywriting is stretched into an alphabet of clouds

some of the dialects roughened by daily use. Or softened, as if the words had been mixed with that silt a spoon stirs up in Turkish coffee. For example, the word *sparrow* in one dialect was pronounced *shparrow,* the sort of bird that takes crumbs from the hands of young lovers and children.

The dictionaries were indifferent to who used them. Or for what purposes. Some made entirely or pictures. And Catullus could get away with a lot because he wrote in Latin. In one story I collected, the writer had made a fetish of darkness. Everything happened in the dark, the characters seeing nothing of one another. But the reader could see them and the darkness. Darkness was the main character. Wings was another character. And Tango. Reading, I could feel how the writer had rolled the darkness between his thumb and forefinger, how he smelled up all its furs and furbelows. Smoked its cigars. I would watch him in his room alone with the darkness, stroking. This was how he got worked up to write. My reading was interposed like an extra heartbeat: an arrhythmia, a tachycardia of listening. This happened on the expressway too, and in malls. It kept fuming through him, the darkness, which he pressed to his mouth like wet panties, like black lipstick.

After he does it with a real girl, he does it with the other one
in the story. Or with both of them together, the one
with wings lying there on the bed.

The girl in the story shines and glares all over his body
like headlights, his wings beating
the glare of her seeing shivering up his body, and his eyes
all gummed with darkness, cocooned

the wings drenched after he comes, matted, the feathers.
That place deep in where Plato said the soul begins, cutting
its teeth on pleasure, the pleasure raw and bloody from the effort.

When they come together, they fragment. First the girl, then
the one with the wings. His feathers as when a bird is shot,
the bird body pulling apart in the air. That's called orgasm.

Or he is up above looking down on her, so far away he thinks she is tied to a
cliff. He's up where the dome is, where the oculus. Or as if he were a hawk and
she the prey. She feels it pull between her legs. And breaks up in his mouth
like shrapnel. Then she comes together again. And he breaks up.

And the one thinking this in malls, thinking there aren't enough tenses for
all this to happen in, the past and the present fragmenting as they bop off
one another. There aren't enough words for darkness to make it different each
time. Darkness with smell and without smell. Darkness with tall buildings, the
blades rubbing against one another, getting worked up. The darkness getting
bigger, reaching the tops of skyscrapers and the one driving the expressway or
huddled under a blanket in the plane, the small laptop resting on her knees

2

I will spread darkness, Darkness said, like a doll on
a bare mattress: broken, the hair matted, silk
scarves and the blackness bunched up, its
boobs and bulbous knobs

Go on, said Tango, feeling it enter her voice,
the unripe, the indigestible, what made
her sick in Crivellis of green

Tango is one character. Speed is another, ablaze and

dripping into the disappearances, the ectoplasmic
rushing away of thinking drizzling off into
fissures, chasms where blackness boils up
uncharted, unimpeded.
                              Along the swagger and irresistible
it's happening so fast there is no space
for breath or wingbeat, only
wave after wave culminating in overmantels and
balustrades with open strings

Speed is waiting for the darkness to go too far, to spoil
go rotten, all its sugars and flambeaus—

I will spread darkness, said Darkness.

Go on, said Tango, forgetting to wipe the excess
from her voice, the scrollwork, she is
strapping herself
into the big boy's wings, lacing up the contraption

for language to change around her
all its green prodigious, as if a parrot
squawking into her ear its guavas, its Cassandras of—

Today, said Tango, the sea is squiggles of stomachache
becoming foam, fat waves crescendoing
into an appetite to be eaten
                              and Speed, Sock it
to me, sock it to me, sock it to me.

                In the soupy
in the drool there are hardnesses
forthrights and aches where the mind
clamps down on the rushing, on the gurge and

confluence, a movie projector running without
film, no images on the screen to happen
in which golds stagger up
columnlike and twisted, with sputter
                                 rusty drippings
screwed into the dilapidation—

Unless, said Darkness, a circle is cut
in the darkness through which, with long lookings and oglings,
at the far end a mirror and across it

to and fro, up and down, from side to side, systematically and also capriciously
with motions herky-jerky and half-cocked. But the phrases were beginning
to stick together like wet leaves, the possible and the impossible, the seeing
getting its jaws around, all foam-flecked. There are, said Tango, twenty-seven
kinds of seeing. Or did she mean twenty-seven kinds of wings? Wings with fluff
and wings without fluff, wings inebriated with flight and wings descended into
their sacs, retracted. The mirror positioned in such a way that looking and
gawking and peeping, and even pinhole rooms where a single drop of vision
was enough, the body suddenly overexposed. Though of course, said Tango,
there is also looking with the mouth open, the mouth like a third eye, as if two
eyes were not enough and now a third, a fourth, a fifth—an argosy of eyes like
the tail of a peacock spread far and wide. Tango wanted eyes all over her body.
But especially an eye between her legs, a great Cyclopean eye blinding her with
its salivas and dilations. Think of those lenses an optometrist clicks into place,
one over the other as his head looms close in the dark. *Is it better this way? Or like
this?* Oh yes, like this, like this. Now it's all so clear it hurts. Yes, unbearable, but
sharper, with the brightness of Yankee Stadium floodlit, with hoses of light at
full force. Yeah, and why not? thinks the one gliding the expressway, gliding
the burning rubber, the acrylic and ammonia. Sometimes this happens with
oil refineries to the right and oil refineries to the left. Now he reaches to where
it's happening: through bridges and tunnels, with the far lane blocked, with

eyes of the mind, with eyes turned inward on stems of
intellect straining back into the brain where a
wick burns round the clock. *Oh there!*

With stems of intellect stretched taut, with eyes tuned up
until there begins to open, an inside. *Oh, eyes
of no color opening!*

It was I, Love, that sent eyes into the world, Love that
knocked holes in the skull and shoved
the tongue out. In there, something

for which no experience exists. *Oh, polish it! Burnish!*
And yes, something like fingers are rubbing,
massaging. *Keep at it! Rubbing*

makes it visible. A form. Antler grown from the skull, cold
prong of sharpness, spicule, barb. An idea.
Oh, idea sealed off like a tomb!

As if a kiss with long velvet gloves were stalking,
sneaking up on the darkness starting to thaw,
to wake up like a gong. The darkness

gaining consciousness. *Oh, give it to me! The full glare
of that looking!* Shall I call it Psyche,
that looking? Shall I call it

Soul, those eyes—newcut, sharp and ferocious
as shark teeth? Oh, what shall I call it,
the darkness popping open

like a jack-in-the-box? The brain knocking down walls, pushing through bone?
And the one driving the expressway thinking, Who will speak to me of this?
Who needs more than anything to speak? It's your tongue I want in my mouth.
Your tongue with its little bubbles, with its slap and tickle. Oh, bubbles, liquid
buds of love. Not only those that cling pebbly to the sides of grass under water
or *bup, bup, bup* from the mouths of fish, but also cartoon bubbles inside which

language blows from the mouths of men and women. Why not the aside as such a bubble? A place in thinking so elastic, so stretchy, it becomes a reservoir of air, an oxygen rush, for those trapped in slow cars of conversation. Or for those mired in rush-hour traffic, some bubbly to the rescue. Now he lets loose a big bubble of fantasy with Tango saying, *Bounce me through the see-through, Baby. I'm all sneezed out.* Clusters of bubbles floating at the surface like eggs, like sexual swarm, geodesic domes of pleasure. And he croons back, *Hey Tango, blow me some slut and sluice.* And Tango, *Some fast and loose?*

Now! says Speed. Now, before anyone cuts into the tender
undersides of darkness. Now, before the lemon is squeezed
and the darkness uncorks, foaming over.

But do not forget, said Tango, looking that is innocent and filled with wonder, the eyes kissing fervently with parted lids. Or did she mean *parted lips?* And was it Tango saying this? Or Wings? All at once she realized this was to be a story about loss in which even the story was lost. For if there was a story, then there was something, and if there was something, then not everything was lost.

Only Speed wanted to go directly to the encryption,
scrambling their favorite places, the possible and
the impossible, birds and men with wings.

No love is true save that which loves forever, said Wings.
At which they all became sad, for Forever towered
above them with its evergreen branches.

Under tuition of the shade, said Darkness. But no one
was listening anymore. So Forever let down its check
boxes and drop-down boxes.

3

Darkness, light, stillness, and movement originate in
one another, said Aristotle, and each exists potentially
in each. To transform darkness into movement and movement
into light, it is necessary to change the proportion
of stillness within them.

But, said Speed, if the proportion of gaze is changed,
wouldn't the borders shift, wouldn't the interior rise
to the surface

Collapsing, said Aristotle, sky onto earth.

And isn't loss only another fetish? Plato asked.

Darkness, light, stillness, and gaze, said Aristotle.

And what is light, said Tango, if not an invitation to look, to press
one's face against looking, to rub one's breath
all over seeing, smudging its transparencies, its sheers
and cellophanes?

To see the darkness lifting its skirts. To see the darkness
undressing to deeper and deeper shades, the hiddenness
pleated, folded over on itself, clavichorded and enrinded
into recesses retiring inward—

Was it a mistake to open it? To let it out of its box?
Impossible now to pack it back in, now that it had sopped up
the sounds of their sex.

What the light interrupted and put a stop to was a process,
said Aristotle, not a process that would necessarily
have culminated in or reached a goal, but a process
in which culmination was always felt as a possibility.

Even when, said Plato, that possibility could not have been
irradiated or developed in the imagination—

It was felt, said Wings, as an expansion of the darkness.
As a throbbing. An aroma pulsing, a song beginning,
breath wafted toward my lips.

In this respect, said Aristotle, the light was like death,
putting a stop to process. Process that was moving
and also process that was not moving.

But that might have moved, said Wings. Its moving
fantasized or felt as a back and forth—

To prolong the throbbing, said Plato, To draw out
the shudder, to rev its wings and engines to erotolepsy.
The way light tattoos the skin with butterflies and lions,
with other lives also desiring, birds with beaks agape.
A love feast of shapes and sensations silk-screening—

My desire, said Speed, is for new desires, new appetites
to hunger and surprise me. To desire tomorrow
what I have not desired today.

There are times, said Psyche, when I need to be addressed by an author, to hear
an author's voice, no other will do, assuring me, explaining my life to me. It is
not so much what the author has to tell me as his tone. It comforts, it sustains
and buoys me. The author's own faith and optimism that all will turn out well.
The pleasure the author takes in relating my misfortunes. Will I speak of my
own life with such joy? Not a trace of bitterness or regret?

And the one driving the expressway thinking he'd like to dribble her misfortunes all over his lips. He'd like to take her disobedience into his mouth. Where
would the story be without her disobedience? Where would any of us be without disobedience? Tango sighed. History could not manage without it. Poetry
would have ended long ago. And all those boxes left unopened. Pandora's and
the Box of Beauty that Psyche—

Though, said Apuleius, it is a mistake to think of the two boxes as similar.
Pandora's was more of a jar, a little house made of clay, with lips—or was that
Pandora? My word for the Box of Beauty was *pyxis*, a small box or casket used
for drugs—

Which proves, said Speed, that beauty is a drug. The more
you get, the more you need. Or, said Tango,

which intoxicates the beholder so that the rest of life
is quickly forgotten, but the one

driving the expressway was no longer listening. He was watching Psyche's lips,
how they opened and closed when she spoke, the upper lip gently pushing
away the lower, then drawing it close again; how her teeth glistened with
syrup. What greeting was worthy of that mouth? Ridiculous to imagine her
saying *hi* or *hello* or *good morning.*

Sometimes, said Psyche, I want a bitter taste in my mouth.
Is this perverse of me? And in my eyes too. To close
my eyes on this taste, so I can make it last. The purpose
of beauty is to wash a bitter taste from the eyes.

And in that respect, said Darkness, beauty is not so
different from sleep. Not to sleep is to fast, to keep
the eyes from devouring, from gorging on

the darkness, said Wings.

Speak, that I may see thee, said Darkness.

4

If the darkness were turned off, said Darkness, what then?
Would memory be enough to sustain it, to keep it going?

Toward dawn, said Psyche, darkness is only a ghost
of itself.

Some poems can be talked about, but not written, Wings
observed. Others can be written, but not talked about.

Which kind of poem are we in? asked Psyche. But by then
it was too late, they were already

in The Darkness Box, where the viewer explores every fault and fracture of
eclipse, gashes crammed with disappearances, fissures descending into zero
visibility. When you turn on the light, the darkness is lit up, darkness still

unspoiled, vast tracts uncharted, not yet memorized. And the light like the whine of a mosquito, like some small seed stuck between your teeth. How Tango got into The Darkness Box kept changing. Sometimes she clicked on Stories Left Unfinished, abandoned structures where the smell of darkness was as fresh as if just painted and the windows like lipstick hastily penciled in. Or she clicked on Spiny Black and descended the darkness as if it were a ladder. Down the windpipe, down the hiatus she went, as

clods of pitch black were spewed up, rough surges that threw open their sarcophagi, stony crypts where darkness hung in clusters like fat grapes. In the infrastructures, in the crawl spaces, it was difficult to breathe, the darkness compressed by the weight of centuries, its molecules following a logic neither straight nor curved, neither active nor passive, but Speed

had already rushed on to Places That Smell of Sex, bathhouses where sand stuck to your legs and the darkness littered the floor like wet bathing suits. Tango lingered in the movie house with its plush seats, well worn, and the gilded gargoyles above the balconies. On the screen the enormous faces of a man and woman. *Click me*, the woman's mouth kept saying.

When they entered The Box of Beauty they saw a beautiful girl asleep or unconscious, a young man straddling her, filling every hole in her body with desire. *Will that be all*? A voice kept asking. The sex performing itself on her, knocking holes in her through which feelings seeped. The sex like a perfume spreading the girl's vulnerability. Or the sex was a shiver in the darkness and the girl spooned out, all idea of her un-ideaed, run back to gruel. Was it beauty that had clubbed her into submission? Or sex? If she could get to where the sex was, Tango thought, but already it was moving on. The box needing her only to open it.

In some places the darkness shone forth like new leaves,
as if it were evolving, putting out stems and branches
almost immediately lost to view,

and a lot of it like badly tied packages, the string coming
loose, hardly any of the darkness in mint condition

nothing stable or permanent and from which lustral sprinklings—

Is this how an idea comes to me? Aristotle wanted to know,
imageless at first, then the way a flock of birds
turns in the air, present, then gone, present, then

the darkness dissipating into troughs which beat up again
as huge wings. Some of the wings tearing away—snotty, phlegmy.

Even so the stream of darkness streams back, reentering.

In The Erotikon the darkness was blindfolded. Tango watched her desire fill in
on the screen, first the upper part, then the lower where the tassels were, the
fringes. The fringes were called fetishes. Ornate rhyme is another fetish. Also
snowflakes. And the rain in Japanese prints which reminded Wings of pick-up
sticks, though Tango said it looked like spaghetti. To get her hands on that
rain, to hold it and rub it, that was a fetish. When someone feels compelled to
say over and over *truffle, ruffle, eyeful*, is that a fetish? Wings asked. But Tango
had already clicked Puns, and now her ears felt like birds flying in different
directions.

In The Erotikon Speed's desire was everywhere at once, but Tango could only
endure short bursts of seeing. Her desire was that unripe, that irritable in its
green and torment of, in the full glare of her temerity looking back at her,
giving double her money, all its brazens and gongs resounding. To taste it
would be foolhardy, to dawdle in its tarts and dangers, and

yeah, he thought, the one driving the expressway, that's the taste he wanted.
More, he said, more,

but Tango clicked on Women Who Disobey and from there she went to Author,
where a woman's voice kept saying, *The author is always a woman when he's writing.*
And a man's voice confessed, *Now I know what it's like to be a woman, to be excited
and have it secret. No one can know what passes through me. When I'm writing, I'm
visible and invisible. With wings wild beating* or with wings folded tight as a bud
and the way a bud opens, that thin line of gold like a crease of light.

It was a disappointment to everyone that Amore, More and Moira all turned
out to be the same place, a room with a weeping girl and a voice repeating,

Loss can be a fetish enacted over and over. It did not help when Plato explained that *moira* was the Greek word for fate. Whatever, said Tango,

and even Wings wasn't listening because he had found a fetish of his own, collecting words that fit one inside the other like boxes. *Ore* inside *core*, he said, and *core* inside *score*. Tango tried to fit *amore* into *more*, but it didn't work. Try it the other way, said Wings. But then she found *emotion*, and they all played with that one for a while.

5

It was when the Darkness said, Forget expressways at night,
    moving chains of light, the golden links opening
    and closing,

it was when the Darkness said, Forget remembering and water
    of all kinds, trilling water and standing water,
    water clear and

Forget species, genus, order, class, subphylum, and phylum,
    even though they are delicious as cutting apples
    into halves, the halves into quarters,

even though they are sweet as cutting into cutting, exposing
    the black seeds, the fibers tough as guitar
    strings, saliva-fine threads,

it was when the Darkness said, Forget reflections of clouds
    in puddles, puddles that dry up, and the skill and
    cunning of insects, the lust of minerals,

also trees. Forget their parasites and diseases, and don't
    think of streets with houses elegant as
    isosceles triangles

Psyche asked, Is there a form that can get the better of
longing? In the beginning, Story said,

story held everything together, the darkness and the light,
the little pieces that would have slipped away, the slightest
of them lifting on the first breeze, and even the breeze
would have blown away. Story

was an illusion, said Plato, but necessary. Without it,
no one would have remembered the sunsets and great feasts
and the first time they made love would have pulsed in their
bodies inarticulate. Afterward would have preceded before,
similar experiences would have stuck to one another,
intensifying like a box of matches.

I would have gone on touching her golden hair, said Wings,
I would have gone on rubbing and

said Aristotle, an excess of touching, an excess of intensity
tactile and contactual, an excess at once tactile and
tactless—

So, said Light. Is it ever possible to feel ready, ready enough,
completely ready, on-your-mark ready, on-your-toes ready?

Have you noticed, said Tango, when you repeat the same word
over and over, it begins to lose all meaning?

Have you noticed, said Darkness, but already

it seemed as if light were blowing in with the wind.
The rain was illuminated, and each gust hung with droplets
appeared to brighten the branches it tossed and shook. Or

it's as if light were wrung from the air, said Psyche, from
the leaves—

Do you mean rung from the air? Tango asked.

But by then there was so much light, it was impossible
to hear what anyone was saying.

SIX REMARKS ON PLATONIC EROS

GLENN W. MOST

Translated from German by Thomas Bartscherer

I

The main sources for Plato's theory of eros are two of his dialogues, the *Symposium* and the *Phaedrus*. Both are central points of reference for Western philosophy and literature; nonetheless, it may be useful to recall some of their details. My emphasis here will be on the first of these two dialogues because eros alone is the main theme in the *Symposium*, whereas the *Phaedrus* addresses a variety of other issues as well. I must ask the lovers of the *Phaedrus* for their forbearance if for my present purposes I use that dialogue only to supplement my remarks on the *Symposium*.

II

The *Symposium* clothes a deep philosophical reflection on the nature, possibilities, and dangers of sexual desire—this is the real meaning of the Greek word *eros*, and not the much vaguer, more modern word *love*, which is cloven between sensuality and idealization—in the trappings of a cheerful, informal Athenian drinking party. At such gatherings, it was the custom that, as the wine flowed and the inhibitions decreased, the cultivated male participants would exchange speeches and songs about whatever was on their minds—that is to say, usually, above all, about sexual desire. This time, contrary to ordinary practice, the pretty flute girls, who normally embodied and intensified the erotic mood of the drinking party, were sent out of the room so that the

An earlier version of this essay appeared as "Sechs Bemerkungen zum platonischen Eros" in *Kunst-Zeugung-Geburt: Theorien und Metaphern ästhetischer Produktion in der Neuzeit*, edited by Christian Begemann and David E. Wellbery (Freiburg im Breisgau: Rombach, 2002).

men could be left alone to deal with the theme, not in deeds but exclusively in words (176e).

The seven speeches that Plato composes, all highly individualized and artfully arranged, constitute a formal structure of paired, complementary discourses (a typical form in Athenian rhetoric, tragedy, and comedy), in this case comprising three pairs and then, as a finale, a comic conclusion reminiscent of a satyr play. In this text, composed with extraordinary care, where nothing is left to chance, it is no mere accident that the central speech is put into the mouth of the comic poet Aristophanes, nor that the fifth (inserted between Aristophanes' speech and that of Socrates) is ascribed to the tragic poet Agathon. Nor is it by chance that, at the very end of the dialogue, the conclusion Socrates, still fully sober, wants to prove to these two sleepy, drunken playwrights is that a poet who is able to write either tragedy (like Agathon) or comedy (like Aristophanes) must also be a master of the other genre. In fact, this did not happen to be the case for Agathon or for Aristophanes (or for any other Athenian poet of the fifth century BC, for that matter). On the evidence of this very dialogue, however, there can be no doubt that we are intended to believe it to be true, in a certain sense, for Socrates' student, Plato, who succeeds brilliantly in devising plausible, indeed irresistibly enthralling speeches not only for both poets, the comedian and the tragedian, but for all the other characters as well, and who not only intersperses moments of genuine comedy throughout this dialogue but also hints unmistakably at perspectives of a genuinely tragic quality all along its course.

In the first pair of speeches, eros is discussed in the context of the prevailing traditions of the earlier phases of Greek culture: Phaedrus begins with an interpretation of the god Eros in terms of (Phaedrus's own idiosyncratically distorted version of) traditional Greek conceptions of religiosity (178a–180b); Pausanias then provides as a counterpart a discussion of eros as a social phenomenon in terms of a (less than fully objective) comparative investigation of traditional Greek legislation in this domain (180c–185c). In this way, the dialogue enters the theme of eros by way of its sociopolitical dimension, since religion for the classical Greeks was first and foremost state religion, consisting of officially recognized cults that were dedicated to the gods and closely tied to political institutions; and the two speeches, precisely by virtue of their complementarity—God is played out against mankind, theology against law—call our attention to the supra-individual, social dimension of the phenomenon of desire.

The next pair of speeches highlights by contrast the bodily, individual side of desire: first the physician Eryximachus gives a rather austere, but for that very reason also quite charming, pseudoscientific account of eros as a medical phenomenon (185e–188e); then the poet Aristophanes returns to a fundamentally comic tone—the tone that dominates the dialogue as a whole and is after all far more appropriate to this theme—by demonstrating the anthropological centrality of eros by means of a humorous myth recounting how human beings, originally circular, were long ago divided into halves and how, ever since, each incomplete half has striven for supplementation and reconciliation (189c–193d). In this case, too, the two speeches are complementary: the newest scientific knowledge is contrasted with an archaic and primitive form of folk wisdom, the severity and earnestness of medicine with the quirky absurdity of Aristophanic myth (which also complements Phaedrus's first, theological speech). Both, however, equally insist upon the corporeality of eros, upon the erotic experiences that all of us have, individually, with our own bodies.

In the third pair of speeches, the main forms of Greek *logos* are finally introduced: first the poet Agathon, speaking from the point of view of poetry and rhetoric, examines the phenomenon of eros in its character—namely, that it is what is most beautiful—and in its effects—namely, that it bestows the gift of the four canonical virtues (194e–197e); then Socrates gives his own philosophical speech, to which we will return shortly (201c–212b). After Agathon's semiphilosophical argument about eros as the foundation for a vulgar aesthetics and ethics, Socrates goes on to reach a deeper, genuinely philosophical dimension, that of metaphysics. Agathon's pretty but unmistakably superficial treatment is explicitly criticized by Socrates and serves as an anticlimactic foil for Socrates' own speech, which follows it directly and provides the high point of the whole dialogue.

The last speech, delivered by the drunken Alcibiades, is offered from the standpoint of a lover and deals with eros as it is personified in such individuals as Socrates and his admirers. It thereby complements the supra-individual, often abstract theories of the previous speakers by supplying the necessary counterpart to them, the passionate confession of the personal experience of eros, with all its urgency, irresistibleness, beauty, and danger. Behind the rollicking gaiety of this conclusion, every Greek reader would have sensed the impending tragedies of Alcibiades' disastrous later career and, inextricably connected with it, of Socrates' own fate. These hints give the phenomenon of eros, as it is presented by the dialogue as a whole, an implicit profundity and earnestness that go beyond even the explicit profundity and earnestness of Socrates' central speech.

That central speech entrusts instruction in the mysteries of eros neither to Socrates himself nor to any other male philosopher, but to a woman named Diotima, a prophetess and a healer. Thus, in the center of a philosophical discourse, it is a religious authority who speaks; in the heart of this masculine symposium, from which all women have been banished, we hear—albeit indirectly and in fragments—a female voice. Diotima explains to the young Socrates what the older Socrates will explain to his dinner companions and to us: namely, that Eros is neither a god nor a mortal, but a *daemon*, an intermediary and a hybrid who unifies and binds together all separated spheres. As the son of Poros (the way or means by which a goal can be reached) and Penia (the poverty or lack of means that is incapable of reaching any worthwhile goal), conceived after a wild and debauched drinking party (a parodic heavenly counterpart to the all-too-human and yet self-controlled symposium reported in the dialogue), Eros exhibits characteristics of both his parents. Like his mother, he is essentially needy, because one only desires what one does not possess; like his father, however, he is always able to overcome this deficit and reach his goal. Like his mother he is absolutely ignorant, but like his father he is the epitome of wisdom—thereby Eros also combines the two characteristics of the Platonic philosopher, who is neither completely wise nor wholly ignorant, who knows that he does not know, and who does not posses wisdom but instead desires it (philo-sophos: "desirer of wisdom"). According to Diotima, Eros is directed not so much toward the beautiful as toward the good, not so much toward the appearance of beauty as toward the possession of the good, and not so much toward temporary possession as toward a lasting possession—all opinions that, in the context of the traditional Greek understanding of eros, must have sounded paradoxical or even absurd. But the greatest paradox of all is reached in Diotima's further assertion that this lasting possession of the good can only be accomplished through "giving birth in beauty, whether in body or in soul" (206b).[1] Socrates' reaction to this obscure utterance, "It would take divination to figure out what you mean. I can't," must have made explicit the baffled reaction of many Greek readers when they first encountered the

---

1. Here and throughout I cite the *Symposium* from Plato "Symposium," trans. Nehamas and Woodruff.

prophetess's oracular riddle. And so Diotima launches into a long speech, in which she develops an astonishing metaphysics of sexuality:

> "Well, I'll tell you more clearly," she said. "All of us are pregnant, Socrates, both in body and in soul, and, as soon as we come to a certain age, we naturally desire to give birth. Now no one can possibly give birth in anything ugly; only in something beautiful. Pregnancy, reproduction—this is an immortal thing for a mortal animal to do, and it cannot occur in anything that is out of harmony, but ugliness is out of harmony with all that is godly. Beauty, however, is in harmony with the divine. Therefore the goddess who presides at childbirth—she is Moira or Eilithuia—is really Beauty. That's why, whenever pregnant animals or persons draw near to beauty, they become gentle and joyfully disposed and give birth and reproduce; but near ugliness they are foulfaced and draw back in pain; they turn away and shrink back and do not reproduce, and because they hold on to what they carry inside them, the labor is painful. This is the source of the great excitement about beauty that comes to anyone who is pregnant and already teeming with life: beauty releases them from their great pain. You see, Socrates," she said, "what Love wants is not beauty, as you think it is."
>
> "Well, what is it, then?"
>
> "Reproduction and birth in beauty."
>
> "Maybe," I said. "Certainly," she said. "Now, why reproduction? It's because reproduction goes on forever; it is what mortals have in place of immortality. A lover must desire immortality along with the good, if what we agreed earlier was right, that Love wants to possess the good forever. It follows from our argument that Love must desire immortality." (206c–207a)

Humans are here defined as beings who are mortal and yet filled with an in-satiable desire to be immortal. In actuality, as individuals, humans can never become immortal, because if they did they would cross the boundary that forever separates humans from gods. Through generation, however, humans can attain a kind of immortality, the only kind available to them. By means of sexual reproduction, animals attain immortality, if not of the individual, then at least of the species. The same goes for inferior human beings, Diotima explains, those who direct themselves exclusively toward the body and think only about bodily reproduction. But those few human beings who understand something about wisdom and poetry—that is, those who know that one can lit-erally exist only in a figurative, metaphorical sense—direct themselves toward the soul and toward a different kind of generation, not that of living, biological children but of metaphorical, ideal children, namely, of speeches like those of Diotima and of the whole *Symposium*:

> "Now, some people are pregnant in body, and for this reason turn more to women and pursue love in that way, providing themselves through childbirth with immortality and remembrance and happiness, as they think, for all time to come; while others are pregnant in soul—because there surely *are* those who are even more pregnant in their souls than in their bodies, and these are pregnant with what is fitting for a soul to bear and bring to birth. And what is fitting? Wisdom and the rest of virtue, which all poets beget, as well as all the craftsmen who are said to be creative. But by far the greatest and most beautiful part of wisdom deals with the proper ordering of cities and households, and that is called moderation and justice. When someone has been pregnant with these in his soul from early youth, while he is still a virgin, and, having arrived at the proper age desires to beget and give birth, he too will certainly go about seeking the beauty in which he would beget; for he will never beget in anything ugly. Since he is pregnant, then, he is much more drawn to bodies that are beautiful than to those that are ugly; and if he also has the luck to find a soul that is beautiful and noble and well-formed, he is even more drawn to this combination; such a man makes him instantly teem with ideas and arguments about virtue—the qualities a virtuous man should have and the customary activities in which he should engage; and so he tries to educate him. In my view, you see, when he makes contact with someone beautiful and keeps company with him, he conceives and gives birth to what he has been carrying inside him for ages. And whether they are together or apart, he remembers that beauty. And in common with him he nurtures the newborn; such people therefore have much more to share than do the parents of human children, and have a firmer bond of friendship, because the children in whom they have a share are more beautiful and more immortal. Everyone would rather have such children than human ones, and would look up to Homer, Hesiod, and the other good poets with envy and admiration for the offspring they have left behind—offspring which, because they are immortal themselves, provide their parents with immortal glory and remembrance." (208e–209d)

Building on three oppositions—body/soul, multiplicity/unity, and human/ divine—Diotima goes on to construct her celebrated ladder of beauty, upon which philosophical men can, and therefore must, climb up toward ever higher rungs, from the lowest one, which is understandable and hence easily reachable for all of us, past various middle steps, and finally to the very highest one, which is reserved for and comprehensible to only the very few:

> A lover who goes about this matter correctly must begin in his youth to devote himself to beautiful bodies. First, if the leader leads aright, he should love one body and beget beautiful ideas there; then he should realize that the beauty of any one body is brother to the beauty of any other and that if he is to pursue beauty of form he'd be very foolish not to think that the beauty of all bodies is one and the same. When he grasps this, he must become a lover of all beautiful bodies, and he must think that this wild gaping after just one body is a small thing and despise it.
>
> After this he must think that the beauty of people's souls is more valuable than the beauty of their bodies, so that if someone is decent in his soul, even though he is scarcely blooming in his body, our lover must be content to love and care for him and to seek to give birth to such ideas as will make young men better. The result is that our lover will be forced to gaze at the beauty of activities and laws and to see that all this is akin to itself, with the result that he will think that the beauty of bodies is a thing of no importance. After customs he must move on to various kinds of knowledge. The result is that he will see the beauty of knowledge and be looking mainly not at beauty in a single example—as a servant would who favored the beauty of a little boy or a man or a single custom (being a slave, of course, he's low and small-minded)—but the lover is turned to the great sea of beauty, and, gazing upon this, he gives birth to many gloriously beautiful ideas and theories, in unstinting love of wisdom, until, having grown and been strengthened there, he catches sight of such knowledge, and it is the knowledge of such beauty.
> (210 a–e)

The apparently irresistible striving upward along a path of ascent is designed to suggest an unbroken continuity in the transition from one level to the next and thereby to divert attention from what is in fact the unmistakable logical dissimilarity of these steps. From the first step (a beautiful body) to the next (many beautiful bodies), there is a simple pluralization; to the next (all beautiful bodies), a generalization within a determinate category; to the next (pursuits), an abstraction together with a category change; to the next (sciences), an increasingly strict family resemblance; and to the last (the beautiful as such), a change in the basic premise or subject matter. Similarly, the plasticity and familiarity of the first steps prepare the way rhetorically for the claim that the last steps are no less visible and comprehensible, a claim that otherwise would be very hard indeed to justify.

III

The *Phaedrus* takes as its theme not only eros but also rhetoric, persuasion, writing, and more. It is no accident that all these themes are brought together in the context of a discussion of eros, for what kind of desire would not want to be persuasive? And what persuasion can be imagined that could succeed without any erotic component at all? For this dialogue, in contrast to the *Symposium*, eros is more a means toward a better understanding of something else than the main theme itself. Thus, at least for present purposes, what this dialogue teaches about eros can be understood as an extension and supplement of the doctrine of the *Symposium*.

The main text on eros in the *Phaedrus* comes from Socrates' palinode (244c ff.). After his initial, sober rejection of eros, Socrates realizes upon further reflection, and after a sharp divine admonition, that not every madness must necessarily be something bad. He goes on to acknowledge four kinds of madness as valid sources of an extraordinary wisdom: prophecy, medicine, poetry, and erotic desire. In order to characterize eros in more detail, he makes a sharp distinction between the soul, which is said to be self-moving and therefore immortal (because anything that is moved by something else stops moving as soon as the origin of its motion stops), and the body, which is said to be purely mechanical and destined to die. The wings of the soul, by means of which it ascends beyond what is purely bodily, are said to be nourished by the beautiful and to reach the condition of greatest arousal and vitality through the sensible stimuli that flow into the soul through the eyes. A common person reacts to such stimuli with the wish for sexual union, whereas a higher, philosophically gifted individual reacts differently (but not entirely so):

> But when one who is fresh from the mystery, and saw much of the vision, beholds a godlike face or bodily form that truly expresses beauty, first there comes upon him a shuddering and a measure of that awe which the vision inspired, and then reverence as at the sight of a god: and but for fear of being deemed a very madman he would offer sacrifice to his beloved, as to a holy image of deity. Next, with the passing of the shudder, a strange sweating and fever seizes him: for by reason of the stream of beauty entering in through his eyes there comes a warmth, whereby his soul's plumage is fostered; and with that warmth the roots of the wings are melted, which for long had been so hardened and closed up that nothing could grow; then as the nourishment is poured in, the stump of the wing swells and hastens to grow from the root over the whole substance of the soul: for aforetime the whole soul was furnished with wings. Meanwhile she throbs with ferment in every part, and

even as a teething child feels an aching and pain in its gums when a toot
come through, so does the soul of him who is beginning to grow his wi
ferment and painful irritation. Wherefore as she gazes upon the boy's beauty, ...
admits a flood of particles streaming therefrom—that is why we speak of a 'flood
of passion'—whereby she is warmed and fostered; then has she respite from her
anguish, and is filled with joy. But when she has been parted from him and become
parched, the openings of those outlets at which the wings are sprouting dry up
likewise and are closed, so that the wing's germ is barred off; and behind its bars,
together with the flood aforesaid, it throbs like a fevered pulse, and pricks at its
proper outlet; and thereat the whole soul round about is stung and goaded into
anguish; howbeit she remembers the beauty of her beloved, and rejoices again.
(251a–d)[2]

Here too, as in the *Symposium*, Socrates freely admits that even philosophical
lovers may end up participating now and then in physical love (256c). But here
too, as there, he gives us to understand: the less, the better.

IV

In summary, we may indicate some of the main features of the Platonic theory
of eros as follows:

1. The common modern conception of Platonic love has very little to do
with Plato's actual theory of love, which is not so much about the idealization,
restraint, or even repression of sexuality as it is about the stimulation, elevation, and channeling of sexuality, so that sexuality can be turned against itself
and redirected toward new objects. In Plato's version of Platonic love, sexuality, so far from being extirpated, is incited, enhanced, and sublimated in order
first to create and then to liberate large quantities of psychic energy that can
be put to the service of philosophical knowledge. To the potential objection
that such an interpretation as the one proposed here might seem Freudian and
thus anachronistic, it can be replied, first, that few other passages in ancient
Greek literature come as close to the Freudian notion of the relation between
conscious and unconscious as does one sentence in Aristophanes' speech in the
Symposium ("It's obvious the soul of every lover longs for something else; his
soul cannot say what it is, but like an oracle it has a sense of what it wants, and
like an oracle it hides behind a riddle," 192c–d), and second, that Freud himself
repeatedly and prominently pointed to the similarities between his own views

2. Plato, *Plato's Phaedrus*, 96–97.

on human psychology and Plato's theory of desire.[3] Therefore, to point out the parallels between Plato and Freud is not to attempt to explain the former by recourse to the latter, but to indicate one of the many paths of the reception of Plato in modern Western culture. But if this is clear, it remains fundamentally obscure whether, on Plato's account, the relationship between philosophical and biological eros is to be thought of as being more in the nature of an analogy or of a substitute. Are the two kinds of eros mirror images, metaphorically related in such a way that each one retains its relative autonomy but is modeled upon the other, or is philosophical eros supposed to take the place of biological eros and completely replace it? This may be considered a variant of a fundamental obscurity in the Platonic theory of mimesis, namely, whether an imitation merely corresponds to the original or whether it might not also threaten to usurp the place of the original. In Plato's theory of eros, homosexuality is evidently preferable to heterosexuality (at least in part because the latter is so much more inextricably bound up with biological reproduction), but in comparison to both of these, the preference goes unquestionably to a resolute abstinence from biological eros altogether. Exceptions are tolerated as a concession to human weakness—and also, no doubt, in order not to make it too difficult to recruit new students. All parents are failed philosophers: sexuality is not merely a metaphor for philosophy; instead, philosophy is the only genuine possibility for an authentic human communication, whereas any form of participation in the common modes of sexuality betrays a misunderstanding of the true destiny of human beings. Plato does not downplay, neglect, or minimize the bodily erotic drive but instead evokes, intensifies, and even demonizes it—only to then explain it away as a misunderstanding or as a metaphor and to turn it against the body itself. In all of this one is struck by a kind of Puritanism that can also be found in many other aspects of Platonic philosophy and that constitutes one of its least attractive aspects.

2. Eros assumes a key role within Platonic philosophy as a mediator between temporality and timelessness. Aristotle recognized that one of the essential aspects of Plato's philosophy lay in the necessity, and difficulty, of precisely this mediation (*Metaphysics* A.6). If we see Plato as the heir, not entirely free from contradiction, to two different philosophical traditions—on one hand, a Heraclitean tradition, which emphasizes the constant mutability of all being, and on the other, a Parmenidean tradition, which locates true being only in what does not change—then bridging the difference between what is subject

---

3. E.g., Freud, *Gesammelte Werke*, 5:32; 13:62, 99; 14:105; 16:20.

to time and what is outside of time certainly must form a central part of his philosophical project. Within the Platonic theory of knowledge, the theory of *methexis*, the participation of individual things in the ideas that give them their being and their intelligibility, fulfills this function. In Plato's psychology of the human soul, one finds similar instances, for example: the drive toward knowledge that strives to go beyond the realm of changeable objects to the unchanging principles of what can be known; the striving of mortals to become as much like the god(s) as possible; and, certainly, eros too, which, because it points outward beyond the limited lifetime of the individual human being, can be interpreted not as a drive for purely sensual satisfaction but rather as a form of participation in the eternal (to the degree that this is possible for mortals), which otherwise would remain fully inaccessible to them. In other words, the sensual pleasure of human erotic experience is derived from the superhuman bliss of the divine; it is neither an enticement nor an instinct but rather the trace of the truly transcendent in the muck of this world.

3. One particularly striking feature of the Platonic theory of sexuality is its fundamental undecidedness with regard to gender specification. It ascribes to men desires and drives that, especially in traditional Greek culture, were seen as belonging only to women. In the *Symposium*, Plato starts from the assumption that men (not human beings) are ruled by an overpowering desire to give birth (not to beget)—precisely as if they were filled with a boundless envy of female pregnancy. In the passage cited from the *Phaedrus*, it is anything but clear whether the basic metaphor is female pregnancy or male erection or, if both are meant, which seems in the end to be most probable, how this is to be understood in detail. The almost clinical precision of the anatomical terminology Plato employs serves only to intensify the difficulty. This feminization of the male philosopher is a curious feature of Platonic philosophy that finds expression, for example, in the fact that the source of Socrates' wisdom about eros, Diotima, is a woman, and in the fact that Socrates likes to identify himself as a midwife (*Theat.* 149a ff., 157c–d, 184a–b, 210b–c, etc.). Should we interpret this as Plato's emancipatory attempt to help women to attain their deserved but long withheld rights? It would perhaps be agreeable if we could do so, but such an interpretation is in fact extraordinarily unlikely. Instead, it seems almost as though Plato wished men alone to take on the sexual functions of both sexes so that women would at last become altogether dispensable and men would finally be able to live on, alone and happily, in a world without women. Similar fantasies can be found haunting other classical Greek texts, such as Euripides' *Hippolytus* (616–24).

V

Although Plato's theory of eros is in many respects absolutely singular within the entire context of Greek culture, it nevertheless derives elements from a number of venerable traditions, which Plato willfully reinterprets for his purposes. At least three such traditions can be easily identified:

1. The Homeric epics start from the assumption of a fundamental contrast between the mortal life of a human being and his immortal fame. Achilles is the paradigm of a man who, given the choice, opts for a short life and eternal glory. And Helen, as beautiful as a goddess and the cause of death for countless men, asserts in one instance that her suffering and that of the others serve to provide future bards with material for their epics (*Il.* 6.357–58). This contrast derives from the temporal remoteness of an ancient and long-vanished heroic world from the present one, a separation that could only be comprehended and mediated by means of the cultural memory deposited in the form of a tradition of oral poetry bridging many generations. Homer bequeathed to Greek culture both an acute awareness of individual biological mortality and an insatiable desire for immortality in *logos*.

2. In early Greek lyric poetry, the temporal immortality of the beloved or of the lover is celebrated in the image of a bird, which is unencumbered by spatial limitations. Theognis furnishes his beloved Kyrnos with wings that allow him to fly out over the sea; Pindar pays tribute in the image of the royal eagle as much to himself as to the victor whom he is paid to immortalize; Horace later supplies an almost comic variant, in which he describes his gradual metamorphosis into a swan in minute, almost embarrassing detail. This imagery celebrates metaphorically the oral dissemination of a successful song beyond the spatial boundaries of its first performance; overcoming space suggests, in turn, overcoming time. In this light, the Platonic theory of eros can be understood as the translation of a topos from love poetry into philosophy: eros bestows immortality in *logos*.

3. There is widespread agreement among philosophers before Plato that the object of genuine philosophical knowledge must be entirely free of temporal change. Just as a statement that is sometimes true, sometimes false, cannot claim absolute validity, so too an object of knowledge for which absolute validity is claimed must be unchangeable. Philosophical knowledge seeks immortality in *logos*. The way of life followed by some schools, in particular by the Pythagoreans and Empedocles, betrays a certain asceticism, but this usually takes the form of vegetarianism, not the renunciation of sexual intercourse. In general, it is not to Greek philosophy that sexual abstinence belongs

but rather to certain highly limited Greek religious institutions, above all, the mysteries. Plato's idiosyncratic attempt to demonize a strenuously repressed homoeroticism derives in part from the social institution of aristocratic pederasty in Athens, in part from a religious prohibition against sexuality that is known to us from the mysteries, and in part from his own psychic needs.

VI

The history of the afterlife of the Platonic theory of eros reaches from Plato's own time to ours, and, for better and worse, extends through all areas of Western culture. To conclude, I would like to call attention to a tiny and almost fully concealed fragment of that reception history, to be found in the works of Marcel Proust. Proust's conviction of the interdependency between homosexuality and certain forms of artistic production is well known, as is his detailed analysis of love as a combination of reflection and projection; in both regards, he proves himself to be a true student of Plato. But even in the lovely episode in the first volume of *À la recherche du temps perdu*, in which he recounts with an enchanting blend of sentimentality, irony, and self-irony how Marcel gives birth to his very first literary creation, a short essay on the church towers of Martinville, Proust is no less true to the Platonic tradition. At the end of the long (self-)quotation from this modest essay, Proust describes the reaction of the young artist to his first artistic accomplishment:

> I never thought again of this page, but at the moment when, in the corner of the box-seat where the doctor's coachman was in the habit of stowing in a hamper the poultry he had bought at Martinville market, I had finished writing it, I was so filled with happiness, I felt that it had so entirely relieved my mind of its obsession with the steeples and the mystery which lay behind them, that, as though I myself were a hen and had just laid an egg, I began to sing at the top of my voice.[4]

The mystery of true being concealed behind appearances; the male's desire to give birth; the contrast between animal reproduction and human creation of an artful *logos*; the contrast between body and soul; the joy in artistic productivity; the citationality that points beyond the boundaries not only of time but even of temporality; the self-stylization, made irresistible by a virtuoso self-irony; and finally, the young Marcel as poet, as lover, and as prophet (and perhaps also as physician of the soul), whose creative genius manifests itself in

---

4. Proust, *Swann's Way*, 256–57 = Proust, *À la recherche du temps perdu*, ed. Tadié, ed., 1:180.

the epiphany of a divine bird, as a—in this case delightfully comical—clucking hen: what could be more Platonic?

BIBLIOGRAPHICAL POSTSCRIPT

The standard edition of the Greek text of Plato's *Symposium* is still the one contained in *Platonis Opera*, edited by John Burnet, vol. 2 (Oxford: Clarendon Press, 1901); it will be replaced in the foreseeable future by a new Oxford edition, and not a moment too soon.

The English-language commentary of choice is now Plato, *Symposium*, edited and with introduction, translation, and commentary by C. J. Rowe (Warminster: Aris and Phillips, 1998); but students should still consult Plato, *The Symposium*, 2nd edition, edited by R. G. Bury (1909; Cambridge: W. Heffer and Sons, 1932), and Plato, *Symposium*, edited by Kenneth Dover (Cambridge: Cambridge University Press, 1980). There is an excellent recent French translation with a long introduction, useful commentary, and fairly full bibliography: *Platon, Le Banquet*, présentation et traduction inédite par Luc Brisson (Paris: Flammarion, 1998).

A conception as difficult and as fascinating and a text as rich and as central as the *Symposium* have, expectably, produced an enormous secondary bibliography. Here I can indicate only a few of the more important and interesting English-language studies of certain aspects of Plato's theory and of this dialogue, leaving aside studies devoted exclusively to the *Phaedrus*.

On Plato's views concerning love, desire, and friendship, I, like many other contemporary scholars, have been much influenced by David M. Halperin, "Why Is Diotima a Woman?" in his *One Hundred Years of Homosexuality and Other Essays on Greek Love* (New York: Routledge, 1990), 113–51, 190–211. There is also a stimulating general account in Giovanni Ferrari, "Platonic Love," in *The Cambridge Companion to Plato*, edited by Richard H. Kraut (New York: Cambridge University Press, 1992), 248–76. For other philosophical discussions, see Dorothea Frede, "Out of the Cave: What Socrates Learned from Diotima," in *Nomodeiktes: Greek Studies in Honor of Martin Ostwald*, edited by Ralph M. Rosen and Joseph Farrell (Ann Arbor: University of Michigan Press, 1993), 397–422; Charles H. Kahn, "Plato's Theory of Desire," *Review of Metaphysics* 41 (1987–88): 77–103; Gerasimos Santas, *Plato and Freud: Two Theories of Love* (Oxford: Blackwell, 1988); A. W. Price, *Love and Friendship in Plato and Aristotle* (Oxford: Clarendon Press, 1989); C. D. C. Reeve, "Telling the Truth about Love: Plato's *Symposium*," *Boston Area Colloquium in Ancient Philosophy* 8 (1992): 89–114; and Martin Warner, "Love, Self, and Plato's *Symposium*," *Philosophical Quarterly* 29 (1979): 329–39.

On the question of the individual as an object of Platonic desire, see still Gregory Vlastos, "The Individual as an Object of Love in Plato," in his *Platonic Studies* (Princeton, NJ: Princeton University Press, 1981), 3–42; and more recently, Christopher Gill, "Platonic Love and Individuality," in *Polis and Politics: Essays in Greek Moral and Political Philosophy*, edited by Andros Loizou and Harrey Lesser (Aldershot: Avebury, 1990), 69–88, and Gill, *Personality in Greek Epic, Tragedy, and Philosophy: The Self in Dialogue* (Oxford: Clarendon Press, 1996); and Martha Nussbaum, "The Speech of Alcibiades. A Reading of Plato's *Symposium*," *Philosophy and Literature* 3 (1979): 131–72.

Plato's strange views on reproduction and immortality are studied by M. Dyson, "Immortality and Procreation in Plato's *Symposium*," *Antichthon* 20 (1986): 59–72; Michael O'Brien, "'Becoming Immortal' in Plato's *Symposium*," in *Greek Poetry and Philosophy: Studies in Honour of Leonard Woodbury*, edited by Douglas E. Gerber (Chica, CA: Scholars Press, 1984), 185–205; Elizabeth E. Pender, "Spiritual Pregnancy in Plato's *Symposium*," *Classical Quarterly* 42 (1992): 72–86; and Paul Plass, "Plato's Pregnant Lover," *Symbolae Osloenses* 53 (1978): 47–55.

Various literary aspects of the dialogue are examined by Diskin Clay in "The Tragic and Comic Poet of the *Symposium*," in *Essays in Ancient Greek Philosophy*, vol. 2, edited by John P. Anton and Anthony Preus (Albany: State University of New York Press, 1983), 186–202; Kenneth N. M. Dorter, "The Significance and Interconnection of the Speeches in Plato's *Symposium*," *Philosophy and Rhetoric* 2 (1969): 215–34; and Michael C. Stokes, *Plato's Socratic Conversations: Drama and Dialectic in Three Dialogues* (Baltimore: Johns Hopkins University Press, 1986). On the rhetorical theories implicit in the dialogue, see William G. Kelly, "Rhetoric as Seduction," *Philosophy and Rhetoric* 6 (1973): 69–80; Andrea Wilson Nightingale, "The Folly of Praise: Plato's Critique of Encomiastic Discourse in the *Lysis* and *Symposium*," *Classical Quarterly* 43 (1993): 112–30; and Wayne N. Thompson, "The *Symposium*: A Neglected Source for Plato's Ideas on Rhetoric," in *Plato: True and Sophistic Rhetoric*, edited by Keith V. Erickson (Amsterdam: Rodopi, 1979), 325–38.

Finally, the reader might also find some stimulating ideas in Luce Irigaray, "Sorcerer Love: A Reading of Plato's *Symposium*," *Hypatia* 3 (1989): 32–44, on which see Andrea Nye, "The Hidden Host: Irigaray and Diotima at Plato's *Symposium*," *Hypatia* 3 (1989): 45–61.

LOVE'S IRONY: SIX REMARKS

ON PLATONIC EROS

DAVID M. HALPERIN

For Valerie Traub

I

Irony consists in meaning something other than what you say. It enables you to say one thing and imply the opposite. It indicates that what you said is not what you meant. Or it can simply warn your audience not to identify you too closely with the view you just expressed. Irony allows the speaker to disappear as a guarantor of authenticity, to become unfindable in the utterance, to escape responsibility for meaning. Irony evades the dichotomies of sincerity and falsehood, belief and unbelief, being for oneself and being for others. It registers a shifting and dynamic tension among different orders of meaning.

That is the formal structure of irony. Irony has a form, then, but it is not itself a formal property of language. It has no fixed or unambiguous linguistic markers. It requires a community of understanding. "I just love this weather" bears no indexical sign that identifies it as an ironic utterance. Spoken by one sunbather to another on a tropical island, it may have nothing ironic about it; spoken in the context of an ice storm, it is ironic only if speaker and audience participate in a shared experience of meteorological discomfort (if the statement is made long distance to someone in a different climate who has no way of knowing what the weather is actually like where the speaker happens to be, it is at most deceptive, not ironic at all—except, perhaps, in the solipsistic mental world of the speaker). Irony is intentional and relational. It is a means of communication, and it presupposes specific social and discursive situations. Irony is a species of rhetoric.

Even when uttered ironically, the statement "I just love this weather" is not a very good example of irony; it does not convey what irony is or what it can do. That is because it does not display the dynamism of irony, because it does not vibrate unstably between belief and unbelief. A more representative instance of irony can be found in the opening sentence of *Pride and Prejudice*: "It is a truth universally acknowledged, that a single man in possession of a good fortune, must be in want of a wife." Perhaps this actually isn't true; perhaps not everyone thinks it is. But who would dare to deny it? Not Jane Austen.

Irony is never completely self-evident. There is no statement so ironic as to ensure that its irony will not be lost. Jane Austen has been taken at her word. Swift's *Modest Proposal* has been read straight. Randy Newman's song, "Short People," an object lesson in the absurdities of social prejudice, caused outrage when it was released in the United States in 1977: audiences understood Newman to be claiming, in all seriousness, that "short people got no reason to live." (Americans have an international reputation for being deaf to irony: they are only ever able to hear, or mean, one thing at a time.)

Irony is unlimited. It cannot be contained. No word, sentence, topic, or subject matter is off limits to irony. There is never any way to know in advance whether the meaning of an utterance will turn out to have been corroded by irony. Nothing is constitutionally immune to irony.

Some experiences, however, are incompatible with irony. In order to have them at all, it is necessary to banish any hint of irony. Conversely, the arrival of irony signals the end of the experience, or its diminution. Irony's opposite is intensity. In moments of intense, overwhelming sensation, we have little awareness of context and no attention to spare for more than one set of meanings. In such states, we become literalists: we can experience only one kind of thing. The three cardinal experiences that demand the elimination of irony, or that cannot survive irony, are raw grief or suffering, religious transport, and sexual passion. Little wonder, then, if they tend to merge.

II

Good sex is not ironic. When sex is passionate, it makes us unaware of our surroundings, indifferent to what we look like, oblivious to the larger context. Intense sexual pleasure is notoriously impervious to competing realities. The very intensity of its focus on its object and on its own sensations excludes a multiplicity of possible meanings.

When those meanings flood back in, when context reasserts itself, then the moment of intensity is past, and we are suddenly overtaken by irony. Which is why we feel an impulse to smile—with embarrassment, affection, or relief.

In backrooms, bathhouses, and sex clubs, no one smiles while cruising. To smile at you would be to acknowledge, and to invite a common awareness on your part, of the one thing that neither of us has ever doubted for a moment but that our mutual quest for self-loss in sex forbids us, temporarily, to admit— namely, that we are both human beings related by our participation in a shared social situation. To admit that would be to allow for the possibility of irony in our apprehension of our circumstances and of each other. The moment you smile at me is the moment I know it's all over. If I smile at you before it's over, I intend for it to stop, and I smile in order to break the contact.

Good sex is not social, not while it lasts. There is nothing polite or friendly or good natured about my desire to break down the limits between you and me, to test how far my body and my desire can be made to fit with yours. For that purpose, what I need is not to situate you in the larger social context of our encounter, of which we are both aware, but to ignore everything except what I feel about you, what I want to do with you, and what it is about you that makes me want to do it.

"Fuck me," pronounced in such circumstances, is the least ironic utterance in the world. There is only one thing it can mean, and it must mean only and exactly what it says.

Actors in pornographic movies do not have to be good at their lines. It is not necessary to sound sincere, or credible, when you say, "Fuck me," so long as the other person's desires, your lover's or your spectator's, are passionately engaged. What is required is not that the words themselves be believable, only that they be uttered. The intensity of the desire they express, and of the desire they mobilize, is sufficient to neutralize, if not quite to banish, the ironic awareness of everything about the utterance that may cause it to sound fake. If it sounds fake to you, that's because your desire is no longer intense: either you're watching a bad pornographic movie, or you're watching a pornographic movie for the second time.

The bad dubbing of Fassbinder's last film, *Querelle*, only enhances the excru- ciating improbability of its dialogue. In a stunning betrayal of Genet's entire design for his novel, Fassbinder puts the words of the narrator into the mouths of the characters. What had made those characters so erotically compelling, both for Genet and for his narrator, was in part their butch inarticulacy: the only language they have in which to express themselves is the salty, macho slang of the merchant marine. To endow Genet's sailors with the capacity to articulate the workings of their own subjectivity in the nuanced speech of the men who desire them is to push gay pornography to its breaking point. Now, instead of saying, "Fuck me" (which he's too virile to say anyway), Querelle is required to say, "I'm on the brink of a shame from which no man ever rises, but only in that shame will I find my everlasting peace." The effect is not just wildly implausible; it is one long assault on psychological realism in the realm of pornography. What keeps *Querelle* teetering, just barely, this side of the completely ludicrous is the aura of erotic intensity in which Fassbinder bathes the entire mise-en-scène and the deliriously rapt contemplation of masculine power and beauty to which he summons the spectator. Fassbinder thereby demonstrates the extraordinary ability of erotic ecstasy to stave off irony, to prevent it from deflating the breathless intensity of sexual excitement, despite nearly irresistible provocations to do so.

The intensity we bring to sex, or that we find in sex, may be predicated on an originary intuition of the impossibility of union through sex, the impossibility of a fusion of bodies, of a merging of subjectivities. And no doubt it is through a calculated heightening of the tension between our recognition and our denial of those impossibilities that we manage to increase the thrill of sex. In that sense, a certain ironic play with the limits of our bodies and our selves, with the surfaces that both separate us and enable us to touch each other, intensifies the excitement, the longing, the desperation of sex. Nonetheless, at the peak of its most ecstatic transports, sex obliges us to suspend all acknowledgment of irony, to keep the absurdity of what we are doing from becoming explicit.

III

Erotic desire, then, would seem to lie at the farthest possible remove from irony. And yet it would be hard to imagine a more powerful or more eloquent demonstration of irony than the lived experience of erotic desire. It is no accident that Plato, the first person on record in Western history to formulate a theory of erotic desire, is also the source of our concept of irony. Plato's best-known version of irony is epistemic, not erotic: it is Socratic irony, the attitude of ignorance assumed by Socrates that paradoxically enables him to rebut everyone else's claims to knowledge. "Irony" is a Greek word, and in Plato's Athens it meant "mockery," the sense it still has today in French. When various characters in the Platonic dialogues call Socrates an ironist, they mean he makes fun of people's pretensions. But Socratic irony, as Plato portrays it, extends the meaning of that word beyond its contemporary Greek signification and endows it with the dynamic rhetorical properties that we now associate with it. By claiming that the only thing he knows is that he does not know anything, Plato's Socrates both affirms and denies that he possesses knowledge, and this ironic stance enables him to profess genuine admiration for other people's expertise even as he sets about to demolish it. Meaning something other than what he says, refusing to surrender either to skepticism or to authority, Plato's Socrates is an ironist in the modern sense.

Platonic eros may be less flamboyantly ironic than Socratic ignorance but it is no less paradoxical. It describes a sexual desire that cannot be sexually fulfilled. It motivates passionate love affairs that do not consist in the love of persons. Erotic attraction is not physical but metaphysical: it intends an object that cannot be grasped without a finely calibrated knowledge of the kinds and degrees of being. Desire ultimately aims not at bodily contact but at self-transcendence. It means more than human beings realize, and it exceeds what can be realized within the limits of any human life.

Love's ironies are many. But they all come down to a single paradox: the object of desire is not what you think it is.

You do not know what you love, or why. What you seek to possess in love is not what you desire. The desire you feel cannot be expressed or fulfilled. No particular object corresponds to your love.

Irony is the very condition of love, its mode of being. Love is the name we give to that state of mind in which we take another person to be the origin and cause of what we feel. In this ascription we may be right or we may be wrong, but, so long as we are in love, we will never know.

When we are unhappy in love, we typically experience a driving epistemic need to find the cause of our unhappiness, to discover whether it lies in ourselves or in the world. But it is pointless for a lover to attempt to locate the true source of his joy or his suffering: to be in love means to be unable to determine whether the desire one feels originates in oneself or emanates from the other, whether the causes of one's suffering lie in the other or in oneself. The wish to escape, in the midst of grief, from this perplexity, or to transcend it, is a wish to step off the world. Plato's transcendental theory of desire offers such a cure for our suffering, a cure shaped from the start by the reality of the suffering it would spare us, but it can provide this cure only by abolishing the epistemic tension in love, by persuading us ultimately to see love as unitary, logical, consistent, whole, and free from paradox—in short, by saving us once and for all from love's irony. That is why Plato's solution to the problem of love is less interesting, and has proven less convincing, than his analysis of it.

IV

Love is an ironic condition insofar as it produces a necessary doubling of perspective. The lover knows that how the world looks to him is different from how it looks to others, but he can't integrate those different views or reduce one of them to the other. Love is defined by the fact that the truth of love, if there is one, never coincides completely with the experience of love.

What I desire exceeds anything I can demand. I may want to have sex with you, but sex does not enable me to actualize what I feel about you, or what you make me feel. Sex does not translate feeling into act. It testifies to the fact of my desire and it acts out to some small extent the turmoil I experience in your presence, but it merely represents my emotions, as if it were a rhetorical figure: it does not express them. To take sexual intercourse for erotic fulfillment would be to mistake a sign for the thing it signifies. Sex is grotesque to the degree that we seek, through physical machinations, to literalize our desire, and perverse insofar as we attempt, through a persistent keying up of effort, to break out of sex's figurality—to close the distance between signs and things, and thereby to refuse the irony intrinsic to erotic desire.

Your body is at once a vehicle and an obstacle. It narrows the field of my desire and gives my desire a focus, a bounded form, a local habitation. At the same time, it gets in my way: it comes between me and what it is about you that I want. My desire for your body also intends both more and less than your body itself: it intends more, insofar as your body, or its parts, are desirable only in some larger context that underwrites their value (the context of a living, conscious human being who trembles at my touch, for example); it intends less, insofar as I do not fixate democratically on every detail of your body.

Your body's meaning inheres in its features but is not reducible to them. As if it were a statue fished out of the sea, your body promises me what I desire but presents it to me encrusted with the "shell and weed and rock" of material contingency (as Socrates says in Plato's *Republic* [611d]), "full of human flesh and color and many other sorts of mortal trash" (as Diotima scathingly puts it in Plato's *Symposium* [211e]). And so to the extent that I take the materiality of your body to be the goal of my desire, I am an idolater, who pursues not a real object but a wraith, such as the gods sent to Troy in place of Helen (according to some versions of the myth) to be an empty focus of heroic strife (*Republic* 586bc).

The secret of my desire for you is written on your body. But I cannot read it; I cannot decipher the hieroglyphs in which it is encoded. There is not the slightest doubt about the significance that your body holds for me: every hollow, every contour, every modulation of your flesh that evokes my desire is

who claim to judge a man on the basis of nothing besides his physique see in that physique the emanation of an extraordinary life.") All passionate love of individual objects is fetishistic, for Plato and Proust no less than for Freud, because it attaches to particularities that are meaningless in themselves and acquire their erotic significance only from an ulterior idea or value in which individual objects participate. So long as that idea or value remains unidentified, so long as the lover does not possess a completed metaphysics, he is liable to pursue a goal that will neither answer to his true need nor fulfill it.

The sexual idea or value that I pursue in loving you cannot be possessed by possessing you: you are merely the medium through which it manifests itself to me. It transcends you. I want you, but you are not what I want.

Plato locates an ineluctable irony in this gap between the subjective experience of love and its truth. The content of the lover's consciousness does not reflect the actual structure of his desire. Without the benefit of revelation, no lover can discover the object he ultimately seeks or the operation he ultimately wants to perform with it. He experiences a transcendental desire even as its logic escapes him. His instinct is infallible: some awareness of the nature and goal of desire is buried in his soul, as Aristophanes says; whether he likes it or not, his erotic longings are structured by the structure of reality. His passion conforms to the order of things. In this, he bears ironic witness to a metaphysics of desire that he doesn't understand.

Love's greatest truth is also its greatest lie: my love for you is stronger than death, more lasting than the universe itself. No wonder Socrates in the *Symposium* presents love under the sign of an impossible immortality. Love imparts to creatures who are going to die an intuition of eternal reality. That is love's final irony.

v

Relations between Socrates and the members of his circle, as they are portrayed in the *Symposium*, dramatize love's irony. Socrates is old and ugly, yet all the golden youth of Athens are in love with him. Their desire for him is well motivated: he has something they want. But their desire is also perverse because they confound him with it. Without a Platonic analysis, they are unable to see Socrates as a vehicle, as a metaphor, or to distinguish Socrates himself from the value he represents to them.

Their mistake is comic. It leads to all sorts of ridiculous errors and misunderstandings—to Alcibiades' failed seduction of Socrates, whom Alcibiades didn't desire anyway, at least not sexually, though he was driven to pursue him as if Socrates were a beautiful boy. But these confusions are also the stuff of tragedy. Misguided eros turns the Socratic community into a theater of frustration and torment. Alcibiades suffers humiliation and inward agony. And he brings about the Fall of Athens.

The drinking party at the center of Plato's *Symposium* is a historical fiction. Plato was writing at least thirty years after the date on which it was supposed to have taken place. It would have been impossible for a contemporary Greek to read the *Symposium* unironically. (It is as if a modern American writer were to depict, on the eve of the congressional vote on the Gulf of Tonkin Resolution, an all-night seminar featuring Robert Kennedy, Mick Jagger, Paul Tillich, Ethel Merman, Robert Frost, Martin Luther King, Rock Hudson, and Michel Foucault.) Readers of the *Symposium* already know how it all turned out, and we bring to bear on our judgment of the characters our retrospective understanding of how their lives and loves have stood the test of time, how well their words matched their deeds, how intimately their desires contributed to their fates. We read the *Symposium* possessed of a tragic knowledge that is denied the characters at the moment of their speaking. They are surrounded by deep shadows of which they are unaware.

Erotic error has potentially gruesome consequences. Coming so inconveniently between the lover and his unknown object, the beloved's body gives rise to increasingly furious resentment in Western literature since Plato. Even Milton, our great champion of embodied human love, registers distinct frustration at the limits imposed on love's expression by the human body: an unmistakable wistfulness can be heard in the Archangel Raphael's boast to Adam in *Paradise Lost* that angels enjoy sexual pleasure "in eminence," inasmuch as they "obstacle find none / Of membrane, joint, or limb, exclusive bars." Human beings are not so fortunate. The horrific and pointless ransacking of the body in search of the qualities that make it erotically desirable to the lover is a prominent theme of Dennis Cooper's novels. In *Frisk*, for example, one boy describes what it is like to be the object of such an erotic assault, "to have an older man so completely, insanely worked up over me, like if I was where someone had buried some sort of treasure or antidote to something malignant in him." Nothing left for it but to cut a pretty boy to pieces. That is the dark side of Platonism.

Given all the tragicomic disproportions between love and its objects, between the desire I feel and what it is I am able to do about it, between the object I seek and the object I really want, between the experience of love and the truth of love, it is eminently reasonable for Socrates to argue, at the end of the *Symposium*, that a poet skilled in comedy should also be good at composing tragedy, and vice versa. Love's irony is a solvent of formal distinction solves the differences between the genres. The reader does not hear $ arguments; we learn only that he defends what to an ancient Greek a would have been a counterintuitive proposition.

But here is how Socrates ought to have defended that proposition. Love breaks down the division between tragedy and comedy because love's irony cuts both ways. Irony undermines the seriousness of high tragedy, but it also registers how much of civilization is at risk in the deceptive balancing act of romantic comedy. Love makes great men ridiculous—and yet that only shows how, even at its most ludicrous, love can still destroy us. Love is one long comedy of errors, an inexhaustible drama of mistaken identity, but a joke so cruel that it can lead to murder and mayhem. Neither tragedy nor comedy alone can contain the irony of love. To write well about love is to refuse to sacrifice either an amused or an appalled perspective on love to the other. And that means that the only way to write well about love is to write about it ironically.

"When my love swears that she is made of truth," Shakespeare said at the end of his life, "I do believe her though I know she lies." Only an ironic mode of representation can manage to convey with the right doubling of perspective the necessarily unironic experience of love—the falseness of sentiments that we genuinely feel, the irrefutable rightness of feelings that are so wrong, the impossibilities that we both deny and do everything we can to heighten. A frank refusal to disavow the irony of love conduces to a sympathy so encompassing that it can span and combine, without exactly fusing, without reducing to each other, a tragic vision of life and a comic one. That is what Shakespeare demonstrated in *Antony and Cleopatra*, and that is what the few great writers about love, without exception, also understood—that love's irony requires a literary form all its own. Hence the formal originality of Dante and Proust, of Nabokov in *Lolita*, of Plato in the *Phaedrus* and, above all, in the *Symposium*.

VI

The unique literary form that love requires does a lot to reveal the formal properties of the literary as such. All great literature finds some way to acknowledge and to incorporate what it does not say. Tragedy and comedy are shadowed by their opposites: a sense of the perennial possibility of a normal, unagonized existence hovers around the edges of tragedy, while comedy keeps us aware that it is only the providential goodness of our luck that prevents our lives from being plunged into horror and despair. But tragedy plays down comic elements, just as comedy plays down tragic ones; neither attempts to give equal weight to the opposed perspective.

Like all great literary forms, the ironic story of love teases us with the contradictions built into its design. What distinguishes it is the way it holds opposed perspectives in unstable and dynamic equipoise. It thereby pushes to an extreme limit what all good writing aims to do—to impress on us a lively consciousness of what it does not, or what it cannot, say. In that sense, the structure of erotic desire ultimately corresponds to the formal practices and properties of literature itself.

So not only is it fitting, it is necessary and telling that Plato's *Symposium* belongs to no preexisting literary genre. Plato composed the *Symposium* in such a way that it could not be classed according to any of the specific formal criteria that had previously been used to define epic or lyric or tragedy or comedy or history or oratory or natural science. The *Symposium* belongs to a category for which not even Aristotle had a word. It is the first surviving work of Western culture that can claim—and that demands we give it—the undifferentiated generic title of literature.

Love's irony will stop at nothing less.

EROS AND THE ROMAN PHILOSOPHER

SHADI BARTSCH

Eros. How natural for us to invoke this word in the same breath as that of philosophy, with Plato's *Symposium* and *Phaedrus* as our patrimony, dialogues in which Socrates' own admiring response to the beautiful young men in front of him enacts the pedagogical and philosophical message the works would convey. As is well known, both Diotima in the *Symposium* and Socrates in the *Phaedrus* posit as the crucial step to true ideational knowledge the establishment of an erotic and mutually admiring relationship between the philosopher-citizen and the young and freeborn adolescent male whom he has made the object of his attention. I will not rehearse here the arguments of these two texts, nor enter into the ongoing debate about the nature of the philosopher-lover's continuing relationship with the beloved in the ascent passage of the *Symposium*.[1] But it might be worth reminding my readers of the language of the famously erotic description in the *Phaedrus*, in which this relationship, both sexual and educational in nature,[2] is incubated in an exchange of the gaze predicated on the sight of the Beautiful. As Socrates explains to the young Phaedrus, it is

---

1. The Platonic treatment of eros is complicated and context driven, and the invocation of the *Phaedrus* and the *Symposium* in this essay cannot make any claim to represent a comprehensive account of Platonic views on eros rather than an account of one aspect of his treatment. For scholarship supporting the perspective taken here, see Griswold, *Self-Knowledge in Plato's "Phaedrus."* For detailed discussions of the continuing role (or not) of physical arousal in the philosopher's pederastic relationship, see Griffith, "Left-Hand Horses"; Price, *Love and Friendship*; and White, "Love and the Individual."

2. For general studies of Greek pederasty, see Cantarella, *Bisexuality,* chaps. 2 and 3; Dover, *Greek Homosexuality,* esp. 81–110; and Percy, *Pederasty and Pedagogy.*

this vision, in its embodied form, that leads to the growth of the wings of the philosopher-lover's soul:

> He whose initiation is recent, and who has been the spectator of many glories in the other world, is amazed when he sees any one having a godlike face or form, which is the expression of divine beauty.... Then while he gazes on him there is a sort of reaction, and the shudder passes into an unusual heat and perspiration; for, as he receives the effluence of beauty through the eyes, the wing moistens and he warms. And as he warms, the parts out of which the wing grew, and which had been hitherto closed and rigid, and had prevented the wing from shooting forth, are melted, and as nourishment streams upon him, the lower end of the wings begins to swell and grow from the root upwards; and the growth extends under the whole soul—for once the whole was winged. (251a–251b)[3]

It is the effluence of beauty from the beloved that penetrates the philosopher-lover's eyes and accordingly causes a rather astonishing response in the wings of his soul, which "swell and grow from the root upwards" as part of the first step in the soul's ascension to the Form of the Beautiful.[4]

Plato here situates his philosophical discussion of the movement toward wisdom in the context of a long erotic tradition in antiquity that focused on the power of the gaze in inculcating *eros*—from Sappho's famous fragment 31

---

3. Plato, *Dialogues of Plato*. ὁ δὲ ἀρτιτελής, ὁ τῶν τότε πολυθεάμων, ὅταν θεοειδὲς πρόσωπον ἴδῃ κάλλος εὖ μεμιμημένον ἤ τινα σώματος ἰδέαν, πρῶτον μὲν ἔφριξε καί τι τῶν τότε ὑπῆλθεν αὐτὸν δειμάτων, εἶτα προσορῶν ὡς θεὸν σέβεται, καὶ εἰ μὴ ἐδεδίει τὴν τῆς σφόδρα μανίας δόξαν, θύοι ἂν ὡς ἀγάλματι καὶ θεῷ τοῖς παιδικοῖς. ἰδόντα δ' αὐτὸν οἷον ἐκ τῆς φρίκης μεταβολή τε καὶ ἱδρὼς καὶ θερμότης ἀήθης λαμβάνει· δεξάμενος γὰρ τοῦ κάλλους τὴν ἀπορροὴν διὰ τῶν ὀμμάτων ἐθερμάνθη ᾗ ἡ τοῦ πτεροῦ φύσις ἄρδεται, θερμανθέντος δὲ ἐτάκη τὰ περὶ τὴν ἔκφυσιν, ἃ πάλαι ὑπὸ σκληρότητος συμμεμυκότα εἶργε μὴ βλαστάνειν, ἐπιρρυείσης δὲ τῆς τροφῆς ᾤδησέ τε καὶ ὥρμησε φύεσθαι ἀπὸ τῆς ῥίζης ὁ τοῦ πτεροῦ καυλὸς ὑπὸ πᾶν τὸ τῆς ψυχῆς εἶδος· πᾶσα γὰρ ἦν τὸ πάλαι πτερωτή. ζεῖ οὖν ἐν τούτῳ ὅλη καὶ ἀνακηκίει, καὶ ὅπερ τὸ τῶν ὀδοντοφυούντων πάθος περὶ τοὺς ὀδοντας γίγνεται ὅταν ἄρτι φύωσιν, κνῆσίς τε καὶ ἀγανάκτησις περὶ τὰ οὖλα, ταὐτὸν δὴ πέπονθεν ἡ τοῦ πτεροφυεῖν ἀρχομένου ψυχή· ζεῖ τε καὶ ἀγανακτεῖ καὶ γαργαλίζεται φύουσα τὰ πτερά. ὅταν μὲν οὖν βλέπουσα πρὸς τὸ τοῦ παιδὸς κάλλος, ἐκεῖθεν μέρη ἐπιόντα καὶ ῥέοντ'–ἃ δὴ διὰ ταῦτα ἵμερος καλεῖται–δεχομένη [τὸν ἵμερον] ἄρδηταί τε καὶ θερμαίνηται.

4. As duBois points out, this passage echoes Sappho's "canonical description of desire"; as such, "the situation of homoerotic desire ensures the mimetic presence of the other sex in the *erastes*" ("Phallocentrism," 99–200).

to long passages in the Greek romances of the first centuries after Christ.[5] It is echoed in the possibly spurious Platonic dialogue *Alcibiades* I, in which, again, the exchange of the gaze between two men leads to self-knowledge. Beyond this, the imagery of the passage in the *Phaedrus*, which has been much studied, is drawn from several different sources: horticulture, medical terminology (especially *febrile*), liquid imagery, and, perhaps most startlingly, the biological arousal of what Anne Lebeck euphemistically calls "an organic part of the body."[6] Françoise Frontisi-Ducroux, not mincing words, has suggested that the swelling psyche that looks at the beautiful object is, in effect, the (philosopher's) phallus.[7] The abstract force of the Beautiful, then, is well grounded in the physiology of arousal and of erotic desire, however far the growth of the soul's wings will eventually carry us from this corporeal response.

I have dwelled on this passage because it is one of the most richly figural descriptions of pederastic love in the Platonic corpus.[8] But Plato's philosophical

---

5. See, e.g., Frontisi-Ducroux, "Eros, Desire, and the Gaze"; Goldhill, "Refracting Classical Vision"; and Walker, "Eros and the Eye in the Love-Letters of Philostratus."

6. Lebeck, "Central Myth of Plato's *Phaedrus*," 274. On the imagery of the *Phaedrus* passage cited here, see also Vries, *Commentary on the "Phaedrus,"* ad loc.; duBois, "Phallocentrism," 97; Halperin, "Erotic Reciprocity"; Van Sickle, "Plat. Phaedr. 255d, 3–6"; Rowe, *Plato's "Phaedrus,"* ad loc.; and Price, *Love and Friendship*, 79. Liquid imagery is not uncommon in treatments of eros; see Walker, "Eros and the Eye in the Love-Letters of Philostratus," on Philostratus *Epistles* 32 and 33 (pp. 138–39), where the imagery is of eyes as fountains and the lover as a drinker. For discussions of this passage in the context of the erotic impulse to philosophy, see especially Frontisi-Ducroux and Vernant, *Dans l'oeil du miroir*, 122–24; Griswold, *Self-Knowledge in Plato's "Phaedrus,"* 126–27; Griffith, "Left-Hand Horses," 31–40; Halperin, "Erotic Reciprocity," 62–63; Vlastos, *Platonic Studies*, 38–42; and White, "Love and the Individual," 400–401.

7. A view confirmed by the analyses of duBois ("Phallocentrism," 97) and Nussbaum ("Eros and the Wise," 249). See also Kristeva, *Tales of Love*, 64. The eyed phallus is not an usual image for the Greeks, for whom the seeing phallus-birds and the one-eyed dildos represented on red-figure vases were a common visual motif; Frontisi-Ducroux, "Eros, Desire, and the Gaze," 95.

8. The ocular and sexual language of these passages will seem less odd to us if we acknowledge the presence of the familiar Democritean terminology of emanations from the object of vision and their ocular penetration of the spectator, a terminology that may coexist in the *Phaedrus* with the extramissive idea of the eye as emitter of a ray. Vries, *Commentary on the "Phaedrus"*; Rowe, *Plato's Phaedrus*, 251b; and Lebeck, "Central Myth of Plato's *Phaedrus*," 274, all make a connection to Empedocles (B 89 Diels-Kranz) here because Plato uses the term *aporrhoe* rather than *eidola*. But not only does Plato's account here *not* support the idea of rays emanating from the eyes, but the term *aporrhoe/aporrhoia* occurs in atomist contexts as well; see Leucippus 3.67 A 29 Diels-Kranz, pp. 78–79; Epicurus 1 Usener, p. 9; and of course Achilles Tatius. Even Democritus speaks of the

evocation of the impact of erotic desire is not limited to the *Phaedrus*. Rather, it is echoed in much of the metaphorical language of the corpus outside the dialogues that deal specifically with the connection between erotic same-sex desire and the growth of philosophical knowledge. To cite just a few examples culled at near random: at *Republic* 501d, Socrates opines that philosophers are *erastai*, lovers, of the truth; when he proposes to interrogate the beautiful young Charmides in the dialogue of that name, he visualizes this action as denuding Charmides' soul (sc. instead of his body, *Charm.* 154e); and he calls himself a lover, *erastes*, of the path of wisdom in *Philebus* 16b.[9] The vision of beauty is both an erotic phenomenon *and* a factor in the growth of self-knowledge; David Halperin puts it well: "Plato refuses to separate—he actually identifies and fuses—the erotics of sexuality, the erotics of conversation, and the erotics of philosophical inquiry."[10] Indeed, it is fair to say that this association of the philosopher and same-sex desire (whatever its social reality) had a life that extended from the classical period as far as the Greek erotic narratives of the first centuries of the common era. To quote the wonderful line of Ps.-Lucian that opens Simon Goldhill's book *Foucault's Virginity*, "Male lions don't desire male lions, because lions don't do philosophy."[11] For Ps.-Lucian's speaker here, the love of (free-born) boys is the only true option for the philosopher; as for Plato, it produces a form of procreation that is intellectual rather than (literally) infantile. And as the narrator Lycinus concludes, "Everyone should get married, but pederasty is to be allowed only to the wise" (*Erotes* 51).[12]

These are, of course, literary and philosophical texts, not social documentary, and the relationship of Plato's treatment of *eros* to contemporary Greek sexual mores has had a long and contested history in the scholarship on ancient

---

aporrhoe of the *eidola* or *deikela* (2. 68 A 135 Diels-Kranz, pp. 114–16). Bychkov, "A Note on Achilles Tatius 1.9.4–5, 5.13.4," gets it right; see also Goldhill, "Refracting Classical Vision."

9. And indeed, even the passage in the *Symposium* in which Socrates, recounting to Phaedrus and the rest what Diotima has told him about love and philosophy, repeats that the true vision of the Beautiful takes its stimulus from physical beauty, the erotic tactility of this sight creeps into his language: in having such a vision, one touches not illusion but truth (212a). Elsewhere, Plato will use imagery taken from birth and midwifery instead.

10. "Erotic reciprocity... mirrors the dynamic process of thought: it reflects and expresses the distinctive, self-generated motion of the rational soul" (Halperin, "Erotic Reciprocity," 79).

11. Goldhill, *Foucault's Virginity*, ix, citing Ps.-Lucian *Erotes* 36.

12. "διὸ δὴ γαμητέον μὲν ἅπασιν, παιδεραστεῖν δὲ ἐφείσθω μόνοις τοῖς σοφοί." See also the discussion in Foucault, *Care of the Self*, 211–27.

pederasty. Not only is it notoriously difficult to make generalizations based on the highly ironic dialogic action of Plato's texts, but one might protest more generally still that even the association of a sublimated form of pederastic desire with the genre of ancient Greek philosophy is a problematic claim; inasmuch as pederastic practice seems to have been understood as a habit of the educated elite in ancient Athens, Plato's texts could simply point to the refinement of a practice not associated by his peers with philosophy per se.[13] Indeed, this aspect of the philosophers may bring to mind the sexual invective flung at political and legal rivals in both the Greek and Roman worlds. Even in Plato's Athens, the charge of being the so-called passive member in a same-sex liaison carried terrible derogatory force outside a very narrow set of criteria of age, class, and context.[14] Aeschines accuses Timarchus of having been a boy prostitute; centuries later, Cicero makes the same allegation against Mark Antony.[15] To call someone a *cinaedus* or a *pathicus* was a pointed insult in these environments in which *continentia* (self-control) and masculinity were seen as prerequisites for entering the public sphere.[16]

However, the purpose of this brief essay is not to examine the sociohistorical issues around Greek philosophical pederasty and its relationship to elite practice in general, but rather to cast a contrasting glance at the received idea of the philosopher at Rome, and at two facets of that reception in particular: the essential absence of a positive role for eros in Roman philosophical texts, in contrast to the metaphorical and literal content of several of Plato's dialogues; and the curious notion—at least as attested to in texts by Roman satirists such

13. As Danielle Allen points out to me. Moreover, texts such as Plato's *Laws* contain apparent stipulations against pederasty as "unnatural." See especially Goldhill, *Foucault's Virginity*, 46–111, for a discussion of *phusis* and same-sex eroticism.

14. The unlikely division of such activity into active and passive may well remind us of the way cultures impose sharp-edged categories upon the confusing variety of actual human behavior. A recent article in the *New York Times* Sunday magazine (August 3, 2003) remarks on a new phenomenon among black gay men: eschewing what they see as the effeminate white culture of homosexuality, these "Down Low" males have sex with their girlfriends/wives and with other men and see themselves as hypermasculine. An interesting echo of ancient sexual categories.

15. Aeschin. *Against Timarchus* 40; Cic. *Philippics* 2.44.

16. On this kind of political invective at Athens, see, e.g., Ober and Strauss, "Drama, Political Rhetoric, and the Discourse of Athenian Democracy"; at Rome, see, e.g., Richlin, "Not before Homosexuality."

as Juvenal and Martial, as well as in snippets and asides in other sources—that the contemporary philosopher was not only no abstaining pederast of the Socratic stamp but, if anything, a man who was so unable to control his desires and urges that under the façade of the philosopher he engaged in the most shameful form of male-male sexuality in both Greek and Roman eyes: the passive role, the role of the free adult male who yielded his body to penetration by others and liked it all too well.[17]

In short, in what follows I would like to unsettle the noble Platonic marriage of *eros* and philosophy—to sue for divorce, as it were. I would like to do so by redirecting our gaze from fifth-century Athens to Rome in the first century AD, where a paradigm rather different from the Greek one (a paradigm that reacted in part to this Platonic imbrication of eros and philosophy, I would argue)[18] brought together ideas about sexuality and the philosopher's public image in a way that can throw light both on Roman anxieties about the philosopher's practice and on the way the very terminology and drive of Roman Stoic philosophizing might be automatically suspect to a Roman audience. For, oddly enough, in the Roman reception of the connection between the philosopher and eros, the Greek identification of the philosopher with same-sex desire loomed large and dangerously, even as philosophers took care to dissociate themselves from the charges lobbed at them in the popular literature—that under their austere exteriors they hid the soft flesh and perverted longings of men who (by Roman standards) were not men at all.

Our starting point may be the curious fact that in a surprising number of popular texts, the philosopher at Rome in the early imperial period is associated with sexual behavior of the kind most despised in the aggressively masculine culture of the ancient Mediterranean, where the gender categories in play were not male and female so much as active and passive.[19] We can search in vain for texts that introduce the beneficial presence of the philosopher-lover and his arousal by the embodied beauty of a young boy. Instead, we find eros entering through the back door, where it is instantiated not as a means to wisdom but as the lie that the philosopher's practice conceals: for the philosopher himself

17. Anathema in both Greece and Rome, of course; for the Greek world, and the delicate position of the citizen *eromenos* who could not show pleasure at his subjection to his older citizen lover, see especially Halperin, "Erotics of Narrativity."

18. On the continuing popularity and influence of Plato's *Phaedrus* in the first century and beyond, see Trapp, "*Phaedrus* in Second-Century Greek Literature."

19. On the basic dichotomy of "active" and "passive," see especially Parker, "Teratogenic Grid," and Williams, *Roman Homosexuality*, 160–224.

is now associated with the unmanly role of the *eromenos*, and though an adult, he has taken on the despised role of the penetratee. Consider the following epigram of Martial's, addressed to such a philosopher:

> You prattle about Democritus, Zeno, and enigmatic Plato,
> And any grubby figure shown hairy on a bust—
> As if you were successor and heir to Pythagoras!
> And sure, your beard is just as long as theirs.
> But you have something those goaty, hairy types abjure:
> That stiff-with-dirt beard over a baby-soft bottom!
> You who know the origins and arguments of the schools:
> Tell me, Pannychus, what's the dogma on buggery?[20]
>
> (*Epigrams* 9.47)

In another epigram, Martial advises the wild divorcee Galla to be careful if she dates a philosopher: they look stern and hairy on the outside, but under that rustic appearance lurks a *cinaedus*, a "pansy-boy" who only wants to be penetrated by other men. The would-be philosophers in these epigrams are represented as perverts: under their rugged exterior, they are said to engage in the practices that Roman sexual ideology depicted as the most debased. Juvenal, too, rails against such false philosophers in his second satire:

> One can't rely on men's faces: every street overflows with
> Austere-visaged perverts. How can *you* reprove immorality,
> most notorious man-hole among the Socratic pansy-boys?
> Your hairy limbs and the stiff bristles on your arms
> promise a stern soul, but the doctor has to mock you
> as he cuts the swollen piles from your depilated anus.[21]
>
> (*Satire* 2.8–13)

20. "Democritos, Zenonas inexplicitosque Platonas / quidquid et hirsutis squalet imaginibus, / sic quasi Pythagorae loqueris successor et heres. / praependet sane nec tibi barba minor: / sed, quod et hircosis serum est et turpe pilosis, / in molli rigidam clune libenter habes. / Tu, qui sectarum causas et pondera nosti, / dic mihi, percidi, Pannyche, dogma quod est?"

21. "Frontis nulla fides; quis enim non uicus abundat / tristibus obscenis? castigas turpia, cum sis / inter Socraticos notissima fossa cinaedos? / hispida membra quidem et durae per bracchia saetae / promittunt atrocem animum, sed podice leui / caeduntur tumidae medico ridente mariscae."

The point of this rather distasteful diatribe is precisely the emphasis on the self-depilation and violated masculine integrity of the apparent philosopher, whose ascetic exterior hides a collection of unmanly desires and practices.

Literally, of course, the expression *Socraticus cinaedus* makes no historical sense: even the most critical reading of the physical practices behind Platonic pederasty would still attribute to Socrates and the other philosophy-laden lovers of these texts the active rather than the passive role; it was the *eromenos*, the young man, who was at danger of losing his qualification for citizenship by allowing himself to be anally penetrated. But Juvenal's and Martial's claimants to philosophy are nonetheless blasted here with the worst possible of Roman insults, the charge of being adult penetratees. Even the established Roman philosopher Seneca comes in for slander in the later sources, where Dio Cassius tells us that he was given over to the love of mature men and taught Nero to like the same; that far from acting out traditional Roman masculinity, he liked to fellate other men (61.10.4).[22] My question, then, is why is the philosopher figured in these texts as a man with deviant sexual mores; why, under the bristly beard that in Roman thinking is the mark of the philosopher, is he said to have the soft and hairless skin associated with self-depilating deviants?[23]

Three possible answers present themselves. One might first suggest that most practitioners of philosophy at the turn of the first century AD at Rome were in fact Greeks themselves, and that as such they were automatically tainted, by association, with what the Romans thought of as "Greek practices."[24] But not only do Roman philosophers come in for the same criticism (as in Dio's comments on Seneca); not only does the usual criticism of Greek philosophers in the republic attack their fascination with logic

22. Contrast this to Seneca's tantalizingly short reference to charges that he played the active role with younger men at *Vit. beat.* 27.5.

23. A further example may be supplied by Persius's *Fourth Satire*, which explicitly takes up the themes of the pseudo-Platonic *Alcibiades I*. When Persius adapts this philosophical exchange between Socrates and Alcibiades to a Roman satire, the results veer in the same direction as the Martial epigrams: after a few lines on self-knowledge, the topic moves surprisingly to effeminacy and self-display. First our young philosopher is shown sunbathing and eating dainty dishes; then a passerby is imagined to pluck the sleeve of our initiate and excoriate him for depilating all his body hair, including that of his genitalia, and showing the results to the populace.

24. On "Greek practices" see, e.g., Polyb. 31.25.3 and Cic. *Tusc.* 4.70 and 5.58, as well as MacMullen, "Roman Attitudes." When Cicero has C. Aurelius Cotta comment, in *De natura deorum*, on his own appreciation for young Greek boys—a sentiment he holds "with the concurrence of the philosophers of old"—Cotta does so on the defensive (*Nat. D.* 79).

rather than their sexuality; but this subgroup of "Socratic pansy-boys" actually sets us at a distance from the reverential treatment normally accorded to Plato's spokesperson for eros and philosophy by his philosophical inheritors. Serious-minded Romans, in their depiction of the virtues of a Socrates, chose to develop Plato's depiction of the philosopher as a shibboleth for sexual abstinence rather than deal with the implications of pederasty with freeborn boys as a good method of philosophical self-advancement. In a clear reference to Plato's *Symposium*, for example, the rhetorician Quintilian praises Socrates (8.4.23) for refusing to do what Alcibiades wanted of him. And even in the randy context of Petronius's *Satyricon*, a novel focusing precisely on the homoerotic misadventures of several lower-class figures from the Roman underlife, the sexy young Giton has this bitter comment to make, after a passionless night with his older lover, Encolpius: "Thanks, Encolpius, for loving me with such Socratic zeal. For not even Alcibiades spent the night in his teacher's bed as unmolested as I" (128.7).[25] The related claim that the Roman philosopher was stained by the sexually problematic origin of his activity in the history of Platonic pederasty, and that his audience was predisposed to think of philosophers as sexually questionable because of the existence of the Platonic Greek precedent (whatever its relationship to the social realities of fourth-century Athens) that posited the best search for knowledge as one based on both dialectic and erotic exchange between an older man and a freeborn adolescent, can be answered with the same objection.

A second solution to our question would be the most unlikely but certainly comical claim that practitioners of philosophy in early imperial Rome (Romans and Greeks alike) were in fact to the best of our evidence *cinaedi*, passive adult participants in same-sex liaisons, to the last man. But any acknowledgment of an actual erotic role for the philosopher or his student is abjured in our Roman philosophical texts, where we find wholesale condemnation of the practice of pederasty as well as critical attitudes toward same-sex eros in general, let alone a passive role for the older man. Indeed, if we follow within a single dominant school, that of the Stoics, the development in attitudes toward same-sex love from the Hellenistic period to early imperial Rome, a clear shift is visible from the tolerant, even encouraging doctrines of a Zeno or a Chrysippus to those of Musonius Rufus and Seneca, both Romans of the first century AD. The Greek

25. A similar usage crops up in Achilles Tatius's *Clitophon and Leucippe*, of which Goldhill remarks: "At crucial points in this narrative . . . 'to be a philosopher,' philosophein, means 'to be committed to sexual chastity and its supporting arguments'" (*Foucault's Virginity*, 98).

founders of Stoicism, Chryisippus and Zeno, seem to have supported the "philosophic" love of boys. Thus, in examining the Hellenistic Stoic response to the tensions present in philosophic homoeroticism, Martha Nussbaum has well delineated the contrast between its beneficial or educational purposes and the fear of falling under the control of lust or losing oneself in love. Stoic doctrine held that all *pathe* (passions) should be extirpated but also that the wise man could—and would—love virtuous and beautiful young men. This "love," however, was specified to be love of "friendship" rather than of "intercourse":

> The wise man will love young men who show a propensity to virtue by means of their appearance, as say Zeno in his *Republic* and Chrysippus in the first book of *On Modes of Life*, and Apollodorus in his *Ethics*. Love, they say, is an attempt at creating friendship by means of the manifest beauty [of the beloved]. Its goal is not sex, but friendship. (Diog. Laert. 7.129–30)[26]

Zeno seems to have defined friendship as involving intercrural sex (Ath. 563e) and suggested that an ideal city could be built around homoerotic ties, recalling Phaedrus's suggestions in Plato's *Symposium* that lovers would fight more bravely in battle because they would be fighting under the gaze of their partner (178e–179b). In the relationships Zeno describes, sexual exclusivity was not necessary (the better to avoid emotional engagement); all *pathe* were to be kept under control, and forms of erotic mania, avoided. These Stoics, then, seem to have taken a stance similar to the Platonic one in focusing on the philosophical possibilities inherent in eros with a beautiful boy and in attempting to identify it with friendship;[27] however, "the *Phaedrus'* doctrine of reciprocal eros or anteros must be rejected by the Stoic sage, who must not comport himself in such a manner as to arouse such an intense feeling in a younger partner."[28]

---

26. καὶ ἐρασθήσεσθαι δὲ τὸν σοφὸν τῶν νέων τῶν ἐμφαινόντων διὰ τοῦ εἴδους τὴν πρὸς ἀρετὴν εὐφυΐαν, ὥς φησι Ζήνων ἐν τῇ Πολιτείᾳ καὶ Χρύσιππος ἐν τῷ πρώτῳ Περὶ βίων καὶ Ἀπολλόδωρος ἐν τῇ Ἠθικῇ. Εἶναι δὲ τὸν ἔρωτα ἐπιβολὴν φιλοποιίας διὰ κάλλος ἐμφαινόμενον· καὶ μὴ εἶναι συνουσίας, ἀλλὰ φιλίας. See also *SVF* 3.650–53. This citation is repeated in Latin by Cicero at *Tusc.* 4.72.

27. See Babut, "Les stoïciens et l'amour"; Rist, *Stoic Philosophy*, 65–68, 79–80.

28. Nussbaum, "Eros and the Wise," 261. In "Les stoïciens et l'amour," Babut voices several reservations about the gulf between Hellenistic and Roman Stoicism. He argues that there is a basic continuity between early and late Stoicism on matters of eros because (a) in all periods, *eros* (homoerotic or heterosexual) is an *adiaphoron*, an indifferent, in Stoic philosophy and (b) even Zeno, Chrysippus, and Apollodorus, who wrote in favor of the philosophical love of boys, held that the wise man should marry and have children (Diog. Laert. 7.121). Babut completely elides the

This Greek Stoic conflation of attitudes toward pedagogic pederasty did not receive a warm reception among its Roman inheritors, even those in the Stoic school themselves. Cicero, for one, would mock the Greek Stoic "amor amicitiae" and the principles on which it stood:

> And so we come to the teachers of virtue, the philosophers: who deny that love is a *stuprum*, and in this matter disagree with Epicurus—who in my opinion, is largely on track. For what is that so-called love of friendship? Why does no one love the ugly adolescent, nor the handsome old man? To me, at least, this practice seems to have begun in the gymnasia of the Greeks, in which those kinds of love are free and allowed. We philosophers have risen up (with Plato as our authority, whom Dicaearchus rightly accuses) to assign authority to love. The Stoics, in fact, both say that the wise man will be a lover and also define love itself as "an attempt to create friendship out of the form of the beautiful." And if there is any such love in nature—without anxiety, without desire, without worry, without sighing—so be it. (*Tusc.* 33.70–71)[29]

In other words, the identification of love and friendship on which the early Stoics rested their arguments seems to Cicero a sleight of hand, especially in its attention only to the beautiful and young. Plutarch, in an essay refuting some common conceptions of the Stoics, similarly acknowledges that Stoic views on love and philosophy are confusing to all; no one would bat an eye if they would simply call the chase a chase, but instead they waffle by calling friendship an activity that involves passion (*Comm. not.* 1072f–1073d).[30] Musonius Rufus, Seneca's Stoic contemporary, condemns male-male sex as

---

different valence of the "love of boys" in the Greek and Roman periods, however, and none of his points address the way Stoic theorizing shifted in its emphases to accommodate this change.

29. "Ad magistros virtutis philosophos veniamus, qui amorem negant stupri esse et in eo litigant cum Epicuro non multum, ut opinio mea fert, mentiente. Quis est enim iste amor amicitiae? cur neque deformem adulescentem quisquam amat neque formosum senem? mihi quidem haec in Graecorum gymnasiis nata consuetudo videtur, in quibus isti liberi et concessi sunt amores. Philosophi sumus exorti, et auctore quidem nostro Platone, quem non iniuria Dicaearchus accusat, qui amori auctoritatem tribueremus. Stoici vero et sapientem amaturum esse dicunt et amorem ipsum 'conatum amicitiae faciendae ex pulchritudinis specie' definiunt. qui si quis est in rerum natura sine sollicitudine, sine desiderio, sine cura, sine suspirio, sit sane."

30. Nussbaum, "Eros and the Wise."

para phusin, against nature,[31] and endorses sex only within marriage and for the propagation of children (86.4–10 Lutz).[32] Epictetus holds that only one's wife should look beautiful to her husband—no other women and no boys (*Discourses* 3.7.21; cf. 2.18.15–18, 3.22.13). Athenaeus remarks contemptuously of the whole school in its Greek incarnation: "You Stoics are oglers of boys" (563e). And the skeptic and philosopher Sextus Empiricus dismisses Zeno's teaching recommending sexual relations with boys as "having nothing to do with real choices in the real world, no more than intercourse with one's mother."[33]

Some of Seneca's writing engages still more directly with the erotic idealism of the *Phaedrus* but, again, only to reject it. In *Epistle* 116, he takes up the question of whether or not the wise man should fall in love in the first place: Panaetius, he says, gave wise advice to the young man who posed the question: "We'll see about the wise man later; but as for you and I, who are still far distant from the wise man, we should not allow ourselves to fall into a state that is unstable, uncontrolled, enslaved to another, and despicable to oneself" (*EM* 116.5).[34] More dramatically still, in *Epistle* 123 Seneca identifies as Stoic

31. On this expression, see Williams, *Roman Homosexuality*, 242. Seneca says the same of *virum pati* in letter 122.7; both, of course, are talking generally about homoerotic sex between males rather than between an older man and a boy. Williams writes: "With this one pointed sentence, then, Seneca is suggesting that maleness itself is ideally incompatible with being penetrated," although, as Williams points out, it was not seen as unnatural to have the desire to be the active penetrator of young (slave) boys (239). But Williams cannot be correct in seeing the origin of this sentiment—real men don't get penetrated—in Seneca's *philosophical* stance.

32. Χρὴ δὲ τοὺς μὴ τρυφῶντας ἢ μὴ κακοὺς μόνα μὲν ἀφροδίσια νομίζειν δίκαια τὰ ἐν γάμῳ καὶ ἐπὶ γενέσει παίδων συντελούμενα, ὅτι καὶ νόμιμά ἐστιν· τὰ δέ γε ἡδονὴν θηρώμενα ψιλὴν ἄδικα καὶ παράνομα, κἂν ἐν γάμῳ ᾖ. συμπλοκαὶ δ᾽ ἄλλαι αἱ μὲν κατὰ μοιχείαν παρανομώταται, καὶ μετριώτεραι τούτων οὐδὲν αἱ πρὸς ἄρρενας τοῖς ἄρρεσιν, ὅτι παρὰ φύσιν τὸ τόλμημα. See Foucault, *The Care of the Self*, 150–85, on the focus on marriage found in the Stoic writers of the imperial period.

33. Quoting MacMullen, "Roman Attitudes," 500, on Sextus Empiricus's *Pyrr. Hyp.* 3.245.

34. "'De sapiente,' inquit, 'videbimus; mihi et tibi, qui adhuc a sapiente longe absumus, non est committendum, ut incidamus in rem commotam, inpotentem, alteri emancupatam, vilem sibi.'" In *De brev.* 18.4, Seneca returns to the imagery of the *Phaedrus* when he portrays the *proficiens* (the Stoic on the path to virtue) as a horse, recalling the horses and charioteer from Plato's famous chariot metaphor. See Torre, "Il cavallo immagine del Sapiens in Seneca," also on *Epistle* 76.20. This borrowing of imagery remains pertinent even if Seneca's position on the theory of the divided mind seems at times Platonic, at times not. Habinek, "Aristocracy of Virtue," underscores the erotic language Seneca uses to describe the irruptive impact of philosophy upon the *proficiens* in letters 90 and 94; here Seneca follows the *Phaedrus* in conceiving of self-knowledge as a form of sexually mediated foray into the soul even as he limits and proscribes elsewhere the place of eros in the philosophical project.

frauds those philosophers who *do* urge their followers to find young men for philosophical loving: "I believe that those men, too, damage us, who urge us to vices under the disguise of the Stoic school. This is what they propound: that only the wise man and the learned man is a lover. 'He alone has wisdom in this art; and the wise man is most experienced of all at drinking and feasting. Let's investigate up to what age young men are to be loved.' Let this be conceded to the Greeks' habits" (123.15).[35] This is an explicit rejection of pedagogic pederasty and its idealist overtones, even as mouthed by men "pretending" (says Seneca) to be Stoics.[36] In short, even if we were to take the extreme case that all Stoic language about boy-love is purely figural, Roman thinkers—including Roman Stoics such as Seneca and Musonius Rufus—explicitly reject this aspect of their doctrine.[37] Nowhere, then, can we find suggestions in Roman philosophical writing that some tolerance might be extended to the kind of roles suggested in the *Phaedrus* and the *Symposium*; and certainly if the Roman philosopher secretly desires to be buggered, there is nothing in his text to suggest it—and this is the best we can do, in the absence of other evidence about what happened in philosophers' bedrooms in the first century AD at Rome.

A third answer to our question, and one that undeniably provides part of its truth, is that broad Roman cultural prejudices about who could be penetrated with impunity probably played some role in generating the kind of slanders we have been looking at—even if Socrates himself usually escaped criticism for his choice of love objects. Unlike the ideological beliefs of at least some segment of the Greek elite, Roman tradition and Roman social mores made no room for same-sex relationships among men of equal class; nor could the penetratee, even if in boyhood, submit to such attention without the complete loss of his reputation and civic standing. Indeed, at Rome, as Michel Foucault, Ramsay

35. "Illos quoque nocere nobis existimo qui nos sub specie Stoicae sectae hortantur ad vitia. Hoc enim iactant: solum sapientem et doctum esse amatorem. 'Solus sapit [Buecheler's emendation of *apte*] ad hanc artem; aeque conbibendi et convivendi sapiens est peritissimus. Quaeramus ad quam usque aetatem iuvenes amandi sint.' Haec Graecae consuetudini data sint."

36. As Brown says of Lucretius's writing, too, "There is no link between philosophy and *eros*" (*Lucretius on Love and Sex*, 86).

37. Here I contradict Babut, who oddly claims that at *no point* could the Stoics be identified "parmi les partisans ou les adversaries de la pederastie ou de l'amour entre les sexes. Cette distinction n'a jamai eu de significance essentielle dans leur pensée" ("Les stoïciens et l'amour," 62–63). This does not seem right: eros may an *adiaphoron*, but that status does not erase all distinctions within eros, at least not in practice. I also disagree with Babut's claim that the Roman Stoic texts we have do not advise against homoerotic "philosophical love."

MacMullen, and many others have remarked, the young boy who served as sex object for an older man (with the older man playing a penetrating, rather than a receiving, role) would be a slave, not a citizen.[38] It is possible that MacMullen overstates when he argues that it was "a disgrace to the community and an outrage to nature for an older man to press himself undesired on a younger man, even a slave," and even "the man who accepted or requested ..., without coercing, submission to his sexual wishes was vulnerable to heavy reproach."[39] Nonetheless, Roman attitudes toward *freeborn* men playing "passive" (i.e., recipient) roles in any sexual activity whatsoever or using other freeborn men, whether adult or youths, to be the passive partners to their lust, were unambiguously hostile; even a more idealized homoeroticism between social equals and without physical acts seems rarely to have emerged into general discussion at Rome.[40] As to the homoerotic relationships that did exist between the Roman elite and their young male slaves, these were obviously not conducive to philosophical idealization: one does not practice self-knowledge with a *servus*.[41]

38. In *Roman Homosexuality*, Williams lists several examples of noncondemnatory language describing the use of male slaves for sex (30–34). Horace, Virgil, Augustus, Domitian—all had their *paidika*. And it is on Roman pottery (and on the Republican-era Warren cup), not Greek, that we see the anal penetration of young slave boys (on the Warren cup, however, the penetrator is a bearded figure who may be intended to be Greek); see ibid., 93–94, and Clarke, *Looking at Lovemaking*, 61–78.

39. MacMullen, "Roman Attitudes," 490, 492.

40. Ibid., 493. It is difficult to know how to treat the poetic idealizing of a Catullus or a Virgil. Note Makowski's argument in "Nisus and Euryalus," in which he suggests that Virgil's portrayal of Nisus and Euryalus and their chaste love in book 9 of the *Aeneid* refers back to Plato's *Symposium*. But in any case, Verstraete has it right: "Unlike the classical Greeks, the Romans never utilized the homoerotic bond between men to build and sustain their culture.... The taint of slavery or service continued to cling to homosexuality" ("Slavery and the Social Dynamics," 235).

41. This is not the place to enter into a long discussion of whether Roman same-sex eroticism should be understood in constructivist or essentialist terms, nor to debate the question of the relationship between categories of behavior, sexual identity, and constructions of gender. However, because I believe that our term *homosexuality* cannot be mapped onto Roman ideologies of sexual behavior (whether or not the *cinaedus* was a category that defined an identity) I have avoided it throughout this essay. For the main texts on such issues, see Cantarella, *Bisexuality*; Edwards, *Politics of Immorality*; Fantham, *"Stuprum"*; Foucault, *Care of the Self*; Gleason, *Making Men*; Halperin, "Forgetting Foucault"; Halperin, Winkler, and Zeitlin, *Before Sexuality*; Lilja, *Homosexuality in Republican and Augustan Rome*; MacMullen, "Roman Attitudes"; Richlin, *Garden of Priapus* and "Not before Homosexuality"; Taylor, "Two Pathic Subcultures in Ancient Rome"; Verstraete, "Slavery and the Social Dynamics"; Veyne, "L'homosexualité à Rome"; and Williams's excellent work,

This general perspective has recently been confirmed in a comprehensive study by Craig Williams, whose conclusions are worth citing in full:

> Relationships on the Greek pederastic model (romantic and erotic relationships between freeborn adult men and freeborn adolescent males that were both publicly acknowledged and endowed with educational and sometimes specifically philosophical meanings) did not form a part of the Roman tradition, because any relations with freeborn Romans of either sex, other than one's spouse, constituted *stuprum*. Moreover, Roman men inherited a cultural patrimony that permitted, even encouraged, them to make sexual use of the slaves, of whatever sex and presumably also of whatever age. Thus it is not surprising that we find in the Roman sources few traces of a culturally encouraged pressure to dichotomize men's erotic objects into women and boys (as opposed to females and males), and less of a tendency to focus specifically on adolescents or boys as the only acceptable male objects of men's phallic desires.[42]

Williams also treats the shadowy evidence for a *Lex Scantinia*, first mentioned in two letters of Caelius Rufus (Cic. *Ad Fam.* 8.12.3 and 8.14.4), which he interprets as a law to penalize *stuprum* (the unlawful penetration of freeborn boys and women) as a whole rather than singling out only pederastic variants directed against the young.[43] If this is correct—and it is supported by much recent scholarship[44]—the law could be invoked against the perpetrators of sexual violation of the free as well as those freeborn who played the receptive role. This is not to say that same-sex love did not occur at Rome even outside the approved boundaries; nor is it to say that Romans and Greeks had different forms of desire.

Roman Homosexuality. For the art-historical evidence, see in general Clarke, *Looking at Lovemaking.* For bibliography, see Verstraete, *Homosexuality in Ancient Greek and Roman Civilization.*

42. Williams, *Roman Homosexuality,* 32.

43. Ibid., 120–24. The clearest definition of *stuprum* comes from Modestinus 48.5.35(34): "Someone commits *stuprum* who keeps a free woman for the sake of sexual relations but not marriage, unless she is, of course, a *concubina*. Adultery is committed with a married woman. *Stuprum* is committed with a widow, a virgin, or a boy." On *stuprum* and the *Lex Scantinia,* see also Berger, *Dictionary of Roman Law,* s.v. *lex Scatinia (Scantinia);* Cantarella, *Bisexuality;* Dalla, *Ubi Venus Mutatur;* Fantham, "*Stuprum*"; Lilja, *Homosexuality in Republican and Augustan Rome;* and Richlin, "Not before Homosexuality," 224. The law is mentioned also at Val. Max. 6.1.7, Juv. 2.44 and Suet. *Dom.* 8.3 and may be connected to the fine of 10,000 sesterces for *stuprum* mentioned at Quint. 2.4.69 and 7.4.42.

44. E.g., Cantarella, *Bisexuality;* Fantham, "*Stuprum*"; Veyne, "L'homosexualité à Rome."

But in terms of a publicly celebrated and condoned form of education, Greek pederasty did not have a parallel at Rome, nor did Roman philosophers make any claim that for them to erotically love adolescent boys would result in the latter's ethical improvement. The philosopher-lover so central to the *Phaedrus* goes undercover at Rome, where finding a young member of the Roman elite to mirror his loving eyes would simply be an act of *stuprum*.[45]

It is worth remarking that even those *Greek* texts of the early empire that invoke the Platonic ideal for the relationship of lover and loved one expand their discussion to include love between men and women. The whole question of which kind of love can better serve philosophical ends is explicitly debated by Plutarch, Ps.-Lucian, Achilles Tatius, and other figures writing in Greek in and after the late first century AD. To take one example: in *Amatorius* 766e, Plutarch argues that there is no reason why beautiful women, as well as beautiful youths, should not emit the simulacra that agitate the body to the production of seed; nor is there any reason why only *male* beauty and *male* virtue should provoke in their viewers the recollection of the Forms. Significantly, when Plutarch's father, speaking at 765c, revisits the role erotic vision has in philosophy, he explicitly rebuts the sexual language and imagery of the *Phaedrus*: the warmth of the gaze does *not* produce semen but rather a plant-like sap that predisposes the lover toward *kindness!*[46] "But those who by sober reason and modesty have excluded the raging element, as if it were literally fire, have kept in their souls only its light and radiance and warmth. This warmth does not, as someone has affirmed, set up a churning that leads to the formation of seed through the gliding of atoms that are rubbed off in the smooth, tickling contact; rather, it produces a marvelous and fruitful circulation of sap, as in a plant that spouts and grows, a circulation that opens the way to acquiescence and affection."[47] Indeed, as the dialogue comes to an end, Plutarch himself seems to establish that it is the reciprocal love characteristic

45. According to Williams, pederasty, but not homoeroticism in general, was felt to be a Greek borrowing (*Roman Homosexuality*, 11). On this point he disagrees with MacMullen ("Roman Attitudes") and a host of others, but is in agreement with Cantarella (*Bisexuality*) and Veyne ("L'homosexualité à Rome").

46. When Plutarch himself later seems to suggest that semen *is* produced (766e), he posits this in order to argue that the effect would be common to the sight of a beautiful woman as well as a boy.

47. Trans. W. C. Helmbold. ὅσοι δὲ σώφρονι λογισμῷ μετ' αἰδοῦς οἷον ἀτεχνῶς πυρὸς ἀφεῖλον τὸ μαντικόν, αὐγὴν δὲ καὶ φῶς ἀπέλιπον τῇ ψυχῇ μετὰ θερμότητος, οὐ σεισμὸν μέν, ὥς τις εἶπε, κινούσης ἐπὶ σπέρμα καὶ ὄλισθον ἀτόμων ὑπὸ λειότητος καὶ γαργαλισμοῦ θλιβομένων, διάχυσιν

of marriage (rather than of pedagogic pederasty) that can teach *sophrosyne* and self-control:[48] as Michel Foucault remarks of Plutarch's language here, "He has borrowed from the erotics of boys its fundamental and traditional features in order to demonstrate that they can be applied, not to all forms of love, but to the conjugal relationship alone.... Pederasty can only be inadequate in view of the strongly marked difference between the *erastes* (lover) and the *eromenos* (beloved)."[49]

To return to the original question: why the association of philosophers at Rome with sexual passivity? I would like to posit a fourth answer: that Roman conceptual givens about sexuality and bodily boundaries, combined with the all-important distinction between agency and passivity in the relationship of one man to another, played a crucial part in generating the slanderous epithet of *Socraticus cinaedus* in the satirical sources. This slander emerged in reaction to some of the main tenets of Roman Stoicism in the first century AD, a school of philosophy whose popularity among the educated classes was most famously represented by Seneca, his contemporary Musonius Rufus (the Roman Socrates, as he was called), and several generations of the so-called Stoic opposition. Roman Stoicism's all-encompassing mixture of received wisdom and Roman tradition in this period is well illustrated by Seneca's invocations of arguably different figures to illustrate the main tenets of its beliefs—not only the Greek

---

δὲ θαυμαστὴν καὶ γόνιμον ὥσπερ ἐν φυτῷ βλαστάνοντι καὶ τρεφομένῳ καὶ πόρους ἀνοίγουσαν εὐπειθείας καὶ φιλοφροσύνης.

48. See similarly Plut. *Dinner of the Seven Sages* 156d and Ps.-Lucian *Erotes* 27–28, where Charicles, arguing in favor of heterosexual love, stresses the equal enjoyment that obtains in heterosexual relationships.

49. Foucault, *Care of the Self*, 193–227 (quote on pp. 205 and 206). As Foucault points out, a similar borrowing of imagery characterizes part of the discussion in the *Amatorius*, where the older woman who kidnaps a youth is described in the language normally used for the *erastes*. As Foucault notes, in both Plutarch's *Amatorius* and the *Erotes* attributed to Lucian, the amorous reciprocity that Plato attributes to ἐρώμενος and ἐραστής is extended by one of the speakers to include, and favor, the heterosexual relationship and its capacity for true mutual benefit. Significantly, when Callicratidas, in Ps.-Lucian *Erotes* 48, protests against this, he invokes the *mirror* to depict, once again, the ideal nature of homosexual love. The dialogue with Plato rages, but the pederastic relationship is clearly suffering ideological slippage. Foucault also discusses the Stoic perspectives of Musonius, Antipater of Tyre, Epictetus, and Hierocles along the same lines. See also Brenk, "Plutarch's Erotikos." For corrections and fine tuning to Foucault's work on sexuality in antiquity, see the cautions of Cohen and Saller, "Foucault on Sexuality." For an excellent discussion of Ps.-Lucian's *Erotes*, see Goldhill, *Foucault's Virginity*.

founders of the sect but also Epicurus and established Roman heroes such as the Catones, elder and younger, and of course Socrates himself.

This form of Stoicism differed in several significant respects from its Hellenistic practice and theory, but the aspect I would like to focus on here is the apparent transformation of Roman Stoic teachings on the worth of the body. For the drastic tenets of this philosophy, more than any other in the West, encouraged the jettisoning of the body in favor of the mind and the will. The texts of Seneca and Epictetus propound a philosophy whose main focus is that the mind and the soul should remain free from dictates of the body; indeed, much of the content of this philosophy was aimed at dulling our instinctive sense that the body must be protected and pain avoided as an evil. The good philosopher yields up his body, the travails of which bear no relation to the health of the soul. In particular, the threats of a tyrant—threats of whipping, beating, mutilation—are not to be feared. As Seneca chides an addressee: "Stop asking, 'Won't it hurt the wise man if he is beaten, if his eyes are dug out?'... You guess at the nature of a noble soul based on your own weakness, and when you have reflected on how much you yourself can bear, you put the endurance (patientia) of the wise man a little further on" (*Constant.* 15.1–2).[50] For the wise man can lose nothing, even as he leaves a trail of body parts in his wake: "We do not deny that it is inconvenient to be lashed and shoved and to lose a limb, but we deny that all those are injuries" (*Constant.* 16.2). Epictetus, himself once a Roman slave, has a particularly winning expression of this attitude: as he puts it, if you take a wise man, flog him soundly, imprison him, and finally behead him, he suffers no harm, so long as he bears it all in a noble spirit (4.1.127).[51] Offering advice to a man whose leg was wounded, the same Epictetus sternly advises him to stop fussing: When the man laments, "Alas, I am lame in my leg!" Epictetus can only respond with: "Slave, do you invoke the universe because you are lame in one stupid leg? Why don't you make a free gift of it to the world? Give it up!" (1.12.24).[52] And Seneca chimes in with the expendability of a hand

50. "Desinite itaque dicere: 'non accipiet ergo sapiens iniuriam, si caedetur, si oculus illi eruetur...' Sed ex inbecillitate uestra coniecturam capitis ingentis animi, et cum cogitastis quantum putetis uos pati posse, sapientis patientiae paulo ulteriorem terminum ponitis; at illum in aliis mundi finibus sua uirtus conlocauit, nihil uobiscum commune habentem."

51. Πῶς οὖν ἔτι οὐ δερόμενος βλάπτεται ἢ δεσμευόμενος ἢ ἀποκεφαλιζόμενος; οὐχὶ οὕτως μέν· ≤εἰ≥ γενναίως πάσχει, καὶ προσκερδαίνων καὶ προσωφελούμενος ἀπέρχεται, ἐκεῖνος δὲ βλαπτόμενός ἐστιν ὁ τὰ οἰκτρότατα πάσχων καὶ αἴσχιστα, ὁ ἀντὶ ἀνθρώπου λύκος γινόμενος ἢ ἔχις ἢ σφήξ;

52. Ἀνδράποδον, εἶτα δί ἓν σκελύδριον τῷ κόσμῳ ἐγκαλεῖς; οὐκ ἐπιδώσεις αὐτὸ τοῖς ὅλοις; οὐκ ἀποστήσῃ; οὐ χαίρων παραχωρήσεις τῷ δεδωκοτι;

or an eye (*EM* 9.4): "If a disease or an enemy lops off the wise man's hand, or if some disaster knocks out an eye or both, what's left will satisfy him, and he'll be as happy with his mutilated and amputated body as he was when whole."[53]

We are looking here at a deliberate and apparently proscriptive change in the valorization of the body that is particularly conspicuous among a small group of writers and thinkers in the early imperial period. It is a way of thinking that deliberately separates itself from the literary, cultural, or even philosophic models this group might have—for there is no evidence that Hellenistic Stoicism shared this attitude on the expendability of the body. In opposition to the Roman model implied in these texts, the Hellenistic Stoics of course did manage to integrate the body and the soul, the physical and the psychic. The famous Stoic doctrine of "total blending," *krasis di'holon*, held that two substances can occupy the same space, even if each is continuous and contains no void; thus *pneuma*, breath that was a particular combination of air and fire, was seen as both, constituting the *psyche* (which was corporeal itself) *and* penetrating all the tissues of the body (cf., e.g., *SVF* II 366–68, *PHP* 3.1.10–12 Galen, and even in the second century AD, Hierocles *El. Eth.* Col. 4.38–53).[54] In the traditional Stoic view, then, spirit (*psyche*, or *logos*) and matter (*hyle*) were seen as conjoined rather than separate; the one did not act as a container for the other. (Similarly, in the macrocosm of the world, the god of the Stoics was understood as a breath penetrating and unifying the whole of the universe.) It is true that a specific part of this psyche was called the *hegemonikon*, or center of command, and worked as the seat of sensation, assent, impulse, and passion. But even from this center there extended seven breaths to the eyes, ears, mouth, nose, and skin to convey the incoming stimuli from the entirety of the body.[55] According to this system, at least, the role of the body is not as a mere casing for the *psyche*. More importantly still, none of the founders of the Hellenistic school seem to have discussed the body in terms of its expendability.

Roman Stoicism may have paid lip service to Stoic theory in this regard, but it is nowhere evident in their vivid renunciations of the body-as-shell. This notion that the human body is a prison for the soul, or a set of chains around its soul, is again a concept more familiar to us from Plato and the Platonic school

---

53. "Si illi manum aut morbus aut hostis exciderit, si quis oculum vel oculos casus excusserit, reliquiae illi suae satisfacient et erit imminuto corpore et amputato tam laetus quam [in] integro fuit."

54. For a more detailed treatment, see Long, "Soul and Body in Stoicism."

55. Sandbach, *Stoics*, 83.

than from Greek Stoicism (*Ti.* 69c; *Phd.* 87b; cf. *Phdr.* 250c on "the walking sepulcher which we call a body, to which we are bound like an oyster in its shell").[56] So it is that in Seneca's best case scenario the body is the clothing of the soul (*Ad Marc.* 25.1), though a temporary and makeshift dwelling (*EM* 70.16–17) that is gloomy, dark, unpleasant (*EM* 65.17), a prison in which the soul is housed (e.g., *Ad Marc.* 23.2). It is falling down and decrepit (*EM* 58.35), a chain around the soul's freedom (*EM* 65.21; *Ad Marc.* 24.5), and altogether unworthy of it (*EM* 120.14).[57] Lest we fail to feel disgust, Seneca hastens to remind us that we consist of a putrid and perishable casing; how can we hope that from this we might give birth to anything solid and eternal? Clearly, he says, this is the meaning of the ancient command to *Know thyself*: it reminds us that the body is merely an earthenware vessel that breaks when it is shaken, a thing unable to bear cold or heat, doomed to decay, quick to sicken and quick to rot (*Ad Marc.* 11.1).[58] (Epictetus even compares the body to a shoe, *Ench.* 39, and a donkey, *Disc.* 4.1.79!)[59] In all these cases, the body is simply a flesh casing for the soul, not something through which the soul is evenly distributed.[60] And although this may seem familiar to us because of its Christian overtones, at this period in time such an emphasis seems particular to a certain brand of Stoicism only.

It is also worthy of note that the Roman Stoic attitude is far removed from the traditional privileged status accorded the body among the Roman elite, for whom its inviolability to assault or even to display for the pleasure of others was crucial to citizenship status. The very concept of liberty, or *libertas*, as Matthew Roller has recently argued, seems to have meant for the Romans a particular kind of freedom—freedom from the force that a master could use against a slave (specifically, his right to inflict corporal punishment).[61] This may

56. On the similarities, see Natali, who agrees that "in Seneca troviamo una netta differenza rispetto alla posizione stoica secondo la quale esso [sc. il corpo] è qualcosa di naturale per l'anima e di inscindibile da essa" ("Gli Influssi Del Platonismo Sul Neostoicismo Senecano," 508).

57. Respectively: "uestes aliaque tegimenta corporum"; "nemo nostrum cogitat quandoque sibi ex hoc domicilio exeundum"; "animus in hoc tristi et obscuro domicilio clusus, quotiens potest, apertum petit"; "aegre has angustias ferunt"; "prosiliam ex aedificio putri ac ruenti"; "vinclum aliquod libertati meae circumdatum"; "nec domum esse hoc corpus sed hospitium."

58. "Mortalis nata es mortalesque peperisti: putre ipsa fluidumque corpus et causis [morbos] repetita sperasti tam inbecilla materia solida et aeterna gestasse?"

59. On Epictetus's negative attitude toward the body, see Long, *Epictetus*, 149, 157–62.

60. For a full list of images of the body as a prison or as a set of chains in Seneca, see Armisen-Marchetti, *Sapientiae Facies*, 154. On the imagery of the weapons with which fortune threatens man, see p. 78; on torture instruments, pp. 164–65.

61. Roller, *Constructing Autocracy*.

seem odd to us, as we associate "liberty" so often with political rights, forms of constitutions, or abstract ideals; at Rome, however, the main examples of the terminology of *libertas* cited by Roller suggest that it was conceptualized in far more concrete terms. Further, this inviolability of the citizen body marked not only the *free* man, but the free *man*: inasmuch as one's status as a man was based on a "perceived bodily integrity and freedom, or the lack of it, from invasion from the outside,"[62] the impenetrability of the body, either at Rome or anywhere else, plugged into gender constructs as well as issues of social status among the male elite. The term *vir*, man, is not applied to just any adult male; not only must he be a freeborn Roman citizen, and not only must he be biologically a male, but he must also demonstrate the requisite dominant behavior, being a penetrator rather than a penetratee, a beater rather than a recipient of a beating. Indeed, there is a strong connection at Rome between sexual activity and literal assaults on the body: whipping or beating, for example. Both were conceptualized under the same rubric: that of a violation of the body that signified, metaphorically, a violation of the citizenship status of the free male. As Jonathan Walters has pointed out, "Sexual penetration and beating, those two forms of corporeal assault, are in Roman terms structurally equivalent."[63] And a quick check in J. N. Adams's book on the Roman sexual vocabulary confirms this: "One of the largest semantic fields from which metaphors for sexual acts were taken in Latin is that of striking, beating, and the like."[64] Examples include the verbs *caedo*, strike, and *dedolo*, cudgel (cf. Apul. *Met.* 9.7), and the noun *ictus*, a blow, which is used of the sex act in Juvenal, Lucretius, and elsewhere (Juv. 6.126; Lucr. 1.1245, 1.1273); verbs of cutting and penetrating such as *scindo*, *inforare*, *scalpo*, and *traicio* also fall into this group.

The Stoic body, unlike the Roman elite body (even though there were practitioners of Stoicism among the Roman elite), is willingly surrendered, at least in theory, to all sorts of violation. This is not to say that Seneca thinks of the philosopher as weak or unmanly in the Roman sense, or that he himself assimilates the philosopher to those of lowly status. On the contrary, as the philosopher gives up his body, it is his mental *impenetrability* that is figured as the new sign of masculinity. Earlier in the same dialogue, Seneca puts to use the same curiously literal language of bodily penetration and violation to describe the detachment of the good Stoic: "Therefore I assert that the wise man is vulnerable to no injury: therefore it does not matter how many spears

---

62. Walters, "Invading the Roman Body," 30.   64. Adams, *Latin Sexual Vocabulary*, 145–54.
63. Ibid., 39.

are hurled at him, since he is penetrable (penetrabilis) by none" (*Constant.* 3.1). Indeed, the philosopher's mental state is a suit of armor; he is like a hard stone (*Ep.* 82.4); "How glorious it is for the mind, impenetrable, as it were, to every weapon, to despise all injuries and insults!" (*Ira* 3.5.8). And it is this impenetrable mental state, rather than the inviolability of the body, that is figured as "male," in contrast to other philosophies (*Constant.* 1.1): "I might say with some justification, Serenus, that there is as great a difference between the Stoics and the other practitioners of wisdom as between women and men, since each group contributes just as much to human society, but one set was born to obey, the other to rule. Other wise men try to cure sick bodies gently and fawningly, not by the best and quickest path, but as it is allowed, as generally do most well-known family doctors; the Stoics, setting out on the virile path, are concerned not that it may seem pleasant to those who undertake it but that it may snatch us up as soon as possible and lead us on to that lofty peak that rises so much above every range of a weapon that it towers above fortune."[65]

However, even as Seneca claims for the practitioners of Stoic philosophy a Superman-like impenetrability, it seems probable that this revolution in attitudes toward the body might draw mixed reactions from an audience of Romans. Seneca and his ilk pride themselves on their impenetrability, but their passive attitude about the boundaries of their own bodies suggests a kind of insouciance about this category that assimilates them to the despised ranks of the actors, gladiators, slaves, and effeminates so despised in Roman culture—the ranks of the *infames*, men without citizenship rights. The new assessment of the value of the body could lead to such striking stories as Seneca's heroicizing anecdote about the German captive who killed himself by swallowing a toilet plunger rather than appear in the arena as a gladiator (*Ep.* 70.20), a story that only makes sense in the Stoic context because a formerly unimaginable form of death—indeed, one suited to a slave—is here elevated to the level of an exemplum for philosophy.[66] A shameful form of bodily violation here becomes

65. "Tantum inter Stoicos, Serene, et ceteros sapientiam professos interesse quantum inter feminas et mares non inmerito dixerim, cum utraque turba ad uitae societatem tantundem conferat, sed altera pars ad obsequendum, altera imperio nata sit. Ceteri sapientes molliter et blande, ut fere domestici et familiares medici aegris corporibus, non qua optimum et celerrimum est medentur sed qua licet: Stoici uirilem ingressi uiam non ut amoena ineuntibus uideatur curae habent, sed ut quam primum nos eripiat et in illum editum uerticem educat qui adeo extra omnem teli iactum surrexit ut supra fortunam emineat."

66. "Nuper in ludo bestiariorum unus e Germanis, cum ad matutina spectacula pararetur, secessit ad exonerandum corpus—nullum aliud illi dabatur sine custode secretum; ibi lignum id

a badge of pride—both in this anecdote and for the philosopher himself, if he can merely think aright.[67]

In Seneca's exhortations, then, the protective armor of philosophy and the frame of mind it can foster must step in for the bodily impenetrability of the elite Roman male. In a reversal of the linkage between freedom from abuse and the status of the citizen, it is no longer the former that is associated with the word *libertas*; it is philosophy that brings liberty: indeed, even servitude to philosophy is a form of liberty, as Seneca puts it paradoxically in some of his formulations.[68] This liberty itself stems from a paradox: the fact that a complete submission to the violation of the body renders it free from the danger of such violation. The despised body, precisely by means of being despised, is the way to ultimate happiness, or at least Stoic happiness, which John Henderson has called "the fantasy-ideology of an absolute control of Self as the boundary and teleology of human freedom."[69]

This linguistic and conceptual revolution finds corroboration in an interesting coincidence of philosophical and sexual terminology that forms around the word *patientia*, endurance, so common in these philosophical texts. The *patientia* of the wise man, his endurance or willingness to suffer, was what enabled this abandonment of the body; for the Stoics, this was a quality to be aspired to. As Seneca puts it, the goal of this philosophy is that the wise man might protect himself from all injury by his *patientia* and *magnitudo* (*Constant.* 9.4; cf. 15.2); and this refrain is echoed before him in Cicero and after him in Aulus Gellius (Cic. *Tusc.* 2.33; Gell. *NA* pr. 2.1, 2.1.1, of Socrates). But the word *patientia* had a rather more sinister sense in Latin as well:[70] it was the noun that described the sexually submissive role of a man having sex with another man

---

quod ad emundanda obscena adhaerente spongia positum est totum in gulam farsit et interclusis faucibus spiritum elisit. Hoc fuit morti contumeliam facere. Ita prorsus, parum munde et parum decenter: quid est stultius quam fastidiose mori?"

67. One might object that Roman heroes were always praised for their indifference to bodily suffering, as the long tradition on, say, G. Mucius Scaevola makes clear. But this was never elevated to the level of a philosophy before Seneca's writing, nor would such examples of heroism normally extend to slaves swallowing toilet plungers, even with the ethnographic tradition of the hardy Germans attested to by Tacitus.

68. On the liberty brought by philosophy, see, e.g., Sen. *Ep.* 8.7–8, 37.4, 104.16.

69. Henderson, "Pupil as Teacher," 127.

70. On *patientia* and its paradoxical meanings, see Kaster, "Taxonomy of Patience."

filled with intense and urgent meaning. But it is meaning of a different order, composed according to some alien logic. Perhaps it is comprehensible to angels; perhaps somewhere there are creatures who speak the mystical language in which it is inscribed. Something is going on, clearly, something that cries out to be understood, but I am not the person who is permitted to understand it. (If I were a tragic hero, this situation would be called dramatic irony.)

Sex, then, accomplishes nothing in the sphere of desire, whatever else it may accomplish in other spheres. My desire for you does not disappear or diminish when I make love to you. I may get tired of you, but unless or until I do, those features of your body that arouse my desire will continue to do so long after I have given up trying to express through sex the attraction you awaken in me. Making love with you is not what I really want to do with you, or to you, although I do want to do it, and I don't know what else to do. But sex achieves nothing, beyond merely "verifying to the point of giddiness the useless objectivity of things."

Or so Baudrillard says. Plato puts it more gently. Those who spend their entire lives together "could not say what they wish to gain from one another," Aristophanes remarks in the *Symposium*. "No one would think it was sexual intercourse," he adds, "or that for the sake of sex each partner so earnestly enjoys his union with the other. But it is clear that the soul of each lover wants something else, which it is not able to say, but it divines what it wants and hints at it" (192c–d; cf. *Republic* 505d–e). A number of characters in the *Symposium*, including Aristophanes himself, attempt to answer this riddle about the aim of erotic desire. And a number of male writers since Plato, such as Augustine, Dante, Freud, Proust, and Nabokov, have also tried to identify what it is that the soul of the lover wants. What is striking about those efforts is not the specific answers they produce but their formal, structural correspondences, their common insistence that passionate desire for an individual object always points somewhere beyond it, that no object contains within itself the secret of its own fascination.

To say that sexual desire intends a transcendental object is to say that there is nothing in the world to which the ultimate object of that desire exactly corresponds. If I am turned on by blonds, it is not because blond hair is intrinsically desirable; I do not get a charge out of holding a detached handful of blond hair. Blond hair is a sexual metaphor: it is the vehicle of a certain meaning or value that has taken up residence in your body. What thrills and fascinates me about your body, then, is not any particular somatic feature in itself but the meaning that one or more of those features conveys to me. (As Proust says, "Even women

and was used in the condemnation of such a man as *infamis* and effeminate.[71] Seneca himself invokes the word in precisely such a sense to excoriate a Roman who was given to a most unphilosophical activity: indulging in orgiastic couplings in which he played both the passive and the active parts, in front of a collection of distorting and magnifying mirrors that lined his bedroom wall. This man, Hostius Quadra, represents for Seneca the reverse image of the philosopher, inasmuch as he uses the mirror not for self-knowledge, as Seneca recommends, but for self-titillation (Q. *Nat.* 1.16.7)—and for precisely the kind of deviant behavior that Martial, Juvenal, and Dio Cassius would paradoxically associate with Seneca. Hostius Quadra's *patientia*—his sexual penetration by another male (the term is used thrice in Q. *Nat.* 1.16.5–9)—forms the shocking kernel of this story about a man whose life represented everything a philosopher's should not be.[72]

In other words, *patientia* is on one hand the self-ennobling standard of the Roman philosopher, who prided himself, under the dangerous and arbitrary rule of such emperors as Nero, on his capacity to endure the violation of his body—if it came to that—with an unflinching will and with devotion to the principles he had spent his adult life endorsing. But *patientia* is also, on the other hand, the mark of the un-man, of the Roman who is forced to accept the aggression of the other; the mark of the stage actor, the man without citizenship, the unmanly *cinaedus* and his ilk: it is, for the Roman citizen, the mark of the absence of aggressive male sexuality. At the center of this paradox, the philosopher takes his stand, in a place where eros as we know it is absent but its violating force is well and alive. This force is no longer figured as the caressing flow of one gaze into the eyes of the other but rather as an assault comparable to a blow against body and mind, a blow that gives us no Socrates but rather works to turn both Plato's beloved and his lover into a single figure of the isolated and violated Roman *sapiens*.

Let us return, in closing, to Juvenal's lines from *Satire* 2 limning the odd relationship between the hypocritical philosopher and his smirking doctor. The doctor's smile as he cuts away the *mariscae* from the philosopher's depilated hindquarters confirms his amusement at the gap between ascetic exterior and unmanly interior. But to drive home his point, Juvenal plays on the double

---

71. OLD s.v.1b: submission to unnatural lust, pathicism, Cic. *Verr.* 2.5.13 §34; Sen. Q. *Nat.* 1.16.5; id. *Vit. beat.* 13.3; Tac. *Ann.* 6.1.1; Petr. 9 and 25; Mos. et Rom. Leg. Coll. 5.3.2.

72. On Hostius Quadra's relation to the rest of this Senecan text on meteorology, see the excellent article of Leitao, "Senecan Catoptrics."

meaning of such surgical intervention. The verb *caeduntur* here (the piles "are cut out") points to the equivalence in Roman thinking between cutting and sexual activity: the philosopher is getting it from the rear even as the results of this activity are being operated on.[73] Is Juvenal also playing with the connection between beating, sexual activity, and the body of the philosopher? Perhaps. But it does seem clear that a multitude of social and historical factors render the Roman philosopher a man in a dangerously liminal position, and if satiric writers of the early empire make a connection between the philosopher and the sexually passive man, we may look not only to these factors but also, as I have been suggesting, to an additional possibility: while Seneca and his ilk pride themselves on their impenetrability, their passive attitude about the boundaries of their own bodies renders them, in the eyes of others in their culture, models par excellence of unmanly penetration. In other words, give up one kind of defense against the violation of the body—its immunity to violence—and in a leap of thought, for your Roman audience, you've given them all up: the philosopher is a *cinaedus*.

73. See Walters, "Making a Spectacle," on this passage.

RESPONSE TO SHADI BARTSCH

CATHARINE EDWARDS

Shadi Bartsch's seductive essay engages with that enigmatic figure *Socraticus cinaedus*, who appears in several of the poems of Martial and Juvenal—and even as a characterization of the philosopher Seneca in Cassius Dio's history. Her argument that this slander can be seen as a specific response to some of the main tenets of Stoicism in the first century AD is an intriguing one (even if the caricature is associated with Academic and Epicurean philosophers as well as the Stoics). Bartsch's emphasis on the degree to which Stoic manliness is divorced from traditional Roman notions of bodily integrity is surely right, and her discussion of the ambiguities of that key term *patientia*, highly suggestive. But the slippery nature of the terminology deployed by Seneca in particular could, I think, be pressed further.

Bartsch explores the often positive association between philosophy and eros in Plato as a source of anxiety for Romans, who reacted by attributing the most shameful desires to those who presented themselves as philosophers. The Platonic tradition is certainly important (I shall return briefly to another aspect of its influence later), but Roman receptions of philosophy—and philosophers—should also, I think, be seen as significantly conditioned by features of the Epicurean tradition. There is some evidence to suggest that Epicurean philosophers were the first to present their doctrines in Latin and that these works had a relatively wide readership, such that Roman notions of philosophy, in the late republic notably, but later, too, were markedly influenced by perceptions of Epicureanism and in particular by the place of pleasure in Epicurean philosophy.[1] The writings of Epicurus and his followers, strictly understood, give

I would like to thank William Fitzgerald for his helpful and perceptive comments on this response.

1. See Griffin, "Philosophy, Politics, Politicians."

little license to the voluptuary, as those Romans who studied them were well aware; in his more philosophical writings, Cicero concedes as much.[2] When defending his young friend Caelius before judges with no particular expertise in philosophy, however, he invokes a cruder version of Epicureanism, characterizing the reprehensible nature of its followers thus: "alii voluptatis causa omnia sapientes facere dixerunt, neque ab hac oratione turpitudine eruditi homines refugerunt" (Cael. 40–41). [Some have said that the wise do everything for the sake of pleasure, and learned men have not shrunk from this shameful claim.] For those who wanted philosophy to be taken seriously in Rome, Epicureanism's popular reputation raised major problems.

The development of Roman Stoicism's distinctive characteristics needs to be seen, at least in part, as a response to this. In particular, the hypervirile image of Stoicism in Seneca can be understood against this background. Here was a philosophical school that had no time for pleasure—and that could be safely embraced by the toughest and most austere of Romans. In Seneca's writing, the image of the Stoic philosopher is repeatedly presented in the most masculine terms; he is a soldier or gladiator fighting against vice or against the ills of fortune.[3] In one of his letters, Seneca seeks to fortify the resolve of his correspondent Lucilius by comparing his commitment to philosophy to that of a soldier who has sworn an oath upon enlisting in the army. This is conceived specifically as a riposte to the mockery of those who term philosophy a mollis militia, a "soft soldiering" (37.1). That was a charge to which Epicureanism, which advocated a life of retirement, might seem particularly vulnerable. Bartsch quotes from the arresting first chapter of De constantia sapientis. Virile Stoicism is, for Seneca, to be contrasted with other philosophical schools, which seek to make philosophy attractive by treating their pupils molliter et blande, "softly and gently." It differs as much from them as the male sex does from the female. That this is a criticism of Epicureanism in particular—at least as generally perceived—becomes clear as the rest of the treatise focuses on refuting Epicurean doctrines.

In another treatise, De vita beata ("on the happy life"), Seneca argues against the Epicurean identification of the virtuous life with the life that is pleasurable by presenting virtue and pleasure as intrinsically opposed to one another. Pleasure is personified, characterized in 7.3 as mollis, "soft," and enervis, "without muscle" (though the use of nervus to mean "phallus" is also relevant here).

---

2. In De finibus, for instance, Cicero is less dismissive of Epicureanism, though he still has many criticisms to make of its emphasis on pleasure.

3. See Lavery, "Metaphors of War," and Armisen-Marchetti, Sapientiae Facies.

Mollis, invoked in 7.3 and elsewhere to characterize Epicureanism, is a symbolically loaded term. The life of pleasure is regularly alleged to "soften" its adherents, to undermine their virility. Conversely, there is a strong association between effeminacy and susceptibility to pleasure in Seneca's writing. At the same time, however, he criticizes those who have miscontrued Epicurean teaching to endorse their own debauched pleasure seeking. Properly understood, he concedes, the Epicureans advocate a very moderate life.[4] And Seneca sums this up with a strikingly vivid characterization of Epicureanism: "The case is like that of a strong man dressed up in a woman's garb; you maintain your chastity, your virility is unimpaired, your body is free from base submission—but in your hand is a tambourine!" (*Vit. beat.* 13.3).[5] Here we have what could be seen as the reverse of the *Socraticus cinaedus*. The Epicurean looks effeminate—dressed like a woman, he brandishes the tambourine, an instrument associated with the orgiastic worship of the goddess Cybele, whose priests were eunuchs.[6] But underneath he is a real man. This paradoxical figure again raises the issue of sexual penetration, with the term *patientia* here qualified by the adjective *turpis*, "shameful." The true virtue of Epicureanism, though belied by its appearance, is attested by the fact that the Epicurean body does not make itself available (*vacat*—implying a willing acceptance) for such usage.[7]

Through this image, Seneca himself raises the issue of the philosopher's availability for sexual penetration. But what if the would-be philosopher has no choice? What if his body is penetrated against his will? Let us return, at this point, to the characterization of the Stoic wise man. Such an experience would count as deeply humiliating, indeed emasculating, according to traditional protocols of Roman manhood but, as Bartsch emphasizes, in theory even penetration of his body need not compromise the manliness of the Stoic. It is how he responds to the experience that is the test of his *virtus*. Yet, while Seneca is always ready to identify with the beaten, the mutilated, or victims of torture, he never identifies or invites his readers to identify directly with the sexually penetrated. And this is perhaps not because of the pain or even the humiliation that might attend such an experience—being beaten could itself

---

4. Especially in his earlier letters, Seneca frequently quotes approvingly from the writings of Epicurus.

5. *Hoc tale est, quale vir fortis stolam indutus; constat tibi pudicitia, virilitas salva est, nulli corpus tuum turpi patientiae vacat, sed in manu tympanum est!*

6. For the effeminate associations of the *tympanum*, see also Quint. *Inst.* 5.12.21.

7. Seneca makes similar comments about Epicurus himself at *Ep.* 33.2.

be construed as an infringement of Roman notions of masculinity—but rather, I would suggest, because of its association with pleasure.[8] Pain, for the Stoic, is relatively unproblematic. Indeed, it may be seen as providing an opportunity for virtue to be tested, to prove itself (*Prov.* 4.3). And *contumelia* or *iniuria* ("insult" or "injury") can be similarly welcomed (*Constant.* 4.3). But while Seneca occasionally presents pain and pleasure as offering parallel challenges to the *proficiens*, the would-be philosopher (e.g., *Vit. beat.* 4.4), by and large the prospect of experiencing pleasure comes across in his writing as much more disturbing to the would-be philosopher's peace of mind. And though, in general, the Romans did not consider a passive sexual role to be a direct source of pleasure for males (to judge from, e.g., Ov. *Ars am.* 2.681–84; Prop. 2.4.17–22; Juv. 6.36–37), exceptions to this might also be cited. Seneca himself provides a lurid picture of the perverse Hostius Quadra (discussed by Bartsch), who loves to watch himself being penetrated by other men (*Q. Nat.* 1.16.7). Even if only perverts such as Quadra are able to experience such pleasure (in accordance with Aristotle's argument, *Eth. Nic.* 1148b15–49a20), to imagine such pleasure could itself be deeply unsettling to the would-be philosopher.

Pleasure, as we have seen, is for Seneca soft and unmanly, and those susceptible to it are similarly characterized. The slippage between notions of effeminacy and sexual passivity in Roman texts generally and in Seneca's work in particular serves also to associate sexual passivity with pleasure. And if the physical experience of being sexually penetrated is not explored in Seneca's writing as a challenge the *proficiens* might have to face, he nevertheless uses bodily penetration as a metaphor for other challenges. The would-be philosopher's body is under constant attack from the insidious infiltrations of pleasure. "Vices steal in (inrepunt) through the avenue of pleasure" (*Ep.* 7.2). "Sensual pleasure . . . flows around us on every side and seeps in (influat) through every opening . . . it softens the mind with its charms and leaves no avenue untried in its attempts to seduce us in whole or in part" (*Vit. beat.* 5.4). It is not too far-fetched, I think, to detect a diffuse eroticism in the representation of pleasure as attacking the body. This, too, could be characterized as *turpis patientia*. Seneca regularly revisits this territory, setting out in fascinated detail those pleasures that the would-be philosopher must avoid at all costs (e.g., *Ep.* 51, 122). For while the *sapiens*, the wise man, can trust himself to know where to draw the line in experiencing pleasure, the *proficiens* will be far safer giving it a wide berth (*Ep.* 116.4–5). For Seneca, "virtue despises pleasure, is its

8. On the associations of being beaten, see Walters, "Invading the Roman Body," 36–39.

enemy, and recoils from it as far as it can" (*Ben.* 4.2.4). Were the Stoics thought to protest too much about the evils of pleasure? It is hardly surprising, when philosophers were accused of every kind of hypocrisy, to find charges of covert sexual passivity (with all its associations) leveled at the Stoics.

At the same time, there is, I think, a more particular sense in which the Platonic tradition of eroticized philosophical discourse has at least an occasional part to play in Seneca's writing. Seneca's most obviously pedagogic work is his collection of letters to Lucilius. In these, he often offers comments on his pupil's philosophical progress (and correspondingly the letters tackle issues of increasing philosophical complexity). Now philosophy here does not involve gazing on beautiful boys. This is not conversation but an exchange of correspondence.[9] Lucilius, as he is presented in the letters, is not a young man but a Roman equestrian who has served as a provincial procurator and is indeed only slightly younger than Seneca himself. Where the relationship between the two is discussed, it is usually in terms of warm friendship.[10] Yet the relations between this pupil and teacher are occasionally presented in what can be read as erotic terms—and with an interesting new twist.

In one letter that seeks to persuade Lucilius that his public career will ultimately bring him less fame than will his role as Seneca's correspondent, Seneca compares him not only to Atticus, made famous by Cicero, and to Idomeneus, made famous as the addressee of Epicurus's letters, but also to two heroes celebrated in Virgil's *Aeneid*—Nisus and Euryalus (21.5, quoting *Aeneid* 9.446–49). Nisus and Euryalus are two young men of striking physical beauty whose regard for one another spurs them on to acts of extraordinary bravery in the conflict between the Trojans and the Italians. When they are first introduced at *Aeneid* 5.294–96, Nisus is figured as the *erastes*—characterized by *amore pio*, "respectful love"—and Euryalus as the *eromenos*. This is as close as Latin literature comes to celebrating the ennobling force of love between beautiful young men—safely located in the heroic, pre-Roman past.[11] And Virgil himself, to judge from Suetonius's biography, was thought to have been particularly susceptible to passions for boys (ch. 9). But elsewhere Seneca rarely seems to be exploiting the context of the passages he quotes from other authors, so one should perhaps not press this allusion too far.

9. Though Seneca does at various points lament Lucilius's absence, exclaiming for instance at 35.3 that his living presence would afford Seneca *vivae voluptatis*, "true pleasure" (cf. also 34.2, 49.1).

10. See, e.g., 75.3.

11. On this passage, see Williams, *Roman Homosexuality*, 116–19.

Yet, in another letter reflecting on the literary nature of his relationship with Lucilius, Seneca does appear to invoke sexual roles—and in a rather disconcerting way. As we have seen, manliness and effeminacy are for Seneca, in particular, heavily loaded terms and ones which he often chooses to invoke. It is not surprising, then, to find references to manliness even in a discussion of literary style, a subject to which Seneca returns on a number of occasions.[12] Letter 114, for instance, excoriates as effeminate the writings of Augustus's associate Maecenas. At 114.8, his style is described as *enervatus*, "without muscle" (and see above for the sexual associations of *nervus*). Seneca sees an intimate link between Maecenas's effeminate literary style and the decadence of every other aspect of his life; even the two eunuchs who—scandalously—attended him in public were more men than Maecenas, *magis tamen viri quam ipse* (114.6). His literary style is loose (*soluta*), just as his tunic is unbelted (*discinctus*).[13] His literary faults—such as inverted expression—prove him to be *mollis* (114.8). "When the soul (*animus*) is sound and strong, the style too is vigorous, energetic, manly" (*illo sano et valente oratio quoque robusta, fortis, virilis est*), comments Seneca; the opposite of this is ruination (114.22). And this is a concern of other letters, too; "elaborate elegance is not a manly adornment" (*non est ornamentum virile concinnitas*), he writes in 115.3. In Seneca's criticisms of effeminate style, the issue is not, of course, how women might actually write but rather how most effectively to stigmatize deviations from stylistic propriety.

To characterize literary composition in gendered terms raises many interesting issues. Some of these come to the fore in letter 46, which has been illuminatingly discussed by Tom Habinek.[14] In this letter, Seneca writes of a book that his correspondent Lucilius has allegedly sent him. The way Seneca characterizes both the text and his own response to it is indeed, as Habinek notes, worthy of our attention. The book Lucilius has sent is *virilis et sancta*, "manly and pure," in its composition (46.2). But there are other comments that perhaps give an erotic dimension to this characterization. The text has a *dulcedo*, "sweetness," which takes possession of the reader (46.1). It charms Seneca, *blanditus est*, such that he reads the whole book when he had only intended to sample it. Seneca is seduced. Indeed he presents himself as the passive

---

12. Seneca was by no means to the first to discuss literary style in such terms. The writings of his father offer a particularly colorful example; see Sen. *Controv.* 1.pr.8–9.

13. Cf. 92.35, where Maecenas is said to have had a genius that would have been *grande et virile*, if only prosperity had not unbelted him, *nisi illud secunda discinxisset*. On the association of an unbelted tunic with effeminacy, see Edwards, *Politics of Immorality*, 90.

14. Habinek, *Politics of Latin Literature*, ch. 7 (first published in *Yale Classical Studies* 29 [1992]).

recipient of Lucilius's manly thrust. *Grandis, erectus es; hoc te volo tenere, sic ire.* (Habinek translates: "You're big, you're taut: stay like that, keep it up!") Lucilius's masculine writing obliges his reader to adopt a subordinate position—but one that brings the reader pleasure: "I was not merely delighted, I rejoiced" (non tantum delectatus sed gavisus sum). Habinek comments, "Far from being humiliated by his 'passivity' Seneca rejoices in what he has encountered—the force, the endurance provide a pleasant surprise."[15] Here Seneca plays with presenting himself in a passive role. However "metaphorical" this may be, it is still a disconcerting move on the part of a writer who is usually so quick to damn the faintest trace of *mollitia*.

And it is not just a question of Seneca succumbing to the charms of his far from boyish pupil. Since Lucilius is also a regular recipient of Seneca's writing (and should no doubt be thought of as modeling his own virile style on that of his mentor), we should presumably imagine him taking his turn as the one seduced. Is it going too far to see Seneca as flirting with the idea of literary intercourse as *mutuum stuprum*?[16] And while *we* do not get to read Lucilius's seductive prose, as readers of Seneca's work are we not implicitly invited to put ourselves in the subordinate position Seneca claims to be adopting in relation to that of Lucilius—with his own writings taking the role of seducer?[17]

Thus it is by no means only the ambiguities of that crucial Stoic term *patientia* that serve to make sexual passivity a preoccupation in Seneca's writings, at any rate. Seneca's playful use of the imagery of seduction in letter 46 is not, I think, directly paralleled elsewhere in his work. Yet, as we have seen, his obsessive concern with the dangerous power of pleasure and his frequent invocation of notions of manliness and effeminacy—particularly in his characterizations of philosophical schools—nevertheless work to bring the erotic back into philosophical discourse, even if in a very different way from that of Plato.

15. Ibid., 145.

16. Elsewhere in the letters, this is characterized as an appallingly deviant sexual practice (99.13). For a rather different earlier Roman example of literary reciprocity characterized in terms of mutual sexual provocation, see Catullus 50 with the discussion in Fitzgerald, *Catullan Provocations*, 46. Note also Ellen Oliensis's deft exploration of a closely related issue, the resemblance between the patron-client relationship and that of the lover-beloved, in "Erotics of *Amicitia*."

17. Several scholars have argued for a sexual model for the relationship between poet and reader with regard to Catullus. See most recently Fitzgerald (ibid., 255n38), who specifically explores parallels between Catullus 16 and Seneca *Ep.* 46.

THE DIVIDED CONSCIOUSNESS

OF AUGUSTINE ON EROS

DAVID TRACY

There seems to be a division in the heart of Western culture on eros. A part of that division—only a part, but a significant part—is the legacy of Plato. More exactly, how, in a still-raging storm of conflicting Platonic interpretations, does one interpret the relationships of eros to *logos*, eros to particularity, and eros to body, given the sometimes contrary positions of Plato in the dialogues? On the same issue of eros, the Christian Platonist Augustine of Hippo bequeathed an even more divided legacy to Western Christian consciousness and, through its influence, to Western culture in general.[1] Western culture's construal of Augustine's transformative *caritas* vision has had a dual effect, contributing both to the great creativity of the West and, at the very same time, to something approaching tragedy in Western confusions on eros. In this brief essay, I will give one interpretation of Augustine on eros and the divided heritage he left. To show the basic outlines of my hypothesis, I will observe, first, the general difficulty any biblical (i.e., prophetic) religion will have with eros and the solutions proposed by ancient and medieval theologians; second, how Augustine believed he had resolved the problem of the ambiguity of eros by his optimistic *caritas* synthesis, in which Christian love as the pure gift of divine agape transforms but does not discard Platonic eros; and finally, how the older, more pessimistic Augustine comes to discover an ever darker vision of the ineradicable human

---

1. The theological anthropology on *eros* in Eastern Christianity (i.e., Orthodoxy) is resolutely non-Augustinian and therefore more optimistic than Western Christianity—at least until the influence of Dostoevsky in modern Russian Orthodoxy. This generalization is true of the classical Greek Fathers, e.g., Origen, Gregory of Nyssa, Dionysius the Areopagite, Maximus the Confessor, Gregory Palamas.

tendency in erotic experience toward self-deception and self-destruction. That strange Augustinian journey affected not only Christianity but Western secular culture as a whole, as the relative optimism on eros of other cultures (Asian, African, Oceanian) amply attests when compared to the still divided (witness the writings of Freud, Lacan, Foucault) Western consciousness of eros.

styled

— THE BIBLICAL RELIGIONS AND EROS

Every religion is grounded in some manifesting or proclamatory event. In the prophetic biblical traditions, this could not be clearer. It is unlikely that we can understand Judaism without interpreting the "founding" revelatory historical events of Sinai and Exodus. It is also probably impossible to understand Christianity without interpreting the revelatory event and person of Jesus Christ. It is equally impossible to understand Islam without knowing that the central revelatory event for Muslims is not a historical-religious event like Sinai or Exodus, nor a religious-historical event and person like Jesus Christ, but the Koran, a text understood by Islam as a revelation given by God to the unsubstitutable prophet Mohammed. Both Judaism and Christianity also need a text—the Bible. But for Christians and Jews, the Bible, unlike the Koran, is not understood as the revelation itself but as the canonical *witness to* the revelatory events. In Islam alone among the three radically monotheistic religions, the revelatory event is the text (Koran) to which the prophet (Mohammed) canonically witnesses.

The distinction in terms of religious types is a classical one: a distinction (not separation) between two basic forms of religion. The first form is one of a manifestation of whatever is construed as Ultimate Reality (the Good, the One, the Open, the divine, the gods) in and through symbols (the cosmic tree, the *axis mundi*, the icon, the ritual, the sacred mountain). Most ancient religions of the West (misnamed "pagan" by their prophetic opponents) are manifestation religions. So are most of the indigenous traditions of Africa, Oceania, and pre-European America, as well as most Eastern religions (Taoism, Hinduism, Buddhism, Shintoism). The key to all religions of this form is a radical sense of participation in the whole—thus the sense of manifesting a religious fullness, or *plenum* for participants. Recall, for example, Thales's famous statement: "The world is full of gods."

The second basic form is one of proclamation. This form is most clearly seen in the Western prophetic radically monotheistic traditions. Here, three moments of a sense of distance from Ultimate Reality, now named "God," occur. There is a profound sense in prophetic proclamation of the distance between God and mortals. God is Other and human participation is deeply ambiguous.

Humans are now proclaimed to be so radically finite and often so sinful that they must be distant from the tremendous power of Yahweh. Thus, the self in history (not nature, as for "pagan" religions) becomes the principal locus for the Transcendent Other, that is, the God proclaimed in the unsettling, distancing words of the prophets. In the prophetic traditions, moreover, the words of the prophets are written down by the community. Writing, therefore, becomes a second, further distancing from any radical sense of participation in God's presence, in either nature or the seeming self-presence of the spoken word. And, if the writings are considered either to be the Word of God (Islam) or an unsubstitutable witness to that proclaimed Word (Judaism and Christianity), then a third distancing, the labor of interpreting the writings (i.e., hermeneutics), becomes religiously central to all three monotheistic traditions.

All three traditions, in my judgment, are fundamentally proclamation-prophetic religions whose distancing reality moves them initially from an earlier, "pagan" manifestation of the whole or divine through nature, eros, and cosmos to a disruptive proclamation by a transcendent God in and through history and a prophetic word in history. Moreover, each of these monotheistic traditions inevitably partakes of the distancing reality of language itself: in all three, earlier oral traditions became written texts of witness. The written texts thus provide a second distanciation from the pagan plenum (the manifesting whole in cosmos, *logos*, and eros). And written texts, once they predominate, demand hermeneutics as intrinsic to the religion itself. Writing, far more distancing than oral language, becomes necessary for recording history as the principal locus of God's self-disclosure. History is the reality that the language of prophetic proclamation understands itself to both interrupt and ground in the Word of a transcendent God. All three monotheistic traditions, therefore, are not only prophetic-proclamatory but also hermeneutical at the core. Each monotheistic tradition has its own ways of performing this hermeneutical task. In Judaism, we find rabbinic exegesis and other oral traditions of the interpretation of texts now written into the classical commentaries of the Talmud. In Christianity, we find liturgical uses (and thereby interpretations) of the scripture, as well as creeds, commentaries, and distinct traditions of emphasis in reading the scripture, in the three main historical forms of Christianity (Eastern Orthodoxy, Catholicism, and Protestantism). In Islam, there is no escape *religiously* from interpreting the text, even for the Sufis, as their mystical and often erotic readings of the Koran witness.

The hermeneutics of Jewish, Christian, and Islamic principles for reading the Bible—even the erotic parts of the Bible like the Song of Songs—are different among the three traditions and also include important differences within each tradition. For example, in Christianity, there is the greater use of Platonic understandings of eros in the allegorical readings of scripture in Origen and Augustine as compared with the insistence on "literal" readings in the distinct senses of the literal in Aquinas, Luther, or contemporary readings of the Bible informed by historical criticism.[2] Sufi readings of the Koran were highly suspect to more orthodox, traditional Muslim readers. However, as the Sufis correctly insisted, their readings were also readings of the Koran, the common revelatory event of all Muslims.[3] Kabbalistic readings of the Bible, which emphasize the very materiality of the Hebrew letters of the Tanach, are still highly suspect to many Reform, Conservative, Reconstructionist, and Orthodox Jews. Nevertheless, the kabbalists, like the Sufis in Islam or such Christian mystics as Bernard of Clairvaux or Angela of Foligno or Dante, always insist that they have not really left the scripture through their erotic readings of it.[4] Instead, like mystics everywhere, these peculiar readers have found some hidden mystical code based on both *logos* and eros to aid, not replace, the traditional interpretations of the scriptural texts.

To reiterate, at every step in this prophetic trajectory, there is some distancing from a sense of "pagan" participation in the manifesting divine whole and from the "pagan" plenum showing itself in nature, eros, *logos*, and cosmos. First, the prophetic word disrupts the pagan plenum (now labeled by the prophets

2. Aquinas was cautious in the use of allegorical readings of scripture in favor of realistic, "literal" readings. Luther rejected allegorical readings as fanciful in favor of literal readings and some typological readings grounded in the literal sense of scripture, namely, for Luther, the event and person of Jesus Christ. Modern historical critics believe in the need to reconstruct the biblical texts by modern historical methods to arrive as closely as possible at the original literal, that is, historical, meaning of the texts. The various quests for the historical Jesus (i.e., the Jesus who can be construed by historical reconstruction of the original scriptural texts) is merely the clearest example of the modern historical-critical search for the literal (i.e., historical) meaning of the Bible. Therefore, paradoxically, *literal* has these different meanings for Aquinas, Luther, and modern critics. What unites all three is not a shared positive sense of the literal meaning but a shared hesitation on allegorical methods (or their modern counterparts) for interpreting the Bible.

3. See al-Ghazzali, *Alchemy of Happiness*; Keshavarz, *Reading Mystical Lyric*; Trimingham, *Sufi Orders in Islam*.

4. Idel, *Kabbalah*, 35–112; Bernard of Clairvaux, *Sancti Bernardi Opera*, esp. vols. 1 and 3 (in English, see esp. the sequence of Bernard's interpretations of *The Song of Songs* in Bernard of Clairvaux, *Works*); Angela of Foligno, *Complete Works*; Gilson, *Mystical Theology of Saint Bernard*; Foster, *Two Dantes*, 15–56; McGinn, "Love, Knowledge, and *Unio Mystica*."

as idolatry) and orients history—not nature, not eros—as the principal locus of revelation. Second, the proclamatory Word of the now utterly transcendent God, as word (i.e., as language), demands testimony or witness (the written scripture). This testimony, in turn, requires constant interpretation (the Talmud, the Church, the mullahs, and scholars in several disciplines), making such hermeneutics the third and last step of distanciation, beyond history, oral language, and writing.

Hermeneutics is also the first step in the generalization of the prophetic reading. For hermeneutics of various sorts were developed for these religious readings long before the modern hermeneutics of historical-critical readings. What happened, for example, when that strange form of interpretive and critical inquiry, Christian theology, first occurred? Christian theology begins as Greek questions (partly focused by *logos* and eros) about Jewish narratives (the Gospels). To be sure, the gospel narratives, written in Koine Greek, are part of the Hellenistic-Jewish milieu from which they emerged, so the Greek element is not foreign to the New Testament. Moreover, the Gospel of John, again, as a Jewish-Hellenistic text, cannot but encourage its reflective Gentile readers to develop exactly what they did first develop—the *Logos* theologies of ancient Christian thought and the love-oriented readings of both agape and eros in what Augustine called this "Johannine Gospel of love."[5]

The move of distanciation, within Christianity, is therefore from Word as the disruptive, proclamatory, prophetic Word of a transcendent God (as in the prophet Jesus's own eschatological sayings, parables, and unnerving proverbs) to the manifesting, meditative Word of *Logos* in the eros-oriented and mystically oriented Gospel of John and in the writing of John's many Christian successors. This trajectory to a meditative form of eros and agape had already begun, of course, in the classical wisdom traditions of the Jewish scripture (now named, for Christians, the First, or Old, Testament). Greek reflective questions and concerns (including those on eros), contrary to the opinion of all anti-Hellenizers, are hermeneutically appropriate on inner-Jewish, inner-Christian, and inner-Islamic terms.[6] Sometimes these questions will take a critical turn.

---

5. See Hardy, *Actualité de la révélation divine*.

6. The anti-Hellenizers have been present in the Christian tradition from Tertullian (third century) through the modern liberal Protestant Adolf von Harnack to the present day. What unites these otherwise disparate voices is a common insistence that Christianity, in fidelity to its biblical Jewish and early Christian roots, betrays its identity by allowing interpretations of the Bible by the "Greeks." Most radical is Tertullian's famous cry: "What has Athens to do with Jerusalem?"

Here the extraordinary achievement of Jewish, Christian, and Muslim readers was the centuries-long struggle to show how the Creator-God of the Bible need not destroy—as distinct from disrupt and transform—the ancient "pagan" participatory, manifesting synthesis of the human, cosmic, and divine realms. In the same way, the biblical religions need not sunder the link between *logos* and eros in all the ancient Greek-inspired philosophies of love.[7]

For these medieval (and earlier) theologians and philosophers, there was no need to choose between the Jewish Creator-God and the ancient synthesis of the self (including the erotic self), the cosmos, and the divine. They clearly held that this critical religious-biblical thinking need not eliminate eros. For the Creator-God need not be interpreted only through Aristotelian efficient causality. The Creator-God would, in that case, be the cause of, but completely transcendent to, not immanent in, the created human and cosmic realms, including eros.[8] But what if the causality of creation is not purely efficient but also—as the Christian Platonists insisted—formal and final? Then the Creator-God of the Bible is not only the origin of all but precisely, as origin, the sustainer of all and the final erotic end (final cause) of all reality.

This remarkable Jewish-Christian-Muslim medieval reflective achievement allowed these early thinkers to philosophically, and thereby theologically, to work through how the Creator-God of the Bible was both transcendent to all creation and, as such, immanent in all creation, including eros. This achievement was aided by the harmony these thinkers found between biblical readings of creation in Genesis and the creation account in Plato's *Timaeus*, as well as multiple commentaries on eros in the Song of Songs.[9] These readings saved the ancient manifesting, participatory synthesis of the human-cosmic-divine realms—of both *logos* and eros—for Judaism, Christianity, and Islam alike. There is perhaps no greater achievement in Western medieval and earlier theologies than this brilliant series of distinct and often conflicting ways (e.g., Aquinas vs. Eckhart on analogy)[10] to make immanent the Transcendent One without the loss of prophetic transcendence and to save the ancient human-cosmic-divine synthesis (and the erotic plenum within it) for thought and life (e.g.,

---

7. Dupré, *Passage to Modernity*, 1–65.

8. Ibid., 29–41.

9. Pelikan, *What Has Athens to Do with Jerusalem?* In Augustine, see Knuuttila, "Time and Creation in Augustine," 103–16. On Christian commentaries on the Song of Songs, see McGinn, "Love, Knowledge, and *Unio Mystica*."

10. Tobin, *Meister Eckhart, Thought and Language*, 31–89; McGinn, *Mystical Thought of Meister Eckhart*, 165–80.

the manifesting-proclamatory Dante in his love for Beatrice). That challenge was as difficult and as complex for the medieval Jewish, Islamic, and Christian thinkers to resolve (and they *did* resolve it) as the crisis of no-thingness is today for all sensitive Jewish, Islamic, and Christian thinkers.[11] The latter crisis is still unresolved, partly because no ancient or medieval synthesis could survive the new cosmology of modern science and partly because the ancient optimism on *logos* and eros is gone, even for many religious thinkers.

Proclamation, by its proclamation, by its insistence on distance, necessarily implies some reality from which it is distanced. Proclamation is always in tension with this other: at its best as a tensive polarity; at the limit as a dialectical opposition. Proclamation is not only logically posterior, it is also historically so in the history of religions. All three proclamatory prophetic monotheistic traditions posited themselves by implying an other (now deemed "pagan") from which they are now distanced: history posits itself by implying nature; language posits itself by implying the nonlinguistic (e.g., claims to a nonlinguistic consciousness or experience); writing posits itself by implying speaking; mediating hermeneutics posits itself by implying a claim to some immediate apprehension of a text.

Religion as proclamatory Word of God posits itself by implying its other—the manifesting participatory Sophia (as feminist theologians have shown).[12] One can see this return in the prophetic traditions in the *Logos* of wisdom traditions and in the radical eros of affective mystics like Angela of Foligno, as well as in the classical retrievals of the ancient pagan erotic *plenum*, disrupted and transformed but not destroyed in the liturgical-sacramental lives of Christians and their Greek-inspired theologies of an erotic Transcendent-Immanent God. One finds that same development in the erotic poetry of the troubadours, in the *Paradiso* of Dante, and later, in John Donne. The ancient synthesis of the self, the cosmos, and the divine (and the erotic *plenum* pervading it) was not destroyed but disrupted, transformed, and reposited by the majority of Jewish, Christian, and Muslim thinkers in the medieval and earlier periods.

AUGUSTINE ON EROS

Before the Jewish, Islamic, and Christian thinkers of medieval times, the Neoplatonic dimension in these three traditions and in polytheistic forms showed

11. Compare Sells, *Mystical Languages of Unsaying*, to Budick and Iser, eds., *Languages of the Unsayable*, and to Ward, *Postmodern God*.

12. See especially Fiorenza, *Jesus: Miriam's Child, Sophia's Prophet*.

the way to generalize the insights on *logos* and eros for both polytheistic traditions (witness Porphyry and Proclus on magical and erotic practices) and for the proclamatory biblical ones. The biblically grounded theologians turned to the different kinds of Neoplatonists to transform and reincorporate the ancient synthesis of *logos* and eros informing self, cosmos, and God with the biblical account of the creating (manifesting), redeeming (proclaiming) God of the Bible and the Koran.[13]

No Western philosophy has ever been so well designed to allow the distancing proclamatory-prophetic traditions to incorporate the participatory-manifestation-meditative and erotic dimensions of the biblical traditions as well as the various forms of middle Platonism (Philo and Origen) and Neoplatonism (especially Gregory of Nyssa and Dionysius the Areopagite in the East, and Augustine in the West). Indeed, no theologian is of greater interest for many thinkers today than the remarkable Syrian-Greek Christian who wrote under the Pauline pseudonym of Dionysius the Areopagite. This is partly due to Dionysius's development of earlier Christian Neoplatonist thought on the apophatic-mystical naming of God. At least as important for this new Dionysian retrieval is the Areopagite's cataphatic or positive naming of God first of all as *erotic Good* (not One or Being). For present purposes, however, it is best to recall the Neoplatonic character of Augustine himself rather than Dionysius. For Augustine is the watershed figure of all Western theology to this day, as well as of several central themes of Western culture and philosophy. Without Augustine, Western culture and Western theology may never have taken certain turns they did: the insistence on the centrality of history; the emphasis on the indomitable power of the will; the increasingly bleak, even tragic account of the human dilemma; the deep ambivalence on eros; the ricocheting between nature-grace paradigms and sin-grace paradigms; and the attempted union of ancient eros and biblical agape into Catholic Christian *caritas*.

What most fascinates at this juncture in the unending study of Augustine is this historical fact: even though Augustine's thought on the human situation became bleaker and bleaker, he never really yielded his Neoplatonism. Should he have, as Luther, Calvin, and Pascal (all of whom owed him so much) thought? Or was Augustine right not to break radically with his Neoplatonic heritage, including that on eros (from his first "conversion" in the *Confessions* through some

---

13. See Courcelle, *Late Latin Writers and Their Greek Sources* and "Plotino e il Neoplatinismo in Oriente e in Occidente"; Morewedge, *Neoplatonism and Islamic Thought* and *Neoplatonism and Jewish Thought*. In Augustine, see Rist, *Augustine*.

"writings of the Platonists," preceding and to a certain degree determining his subsequent Christian conversion)?[14] By not breaking with that Platonic heritage on eros and *logos*, even in the midst of his tormented portrait of humanity turned in upon itself, deceiving itself and disrupting itself as we see in his later, anti-Pelagian writings, Augustine bequeathed to Western medieval theology (e.g., Anselm, Aquinas, Bonaventure, Dante) an unbreakable bond with the ancient synthesis of the human-cosmic-divine realms, including (especially in Bonaventure and Dante) eros. Even later medieval additions and modifications of this Augustinian heritage never broke this bond. Anselm did not with his understanding of *intellectus* and *ratio* as intuitive and participatory even if more rationally rigorous than Augustine's purely intuitive understanding of intellect.[15] Aquinas did not, by bending the new set of Aristotelian-Scholastic methods and system making into a basically Neoplatonic (*exitus-reditus*) and Augustinian (the power and meaning of intelligence-in-act for naming God) mode.[16] Bonaventure did not in his amazing synthesis of Francis of Assisi's new nature-mysticism spirituality[17] with the Augustinian introspective journey of *logos* and eros within.[18]

Indeed, it is difficult to overemphasize three facts (possibly three conflicting facts) about Augustine on eros. First, as we know from the *Confessions*, Augustine

14. Even as relatively late a text as *De Trinitate* is representative here: see Augustine, *Trinity*, esp. 241–86, 388–95, 426–36. Despite the pronounced turn to a much bleaker view on the human situation in his later, anti-Pelagian works, Augustine never retreats in his Neoplatonic affirmation of eros in his reconsiderations of his earlier works near the end of his life in *Retractiones*. For an excellent collection of texts from every stage of Augustine's life and writings, see Augustine, *Selected Writings*.

15. This is also the case in the works of Anselm that are more focused on logical issues; the most influential of all is the *Prosloquium*, wherein one may find what Kant (not Anselm) named the "ontological argument" for the existence of God: Anselm and Deane, *Prosloquium, Basic Writings*, 6–206. For the debates on Augustine's understanding(s) of intuition, illumination, and reason, see Du Roy, *L'intelligence de la foi en la Trinité*; Markus, "Augustine, Reason, and Illumination," 362–73; O'Daly, *Augustine's Philosophy of Mind*.

16. Lonergan, *Verbum*.

17. Through Francis, that amazing love-troubadour, the pagan *plenum* returns to Christianity in force, in his understanding of all creatures—not only humans—as God's erotically beloved creatures. See Francis and Clare, *Complete Works*, espescially the extraordinary, troubadour-like love poem "The Canticle of Brother Sun" (38–39), where even death is loved and praised: "Praise to you, my Lord, through our sister bodily death" (39).

18. Bonnefoy, *Le Saint Esprit et ses dons*; Cousins, *Bonaventure and the Coincidence of Opposites*. For representative texts, see Bonaventure, *Bonaventure*.

was clearly a passionate, carnal man. He believed that all thought is driven by and weighted by *amor*, love, eros. ("Pondus meum, amor meus.") Augustine uses the weight (*pondus*) metaphor frequently. Our loves as our weights can either push us forward or hold us back. Our loves can either draw us up to the true object of eros—God—or drag us down into lesser objects of eros. Thus the self becomes curved in upon itself (*curvatus in se*) and cannot help itself out of its own perverse trap. Only God's grace can free the self from its self-imposed overwhelming "weight." Analogously, Pure-Land Japanese Buddhism states the same kind of emphasis against the confident "self-power" of Zen Buddhism: our situation is so bleak that only "Other Power" can help us now. Recall as well the tragic (not sinful) resonances in Freud, Nietzsche, and the Heidegger of *Being and Time* (a text deeply influenced by a reading of Augustine). For myself, one of the tragic errors of Augustine's otherwise brilliant account of our perverse tendency to trap ourselves in our hardened and recalcitrant egos is this: unlike Freud, Nietzsche, Heidegger, and their Greek tragedic ancestors, Augustine rejected "fate" and "chance" as inconsistent with providence (as did the Stoics and the Platonists). Hence Augustine also rejected a tragic vision and imposed (tragically, in my judgment) a reading of the biblical Fall as "original sin." That doctrine of original sin as transmitted through sex was Augustine's own great eros-driven original sin. That doctrine is also one of post-Augustinian Christianity's greatest tragedies.

Augustine was not, of course, solely responsible for this move. Indeed, in his time, he was a moderate in his teaching on sex and marriage. Nonetheless, by his move away from fate and therefore tragedy to having *all* depend on "sin" (original and actual), Augustine damaged his own classical heritage. That human beings often trap themselves through the perversity of turning all eros-driven objects ("flesh" and "spirit") into objects for the ego is true. We are responsible for what we have done to others and to ourselves. There is responsible guilt. However, that human beings are also "thrown" (Heidegger) into a specific world, body, language, and history, which becomes our "fate," is an insight that Augustine rejected. There is, moreover, pure chance in existence. Nevertheless, Augustine's metaphor "pondus meum, amor meus" remains to haunt us:

> Love lifts us these and "your good Spirit" (Psalm 142:10) exalts "our humble estate from the gates of death" (Psalm 9, 15). In a good will is our peace. A body by its weight tends to move towards its proper place. The weight's movement is not necessarily downwards, but to its appropriate position: fire tends to move upwards, a stone

downwards. They are acted on by their respective weights; they seek their own place. Oil poured under water is drawn up to the surface on top of the water. Water poured on top of oil sinks below the oil. They are acted on by their respective densities, they seek their own place. Things that are not in their intended position are restless. Once they are in their ordered position, they are at rest. My weight is my love. [Pondus meum, amor meus.] Wherever I am carried, my love is carrying me. By your gift we are set on fire and carried upwards: we grow red hot and ascend.[19]

For Augustine, eros is always determined by two realities: the object loved and the character of the self desiring the object. The main problem is the self (the ego in modern terms). The self can become so self-centered that it traps itself and cannot escape its own ego. By its twisted weight, the self then drags all objects (even good ones) into itself. Thus the self curves in upon itself (curvatus in se) and finds itself in an abyss, a labyrinth wherein it is trapped without hope of release on its own. Only Other Power (grace) can save the self now.

Second, Augustine believed he had transformed but not replaced the ancient Platonic synthesis by a distinct Christian intellectual move against his own earlier Manichaeanism and, in a milder way, even the Platonism of Plotinius and Porphyry. For Augustine insisted that the doctrines of creation and incarnation forbade a Christian thinker from sharing any Manichaean despisement of the flesh (including sex) or even from sharing any overspiritualization of eros by the pagan Platonists. This enabled Augustine to claim what is held by Western Catholic and most Protestant theology to this day:[20] the Christian should affirm the positive creative and incarnational (as John Donne insisted, even erotically carnal) reality of eros (in caritas). The Christian should also be suspect of the power of self-delusion and self-destruction in eros (as cupiditas) and realize that only the divine, pure gift of God's love (agape) can sustain and transform eros from our hardened egoism. Thus his favorite word for love: caritas—the transformation of eros by agape. Thus also his favorite word for eros gone wrong: cupiditas—the love of the self alone.[21]

19. Augustine, Confessions, XIII, 9.

20. For an exception, see Nygren, Agape and Eros, 449–563. The definitive response to Nygren's famous attack on Augustine "caritas synthesis" as far more Platonic (eros) than biblical (agape) may be found in Burnaby, Amor Dei. To sense the importance of Platonic eros even for Augustinian caritas it is not irrelevant to note that Augustine at times did not hesitate to use interchangeably for "love" the eros words amor and dilectio, as well as caritas.

21. This dual metaphor is most developed in Augustine, City of God: "We see then that the two cities were created by two kinds of love: the earthly city was created by self-love reaching the

The third (and possibly conflicting) fact of Augustine's interpretation of eros must be stated starkly: as Augustine's thought developed late in his life in his debate against the Pelagians, he believed (here following Paul, not John) that our wills were so distorted that the possibility of self-delusion and self-destruction in erotic experience was inevitable. Hence, the profoundly divided, even tragic, consciousness of Augustine on eros.

All three of these Augustinian positions are still continued, refined, and transformed in contemporary Catholic theologies: as in Bernard Lonergan on intelligence-in-act to name God as Pure Intelligence;[22] as in Karl Rahner's increasing insistence late in his life that theology must become, more and more, a "reduction" into mystery as Augustine's whole thought so clearly is;[23] as in Hans Urs von Balthasar's recovery of the aesthetic dimension of Augustine's achievement on the good as beauty.[24]

Furthermore, contemporary theological heirs of the Reformation, in their recasting of Augustinian insights, have also begun to recover the Neoplatonic, participatory side of Augustine without loss of the sin-grace, tragic sensibility of the Reformation, with Luther's classic insistence on the bondage of the will.

In modern Protestant theology, no one was as successful as Paul Tillich in insisting on the theological need for both "Protestant principle" and "Catholic substance." In his three-volume systematics, Tillich structured his whole theology in Augustinian terms: volume 1 on human essential goodness (including eros); volume 2 on our existential estrangement; and volume 3 on uniting our essential goodness and our existential estrangement to develop the category *ambiguity* for history, society, and self in ways deeply reminiscent of *The City of*

---

point of contempt for God, the Heavenly City by the love of God carried as far as contempt of self. In fact, the earthly city glories in itself, the Heavenly City glories in the Lord. The former looks to glory from men, the latter finds its highest glory in God, the witness of a good conscience. The earthly lifts up its head in its own glory, the Heavenly City says to its God: 'My glory; you lift up my head.' In the former, the lust for domination lords it over its princes as over the nations it subjugates; in the other both those put in authority and those subject to them serve one another in love, the rulers by their counsel, the subjects by obedience. The one city loves its own strength shown in its powerful leaders; the other says to its God, 'I will love you, my Lord, my strength.'"

22. Lonergan, *Verbum*.

23. Rahner's entire final work can be read as a radical change from his earlier Thomist intellectualism to his later more Augustinian sense of ultimate mystery. For a major example of this, see Rahner, "Thomas Aquinas on the Incomprehensibility of God" (also published in *The Journal of Religion* suppl. 58, no. 5 [1978]: 107–25).

24. Balthasar, *Glory of the Lord*, 2:95–211.

God. No theologian was as successful as Tillich in finding a way to try to unite the two sides of Augustine (the Platonic-participatory, erotic side and the later, anti-Pelagian side, with its emphasis on the self as inevitably turned in upon itself—*curvatus in se*).[25] Augustine himself, however, for all his unquestionable genius in addressing the dilemma of the self and all his willingness to retract former opinions, never, in my judgment, rendered coherent his earlier Platonic understanding of eros and *logos* with his later account of human brokenness and sin.

One of Augustine's last enemies, the brilliant Pelagian Julian of Eclanum, accused him late in life of having returned to Manichaeanism and its hatred of the flesh. It is an unfair charge. Nevertheless, Julian had a point, for even Augustine's admirers (I am one) find that he left, at best, a deeply divided heritage on eros. This heritage was determined by Augustine's own divided theological, philosophical, and personal consciousness of eros: the theological transformation of eros into the hopeful Johannine vision of *caritas*; the inevitable degradation of eros by the ego into *cupiditas* (which he understood to be the position of Paul).

Mid-twentieth-century existentialism, with its tragic portrait of humankind, may well have been, as Paul Tillich said, "good luck" for twentieth-century Christian thought. It can also be said, however, that Augustine himself, once revised, has proved "good luck" not only for Western Christian theology but for any Western thought that attempts to recover the ancient Greek sense of tragedy. Consider, for example, these typically Augustinian insights: our propensity for self-delusion, especially in erotic affairs (witness Racine); our need to try to read our concrete histories (not only the cosmos) for whatever clues to ultimate meaning may be available to us; the power of the will to becloud even the most stunning intelligence and to render ambiguous even our most noble and virtuous exercises of *logos* and eros; the inevitability of *cupiditas*; the political-historical acknowledgment in *The City of God* that all empires (not only the ancient Roman but all—including that of the United States of America and that of global capitalism) are "robber-bands" writ large. Augustine's view of our situation was and still is a powerful, tragic, and provocative vision. Significant aspects of the sensibility of contemporary Western culture lives in half-remembered memories of Augustine's views.

As Peter Brown colorfully insists, Augustine, in his portrait of the erotic self *curvatus in se* shocked his fellow Platonists as much as Freud in his portrait of

---

25. Tillich, *Systematic Theology*, vol. 1; the categories *curvatus in se* and *cupiditas* in Augustine are discussed in notes 20 and 21.

the Unconscious and the polymorphous sexuality of infants shocked the optimistic psychologists of his Victorian day.[26] In another way, Augustine himself on eros remains, in Whitehead's famous phrase, another footnote to Plato. But Augustine (like Aristotle or Plotinus or Descartes or Kant or Hegel or Whitehead himself) is one of those Platonic "footnotes" that made an ineradicable difference to all Western thought. Western Christian theology, for example, is unimaginable without Augustine. One need only observe how it differs from non-Augustinian Eastern Christian thought, which offers an uninterrupted cosmic Christianity; a form of Christian life and thought that finds the basic correspondences of the human-cosmic and divine realms damaged but fundamentally stable and healthy, including on eros; a theology in which John's gospel and Neoplatonism live in all their iconic glory; a form of Christianity where proclamatory-prophetic history is of course acknowledged but never plays the central role it does in Western Augustinian Christian thought. It is as difficult to imagine an Augustinian Eastern Christian theologian as it is to imagine a German Doctor Johnson. More exactly, to find an Augustine-like Eastern Orthodox thinker, one must read the modern Russian theologians and philosophers influenced by the tragic vision (including on eros) of that most Augustinian of novelists, Fyodor Dostoyevsky. Only after those novels did Eastern Christianity, for good and ill, begin to sound like the relentlessly Augustinian dividedness on eros of Western Christianity, whether Catholic or Protestant.

Nevertheless, in his own possibly incoherent but always brilliant way, Augustine combined Neoplatonic optimism, both regarding the beauty and glory of all creation (especially of his beloved North Africa) and regarding the human abilities to think and to love, with an undertow of tragedy in his melancholic courage at facing the evil and suffering that results from the inevitable (for Augustine) self-deceptions of eros, both in individuals and in history. Thus did Augustine bequeath to Western theologies a basic paradigm: the need to find some way to allow the sin-grace paradigm of biblical (especially Pauline) and later Augustinian prophetic religion to posit itself by implying its manifesting erotic other (or vice versa, as in much Catholic theology).

One of the great scholarly retrievals of our period is the extraordinary recovery of Christian Neoplatonism, that is, its power to allow a fundamentally proclamatory, prophetically oriented religion to expand its range to recover the self-manifesting Good in all nature, sacrament, eros and cosmos in acts of intelligence and love—a highly reflective, indeed meditative and contemplative

26. Brown, *Augustine*, 261.

way of thought and life. In modern Christian theology, Balthasar is the leading figure in recovering the Neoplatonic tradition for contemporary thought. His influence (including on philosophers like Jean-Luc Marion) is notable.

But even that series of recoveries will prove in vain, I fear, if the other, bleaker, tragic side of Augustine is not also acknowledged. Just as Augustine could transform the Neoplatonism of Plotinus and Porphyry by his Christian insistence on the fleshly reality of incarnation, so today all Christian attempts to recover a sense of embodiment and a sense of participation in nature can learn anew from Augustine's Johannine incarnationalism and philosophical Neoplatonism. Christian theology today also needs to keep alive the bitter and tragic reality of the latent possibilities of self-deception, self-disruption, and self-destruction in the power of eros. In the meantime, it is enough to state that Western Christian thought and life owe to Augustine not only a recovery (unusual for a Platonist) of a sobering biblical view of humanity and history and eros, but that it is in debt as well (and perhaps especially) to Augustine's powerful recall—through transformed Neoplatonic resources—of the erotic, meditative-contemplative expansion of that biblical prophetic tradition into a Christian Neoplatonism. Without Neoplatonism, Western Christian thought on eros would have found it very difficult indeed to assure that Christian proclamation could posit itself by implying its manifesting, participatory, erotic other. No reflective philosophy in the West has ever replaced, as distinct from transformed (Aristotle, Aquinas, Bruno, Hegel, Whitehead), Platonism as the philosophy best positioned to aid any new outreach to participation, manifestation, contemplation, and eros. In our period, Christianity has finally ceased to be merely a European (indeed Eurocentric) religion and finally become a global religion more open to the philosophies and theologies of the non-European world, especially Asia and Africa. Whatever future form (e.g., Buddhistic) Christian thought may take on eros, it is the pluralistic and ambiguous Platonic-Augustinian heritage that will always be there to help focus and thereby work both with and against newer insights from non-Western cultures. After all, Augustine himself was African.

Moreover, Augustine still lives not only in the Christian world but in our common cultural divided consciousness: in such poets as John Donne, for example, with his lifelong effort to unite his erotic poetry and his metaphysical-theological poetry. Donne wanted a carnal Christianity. So do many now. Perhaps even Augustine did: he loved the body so much that he became, as his tragic vision of our unconscious but systemic self-delusion darkened, fearful of it; he honored creation and incarnation so seriously that he became not only a Platonist but a Christian Platonist; he knew from within the power and beauty of eros; he never fully abandoned the erotic vision of his youth, but he could not believe that vision could ever again work without constant self-deception. Augustine believed, one might say today, in an unconscious so ultimately unknowable that even eros needed agape to transform it into a symbol of hope—the *caritas* synthesis whereby the gift of divine agape could transform but not destroy desiring eros. But the more we read the later Augustine on the *cupiditas* affecting all persons, states, and civilizations, the more Augustine seems, at the end, what one commentator (Ronald Knox) says about that most unrelenting of Augustinian philosophers, Blaise Pascal—"He should have been the village atheist but somehow grace caught him and he became a Christian pessimist":

> You, Lord, are my judge. For even if "no man knows the being of man except the spirit of man which is in him" (1 Cor. 2:11), yet there is something of the human person which is unknown even to the "spirit of man which is in him." But you, Lord, know everything about the human person; for you made humanity. Although in your sight I despise myself and estimate myself to be dust and ashes (Gen. 18:27), I nevertheless know something of you which I do not know about myself. Without question "we see now through a mirror in an enigma," not yet "face to face" (1 Cor. 13:12). For this cause, as long as I am a traveler absent from you (2 Cor. 10:13), I am more present to myself than to you. Yet I know that you cannot be in any way subjected to violence, whereas I do not know which temptations I can resist and which I cannot. There is hope because "you are faithful and do not allow us to be tempted beyond what we can bear, but with the temptation make also a way of escape so that we can bear it" (1 Cor. 10:13). Accordingly, let me confess what I know of myself. Let me confess too what I do not know of myself. For what I know of myself I know because you grant me light, and what I do not know of myself, I do not know until such a time as my darkness becomes "like noonday" before your face (Isa. 58:10).[27]

27. Augustine, *Confessions*, 182–83.

AUGUSTINE DIVIDED: A RESPONSE
TO DAVID TRACY

VALENTINA IZMIRLIEVA

It is the doubt that is the destiny of man, who after having tasted nearness must
experience distance and learn from distance what it alone can teach.

MARTIN BUBER, «ON THE BIBLE»

David Tracy's essay on Augustine offers a series of delectable surprises. Most
of them come about as subtle optical shifts within our traditional vision of
Augustine's erotology: a paradigm shift from sin to tragedy; a shift in perspective from a divided eros toward a divided Augustine; a shift in focus from a
surface contradiction between the Augustinian *caritas* and *cupiditas* toward a
deeper conflict between eros and logos discovered right at the heart of biblical
religions.

Tracy presents his argument against a sweeping religious panorama, where
Paul Ricoeur's juxtaposition of manifest and proclamatory religions is reinter-
preted in the terms of an eros-logos polarity. The argument itself, if I read
it correctly, is threefold. Its bedrock is the claim that reconciling eros and
logos was never an easy task for Christian theology. Admittedly, the Gospel of
St. John had opened from the start the way to an optimistic synthesis; but
it might never have come to fruition had it not been for the sixth-century
Christian Neoplatonist who hid himself under the pseudonym of Dionysius
the Areopagite. The ripe fruit of a ripe time, his remarkable erotic synthesis
could recover all the healing, connecting, "agapeic" powers of *Logos* within the
most positive version of "fleshy" Johannine Christology.

Augustine was a man of an earlier age. He lived in the turbulent time of a
doctrine in flux and died two whole decades before the Council at Chalcedon
(451) concluded, at least for the West, the seemingly endless Christological

controversy. Should it surprise us then that he never quite managed to pull off his own brand of an optimistic erotic vision? In his neophyte enthusiasm, Augustine attempted a *caritas* synthesis only to see it collapse almost immediately into its *cupiditas* antithesis; and then he saw it disintegrate into an even darker vision of the human erotic that, in Tracy's own words, has the feel of an ancient Greek tragedy: a premonition of humanity at an impasse that brings to mind the notorious double bind of the Sophoclean Oedipus.

The reason Augustine failed to achieve an erotic synthesis—and this is the second stage of Tracy's argument—was his ambivalence about Neoplatonism. Tracy remains deliberately vague about Augustine's problems with the Neoplatonic stance that might have undermined his commitment to it. I, personally, was left wondering whether the crux for Augustine was not that old question of evil. In his youth, he had embraced with zeal the Neoplatonic weapon against his radical Manichaean good versus evil dualism. But did not the problem come back to haunt him in his later years, when the impending doom of the Roman Empire fired in Augustine a profound skepticism about human nature, and when his debates with the Pelagians forced him to confront yet again some of his old Manichaean patterns and doubts that he thought he had overcome? Still, this wondering is entirely my own, unencouraged by Tracy's analysis.

I was encouraged, however, to infer that in the province of the human erotic, Augustine's reservations with Neoplatonism centered around the hopeful assumption that our libidinal tendencies are bound to be uplifting and developmental. Translated into a Christian context, such an assumption would mean—as it did later for Pseudo-Dionysius—that God, who *is* Love, is the Final Cause always already erotically; and so all erotic ways, however long and winding, must lead to His door. Augustine intuited otherwise, Tracy suggests: the erotic subject has the nasty habit of "turning in upon itself," thus curving, in a manner of speaking, Diotima's ladder into the vicious circle of Alcibiades' obsession. Put in slightly different terms, this egocentric tendency means turning the other into the self, a narcissistic bend that threatens to undermine human relations with *every* Other, even if He be the transcendent and personal divinity of a monotheist religion.[1] Tracy's thesis thus moves from a general

---

1. I have to admit that, at that juncture of Tracy's interpretation, Augustine begins to sound distinctly Levinasian, almost as if anticipating one of the central claims of Levinas's ethical alterity, that the egotistic spontaneity of the self—its "totality"—admits no outside; cf. Levinas, *Totality and Infinity*. In fact the resemblance is so strong, one is tempted to suspect a retrospective projection.

claim about the principal difficulties of proclamatory (or logos) religions with eros toward a specific claim about Augustine's personal version of the same dilemma.

At its third and final stage, Tracy's argument progresses from claims to an assessment: a valuation of Augustine's tragic dividedness between Neoplatonism, which he could never fully integrate with his Christianity, and some new style of Christian pessimism that he could only vaguely anticipate in the dark. That double predicament might first appear as a double disadvantage. Yet Tracy manages to reverse the negative at both ends. He urges us to salute Augustine for never yielding his loyalty to neo-Platonism, despite all his doubts. In other words, where one might suspect a failure, Tracy discovers only an admirable fidelity.[2] And as for the pessimism, he sees in it perhaps the most significant, albeit still unappreciated, contribution of Augustine to the Christian vision, contending, in the vein of William James, that pessimism in a religious vision is a sign of maturity and completeness, and the way to a sober and more authentic religious experience.[3]

That last step of the argument, stimulating and inspiring as I find it to be, might also be its most vulnerable part. For one, it embraces the Jamesian preference for the "sick (divided) soul" over the "healthy-minded," as if it were an axiom and not just a powerful assumption. But there is a trickier trap down that road: the risk to psychologize Augustine too much, all the more natural perhaps, because we know—thanks to the Doctor's *Confessions*—so much about his "unconscious," we feel as if we know him well enough! I believe that Tracy would be the first to warn us against this trap, or as he would say, against the temptation to "domesticate" Augustine.[4] For if we yield, we might end up projecting upon a stranger from late Antiquity an entirely modern experience, all in the noble ambition to make familiar that enigmatic part of his appeal which remains forever beyond the grasp of our "totality."

---

2. If indeed there is some ground to my suspicion that the real conflict in Augustine's Christianity is between Neoplatonism and Manicheanism, his loyalty to Neoplatonism is all the more significant, for the very condition for possibility of Augustine's Christianity hinges upon it.

3. Consider, for example, the following characteristic passage from James: "Systematic healthy-mindedness, failing as it does to accord for sorrow, pain, and death any positive and active attention whatever, is formally less complete than systems that try at least to include these elements in their scope. The completest religions would therefore seem to be those in which the pessimistic elements are best developed" (*Varieties of Religious Experience*, 184).

4. For Tracy's critique of scholarly "domesticating impulses," see Tracy, *Plurality and Ambiguity*, 15.

I would like to suggest a slightly different approach toward the same set of questions that Tracy lays out so compellingly for us in his essay. Whatever Augustine's problems with eros are (and they are numerous!), his divided consciousness on the subject is only an aspect of a more general and pervasive split. In fact, it would not be an exaggeration to claim that Augustine's vision is fundamentally polarized: not only on eros and logos but all the way across. There is hardly anything in this vision that does not come in two. One may say that Augustine proliferates binaries faster than a Russian structuralist, and with the same uncompromising intensity. There are two loves, two wills, two cities, two communities: one predestined to heaven, the other damned to hell. And then there is the overarching Pauline dichotomy of flesh (*sarx*) and spirit (*pneuma*), which comes to dominate Augustine's vision so completely in his old age and is pushed to such an extreme there, it almost recaptures the fervent pitch of the Manichaean radical dualism between the spirit of Light and the matter of Darkness.

I am not trying, of course, to revive here the old Pelagian charge that Augustine reverted back to his Manichaean ways when pushed by the "optimistic" Pelagians to reconsider the question of evil. Rather, I suggest after Peter Brown that the Manichaean residue in the late Augustine is to be found not in the doctrinal solutions, but in the general way the questions are framed, in the focus where the predominant religious concerns meet and interact.[5] It is the split that fascinates (while horrifying) Augustine, and it is the chasm that holds his gaze and commands his attention. Note that the historical focus of his theology is oddly not Incarnation but the Fall: the event of separation, of driving apart, of opening a ghastly wound across the body of humanity that, he feared, not even the Coming of Christ could close up to the end and heal. There is an extremism in the way Augustine frames questions, and that extremism is the main force which keeps his antitheses from collapsing into syntheses. He is the archetypal "either-or" man: a master of positing impossible alternatives, of inventing artificial polarities where for others there exists a whole spectrum of intermediary alternatives. (A classic example would be his radical dilemma in the *Confessions*, debauchery or celibacy, which forces us—quite to our displeasure—to imagine the Christian populace as split into two equally awkward communities of saints and slimebags.)

The broad schema that Tracy charts in the first part of his essay is the theater of two forces: the connecting, cohesive, coalescing force of eros that

5. See Brown, *Augustine*, 393–94.

(re)generates the plenum in the immediate experience of immediate presence, and the divisive force of logos that creates meaning by distancing and differentiation. Within this framework there is an optical paradox. If you look at the dynamic between eros and logos from the vantage point of eros, the tension between them is but the flip side of their affinity. It is only if you take the logos stance that things turn problematic, the productive conflict disintegrating into a series of unbridgeable chasms. It seems to me evident that Augustine had a logos vision. And that optical slant by itself not only presumed that he should choose between eros and logos but also predetermined his choice. Pseudo-Dionysius, having sided with eros (that "innate togetherness of everything" which "do[es] not obliterate identity"; "a capacity to effect a unity, and alliance, and a particular commingling in the Beautiful and the Good" [*On Divine Names* 704C, 709D]), could embrace a world of antinomies where, contrary to the assumption of Aristotelian logic, negation is not the opposite of assertion. Augustine's way was the opposite way: not of synthesis but of relentless analysis, of uncompromising self-reflection—all the way to the bare bone, despite the pain. It is not an accident, after all, that postmodern critics of Augustine trace back to him the origins of the Cartesian cogito (Marion) and even see him as the cornerstone of Western logocentrism (Derrida).

To be sure, Tracy is no stranger to those intellectual landscapes. So, I suppose, it would not be too far fetched to discern in his argument the invitation for still another road, a road not taken by him, yet no less promising for a general assessment of our debt to Augustine. That path is implied in the alternative handling of the tension between eros and logos in the Christian East and West: an Eastern synthesis at the place of a Western conflicting juxtaposition. What I find particularly intriguing in the context of our discussion is the fact that this East-West rupture is oddly reinforced by a split in the evaluation of Augustine's heritage: while Augustine and his vision always remained a focus of intense preoccupation for the Catholic and the Protestant West, the Orthodox East could hardly have been more indifferent to them. Is this overlap of faultlines a mere coincidence, or is there a relation between the two? The question looms even larger when we consider that the ability for synthesis is the one quality most frequently brought up by Eastern theologians to characterize both the Orthodox theological vision and the Orthodox sacramental experience in opposition to their Western counterparts.[6]

---

6. Meyendorff, for example, claims that the Eastern Orthodox experience emphasizes antinomies and thus preserves "a sense of inadequacy between the formulae and the content of the

Would it be too audacious, then, to see Augustine—Tracy's Augustine, with consciousness on eros so tragically divided—also as a figure that divides? Would it be a fallacy to place him at a crossroad of Christian experience, where alternatives meet and acknowledge one another so that they may define themselves; where the search for synthesis and the drive for analysis, the (Johannine) aesthetic sensuousness and the (Pauline) ethical trust in the rational, the pull to the mystical ecstasies and the commitment to practical concerns confront one another the moment they go their separate ways? And could we be justified in the end to discover in that Augustine the beginning of the Christian split along the same divide between eros and logos that he had to face—as in a mirror, dimly—at the core of his most private Christian vision?

---

faith" in opposition to the Western emphasis on "conceptual rationalism" and analytical formulae, see Meyendorff, *Byzantine Theology*, 124 ff.; cf. the more general scheme of synthesis/antithesis drawn by George Fedotov in Fedotov, *Russian Religious Mind*, 23–57; cf. also the emphasis on the synthetism of the Orthodox liturgical experience in Florenskii, *Iconostasis*.

LOVE OF LIFE: LUCRETIUS TO FREUD

JAMES I. PORTER

> I find ecstasy in living—the mere sense of living is joy enough.
> Life is death we're lengthy at, death the hinge to life.
>
> EMILY DICKINSON

What binds us to life? At issue in the question is not simply what makes us want to live rather than not live, but also what attaches us to the existence we have. Attachment to life needn't be imagined as being so strong that it binds us even when (say) it is an existence that, other things being equal, we wouldn't choose to have.[1] Attachment need only affect us—bind us to life and to living—whenever we are alive, and possibly, and perhaps most powerfully of all, without our knowledge or conscious assent. And it need only provide us with a reason to value life without also giving us a reason to accord life any intrinsic value. So, for example, life viewed from a first-person perspective can be a source of goods even if from a third-person perspective (for instance, that of physics) life's value seems negligible—nor is there any inconsistency in holding these two views simultaneously. Of course, attachment could come

For comments on earlier versions of this essay, I am grateful to Mark Buchan, Eric Downing, Tony Long, Arthemy Magun, Sara Rappe, Tom Rosenmeyer, and George Rosenwald; to audiences in Chicago, Berkeley, Ann Arbor, Philadelphia, and Atlanta; and to the editors of this volume.

1. "Other things being equal" presupposes a "we" that does the choosing. By framing the question in terms of "wanting to live," I am hoping to bracket, but not to exclude, the case of vegetative existence—for example the medically supported life of a brain-dead person. That is, my discussion is limited to cases of the survival of a recognizable self. This is not to say that my remarks won't have any bearing on vegetative survival. They may even throw some light on the continued survival of a human organism despite the failure of its central neural functions. (My discussion will by no means be limited to desires and wishes.) For a fascinating portrait of the problem and its ethical dilemmas, see Singer, *Rethinking Life and Death*.

in a stronger form still. It could conceivably bind us to life even when our existence is one we wouldn't choose to have and one we might, at the extreme, willingly throw away. Here, attachment to life, in nullifying the attempt to eliminate it (again, without our knowledge or conscious assent), looks to be an irrefragable constituent of life and the living.[2]

So what is it that binds us to life? One possible answer will be pleasure in living, our enjoyment of life. Pleasure is surely a factor, or at the very least a symptom, but how far down does it go? Isn't pleasure frequently belied by pain or displeasure? And isn't pain at least occasionally a source of enjoyment? How stable are the terms? Another, more satisfying answer to the question will be our love of life: we live and want to live because deep down, in our heart of hearts, we value life itself, irrespective (say) of any pleasures or pains we may experience. True as this may be, it may not be true enough, or provide a strong enough reason to make a satisfying answer to the question. I can love life and I can love a friend, and the two impulses can come into conflict. But what we need to know is why it is that to love a friend even at the cost of my own life is in some fundamental way an expression of my love of life. That is, we need to know why a life lived is a life loved irrespective of the desire to prolong life. A stronger answer to the question would be that we live and want to live *insofar as* we love—are attached to and value—life itself. Here the two states, living and loving, might appear to be one continuous state with no clear distinction: we live with a powerful attachment to life, and life just is this attachment. Life here isn't an object of an emotion such as love, even if love the emotion may be modeled on the bond of life. Rather, life is the constitutive result of a valuation that obtains at a more primitive level of our emotions—for instance, in the mere exercise of our conscious faculties and in the pleasure this brings. In a more concrete but also more reduced form, the attachment could be said to be libidinal, a drive to life that is inextinguishably rooted in us. Let us call attachment in either of these forms—existential (or constitutive) and libidinal—"love of life."

Putting the problem in this way, awkward as it may sound to our contemporary ears, was once traditional within philosophy. That it was is shown by Kant, who makes the rather harsh-sounding claim that one should live not out of a love of life and a "taste" for living but only out of a duty to live.[3] Kant has

2. I am thinking of a claim like Nietzsche's at the close of *On the Genealogy of Morals*, namely, that "*a will to nothingness*, an aversion to life, a rebellion against the most fundamental presuppositions of life . . . is and remains a *will*!"

3. *Critique of Practical Reason*, A157, in Kant, *Practical Philosophy*, 211. Cf. *Metaphysics of Morals*, in *Practical Philosophy*, 543–44, esp. 546 ("On Killing Oneself") and 548–49 (on "love of life"). In

historical antecedents in mind. His own view recalls the Stoics, inasmuch as they held life to be morally indifferent (though not a duty);[4] and he is prepared to identify the thesis he opposes with Epicureanism, even if the Epicureans in fact stand closer to the Stoics than to Kant on this issue.[5] But the intuition that love of life is a worthwhile attachment has deeper roots still. Were there space, it would be possible to survey a line of thinking that begins somewhere in the ancient Greek past, starting with Homer, and enjoys a continued if for the most part inconspicuous afterlife into the present.[6] In this tradition of sorts (it is really just an amalgam, albeit a distinctive one, of intuitive folk psychology and of subsidiary philosophical debate), love and life are variously connected with each other. In its weaker forms, love of life comes to imply a preference, a pleasure or desire, or a quasi-erotic attachment. In its strongest form, the con-substantiality of love and life is affirmed: attachment to life is the existential condition of life when life is looked upon as constituting or as constituted by this attachment. Let us call this last view the "identity thesis." Important re-lays in the modern period are Spinoza and Nietzsche, each of whom articulates a strong version of the identity thesis—Spinoza in a pure and what he takes to be unproblematic form (that of the indomitable life force he calls *conatus*); Nietzsche in more disguised and troubled ways (under the rubrics of "the will to life" and "affirmation"). Obviously, all of this is far too much ground to cover in a single essay. Instead, by way of broaching the problem and treating some

---

The Conflict of the Faculties, Kant blurs the distinction between the two faces of this problem: life viewed apart from moral considerations is driven by a "natural instinct" (*Naturinstinct*) to life (intellectual pleasures are one index of this instinct), which in turn becomes a motivation (*Triebfeder*) guiding reason, in view of which the instinct to life constitutes a "duty" (179). For Kant, prolonging life and loving life are related instrumentally to one another (ibid., 185; cf. 189). Not so on the views I will be considering here. Finally, there is another strand in Kant in which "interestedness" is actually recognized as a basic requirement for living, as in the Analytic of the Beautiful in *The Critique of Judgment*, where interest, pleasure, consciousness, and *Lebensgefühl* (feeling of life) are intimately connected. If so, then Kant is strangely at odds with himself. But this is not the place to explore Kant.

4. As A. A. Long reminds me (personal correspondence).

5. Kant, *Practical Philosophy*, 212.

6. Consider the example of Achilles in *Odyssey* 11, who would fain trade his existence as a shade with that of a toiling slave. And even with the heroic ideal of a "beautiful death," epic heroes avenge *lives lost*. The terms *philopsuchia* and (more often pejoratively) *philozōia*—"love of one's soul" or "life"—and the associated verb *philopsuchein*, from Herodotus to Euripides to Plato and beyond, are good but only partial clues to the problem.

of its thornier aspects, I want to take up two rather unlikely exponents of this line of thought: Lucretius and Freud.

What is perhaps most remarkable about these two figures is not that they attempt to answer the question of what binds us to life but that they ask it at all. It is remarkable because what they share in common is a dark view of human potential: they are pessimists about life and its possibilities. But for all their darkness of mind, they also share one further trait: a basic fascination with human life and its possibilities. Is it possible to love life while despairing of life—to love a life one despairs of, or to love life even when it is felt that, objectively, life lacks all intrinsic value? This problem, which is one of the more troubling facets of the line of thought I want to consider, happens to lie at the heart of the writings of Lucretius and Freud. By addressing these two theorists of life and death, we can also address the problem directly in some of its complexity.[7] My more specific aim will be to inquire into the place of death in what I want to call these two philosophies of life, each of which has too often been read *sub specie mortis* (that is, as fixated upon the ineluctable term of death), by asking the reverse question: What binds us to life while we are on the road to death? In the case of Freud, this will come out as the further question: When is the death drive not a drive to death? Both philosophers are keenly aware of the fact of our attachment to life. In order to see how this is so, we will first consider Lucretius, from whom I have borrowed the title of my essay, and then we will turn to Freud, a latter-day Lucretian in more than a few respects.

7. Other facets typical of this line of thought are the following: (1) the life loved is implicitly that of mankind, or is at least viewed from a human perspective (even when it is acknowledged that humanity hardly exhausts what there is to life: this is a *tempered* humanism, a critical humanism if you like); (2) life is a (happy) accident; (3) life is inextinguishable in its immediate expression, whence it draws the sole source of its value; (4) death, the conventional concept and the reality, is incoherent for a subject, and yet it (wrongly) dominates mental life, far more than is ever acknowledged (especially in the widespread fear of death), and consequently the very idea of death needs to be reconceived; (5) death, the revised concept, is either a component or an essential constituent of life; alternatively, both death and life are subsumed under a more basic idea of existence; (6) suicide is not well received, but in cases it is tolerated; and finally, (7) the desire for immortality is rejected (that is, the aggrandizement of life in the form of an imagined immortality is taken to be a sure sign of a turning away from life). At its most striking, this amalgam of ideas, especially in its open embrace of life and death, allows for sheer but only apparent contradiction, as is shown by the contrasting attitudes to life in the epigraphs to this essay and as will be seen in each of the two case studies discussed in this essay.

"DIRA LIBIDO" (LUCRETIUS)

Lucretius, the Roman poet who set to verse Epicurus's philosophy in *On the Nature of Things* (*De rerum natura*) sometime during the first half of the last century BC, opens his poem with a hymn to Love:

> Mother (genetrix) of Aeneas' sons, joy (voluptas) of men and gods, Venus the life-giver (alma Venus), who beneath the gliding stars of heaven fillest with thy presence the sea that carries the ships and the land that bears the crops; for thanks to thee every tribe of living things is conceived, and comes forth to look upon the light of the sun. Thou, goddess, thou dost turn to flight the winds and the clouds of heaven, thou at thy coming; for thee earth, the quaint artificer (daedala), puts forth her sweet-scented flowers; for thee the levels of ocean smile, and the sky, its anger past, gleams with spreading light. For when once the face of the spring day is revealed and the teeming (genitabilis) breeze of the west wind is loosed from prison and blows strong, first the birds of the air herald thee, goddess, and thine approach, their hearts thrilled with thy might (perculsae corda tua vi). Then wild beasts and cattle bound over the fat pastures, and swim the racing rivers; so surely enchained by delight (capta lepore) each follows thee in hot desire (cupide) whither thou dost hasten to lead him on (inducere pergis). Then, through seas and mountains and tearing rivers and the leafy haunts of birds and verdant plains thou dost strike fond love (blandum per pectora amorem/efficis) into the hearts of all, and makest them in hot desire (cupide) to renew the stock of their races, each after his own kind. And since thou alone dost guide the nature of things, and nothing without thine aid comes forth into the bright coasts of light, nor waxes glad nor lovely (nec sine te quicquam dias in luminis oras/exoritur neque fit laetum neque amabile quicquam), I long (studeo) that thou shouldest be my helper in writing these verses, which I essay to fashion on the nature of things. (Lucr. 1.1–25)[8]

This address to Venus, a mythical goddess fully active in the human world and not serenely detached from its workings, is extraordinary in an Epicurean context, and indeed the near equivalent of a philosophical howler. And so too the contrast with the blank, featureless world of atoms and void to which all this color and variety will be reduced, and which is soon to be expounded in relentless detail, could not be any greater than it is. Not that the materialism of the poet isn't to be felt even here. There is a slight reductionist tendency to the passage. Mankind is not mentioned but is only implied in its animality.

---

8. All translations of Lucretius are from Bailey, ed., *Titi Lucreti Cari*, vol. 1.

Love, recognizable as the mythical (or if you like, ideological) trappings of Eros, has a functionalist tinge to it: reproduction is the aim, if not the goal (the *skopos*, though not quite the *telos*, as it were), while eros is seductively complicit, like honey spread around a more sinister rim. An undercurrent of violence runs through the whole, which is a conventional association to be sure: love is compulsive, it "strikes" and "captures" hearts, enslaving them. But enslaves them to what end? To the task of propagation? Or to the labor of life itself?

Renewing the generations of the natural kinds, nature (which Venus also is) renews itself, extends itself forward in space and time: the self-propagation of nature is what life is, and under this aspect Nature, the mythological force, appears as *Venus genetrix* (see figure).[9] Plainly, the burgeoning of life is what love is. But there is more, or rather there is less, *for life is nothing but this burgeoning*, which leaves little room for love in the picture, whether of the romantic variety or simply as distinct from life. The erotics of nature seems madly exhausted in its own internal finality and efficiency, as though biologically driven rather than erotically drawn.

Consider the option, which is also on offer in Lucretius's picture: what would nature be like in the *absence* of this desire for futurity and for continued existence? Because they have no duty to life, no rational and certainly no objective reason to be rather than not to be, creatures need some other motive to cooperate in the business of life and its laws. The kinds of nature are as if reluctant victims of life; they would be unwilling helpmates, were it not for love. It seems pretty clear that they would not be at all, minus the love that induces them to be. "And nothing without thine aid comes forth into the bright coasts of light, nor waxes glad nor lovely" is a way of saying just this. Life absent love would not be. But what is more, love *deceives* things into life, drawn forth by the light as they are. And so things come into the world, to look upon the light and upon life and then to leave again. Love is their minimum condition of existence. And existence evidently requires coercion—the coercion to be. Is love anything other than this coercion? It is as if life were not for the sake of the living but the other way around: the living seem to be for the sake of life, even if life is not for the sake of anything at all. And that is just what one ought to expect from a materialist vision of life.

9. P. Michael Brown comments that the Venus of the prologue would conjure up to a Roman mind the *Venus physica* of Roman religion, who was the embodiment of what he suggestively calls a "life-urge" (*Lucretius: De Rerum Natura I*, 41 [ad loc.]).

Venus Genetrix, Roman version of a Greek original. Vatican Museum, Rome.
(Photo courtesy of Alinari/Art Resource, NY.)

The poem, which opens on a note of hurried sexuality and bustling existence, thus resounds to another, darker chord, which ought to make us pause over the phrase that appears in a much later context, *amor vitae*, or "love of life." Indeed, the later passage offers a stark contrast with the opening prelude to the poem, with its appeal to the bloodless life of the gods and their strangeness to human nature and the strangely coupled thought of blank void, not so much of death as of inexistence:[10]

> For what profit could our thanks bestow on the immortal and blessed ones, that they should essay to do anything for our sakes? Or what new thing could have enticed them (*inlicere*) so long after, when they were aforetime at rest, to desire to change their former life? For it is clear that he must take joy in new things (*gaudere novis rebus*), to whom the old are painful (*obsunt*); but for him, whom no sorrow has befallen in the time gone by, when he led a life of happiness (*cum pulchre degeret aevum*), for such a one what could have kindled a passion for new things (*novitatis amorem*)? Or what ill had it been to us never to have been made? Did our life, forsooth, lie wallowing in darkness and grief, until the first creation of things dawned upon us? For whosoever has been born must needs wish to abide in life (*debet . . . velle manere/in vita*), so long as enticing pleasure shall hold him (*donec retinebit blanda voluptas*). But for him who has never tasted *the love of life* (*vitae amorem*), and was never in the ranks of the living (*nec fuit in numero*), what harm is it never to have been made? (Lucr. 5.165–80)

The second half of this passage helps confirm the suspicion that mortal creatures cling to life only by virtue, as it were, of this act of clinging itself; that without this bonding or attachment to life, and without the pleasurable sensation that life alone brings, no creature will abide in life for long, or at all. Just what does this sensation consist in? The commentators are on this point remarkably silent. They seem not even to perceive the claim that life taken as a constitutive object of love presents a problem—namely, that life can be loved insofar as it is lived, not insofar as it is loved and the object of a first-person

10. See Cic. *De natura deorum* 1.48–49: gods do not have a real body, but only a quasi-body (*quasi corpus*), nor real blood but only quasi-blood (*quasi sanguinem*). The status of the gods in Epicureanism is complex and at times contradictory, but also characteristic of the problems I will be discussing in this essay. The desire for immortality is not in itself a direct expression of a love of life, even if it ultimately is a celebration of vitality, the way true gods ultimately represent the divinity of vitality itself, a "divine feeling" (*divinus sensus*, Lucr. 5.144) and uninhibited life.

emotion. But surely the problem is one that drives Lucretius's poem and, indeed, his entire worldview. It is one that insists itself upon the reader at every turn, in a way that runs parallel to the further question that likewise runs through the poem, namely, Why is there something and not nothing? (In human terms, Why are we alive and not dead?)[11] And the same problem is the specific burden of book 5, in which the phrase *amor vitae* makes its appearance: life is short, it is finite, the world as we know it is mortal; only atoms and the gaps between them, the void spaces of the universe, are eternal, like the gods themselves. Our current world (for the universe consists of a succession of worlds), though young, is on the way to relentless decline: "all things are constantly flowing away," no phenomena are forever, and the very process by which life cycles into death and back again into life has to be viewed in its most reduced aspect, that of atoms assuming shifting configurations (which is not the same thing as life: atoms are neither alive nor dead); and so, "without doubt the parent of all is seen herself to be the universal tomb of things" (omniparens eadem rerum commune sepulcrum).[12] Nature is an impatient grave. And so too, famously, death, *sub specie aeternitatis*, is nothing to us.[13] Yet Nature, like some magnificent femme fatale, imperiously seduces creatures to life. Why? And how?

However it does, love of life has to precede the fear of death: it occurs at a more primitive level of one's psychic attachments, and it may even precede what I believe is the most primitive root fear present in the fear of death—namely, the fear of blank void, or *horror vacui* (an idea, but not a phrase, that is everywhere to be felt in the poem).[14] Nor can the answer to the question of what makes things cling to life lie in the constant novelty of things, for the simple reason that love of novelty seems to be a consequence of love of life, not its cause. More to the point, love of life tends to produce a *sense* of novelty and of the passé, or rather the illusion of these things, though it needn't (the gods, Lucretius's control group, know neither passion); valuation produces unwarranted (or else an implied) disvaluation: "For what is here at hand (quod adest praesto), unless we have learnt anything sweeter before (quid suavius), pleases us above all, and is thought to excel, but for the most part the better thing found later on destroys or changes our feeling for all the old things"

---

11. See Porter, "Lucretius and the Poetics of Void."

12. Lucr. 5.280; 5.258–59.

13. Lucr. 3.830; Epicurus *Letter to Menoeceus* 124.

14. Porter, "Lucretius and the Poetics of Void."

(5.1412–15). But nothing is sweeter than life itself when it is experienced as an immediate object of the senses. That is the only value there is.

It is as if attachments come in tenses: attachment to the present ("what is here at hand") gives an immediate pleasure that has no comparative value; attachments to the novel and the old are contrastive.[15] Presumably, Epicurean value is modeled on present-tense pleasures that to all intents and purposes fall out of the framework of time itself (again as with the gods, who live in an eternal present). Value and pleasure are identical states: to take pleasure is to make a positive judgment of value; it is to make this judgment in an immediate way with no contrastive disvalue being involved. The value this judgment posits is that of a pure affirmation. I suspect that by the same token pleasure is bound up not only with Epicurus's moral hedonism but also with his epistemology, as a criterion of truth, which is to say as one of the affections (*pathē*) by which we feel our way through the moral universe, thanks to the vividness of present impressions (*enargeia*). If so, then pleasure is integrally bound up with Epicurus's attitudes about the moral value of living. The state of being so drawn to reality, of this immediate connection to the world, is an experience of life as a source of pleasure and moral value, which is to say it is an experience of the pleasures of life and of living *tout court* (*to hēdeōs zēn*).[16] Probably, this is a strong reason why death is nothing to us according to the Epicureans: it is not an experience and therefore not a source of pleasure or pain. In Lucretius, this comes out as the interesting claim, which has a long history after him, that we cannot coherently imagine our own deaths.

To love life is to be in an unqualified state of affirmation of what lies most immediately to hand: it is the pleasure, the unalloyed passion and even thrill, of living in itself. This is the farthest-reaching meaning of the Epicurean claim, "When we live, we feel pleasure (chairomen) just like the gods."[17] The point, I take it, is not that happiness can be maintained indestructibly while we live,[18] but that our highest happiness actually consists in the pleasure of living as analyzed above. But to say this is not to say that love of life or the pleasure we take in living constitutes an unqualified or unquestioned value. We have already seen how Lucretius frames the value even of life with an irony.

---

15. Cf. Epicurus *Letter to Herodotus* 82; Diogenes of Oenoanda fr. 44.iii.3–10 Smith.

16. For a development of this argument, see Porter, "Epicurean Attachments."

17. Epicurus *Letter to Mother* (Diog. of Oen. fr. 125.iv.8–10 Smith).

18. Warren, "Epicurean Immortality," 250.

His qualification of love of life as a coercion on the part of nature reflects a qualification of the value of life and of our attachment to it. And Epicurus's exhortation to *enjoy our mortality* (*Letter to Menoeceus* 124) is his own way of coloring (darkening) the problem. Love of life for Epicurus, as for Lucretius, is not a longing for life but rather an immediate expression of what is dear about life, what is most life-worthy in life. Epicurus's view is that the best artists of life ("sages" in a more conventional terminology) will give up on their longing for life while loving life in the mere practice of living: they stand impartially, as it were, toward the desirability of living per se and reap what there is to enjoy in life.[19] Attachment here paradoxically consists in disattachment. Realizing this truth is the hoped-for goal, in Epicurean philosophy, of *ataraxia*, or psychic calm.

Love in this sense is an attachment that we have, a bond that, pleasurable in and of itself, is fragile and easily ruptured. "All things are constantly flowing away"; the life of an individual exists in a fragile state of unity that is continually threatened with dissolution. Shocks are suffered whenever the material world impinges on our senses; sleep is a daily threat of disruption, and each time we awaken we snatch ourselves from the jaws of death (the thread of life is nearly broken by sleep).[20] Meanwhile, the soul is in a constant state of dispersion even when it is safely contained within the body, and it tenuously

19. The point needs to be stated clearly, because it rarely is: what an Epicurean enjoys is not some pleasure that is distinct from life but life *qua* source of pleasure. Epicurus's views on the desirability of life are complex. Contrary to common misperceptions, many of them originating in antiquity (e.g., Plut. *That Epicurus Actually Makes a Pleasant Life Impossible*, e.g., 1105A), Epicurus's claim is not that life is nothing to us. He does not disdain life ("The wise man does not deprecate life.... The thought of life is no offence to him," *Letter to Menoeceus* 126) and even accords it a certain desirability (*to tēs zoēs aspaston*, ibid.). He disparages the famous quip found in Theognis, Sophocles, and Alcidamas, "It were good not be born, but when once one is born to pass with all speed through the gates of Hades" (126–27): "For if [anyone] truly believes this," Epicurus retorts, hurling the charge of self-refutation against all objectors, "why does he not depart from life?" What he seems to be getting at here is the question from which we began: what is it that binds us to life, even when we seem to despair of it? Further, for Epicurus, "the same exercise [viz., philosophical instruction of the kind he approves of] teaches to live well and to die well" (126). Thus, "a right understanding that death is nothing to us *makes the mortality of life enjoyable*" (124). This last dictum raises some interesting questions. Does one enjoy life or its mortality, or is it the inseparable union of these features that one enjoys? At any rate, in Epicureanism, *love of life is a love of mortal life* and not a love of life as abstracted from death, much less of immortal life—a thought worth bearing in mind when we turn to Freud.

20. Lucr. 5.280; 4.929–53; 3.163; 3.921–30; 4.920–28 (with 3.851).

clings (*adhaeret*) to the unity it has. We die thousands of little deaths at every moment, and health is a precarious balance that is never perfectly attained (thus making life an ongoing flirtation with mortality).[21] Such is the objective mortality of life, against which the soul strains. But occasionally one also glimpses something like a subjective desire or willingness to die, the soul's unequivocal wanting to be released from the body it also clings to, as if the fragility of life at the organic level (the tendency to dispersion) were a sign of a drive to return to the inanimate condition of the world itself.[22] And indeed, this tendency in the atomistic picture of the nature of things functions like a primordial question mark, and it hangs over all that we call life, psychology, and culture generally. Is culture, with its successive rejections of momentary pleasures (its love of novelty) and its historically proven fatal tendencies, a betrayal of the innate love of life or the express fulfillment of a deeper ambiguity and of a darker tendency? However we may decide to answer this problem, one thing is sure: love of life, understood as our attachment to life, is a weak force in the world for Lucretius and for Epicurean philosophy, even if it is the strongest force known to us.

MYRMIDONS OF LIFE (FREUD)

Meine liebe Marie: The moment one inquires about the sense or value of life one is sick, since objectively neither of them has any existence. In doing so one is only admitting a surplus of unsatisfied libido, and then something else must happen, a sort of fermenting, for it to lead to grief and depression. These explanations of mine are certainly not on a grand scale, perhaps because I am too pessimistic. There is going through my head an advertisement which I think is the boldest and most successful American one I know of. "Why live, when you can be buried for ten dollars?" (Freud to Marie Bonaparte, letter dated August 13, 1937)[23]

Freud recognized how tenuously life clings to its own affirmation: the thread of life is a fragile one, and love of life accounts for only a small part of what there is to life. While this could be illustrated by any number of texts, in

---

21. Lucr. 3.557 and 3.756–68.

22. "Yet often from some cause [such as a mortal blow] the soul seems to be shaken and to move, and to *wish to be released.*... Even so it is, when, as men say, the heart has had a shock, or the heart has failed, when all is alarm, and one and all *struggle to clutch at the last link with life*" (Lucr. 3.592–99); "Why does [the soul] desire to issue forth abroad from the aged limbs? does it fear to remain shut up in a decaying body?" (3.772–73).

23. Jones, *Life and Work of Sigmund Freud*, 3:465 (= Freud, *Briefe*, 452).

what follows I will restrict myself to *Beyond the Pleasure Principle* (1920) for two reasons: It contains Freud's most fully developed reflections on the problem. And of all his writings it evinces the most evident links, though not exactly debts, to Lucretius—with its emphasis on pleasure, its materialist view of life, its reliance on a model of quantitative elements (in Freud: energies), and what amounts to the same thing, its tracing of life's complexities and its deepest urges back to life's most primitive arenas.[24] It is this conceptual distillation, rather than reductionism, that makes Freud's essay so powerful a statement on the workings of life, despite its discovery of what he was only the first to call "the strange assumption" of a drive to death.[25]

I say "despite," but in fact what is so shocking about *Beyond the Pleasure Principle* is not its lurid fascination with death, or its insight into the magnetism of death (a magnetism that operates inexorably and below the level of, yet guiding, human emotion), let alone its bleak pessimism, but something that is in a sense far worse: it is Freud's insight into the inextricability of the passions for creation and destruction in a living subject, the fact that they are mingled together, compulsively and pleasurably, in a way that may strike some of us as improper, if not obscene. Indeed, so closely are these two passions intertwined for Freud, he makes it effectively impossible to tell them apart, let alone to sunder them. Worse still, at the point where they meet they no longer resemble passions or desires but are simply instinctual forces, blindly driven to their work. Together these factors have produced a resistance to the notion of a death instinct or drive (*Todestrieb*), not only among the lay public but even in the heart of the psychoanalytic community.[26]

24. Although Freud's only mention of Lucretius comes early on in *The Interpretation of Dreams* (Freud, *Standard Edition* [hereafter, *SE*], 4:8), Lacan makes the connection again, albeit whimsically and in passing: "nous ne pouvons parler adéquatement de la libido que d'une façon mythique— c'est la *genitrix* [*sic*], *hominum divumque voluptas*. C'est de cela qu'il s'agit chez Freud" (Lacan, *Le séminaire*, 2:265, alluding to *New Introductory Lectures* [*SE*, 22:95]: "instincts are mythical entities"); cf. also Laplanche, *Problématiques IV*, 231 (mistaking Epicureanism as aiming at the "death of desire"—Epicurus, on the contrary, fully embraces "natural and necessary" desires).

25. *Beyond the Pleasure Principle*, in *SE*, 18:47. Subsequent citations to this work, henceforth in the notes "*PP*," will be by page only.

26. "The assumption of the existence of an instinct of death or destruction has met with resistance even in analytic circles" (*Civilization and Its Discontents, SE*, 21:119); Jones, *Life and Work of Sigmund Freud*, 3:266, 3:277–78; Kastenbaum adds an intriguing wrinkle: despite being officially banished and theoretically dead, the death drive "seems to be enjoying a surprisingly active, if mostly invisible, afterlife" (*Psychology of Death*, 161–203, quote on 203).

Although this resistance is primarily directed against the death instinct, it is a fair question to ask why there is no corresponding resistance to the life instinct, which can be as mysterious and as strange, and as blindly driven, as any psychic force postulated by Freud.[27] In the next part of this essay I will try to rehabilitate, to a degree, Freud's notion of the death instinct, which I believe has been badly served by his readers, while at the same time trying to put it in a clearer relation to the life instinct. Doing so will oblige us to reevaluate the meaning of life and death in Freud. This in turn will allow us to develop the range of meanings that "love of life" can have, and to extend our findings from the analysis of Lucretius above. But first we need to get a better sense of what it is about Freud's "discovery" of the death instinct that could be so repellent, not only initially for Freud but also more lastingly for his followers and heirs.[28]

In the most general of terms, the resistance among Freud's readers to the idea of the death instinct, that "strange assumption," is likely to be a product of several factors: a resistance to death (whether we call this fear or repugnance);

27. It is surely symptomatic of this bias that in discussions of Freud the death drive is almost never conceived of as a plurality (it is a solitary, dark drive), while the life drives typically, and almost exuberantly, are. Freud, on the contrary, allows both instincts (or drives: Freud is not concerned with instincts in a narrow sense in *PP*) to be singular or plural.

28. "I remember my own defensive attitude when the idea of an instinct of destruction first emerged in psycho-analytic literature, and how long it took before I became receptive to it" (*Civilization and Its Discontents, SE*, 21:120). Neither Freud nor his editors indicate which prior literature he has in mind here—unless he is obliquely referring to his own earlier work. See Singer, *Meaning in Life*, 2–3, for a critical response to Freud's "pessimism." Early Lacan likewise overstates the pessimism of Freud's conception: "La vie ne veut pas guérir" (*Le séminaire*, 2:271). Further, Laplanche, who is prone to see Freud as threatening healthy vitalism with the "obscure" introduction of a death instinct, strangely read by Laplanche, with a clear hint of panic, as "a compulsion to demolish life" (*Life and Death in Psychoanalysis*, 123; cf. ibid., 124; Laplanche, *Problématiques IV*, 230). Lear, in *Happiness, Death, and the Remainder of Life*, eloquently attacks the postulation of the death drive, not only as an unwarranted postulate about the mind (a "fantasy" of a theory, 89; similarly, Jones, *Life and Work of Sigmund Freud*, 3:278–79) but also as a teleological principle (a reductive "tendency," 81). The objection falls away once it can be shown that the death drive has no teleological features for Freud and is not neatly opposable to pleasure, love, or life, which is to say that it is not a drive to death. What is objectionable is not Freud's "teleology" but a teleological reading of Freud. Phillips offers one possible way out—"aim" represents not teleological direction but "desire" (*Darwin's Worms*, 75)—before falling back into a teleological reading again (78). Early Lacan would concur on this last point: the death drive is a desire (*Le séminaire*, 2:259–74). A decade on, in *Four Fundamental Concepts*, Lacan will offer a more sophisticated reading of drive that actually opposes it to desire; see Žižek, *Ticklish Subject*, and Zupančič, *Ethics of the Real*.

a resistance to death as a desired object (which, as we shall see, is a misleading way of putting Freud's reasoning); and finally, odd as it may sound even for a psychoanalytic community steeped in this kind of thinking, a resistance to the prospect of instinctual life itself (to the life of the drives operating behind, as it were, desires). Could there be a further fear at work here, a fear of life itself in its most vital dimensions? Surely the problem owes something, indeed possibly everything, to the incorporation of death into a model of mind, as though the mind's life (generally felt to be aligned with love or Eros) had no place for this radical antithesis to life.[29] As I hope to show, Freud to his credit was unafraid to acknowledge the place of death in the mind, even if he recognized the possibility is one we naturally shrink from.

On a first approach, as we saw, the objectionable substance of Freud's claim is that there is something attractive and pleasurable about death: "beyond" the pleasure principle lies not a drive to death but rather the pleasure that only the approach to death can bring. Freud's infamous statement, "The aim of all life is death," captures only half of this claim. The other half of the claim, more implicit than explicit perhaps, is that this "aim" is less an aim with a teleological direction (as some of Freud's readers object) than it is a fundamental expression of vitality itself—or as Freud says, "an expression of the *conservative* nature of living substance." The essential tie to pleasure can be read off the confluence of Freud's descriptions of the principles of death and life in what he briefly calls, in a borrowed terminology, "the Nirvana principle" and what he more frequently calls the principle of constancy: "The dominating tendency of mental life, and perhaps of nervous life in general, is the effort to reduce, to keep constant or to remove internal tension due to stimuli (the 'Nirvana principle'...)—a tendency which finds expression in the pleasure principle; and our recognition of that fact is one of our strongest reasons for believing in the existence of death instincts" (55–56). The inference to the death instincts is possible because death is defined just a few lines earlier (and throughout the essay) as "an abolition of chemical tensions, that is to say, ... death." The vital instinct of pleasure and the morbid instinct of death here seem to collude, disconcertingly. And their functional identity is reaffirmed in the final

29. Lear, *Love and Its Place in Nature*, e.g., 140–55; and see ibid., 14: "Since our concern is the philosophical implications of Freudian *psychoanalysis*, there is reason to set death aside." Freud's contrasting point is that there can be no love or life in the absence of the death instinct (e.g., *Why War? SE*, 22:209–10; see also *New Introductory Lectures, SE*, 22:107: "a 'death instinct' which cannot fail to be present in every vital process," etc.).

paragraph of the essay, where we read: "The pleasure principle seems actually to serve the death instincts" (63).[30]

It is in this way that Freud arrives at his famous, if to us illogical, hypothesis about the circularity of life and death: namely, that life is unconsciously working its way back to death and that this regression is the essential work of life. Life, so viewed, is redefined—as a "circuitous path to death" (39). The statement is alarming. But in order to understand its meaning we need to place the accent where it belongs, on the word *circuitous*. Freud's claim is not that the death instinct leads away from life but that it is, as we saw, "an expression of the *conservative* nature of living substance." By *conservative*, Freud can only mean life preserving and life restoring.[31]

I want to underscore this last idea. Despite what his critics and proponents alike say (and I realize the heretical-sounding nature of my counterclaim), Freud's concern in *Beyond the Pleasure Principle* is exclusively with *life* and not with death. This also applies to the death instinct itself, which after all represents "the aim of *life*," and which, moreover, has a life all its own (and, surprisingly,

30. The two kinds of instinct are approximated again in *The Ego and the Id*: "Acting in this way [as defined in *PP*], both the instincts would be conservative in the strictest sense of the word, since both would be endeavouring to re-establish a state of things that was disturbed by the emergence of life" (*SE*, 19:40); and, e.g., in *New Introductory Lectures* (*SE*, 22:107–8). The fact, which appears elsewhere in Freud's writings, that the death instinct and pleasure tend toward a mutual conflation ought to be uncontroversial. The connection can be noticed and rejected as nihilistic (Dufresne, *Freudian Crypt*) or else as confused (Laplanche, *Life and Death in Psychoanalysis*, e.g., 117 and 122; Boothby, *Death and Desire*), and occasionally—here, by way of Lacan—embraced (Ragland-Sullivan, *Pleasures of Death*). See further *The Economic Problem of Masochism*: "the Nirvana principle, belonging as it does to the death drive, has undergone a modification in living organisms through which it has become the pleasure principle" (*SE*, 19:160). Freud takes this as a reason to "avoid regarding the two principles as one." But it remains hard nonetheless to keep them apart. At the close of the same essay, we read that masochism testifies to "the existence of fusion of instinct (*Triebmischung*)"; and further, "since [masochism] has the significance of an erotic component, even the subject's destruction of himself cannot take place without libidinal satisfaction" (ibid., 170). The theoretical possibility of "primary masochism" (*PP*, 55) would lodge this fusion at the most primordial levels of instinctual activity. At issue here is Freud's inability, or unwillingness, to draw hard and fast distinctions among the instincts, which forever remain "magnificent in their indefiniteness" (*New Introductory Lectures*, *SE*, 22:95). It would perhaps be more true to say that the two instincts serve each other, and that they are united in a single contradictory process, "the process of living" (ibid., 107).

31. The term "conservative" has a range of meanings and degrees (cf. *PP*, 40), all of them in *PP* compatible with its application to both instincts. Freud's point here is unequivocally clear and couched in terms that are "universal."

has no way to take death in its aim—more on that in a moment). "The instinct to return to the inanimate state," which is to say the death instinct, "*came into being*" (38, my emphasis), and it is the emergence of this impulse that is of keenest interest to Freud. The death instinct has its vicissitudes, and it is these that are of primary concern, their curriculum vitae, and nothing else. That is why Freud can happily say about his image of the death drive that it gives us the very "picture of *life*": the instinct for death is bound up at one and the same time with "the origin and aim of life" (39, my emphasis).[32] Somehow, Freud wants to say, the death drive is, as it were, instinct with life, the very source of life and of life's strivings. Technically, the death instinct is difficult to distinguish from a libidinal force, which is to say from "a surplus of unsatisfied libido."[33] Logically, the death represented by the drives cannot be the supreme *telos* of life, let alone something entirely distinct from life and standing outside of it, because death is actually "immanent" to the living organism (39), not beyond it but within it and constitutive of it. As Freud writes elsewhere, "The struggle [between Eros and death] is what all life essentially consists of."[34] Life consists precisely in the struggle between the two principles, not in the vindication of one or the other.[35]

Now, it is a plain but consistently ignored fact that in *Beyond the Pleasure Principle* Freud is uninterested in self-elimination as anything other than a goal or tendency that is aimed at but not arrived at, indeed as anything other than an *unreachable* goal—if it is even a goal. "Direction" might be a better way of describing this tendency, although, as we are beginning to see, the direction the death drive takes is not pointed at death but instead traces a pattern of life. Small wonder, then, if Freud should offer *no* examples of self-elimination in his treatise on the death drive, and indeed, no examples of death, let alone of death as an outcome of the death drive—with one possible exception: only

32. Cf. *New Introductory Lectures*, SE, 22:107 (e.g., "We are not asserting that death is the only aim of life").

33. Libido is generally taken to be an equivalent of life-preserving instincts in Freud, and specifically of love and sexuality (Eros). But Freud vacillates on this in a way that leaves the meaning and function of libido open to further interpretation (see *Ego and the Id*, SE, 19:46–47, and, e.g., n. 36 below).

34. *Civilization and Its Discontents*, SE, 21:122.

35. "Life itself" is "a conflict and compromise between these two trends" (*Ego and the Id*, SE, 19:41). "Neither of these instincts is any less essential than the other; the phenomena of life arise from the concurrent or mutually opposing action of both" (*Why War?* SE, 22:209). Further, *PP* 38, 39, 61; and at n. 56 below.

here, the "sacrifice" in question, which seems to involve self-annihilation, is driven entirely by the instinct for *life* (it has to do with what Freud calls the "narcissism" of germ cells acting on a libidinal impulse).[36] For a work purportedly about death, Freud's treatise has remarkably little to say about its subject matter! The essential confusion to avoid here is that Freud's death instinct is not a death *wish*. It is not aimed at death because, *qua* instinct, at the very least it is aimed at its own satisfaction, however this comes to be defined, and at most it is aimed at some psychic representation of death, which is one reason why the death instinct never appears in a pure form, but only in a "displaced" form.[37] The death instinct is arguably a paradigm of satisfaction resulting from *missing* an object. Consequently, if we wish to say that death in some literal sense is the object of an instinct or that it is what defines what an instinct does, then we will have to acknowledge that death in this form is a representation: it is a purely psychical entity, and a phantasmal one at that. Keeping this representational content within (or else out of) view just is what a living subject does; it defines the most basic activity of the living.

If this is right, I think it helps to explain why the apparent struggle *for* death, for Freud, is in fact a struggle *against* death and a sign of life. Inclined toward an

---

36. Illustrating the relevance of libido theory to cellular life, Freud notes that while some cells preserve life by "neutralizing" the death instincts, "still others sacrifice themselves in the performance of this libidinal function" (*PP*, 50). Here, self-immolation is in the service of life. The general claim that death is conspicuously absent from *PP* holds even if originally, at the dawn of time, "it was still an easy matter...for a living organism to die." The reason Freud gives is nicely equivocal: "the course of its life was probably only a brief one" (38). Similarly, the natural death of "infusoria," which perish "as a result of their own vital processes" (*PP*, 48). At the level of complex psychic organization the question of self-elimination becomes moot, not least because of the inextricability of the instincts in the shaping of desires. Suicide would no longer serve a single instinct (see *Problem of Masochism, SE,* 19:170; *Outline of Psychoanalysis, SE,* 19:180; and, more generally, *Why War? SE,* 22:210), a point on which Freud can vacillate. Whether a death wish requires activation of a death instinct is unclear; perhaps it does, but it can as easily draw on other kinds of instinct. At the very least, the death instinct is probably not sufficient for an act of death or destruction (of oneself or another), given Freud's general principles of overdetermination and of *Triebmischung* (fusion of instincts). Whether it is a necessary or leading factor, Freud does not say—certainly not in the present essay. Nor is there any obvious reason why he should. And mutatis mutandis, the same applies to life-preserving behavior, which not infrequently, and possibly always, requires the activation of the death instinct. See n. 29 above.

37. *PP,* 54; cf. *Outline of Psychoanalysis, SE,* 19:148. See further *PP,* 34; *Three Essays on Sexuality, SE,* 7:168; and *Analysis Terminal and Interminable, SE,* 23:343, for similar reflections on instincts as psychic representations (*psychische Repräsentanzen*) of prior forces; and n. 56 below.

immanent death, life keeps death in abeyance. "Hence arises the paradoxical situation that the living organism struggles most energetically against events (dangers, in fact) which might help it to attain its life's aim rapidly—by a kind of short circuit" (39). Self-preservation is in the service of self-termination (death by internal causes), while the latter is in the service of life and its aims. But what, for Freud, is life? Life, as we saw, cannot be located in, nor is it reducible to, the instinct for the preservation of life, whether as that instinct's aim or result. Nor is life realized in death.[38] Rather, life is realized in a tension that does not so much stretch between the two ends of Freud's initial polarity, the so-called life and death instincts, as it inhabits each of these two poles. The result of this tension, which is irresolvable and vital (it traces, if you like, the self-disrupting logic of vitality itself), is nothing less or more than the object of psychoanalysis, namely, the efflorescence of psychic *life* (what Freud calls *Seelenleben* or *psychiches Leben*), with all its innumerable complications—the illogical behavior that Freud's essay sets out to explore (traumatic neuroses, repetition compulsions, masochism, etc.) and symptomatic behavior in general, of the sort that Freud's life and work were dedicated to understanding. "As contrasted with intelligent efforts" that would bring life to its end immediately, life is rather a kind of short circuit—a stupidity of sorts—in the otherwise intelligent logic of life and death, which is then drawn out to excruciating lengths in endless detours and in a lurching, "vacillating rhythm."[39] Psychic life, in all its fascinating manifestations, is the consequence—indeed, the symptom—of this oddity about life in its most primitive dimensions.[40]

Freud's essay strikes many readers as overbearingly dark and pessimistic. In point of fact, his image of psychic life is so overpowering and so vital that the

---

38. Unlike many of his readers, Freud avoids the clichéd approaches of Romanticism (sex is death) and of nihilism (we live to die, death is the actualization of life).

39. The rhythm could be defined as the fluctuation or just the tension represented by the (ever changing) "difference in amount between the pleasure of satisfaction which is *demanded* and that which is actually achieved." This perpetual asymmetry is both a cause and an effect of the process: Freud calls this, and not the demand for satisfaction, "the driving factor" (das treibende Moment) that "'presses ever forward unsubdued'" (ungebändigt immer vorwärts dringt) (*PP*, 42). "The backward path that leads to complete satisfaction" is self-obstructing when viewed in this dynamic light. Nor are either of the drives self-evidently correlated with one direction or the other.

40. Can psychic life ever know a literal death? Perhaps it can, in the case of catatonia or brain death (see n. 1, above), but so far as I am aware Freud shows no interest in these phenomena or in attributing to them as a cause anything like the death instinct.

very coherence of the idea of death begins to fade away—or in Freud's words, begins to "melt away" under his own hands. Somewhat wickedly, and in any case gleefully, he observes "how little agreement there is among biologists on the subject of natural death and in fact...the whole concept of death melts away under their hands." Death's coherence fades because, as Freud shows, the results of the inquiry into biology are frustrated by the very indeterminacy of the idea of death and, correspondingly, of life. The boundaries of death are disputed in biological terms; no consensus reigns; and the very idea of death as a stark alternative to life is shown to be incoherent.[41] The same holds in psychoanalysis. For psychoanalysis, death's coherence fades, not despite all the attention paid by Freud to the supposition of a drive to death but precisely because death (or rather, its displacement by the instincts) is conceived by him as the aim of a vital and active *drive* that brings satisfaction to a *living* organism. That is, the representation of death by the instincts is conceived by Freud as an activity of the living. Indeed, the death drive is a sign, precisely, of healthy instinctual life. If so, then the question now becomes not: What is life or death? (the problem put by biology) but rather: What is the meaning of death in relation to life? As Freud frames this puzzle, at issue is not even whether death has a meaning beyond life and its principle of pleasure but *whether it has any meaning at all within life.*

Freud's answer is astonishingly clear. It is that death, from the point of view of life, is an impossible conceit. Death is literally inconceivable from within life—which is not to say that it is not a possible object of fear or phobia or pleasure but only that death's only meaning will be imaginary, a halo of images draped around an empty core. It can have a psychic form, as manifested in behavior, but it can have no psychic content.[42] Elsewhere, this comes out as the famous claim that in our unconscious we are all convinced of our immortality: we cannot conceive ourselves as dead.[43] Death for Freud thus combines two puzzling features: it represents the greatest negation one can ever conceive, and no one can ever truly conceive it. (For the very same reason, the unconscious cannot represent negation to itself.)[44] As with Lucretius, death for Freud is not

41. *PP*, 45–59. For a contemporary offspring of this same debate, see Natalie Angier, "Defining the Undefinable: Being Alive," *New York Times*, December 18, 2001.

42. For this kind of distinction, see *Extracts from the Fliess Papers, SE*, 1:192; *Inhibitions, Symptoms, and Anxiety, SE*, 20:135; and *Interpretation of Dreams, SE*, 4:332 and 5:506–7 n. 2.

43. *Thoughts on War and Death, SE*, 14:289, 296.

44. *Negation, SE*, 19:239.

a coherent thought a subject is permitted by its nature to have.[45] The rejection of death, in other words, is built into the very foundation of Freud's model of the mind—even as the principle of death slips in through the back door again, in the very form that the mind's workings assume (for example, in the—forever imperfect—negation of consciousness that governs how subjects act).[46] And so, here too Freud moves closer to the tradition, mentioned at the outset of this essay, that denies the coherence of death and simultaneously puts the accent on the sheer affirmation of life from within the perspective of life, even as he shares that tradition's fundamental ambivalence toward the intrinsic value of life.

I have been treating Freud's essay as circulating around a primary tension rather than a dualism. I mean to suggest that there is a tension to Freud's dualistic program and that Freud is well aware of this fact. For all of his emphasis on opposite tendencies in instinctual life, Freud at times confesses to the difficulty of maintaining these very distinctions. We need to be attentive to these confessions. But perhaps the problem lies not in Freud's maintaining the distinctions, but in his maintaining their meaning and their validity as such. That is, the problem may have to do with the questions Freud was willing to entertain about the validity of his image of mental life as a whole. More on that in a moment.

When Freud describes instincts as urges "to restore an earlier state of things," the assumption has typically been that the regression is to death. But this assumption isn't justified. At the end of his treatise, Freud returns to the thesis about the regressive tendency; only, what the tendency aims at is not death but an earlier state of *life*. That is what the parable from Aristophanes, of the return to a primordial whole, is designed, after all, to illustrate.[47] Translated into modern biology, the return to wholeness is a return to the original state of the "living substance," prior to its being "torn apart into small particles" in the name of cellular division, growth, sexual union, combination and coalescence into "ever larger unities," further libidinal attachment, more complex forms of life, and so on.[48] Fatal regression, in that case, would be to a

45. The same is true of Nietzsche and, before him, Spinoza and, later, Wittgenstein (among others).

46. *Negation, SE*, 19:235–36; and cf. ibid., 237–38, where we find a kind of *fort/da* of negation that resembles the compulsion to repeat.

47. Contrast *Outline of Psychoanalysis, SE*, 19:149, which PP seemingly revises.

48. *PP*, 43, 444, 58.

primordial form of *attachment*. I think this is a very different picture from that of the *textus receptus* of the received Freud. But this is what Freud's text actually says. "Love of life" need mean no more and no less than this deepest form of attachment, a form of binding that does not lie beyond the pleasure principle because it in fact antedates it.[49]

Freud's essay ends here, but his thinking prematurely ends on a different note a few pages earlier, at the beginning of the penultimate section (section 6). There, Freud makes a startling revelation about the hypothesis of "the internal necessity of dying," which the essay takes on board as an unexceptionable "truth" and which henceforth stands at its conceptual center, namely, the view that all life seeks out a natural death from "internal causes." The view, Freud now worries, is worse than a hypothesis: it may turn out to be a piece of psychological rationalization, a mere metaphysical comfort. If so, the "sublime Ἀνάγκη" of this law may be no more than "only another of those illusions which we have created '*um die Schwere des Daseins zu ertragen*' (to bear the burden of existence)." The resort, in the sequel, to biology and its grappling with the problem of the immortality of protista (the question whether germ cells undergo a "natural death" or not) was an attempt on Freud's part to confront the problem on physiological grounds, and it too remained inconclusive. If Freud's central hypothesis merely repeats a common delusion, and self-consciously at that, where does this leave us? Is the idea of a death instinct, of a drive to death, conceivably itself a comforting *illusion*?

CONCLUSIONS: DEATH, LIFE, AND MEANINGFULNESS

It is time now to stand back and take stock. Earlier I proposed that Freud's theory of the mind disturbingly mirrors some of its own features, as though the theory were caught in a narcissistic self-reflection, or else were propelled by a death drive of its own—toward the death (say) of the familiar features of mind, in their ultimate estrangement, that of their representation as drives, energy flows, cathexes, and the rest. If this kind of reduction is indeed best understood as a distillation of psychological activity, as I was suggesting, we might want to ask just what it is that is being distilled in the picture of life as a flow of energies. Could Freud, in the very picture he is constructing and offering to us, be probing another kind of drive, a drive to *reduce* and *distill*? Is this reductive tendency (if it is one) somehow in line with the regressive

49. Cf. *PP*, 52, on libidinal attachment; ibid., 58, on the "chemical affinity" of inorganic matter (unbelebte Materie) that "persists" *in* the instincts.

tendency? Is *any* theory of the mind, not to say of the world, possibly a product of just such a regression?

Theory, be it of the mind or the world, is always a regression from experience: it simplifies what is given in phenomena, with the aim of returning the phenomena to their original condition, namely, that of their schematic truth. This self-evident fact about Freud's theory—its own regressive tendencies—doesn't so much invalidate his theory as it requires us to ask fresh questions about it (with implications for Lucretius as well). Are Freud's theoretical regressions a refutation or a confirmation of the death instinct? What are the pleasures taken in this kind of reduction? Was the death instinct postulated as an entity in its own right or as a paradigm case of a tendency of the mind that may have no ontological correlative (say, in some drive-like mechanism), but that is only to be found in a range of behaviors that cuts across the categories of life's maintenance and endangerment (as exhibited, for instance, by the act of proposing a theory of the death instinct, not to mention a life instinct or a pleasure principle)?

Not even Freud's blatant self-refutation in section 6 of *Beyond the Pleasure Principle* changes the force of these questions. Just a moment ago we saw how Freud rips the rug out from under his own theory when, toward the end of his essay, he casts doubt upon its central premise: death by internal reasons is a myth of the mind; therefore, it would seem to follow, the postulate of the death drive as a drive to this kind of death (summed up by the motto, "the aim of all life is death") is invalid. But this last conclusion doesn't follow. What is invalidated is only the motto, or rather the narrow conception of death that it is felt to express. If death is understood most broadly as a rupture in meaning, a direction I would like to pursue for a moment, then Freud's self-refutation (and not just inconstancy or vacillation) is a further instance of a tendency to death in this broader sense. Casting illusions and ripping them open again, in a way that is reminiscent of the Schopenhauerian Will, Freud is modeling the mind either as a dupe or as desperate for the assurances of meaning, and especially for meaning about itself (the only meaning it finally recognizes). And so, too, his ultimate concern is with the meaning of life—not as a real or scientifically true entity, but as a meaningful one. Projecting the lesson of his scientific paradigm (it is really a scene of instruction) back onto a more familiar level, we can say that love of life for Freud is inseparable from a fascination with death and that it may be constituted solely in relation to this latter. This is also the lesson of an earlier essay, in which Freud puts forward the striking thesis that "life is impoverished, it loses in interest, when the highest stake in the game of living, life itself, may not be risked." It is only when life runs the risk of forfeiture, or incoherence, that it can "retrieve its full content" and its full value—the only value that it has.[50]

To claim, as Adam Phillips does, that "Freud asserts in 1920, above all, or rather beneath all, we desire to die; or rather to fashion a death," is to misrepresent Freud in a grotesque way.[51] Phillips is on a better track when he tries to see in Freud's view of death a view of how people go about constructing stories about themselves and their lives. "Freud needed the notion of a death instinct—a curious notion in itself—to tell more persuasive, more convincing life stories: stories about how people actively, if unwittingly, undo their lives; and how this is a source of satisfaction to them" (78). One should probably contest the notion of a life "undone": it leaves all too vague the idea of a life "done"; and it places too much positive value on "life." It would be wrong to believe that death can be tidily swept away from the picture of life, leaving us with a clearer view of life in some intact condition. That is, it would be wrong to imagine that we can conceive, have, or love a life that shares none of the features of death. There can be no instinct for life as distinct from an instinct for death. On an alternative view of Freud's theory, one I would like to propose for consideration, the only difference between the two so-called instincts to life and to death is at most a perspectival one, depending upon whether life is viewed *sub specie mortis* or *sub specie vitae*.

What I have been trying to do here, to sum up and to begin to conclude, is to explore a space for life within two theories of death and thus to revise our notion of the place of death in life. So let us begin our revision by underscoring the fact that the desire located by Freud is not a desire for death but is rather a desire to see death as a permanent element in the logic of life. Freud's reputation as a nihilist who placed no value on life notwithstanding, we can sum up his oeuvre as a whole by saying that it is in fact obsessively concerned with the value of life, and of any particular life, which is to say with the question about how we construct that value and find ways to reach after it. And if Freud is dismissive of the objective reality of this value and its attainability as such, he in no way dismisses the value of the activity he describes, which is to say the constructing and the searching for life's value—and for values generally, especially if it is the case that life's value is premised by every value we hold dear, and indeed by the very act of valuation itself.

50. *Thoughts on War and Death*, SE, 14:290, 291.
51. Phillips, *Darwin's Worms*, 79.

At stake and implicit throughout my discussion has been the transformation of death from a fact into a fascination. The fascination with death, which is undeniably present in all societies and not just our own, is an attempt to locate meaning in life. Death is a crucial narrative element in stories about life. One couldn't tell such stories, or live them, without this element being present in them. This is not just because death gives a final shape to life projects or their conception (these are one and the same). Death ends stories, and it begins them. It can be a period, a parenthesis, or a new paragraph marker. It would seem hard to deny the generative nature of death in the quest for meaning, and so too, viewed in this light, death, the fascination, takes us a long way away from nihilism. Freud's perpetual struggle with meaning, his repeated and combative attempts to lay hold of something ("whereas what *we* seek to understand is … "), is likewise a problem for anyone who would saddle him with sheer pessimism or nihilism or with devaluing life. "It is not a question of an antithesis between an optimistic and a pessimistic theory of life," Freud writes elsewhere. "Only by the concurrent or mutually opposing action of the two primal instincts—Eros and the death-instinct—, never by one or the other alone, can we explain the rich multiplicity [*Buntheit*, or "colorful variety"] of the phenomena of *life*. How parts of these two classes of instincts combine to fulfill *the various vital functions* … are problems whose elucidation would be the most rewarding achievement of psychological research."[52] Much the same can be said of Lucretius.

52. *Analysis Terminable and Interminable*, *SE*, 23:243; my emphasis. Indeed, as a glance at another of Freud's writings, *The Future of an Illusion*, would show, Freud at times runs the risk of being found guilty of *optimism*. But what remains certain, even here, is his steadfast "interest in" (or else "love of") the human world and and human life (*SE*, 21:53, 54). Freud may in fact be closer to Lifton's *Life of the Self* here than Lifton would have us believe—or to Lacan than many Lacanians might believe today. For despite all of its attention to the "primordial dis-attachment" that allegedly founds subjects but is arguably also no more than a fantasy entertained by them (or by psychoanalysts), contemporary Lacanianism is in fact concerned to show the effects of "primordial passionate attachment" in subjects—and not least of all their peculiar attachment to disattachment (viz., to the voiding of meaning). In other words, there is a certain—or rather *excessive*—vitality to the death drive. See Žižek, *Ticklish Subject*, esp. 288–94. At the bottom of everything is not the question, Why is there nonsense, void, death, etc.? but, Why do we *produce* nonsense? What is the source of this *fascination* in us? To answer, "the death instinct," if by that we mean something other than some vital activity, is to go again in circles, as I have been trying to show. The problem is that in the attempt to produce meaning, subjects inevitably *over* produce meaning. This excess of meaning is what Freud calls death; the tendency to produce this excess of meaning corresponds to what he calls the death instinct. (Thus, asking about the meaning of life can be a life-sustaining activity, even if the question in itself is a nonsensical one.)

The fascination with death is a vital sign, not the opposite. It may even have a defensive function, for instance by being aimed at defending a psyche against its own avowed or disavowed fears of death. The figure of Leontius is a case in point. As Plato tells the story, Leontius went about the Piraeus trying in vain to wrest his eyes from the sight of corpses. While a sign of morbidity in one sense, in another the gesture is entirely life affirming: wasn't Leontius thereby assuring himself of his own valid existence?[53] We should not forget, moreover, that the compulsion to repeat is a salient trait not of suicidal victims but of traumatized *survivors*. Their reenactments of trauma are not death seeking but are on the contrary meaning seeking. Delusions about "destiny" have a similar explanation. They are an attempt to read a "sublime" and "compulsive necessity" into a fragile and contingent world (*PP*, 23). Freud and Lucretius both resist this kind of delusion, in the name of its rational intelligibility. (The delusion reflects, they would say, a genuine human need.) The very behaviors pointed to by Freud—the compulsion to repeat, the imaginative flirtations with pain (with their increment of pleasure) and the reality principle—are all one needs to establish that meaning is being constructed even where none exists to be found. The bare recognition that there is no clear or essential meaning to perfection, fate, or the rationality of the world is itself a meaningful discovery, and so again hardly a sign of nihilism or morbidity.

That said, a number of issues clamor for attention. Is Freud's work about death or is it about the idea of death (its fantasy)? Is his work about the simplification of life and thus (by correlative symmetry) itself the sign of a regressive tendency? Or is it about the complications in life and in our view of it that such a regression necessarily entails? Does Freud's death drive exist to illustrate the simple necessities of death or the ever curious ways in which people contrive to make their lives? Surely it is for the sake of the latter kind of explanation that the death drive is postulated by Freud at all.[54]

53. Plato *Republic* 439e–440a.

54. See Lear, *Happiness, Death, and the Remainder of Life*, 135: "Instead of treating 'the death drive' as a permanent and peculiar possibility of mindedness, [Freud] substantializes it into a basic metaphysical principle." Lear, while content to perpetuate Freud's apparatus of energies, tensions, discharges, breaks, and the like, goes the first route, which (as I have been arguing) comes closer to Freud's own. The problem will always remain that "death instinct" signifies too many things in Freud to be reduced to anything other than a puzzle of meanings, attractions, and repellencies that are *included* in the definition of life and so too in that of the "life instinct." This, at least it seems to me, is the most productive way of reading Freud.

When Irving Singer writes against Freud, "To ask for the meaning of life would…be an expression of one's humanity rather than just a symptom of psychological or moral disability," he seems not to notice that this was, precisely, Freud's point.[55] Freud, like Lucretius, can have been a lover of life without allowing himself to be duped by that love. To love life, as I have been defining it here, is not necessarily to affirm life in a propositional way, nor is it necessarily to be in a state of emotion. It is a kind of attachment, deep and unwilled.[56] Love or attachment (the emotions) will often follow as a consequence of this deeper kind of attachment, but they needn't do this, and they needn't come in a pure form when they do—they can be ambivalent, involve hate, repulsion, fear, and so on. Perhaps we need to complicate our own sense of what loving life entails so that it can encompass or else be compatible with a full range of human emotions and of possible stances toward the world.

But even with this complication, love of life needn't entail an immediate and total grasp of the being of life. Life is not somehow more immediately apprehensible and less opaque than death, nor is it somehow brighter, more transparent, and therefore more desirable than death.[57] To say it is any of this is to suggest that love of life, death's alter ego, provides all the value we need and want, while death merely does the work of underscoring this value, as though by contrastive shading. In the spirit of the tradition I have been exploring (or assembling), I want to question the value of the love of life, not as a valuable activity but as an unqualified and self-sufficient source of value. This also means questioning the detachability of life as an object of love. Love is more complex than positive wanting or desiring. And yet there is no attitude or stance toward things that does not involve love in the sense of a lavishing of attention on an object, or simply a directing of the mind or the senses upon themselves. This is the affirmative quality of love, which does not always entail a final affirmation: we are not compelled to value and affirm in

55. Singer, *Rethinking Life and Death*, 3.

56. Cf. Hazlitt, "On the Love of Life."

57. See also Laplanche, *Life and Death in Psychoanalysis*, in the spirit of Freud: "every unmediated reference to life, self-preservation, and reality falls outside of our grasp" (122). One suspects this is why Freud could hold, in *Civilization and Its Discontents* (SE, 21:138–39) and in *Why War?* (SE, 22:209–10), that *neither* the life *nor* the death instinct ever appears "in a pure form": the phenomena of life and death are themselves too various, and their respective instincts too intertwined, to admit of such clarity.

the narrower sense all that we love and affirm in this broadest, most generous sense.[58]

There is much more to be said here.[59] But let us simply note for now how life is not a determinate object, any more than death is, and for this reason alone it cannot be made into an object of thought or desire: it has no essence. We might as well admit that life can be no more coherently represented to the mind than can death, and for the very same reasons that death escapes representation. To love life is to love an elusive object, or perhaps it is to love no object at all, because love of life is not object-love but only a constitutive practice—a meaning-constituting practice. The instinct for life, as Freud knows, is the instinct for an ever greater and thus ever receding and ever more elusive complexity. It is what, in Lucretian language, draws us to "the shoals of light," and in drawing us up draws us out. Its path is that of a detour that has no direction to it, but only a movement or rhythm. These vacillations are the "ever more complicated detours" traced by the curriculum vitae of an organism as it "diverges ever more widely from its original course," however this comes to be defined. It is in the dance with death and negation that life becomes the complex, enchanting, frustrating, and often self-frustrating phenomenon that it is, full of hopes and despairs, imaginings and illusions. It is this complexity that never ceases to amaze the mind of a Lucretius or a Freud as they look upon the dazzling richness of human life and the world, which life acts in responson to and, in responding, fashions and refashions.

To love life is to love the limits of life, its whole variegated economy of waxing and waning powers. It is surely also to love death, for without this final component, love of life remains incomplete and life becomes a deathless illusion. To fail to love life *even in its absence* is, quite simply, not to love life at all.

---

58. This kind of affirmation is the underlying motif of Elaine Scarry's recent book, *On Beauty and Being Just*. Beauty is for her ultimately life affirming. My only quarrel with her argument, which at bottom is an aestheticizing version of Spinozism, is that life affirms far more than comes to be denominated as beautiful: the affirmative quality of the senses or the mind can be life enhancing (and, if we so wish, beautiful) even when their object is not felt to be beautiful; correlatively, that object, when sensuously perceived or mentally grasped, will nonetheless be life sustaining. Even to reject an object is, in true Spinozan (and later, Nietzschean) logic, to embrace that object affirmatively (cf. Spinoza, *Ethics*, 170–71 [*Ethics*, part 3, proposition 4]). Negation here is not an option for the mind, or for life.

59. In particular, see Williams, "Markopulos Case"; Wollheim, *Thread of Life*; Nagel, *View from Nowhere*; and Nussbaum, *Therapy of Desire*. I hope to develop these arguments elsewhere, and eventually in a longer form.

And so, contrary to all expectation but fully in keeping with his philosophical bearings, we find Lucretius pouring out golden verses in honor of the most mundane and simplest of pleasures, as when he describes how "the golden morning light of the radiant sun reddens over the grass bejeweled with dew, and the pools and ever-rustling streams give off a mist" (5.461–63). Hundreds of similar details of nature and of human life are found scattered throughout Lucretius's poem, each lavished with the kind of attention that only a lover of verses and of appearances could supply. And then there is Freud, the entirety of whose work is devoted to exploring the magnificent, because deeply flawed, edifice of the soul that so detained Lucretius before him. Neither of these writers is deceived for a minute about the severe limitations of what both of them are trying to describe. On the contrary, each of their gazes is trained precisely on those limits, which is where all the interest lies. For it is at the edges of existence and where death looms near that life comes alive, only to produce a fleeting but fully mortal experience, thanks to the complications that bring this experience into being and that finally must surrender it to nothingness.

RESPONSE TO JAMES I. PORTER

RICHARD WOLLHEIM

James Porter is not the first interpreter of Freud, nor will he be the last, to claim that there is, for some part of that theory at any rate, a parallel so strong between it and the psychological reality it professes to theorize that the theory comes to take on some of the salient characteristics of what it is about. Nor is he the only one to be led astray by what is in essence a playful project. Thus, in discussing Freud's theory of the death instinct and its inherently regressive nature, Porter draws attention to the "self-evident but little noticed fact" that Freud's own theory, like indeed all theory, is a form of regression. Why is this? It is so because, according to Porter, theory in its nature is "always a regression from experience," and this claim he tries to clarify by remarking that theory inherently "simplifies what is given in phenomena."

However, in the sense in which this remark is intended, theory does no such thing. For, if the remark is to support the conclusion that Porter draws from it, it must tell us that theory affirms that things are simpler than they are. Only in that way would theory be a form of "regression." But that things are simpler than they are is something that theory asks us to imagine: to imagine, not to believe. And it does this so as to get us to recognize similarities between things that, so long as we continue to think about them in the fullness of their empirical detail, will always seem very different. If theory went beyond this and systematically asked us to believe of things that we recognize to be complex that they are other than complex, it would fall into absurdity, and it could not aid us in acquisition of knowledge about the world. Porter's point would have been better put by saying that theory abstracts from experience: theory asks us to bracket our knowledge of that detail which obscures the perception of pattern.

If I have labored this point, it is because I think that it is of general relevance to Porter's essay. For optimism and pessimism about the human condition, one of which is covertly, the other overtly, the topic of the essay, resemble theory in that they too depend for their hold over us more on the imagination, or on how we see the world, than on belief. And, since the imagination is invariably influenced by how the matter over which it then casts its spell is initially presented, it follows that the rival attractions of optimism and pessimism cannot be divorced from the way in which we pose to ourselves the fundamental issues of our existence and its value. It is on this matter that I have a suggestion to make.

Porter introduces us to Lucretius and Freud as though they ask, What— that is, What if anything—binds us to life? and, in working out a reply to the question, find it natural to think that the very existence of death as the conclusion of life ensures that the right answer is, Not enough. It would, I suggest, be only a small emendation that would make this answer seem less compelling: to ask our question not about life, but about *a* life, about *the* life that we lead. And, before I try to draw out the consequences to this small shift, let me say that I suspect that I may only be articulating something to which Porter is as deeply committed as I am.

The difference on which my suggestion trades is this: If we ask our question about life, what we are asking about is an aspect of ourselves that we possess while we are alive and to query its value makes little or no sense unless we specify the conditions on which we may be expected to possess it. However, if we do specify these conditions, which, of course, will include death, it will look as though we are asking what value life, or living, has on those conditions compared to other conditions on which we might have been offered it. And then it can come to seem as though life as we have it is at best a second best: a second best because to get the very same thing without death would be better.

But ask the question not about life but about our life, about the life that we are leading as we ask it, and that absurd option vanishes. For the lives of persons are the lives of finite creatures. Death is not the condition on which creatures have lives, and which they could, in their imagination, abstract from those lives.

One way of appreciating this last point is to see that we go wrong when we think that death impinges upon our lives only at a certain moment: specifically, when we die. That would make death rather like, say, our sixtieth birthday. But in fact mortality colors the whole of our life. For instance, it determines that we should choose to do this and not to do that rather than, as would seem consonant with immortality, what to do first, what to do next. We would indeed, were we to live but not to lead a life, have "world enough, and time."

THE ARCHITECTURE OF LOVE
IN BAROQUE ROME

INGRID D. ROWLAND

> And he gave some, apostles; and some, prophets; and some, evangelists; and
> some, pastors and teachers; for the perfecting of the saints, for the work of the
> ministry, for the edifying of the body of Christ: till we all come in the unity of
> the faith, and of the knowledge of the Son of God, unto a perfect man, unto the
> measure of the stature of the fulness of Christ: that we . . . speaking the truth in
> love, may grow up into him in all things, which is the head, even Christ: from
> whom the whole body, fitly joined together and compacted by that which every
> joint supplieth, according to the effectual working in the measure of every part,
> maketh increase of the body unto the edifying of itself in love.
>
> PAUL, LETTER TO THE EPHESIANS

When Paul described the Christian Church as a building whose structural parts
were the people of its congregations and whose joinery was love,[1] the architects
of papal Rome took him at his word. No less than the beauty of a mortal lover,
the beauty of their designs was intended to capture the souls of the faithful,

---

1. "[11] et ipse dedit quosdam quidem apostolos quosdam autem prophetas alios vero evan-
gelistas alios autem pastores et doctores [12] ad consummationem sanctorum in opus ministerii
in aedificationem corporis Christi [13] donec occurramus omnes in unitatem fidei et agnitionis
Filii Dei in virum perfectum in mensuram aetatis plenitudinis Christi [14] ut iam non simus
parvuli fluctuantes et circumferamur omni vento doctrinae in nequitia hominum in astutia ad
circumventionem erroris [15] veritatem autem facientes in caritate crescamus in illo per omnia
qui est caput Christus [16] ex quo totum corpus conpactum et conexum per omnem iuncturam
subministrationis secundum operationem in mensuram uniuscuiusque membri augmentum
corporis facit in aedificationem sui in caritate" (Eph. 4:11–16). Translations are taken from the
King James Version for their stylistic grace.

binding their affection as securely as (and, according to contemporary belief, by essentially the same mechanism as) a magic spell. Like most of their contemporaries, the builders of this new Rome were convinced that the keys to the divine realm of beauty, love, and magic lay concealed in the ancient ruins that loomed over the much smaller medieval city; whoever could infuse those elegant forms with Christian faith would not only create a new architecture for the renewed capital of a Christian empire but also create an architecture of unprecedented persuasive power.

The thought that Rome's ruined cityscape could be restored to something resembling its ancient splendor thus became something of an obsession in the fifteenth century, especially after the Turkish conquest of Constantinople in 1453 brought down the last great capital of Christianity. To meet this Islamic challenge, the popes and patrons of Renaissance Rome resolved to remake the ancient city as the new heart of Christendom. The economic conditions of fifteenth-century Rome were not especially favorable for an undertaking of such epic scope; what drove the project of Rome's renewal was rather the sheer force of the idea itself and the passion it excited. That passion itself took on powerfully erotic overtones, in the first place because of the Greco-Roman (and probably also Etruscan) linguistic quirk that made cities feminine, to be won over, captured, or conquered.[2] At the same time, however, the very elusiveness of the ancient past made it as alluring, and as frustrating, as an evasive lover.

The eros of classical antiquity is nowhere more eloquently presented than in the woodcuts for a strange, beautiful book published in Venice in 1499, the *Hypnerotomachia Poliphili*. Its publisher, Aldus Manutius, probably hoped to sell the steamy vernacular novel in order to increase his capital for more scholarly ventures, spicing its text with daringly explicit woodcut illustrations (fig. 1). The price was high, the novel was boring, and its sales were dismal, but the haunting woodcuts captured the spirit of Aldus and his own enterprise with perfect precision: a spirit of pure desire for the lost world of classical antiquity, a desire inflamed all the more by its eternal frustration. The very title of the novel, *Hypnerotomachia Poliphili*, erotic to its roots, played on every ramification of the longing for antiquity; a mixture of Greek and Latin that meant, roughly, "Poliphilo's Sleep- and Love-Battle" and suggested to readers that the book would provide a dream world of sex, strife, and high culture.

2. Also see Song of Songs 8:10: "I am a wall, and my breasts like towers: then was I in his eyes as one that found favour."

1. Benedetto Bordon (?), illustration for Francesco Colonna,
Hypnerotomachia Poliphili (1499).

And true to its promise, the *Hypnerotomachia* plunged its hero, Poliphilo, into
an ancient world that was sexy, turbulent, ineffably beautiful, and ineffably
elusive. Tellingly, moreover, Poliphilo can never quite decide whether he cares
more about women or ruins; he yearns for them both insatiably. When, after
many adventures undergone, trials endured, inscriptions read, and ruins explored, he embraces his lover on the novel's final page, she breaks away from
him to leave behind a motto as her epitaph: "A wilted rose can never live again."
However deeply Poliphilo loves antiquity, antiquity is dead.

Or perhaps not so dead after all. Aldus had made his career by applying a
new technology, print, to the great works of ancient Greece, helping thereby
to make antiquity live again, in a new age, in a new way. He and his contemporaries may not have used the specific term *Renaissance* to describe their
activities, but they certainly spoke constantly of antiquity's rebirth, born as
the child of a distinctly erotic ancient sensibility. Yet Aldus and his contemporaries did not necessarily see the ancient eros as a licentious paganism in
conflict with their Christian faith. Quoting a speech from Plato's *Symposium* as
if it were Plato's own opinion, they observed that the ancients had identified

two kinds of love, earthly and heavenly, one aimed at reproduction and one at philosophical truth. Furthermore, they recognized that it was only thanks to the long development of Greek philosophy, the heavenly love of the *Symposium*, that the Gospel message could combine with Hebrew wisdom and the Romans' imperial government to spread so quickly to so many people.

Most of the eros in the *Hypnerotomachia Poliphili* runs distinctly to the earthly variety in all its unbridled fertility: nymphs cavort over lush meadows and bring tribute of fruit and flowers to the phallic god Priapus, who is shown by the woodcut in a frank and triumphant state of arousal (fig. 2). Poliphilo stops to drink at a fountain carved in the form of a sleeping nymph newly unveiled by an overexcited satyr with a corkscrew penis; one of her sculpted breasts spurts hot water, one cold, and Poliphilo drinks deeply from the latter. Another fountain centers on the fertility goddess whose temple was one of the seven wonders of the ancient world, Artemis of Ephesus: her hat, a city wall; her hood and lap sprouting fabulous beasts; lions crawling up her arms as if they were kittens; hung with layer upon layer of pendants. The most impressive of these pendants were thought until modern times to be multiple breasts (they are probably tear-shaped amber beads), and as breasts they duly spray water in every direction in the *Hypnerotomachia*. Just as the Roman poet Lucretius traced all creation back to "nurturing Venus," so, too, in the *Hypnerotomachia*, nature is entirely subject to the rule of love, and human beings, to the rule of nature. The contrast with Christianity seemingly could not have been more stark.

Ancient sexuality, therefore, seemed to pay proper homage to nature in all her power; it is no accident that the age of Aldus Manutius was an age of exploring new worlds and natural phenomena. Rather than maintaining an ascetic contempt for the body and its senses, the ancients, especially in their works of art, had reveled in the beauty and abundance of the physical world. It may have been no wonder, then, that eros in the Renaissance nearly always went back to antiquity, where sex and piety could coexist in perfect contentment.

And yet the author of the *Hypnerotomachia Poliphili* was in all probability a Venetian friar, Francesco Colonna, who could have pointed to all the instances in the Bible that describe the relationship between divinity and humanity as an explicitly erotic one: the book of the prophet Hosea, for instance, memorably shows God and Israel in an amorous give and take for which the final prospect of reconciliation is specifically portrayed as betrothal: "And I will betroth thee unto me for ever; yea, I will betroth thee unto me in righteousness, and in judgment, and in lovingkindness, and in mercies. I will even betroth thee unto me in faithfulness: and thou shalt know the LORD. And it shall come to

2. Benedetto Bordon (?), illustration for Francesco Colonna,
Hypnerotomachia Poliphili (1499).

pass in that day, I will hear, saith the LORD, I will hear the heavens, and they shall hear the earth; And the earth shall hear the corn, and the wine, and the oil; and they shall hear Jezreel. And I will sow her unto me in the earth; and I will have mercy upon her that had not obtained mercy; and I will say to them which were not my people, Thou art my people; and they shall say, Thou art my God" (Hosea 2:19–23).

In the same way, the love poetry of the Song of Songs, already read as an allegory in Jewish tradition, became a Christian allegory of the love between

Christ and the Church, a love attuned to pain as well as sensual delight:[3] "I rose up to open to my beloved; and my hands dropped with myrrh, and my fingers with sweet smelling myrrh, upon the handles of the lock. I opened to my beloved; but my beloved had withdrawn himself, and was gone: my soul failed when he spake: I sought him, but I could not find him; I called him, but he gave me no answer. The watchmen that went about the city found me, they smote me, they wounded me; the keepers of the walls took away my veil from me. I charge you, O daughters of Jerusalem, if ye find my beloved, that ye tell him, that I am sick of love" (Song of Songs 5:5–8).

Using the sensual appeal of classical line and Hebrew poetry, the popes and patrons of Renaissance Rome set out to make the beauty of the city as powerful a weapon of conversion as an Ottoman scimitar.[4]

In order to change lives, they knew that this new kind of Christian beauty had to be more than simply admirable; it had to engage the passions of view-ers and hold them in a relentless grip. Contemporary theologians and artists agreed that the essence of divine beauty lay in harmony, but in order to attain that harmony, the soul first underwent every torment of desire, separation, and ecstatic reunion that a lover might endure; eros was, after all, only a more worldly expression of the same passion as the love of God. In descriptions of Jerusalem, this new Christian Rome found words for a divine mission expressed specifically as architecture. Psalm 125 describes Jerusalem as an eternal city protected by God but also emphasizes that this holy city consists above all in a faithful people: "They that trust in the LORD shall be as mount Zion, which cannot be removed, but abideth for ever. As the mountains are round about Jerusalem, so the LORD is round about his people from henceforth even for ever" (Psalm 125:1–2). And it must have been on the basis of imagery like that of the Psalms that Paul conceived his own powerful image of the Christian Church as a building: "The household of God . . . built upon the foundation of the apostles and prophets, Jesus Christ himself being the chief cornerstone; in whom all the building fitly framed together groweth unto an holy temple in the Lord: in whom ye also are builded together for an habitation of God through the Spirit" (Eph. 2:19–22).

3. Although the Song originated as Hebrew love poetry, it was eventually taken as an allegory, first of God and Israel, then of Christ and the Church. See Pope, *Song of Songs*.

4. This is not to say that in the same period the popes did not also resort to hand grenades, assault troops, and the Inquisition; they used all these means as well, but beauty was regarded as more immediately conducive to love, which was the ultimate point of conversion.

From the outset, architecture in Renaissance Rome expressed this "habitation of God through the Spirit" in a tension between serene faith and anguished pilgrimage; circular spaces like the Pantheon or the dome of St. Peter's fostered a sense of arrival and repose, whereas the city's streets and the river Tiber, with its shoals and periodic devastating floods, implied not only constant movement but, often enough, insecurity.[5] In many ways, however, the tensions of this new Roman architecture did not reach their peak until the seventeenth century, with the advent of the style we now know as Baroque. By then the grand dream of Rome as a Christian capital had foundered on the Protestant Reformation, which brought political as well as theological warfare to Italy and its neighbors. At the same time, thinkers like Nicolaus Copernicus, Giordano Bruno, Johannes Kepler, and Galileo Galilei had brought the whole structure of the universe into question; the harmonious system of crystalline spheres that Aristotle and Ptolemy had described for the Hellenistic world had given way to a central sun, oval orbits, and the terrifying suggestion that the universe itself might stretch on into shapeless infinity. The commanding central dome of St. Peter's no longer seemed so perfectly to represent the universe in microcosm, and Rome's claim to its status as the capital of Christendom no longer stood uncontested.

In 1600, Bruno, the most radical of these cosmologists, was burned at the stake; in 1633, Galileo, the most eloquent, was condemned to silence. Their ideas, however, persisted in Protestant lands, propagated by the medium of print. Even in Rome itself, the new science endured, even in apparent bastions of orthodoxy like the Jesuits' Roman College, where most of the professors of astronomy were probably Copernicans at heart. Under these circumstances, the mission of Roman architecture to capture souls and convert them burned brighter than ever; so did the zeal of Rome's architects. If ever architecture has set out to seduce and capture its beholders, it is the architecture of Baroque Rome, whose two chief creators—Gian Lorenzo Bernini (1598–1681) and Francesco Borromini (1599–1667)—were also bitter rivals.

Born within a year of one another, both men served as apprentices to Borromini's uncle Carlo Maderno during the final completion of St. Peter's, but otherwise they could not have been more different. Bernini, born in Florence of a Neapolitan family, trained as a sculptor in his father's studio; a child prodigy, he grew into a socialite of quicksilver temper and myriad interests; Borromini, who grew up among the Alps of what is now the Swiss

---

5. For the renewal of Rome in the Renaissance, see Portoghesi, *Roma del Rinascimento*; Stinger, *Renaissance in Rome*; Rowland, *Culture of the High Renaissance*.

canton of Ticino, began as a stonecutter, maturing slowly into a morose celibate who devoted his talents to architecture alone and died a suicide at the age of sixty-eight. Yet both turned the carving of stone in the service of God into an art form of incomparable sensuality.

Bernini always worked instinctively as a sculptor, even though statues like *Saint Teresa* (1647–1652) and *Blessed Ludovica Albertoni* (1671–1674) have been carefully placed within architectonic settings that he designed with no less care. Both of these extraordinary works approximate the sensation of religious rapture by likening it to sexual fulfillment, an analogy for which the writings of Teresa of Avila provided a richly suggestive starting point. Teresa, a shrewd, down-to-earth Spanish noblewoman who alternated her mystic experiences with clear-headed administrative decisions about her order, the Discalced Carmelites, described one of her recurrent visions in terms that Bernini exploited to the full:

> It pleased the Lord that I should sometimes see the following vision. I would see beside me, on my left hand, an angel in bodily form. . . . He was not tall, but short, and very beautiful, his face so aflame that he appeared to be one of the highest types of angel who seem to be all afire. They must be those who are called cherubim. . . . In his hands I saw a long golden spear and at the end of the iron tip I seemed to see a point of fire. With this he seemed to pierce my heart several times so that it penetrated to my entrails. When he drew it out, I thought he was drawing them out with it and he left me completely afire with a great love for God. The pain was so sharp that it made me utter several moans; and so excessive was the sweetness caused me by this intense pain that one can never wish to lose it, nor will one's soul be content with anything less. It is not bodily pain, but spiritual, though the body has a share in it—indeed, a great share. So sweet are the colloquies of love which pass between the soul and God that if anyone thinks I am lying I beseech God, in His goodness, to give him the same experience.[6]

Aside from putting the angel to the viewer's left rather than to Teresa's, Bernini translates the saint's description of her rapture into powerful physicality, a feat all the more remarkable because her hands, feet, and face are the only visible parts of her body (fig. 3).[7] The rest of her pain and joy are conveyed

---

6. Lavin, *Bernini and the Unity of Visual Arts*, 107.

7. See Fagiolo dell'Arco, "Bernini: 'Regista' del Barocco," 25–26; Lavin, *Bernini and the Unity of Visual Arts*, 77–145.

3. Gian Lorenzo Bernini, *The Ecstasy of Saint Teresa* (1645–52). Cornaro Chapel, S. Maria della Vittoria, Rome. (Erich Lessing/Art Resource, NY.)

entirely by marble drapery and the play of light that Bernini has effected with the use of a hidden window. Teresa's right foot curls around a spur of rock; her left hand hangs limp, almost entirely relaxed except for a suggested twitching of her fingers that makes the stone seem to tingle. Her lolling head and slack mouth contrast with the agitation of her heavy robe, which the mischievously smiling cherub has begun to lift away; although Teresa herself expresses doubt

4. Gian Lorenzo Bernini, *Beata Ludovica Albertoni* (1671–74). S. Francesco a Ripa, Rome.
(Scala/Art Resource, NY.)

about what kind of angel her visitor was, Bernini confirms her description of
him as "all afire," by aiming a beam of sunlight on him and carving his thin
robe in flamelike pleats; he is a cherub, Hebrew for "fiery." Teresa herself recognizes how closely her experience resembles sexual ecstasy, but she insists that
it was an entirely different sensation and that of the two, the spiritual rapture
is by far the more consuming; so, in Bernini's dramatic assemblage, the gilt
rays that shower down on her from heaven go far beyond any human climax.

At the very end of his life, Bernini designed his image of Blessed Ludovica
Albertoni (fig. 4) with a similarly dramatic side lighting (from a window that
has since been bricked up) that plunged the dying woman into a stark contrast
of dark and light—just at the moment, appropriately enough, when she meets
both death's absolute darkness and the absolute light of salvation (and Bernini,
well beyond the normal lifespan of a seventeenth-century man, must have
been well aware by this time of his own mortality).[8] Unlike the spent, languid

8. Fagiolo dell'Arco, "Bernini: 'Regista' del Barocco," 27; Perlove, *Bernini and the Idealization of
Death.*

5. Gian Lorenzo Bernini, *Fountain of the Four Rivers* (completed 1651).
Piazza Navona, Rome. (Author's photo.)

Teresa, Ludovica Albertoni writhes in her death throes, contorted in physical agony; but at the same time, she, too, welcomes a "sweetness caused by intense pain" with the prayerful gesture of her arms and the ecstatically agonized expression on her face. Like *Saint Teresa*, *Blessed Ludovica* conveys the feeling of heavenly release with the tiny patches of her exposed flesh, while her bodily anguish shows through the roiling movement of her clothes. Whether or not we ourselves can touch these sculptures, they both revel in texture (and though, ironically, "texture" is a word with no Italian equivalent, Bernini has mastered the concept all the same).

Bernini gave a sexual edge not only to ecstatic saints (and, notably, the portrait of his mistress, Costanza Bonarelli) but also to abstract nature. Between 1648 and 1651, by order of Pope Innocent X, he designed a fountain for the center of Piazza Navona in Rome, the centerpiece of which was an Egyptian obelisk rescued from the ruined Circus of Maxentius just outside the city walls on the Appian Way and erected again to honor the Jubilee Year of 1650 (figs. 5 and 6).

6. Gian Lorenzo Bernini, *Fountain of the Four Rivers*, detail. Piazza Navona, Rome.
(Author's photo.)

As with those for *Saint Teresa* and *Blessed Ludovica Albertoni*, this commission enjoined him to illustrate the workings of God in the world, the better to bind the emotions of viewers to the Catholic faith by the magic bonds of beauty. To create a work with an obelisk as its centerpiece, Bernini felt the need to collaborate with an Egyptologist, the Jesuit scholar Athanasius Kircher, who claimed to read Egyptian hieroglyphs (as well as twenty-three other languages, ancient and modern). Kircher helped Bernini restore the inscriptions on the obelisk's battered surface and explained to one and all what the carved texts might really mean.

His translation, of course, was pure fiction by present-day standards; Jean-Louis Champollion would not decipher the Rosetta Stone until 1822 (though when he did, he would use Kircher's books as a beginning).[9] Kircher declared that the ancient Egyptians had consigned a whole ancient tradition of wisdom and magic to the hieroglyphs: "Secret Symbols by which [they] might present the mysteries of divinity and the laws of Nature, so that they would be manifest

9. Champollion's books are in the Bibliothèque Nationale in Paris. For an evaluation of Kircher's role in the decipherment of the hieroglyphs, see Iversen, *Myth of Egypt and Its Hieroglyphs*; Adkins and Adkins, *Keys of Egypt*.

only to the wise, and those conspicuous for intelligence, [leaving] nothing attainable to the masses and to Idiots but wonderment."

One of these "laws of nature," to Kircher's mind, was the existence of a universal spermatic power that was projected to earth on the rays of the sun: "The whole mass of this solar globe is imbued, not with one single property, but rather with a certain universal seminal power (panspermatica quadam virtute), by means of which, as the nature of the various parts of the sun, in various ways, hides its riches within the hidden bowels of the Solar World, a fiery liquid, blended in various ways, touches things below by radiant diffusion...and produces various effects."[10] Obelisks, he declared, had served to attract this solar spermatic power in ancient Egypt; atop Bernini's *Fountain of the Four Rivers*, the Piazza Navona obelisk, as of 1651, was providing the same service in a Christian spirit. One wonders whether the golden rays of stucco sunshine that pour down on Bernini's *Saint Teresa* may not have been performing something of the same role, in which case they are at least as responsible for her ecstasy as the cherub's single, modest arrow.

The fiery Bernini's great rival, Francesco Borromini, was a big, melancholic man whose fixation on architecture is said to have consumed every other aspect of his life. Although he never joined a religious order, he maintained a rigorous celibacy, and he never carved any figures, human or animal, except as architectural ornament.[11] Yet however sophisticated his designs, with their intricate geometries and complex architectural detailing, they are both powerfully abstract and intensely sensuous. Trained as a stonecutter in the mountainous Swiss canton of Ticino, he insisted as fanatically as Bernini on the perfect execution of his designs, and his textures are no less remarkable than Bernini's, however differently they are deployed. The fruits and flowers that hang from the staircase at the Palazzo Carpegna (1643–1649) are as fat and fertile as the spilling cornucopias of the *Hypnerotomachia Poliphili*, but they are huge, so disconcertingly larger than life that they take on an overgrown vitality (and breed, among other living things, a baby, tucked under the abacus of the left-hand

10. "Hoc tibi certo persuasum habeas, totam hanc solaris globi molem, non una tantum facultate, sed panspermatica quadam virtute imbutam esse, qua quidem pro diversa diversarum partium solarium natura, intra abdita Solaris Mundi viscera divitias suas abscondente, humor igneus diversimode tinctus, per radiosam virtute varia et multiplici imbutam diffusionem inferiora attingit, et pro subiecti cuiusvis natura diversos effectus producit" (*Iter Exstaticum Coeleste*, 201).

11. On Borromini's personality, see Schütze, "L'architettura come esercizio morale," 312–18, with bibliography. Although Borromini owned a thousand books, we do not know their titles.

7. Francesco Borromini, Oratory of the Filippini (1637–50), window frame.
(Author's photo.)

column).[12] The broad cornice that overhangs his Collegio della Propaganda Fide (completed 1664) is hung with pomegranates ripened to bursting and ready to shower passersby with seeds—more "universal seminal power" shed from on high. Within the pediments that surmount the small doors in the corner of his glorious Sant'Ivo alla Sapienza, palm fronds bend gently within their architectural frames, caressing the moldings with the same teasing lightness as the wing from Goliath's helmet that strokes the inner thigh of Donatello's *David* in Florence (a motif he had anticipated already in his Oratory of the Filippine Order of 1637–50; fig. 7). It is clear from the silken curves of his moldings that Borromini loved architecture—the line of it, the texture, the play of light—but like his contemporaries he used its sensual attraction as a way to convey the supreme joy of meeting God. The basic symbolism of Sant'Ivo is revealed in a humble payment slip from 1653 that mentions "the descent of the Holy Spirit which brings true Wisdom" for a church that served as chapel for the University of Rome; the endless triangles in his first church commission, San Carlo alle Quattro Fontane, express the Holy Trinity.[13] The arcades of the side aisles

12. Connors, "Palazzo Carpenga," 30.

13. The telltale payment with "[la] venuta dello spirito santo che porti la vera Sapienza" is explained in Rice, "Pentecostal Meaning," 259–70, esp. 259; see also Scott, "S. Ivo alla Sapienza

in the Basilica of St. John Lateran (completed 1655) seem to be lifting away on cherubs' wings and leading the thoughts of the congregation to heaven. The senses have never been at once so abstract and so intensely literal. Borromini's architecture is, in short, as sexy as Bernini's *Saint Teresa*, testimony to an ecstatic sense of religion not as repression and guilt but as fulfillment of all five bodily senses and, in addition, a transcendent soul.

And yet these two designers, once colleagues, then enemies, go about their mission in almost diametrically opposite ways. Bernini melts one surface into another, as in his windows for Palazzo Montecitorio (circa 1650), where the frames seem to emerge from native rock as the rock in turn gives way to weeds, these, too, carved in stone. The fountain of Piazza Navona plays host not only to Bernini's carved weeds but also to the real weeds whose seeds nest in the holes of its travertine. Bernini's world, from its ecstatic saints passing between life and death (both the "little death" of love and the throes of real mortality) to its metamorphosing fountains, is made up of appearances and flux, of burgeoning fertility and implicit decay. Borromini keeps every line of his geometries intact: a molding is always a molding, an angel an angel, a curve a curve. Nothing in his architecture will ever break their integrity. If Bernini expresses energy by breaking down architecture into sculpture, or mineral into vegetable, Borromini conveys energy through geometry itself, bending flat walls into curved space and warping arches in three dimensions so that they bend in and out as well as over.[14] Some of his complex curves seem to have been drawn using a compass with a moving center, as on the facade for the church of Sant'Agnese in Agone (1650–1657).[15] The round arches over the windows of his Palazzo della Propaganda Fide (completed late 1664, fig. 8) look semicircular, but they actually bow inward, slightly past the halfway point, just enough to charge the shape with a taut energy, as if it might spring apart at any moment. With the same sense of contained force, the whole arch itself flares outward at the lower edges. And yet these tightly controlled forms also burst free from time to time, and when they do, the effect is so dramatic that Borromini's detractors called his work "bizarre": the spiral cupola of Sant'Ivo

---

and Borromini's Symbolic Language," 302–3; the classic presentation of the trinitarian imagery in San Carlo alle Quattro Fontane is Steinberg, *Borromini's San Carlo alle Quattro Fontane*.

14. See Jung, "Borromini e il 'foror mathematicus,'" 271–78; Camerota, "Architettura obliqua"; "Geometria"; "Scienze Naturali," 26–38, 317–23; Bösel, "Morfologia spaziale," 333–45; Simona, "Le geometrie del Borromini," 453–455.

15. I owe this observation to my father, F. Sherwood Rowland, and his scientist's eyes.

8. Francesco Borromini, Collegio della Propaganda Fide (completed 1664),
window frame. (Author's photo.)

(completed 1660) erupts in a travertine firestorm and flickers into pure air
(in the same upward surge as that of the huge cherubs of the Lateran Basilica, already mentioned above, whose flight suggests that the building itself is
lifting off). The interior of Sant'Ivo performs the same miracle by pure design;
insistent verticals and its precipitously tall space compel the eye upward to
the cupola, where the dove of the Holy Spirit flies against a field of light. First-
time visitors often gasp audibly (as, on occasion, do veterans); the old parish
priest could never keep himself from looking up repeatedly any better than
his congregation could. But Borromini also insisted that Sant'Ivo was a space
in which the Holy Spirit came down to meet the faithful; hence here, as with
Bernini's carefully staged sculptures of Saint Teresa and Blessed Ludovica (and
as elsewhere in his own buildings), he bathes the space in carefully channeled
showers of light.

In 1623, at about the time when Borromini arrived in Rome,[16] Galileo Galilei
wrote: "Philosophy is written in this great book that stands ever open before our

16. Borromini's arrival in Rome is now dated to sometime between 1619 and 1621; see Scotti
and Soldini, "Borromini milanese," 71. The passage from Galileo Galilei's *Il Saggiatore* of 1623 is
one of his most quoted; it can be found in Galilei, *Le Opere, Edizione Nationale*, 232.

eyes (I mean the universe), but it cannot be understood without first learning to understand the language and recognize the characters in which it is written. It is written in mathematical language, and the characters are triangles, circles, and other geometric figures; without these tools it is impossible for a human being to understand a word; [to be] without them is to wander aimlessly through a dark labyrinth." Although Galileo understood mathematics in a sophisticated sense, he was also, intentionally, repeating an ancient trope. Long before him, Pythagoras and Plato had insisted that the secrets of the universe, and thus of God, were couched in number and geometry, and the Platonic tradition in turn shaped Saint Paul's description of a Christian Church where measure is essential to the architecture of love: "Unto the measure of the stature of the fulness of Christ: that we ... speaking the truth in love, may grow up into him in all things, which is the head, even Christ: from whom the whole body, fitly joined together and compacted by that which every joint supplieth, according to the effectual working in the measure of every part, maketh increase of the body unto the edifying of itself in love."

In their very different ways, both Bernini and Borromini took Saint Paul at his word, creating a way, through art, of expressing love of the very highest order, in which, paradoxically, the heavy materials of stone sculpture and monumental architecture capture the moment when matter melts and the universe is reduced to its elemental passion and its elemental geometry.

ARCHITECTURES OF LOVE AND STRIFE

ANTHONY GRAFTON

Many men built papal Rome. Popes, cardinals, bankers, and diplomats imagined and paid for the city's new streets, squares, and palaces. Architects, engi-
neers, artists, and craftsmen carried out their plans. Together they transformed
a wasteland of swamps and pastures surrounding a labyrinth of narrow streets
lined with gloomy, squalid arcades into something that they—and we—could
genuinely see as a paradise on earth. The fountains with which they watered
dusty streets and squares still attract—and cool—crowds from around the world.
The obelisks they pieced together and raised to pierce the Roman skies still
punctuate and give order to the city's public space. Even now, Rome enchants,
as it enchanted the Viennese librarian Peter Lambeck when he visited the Piazza
Navona in 1662: "It made a delightful spectacle.... The water rose above the
splendid shell of the fountain, and since the underground outlets were shut,
it filled most of the Piazza. Waves came more than halfway up the carriages,
in which a vast throng of nobles drove around the obelisk, seeking relief from
the heat of summer. Where once upon a time men fought in the dust, they
nowadays play in the water."

Ingrid Rowland shows that the patrons and service providers who built this
Catholic wonderland by the Tiber used precise methods to attain specific goals.
They deployed every resource of form and contour, color and texture, that
ancient models and modern practices could suggest, in order to make their
city and their church irresistible. Often they succumbed even more rapidly
than the tourists to the charms that they themselves financed and devised.
When Pope Innocent X saw Bernini's *Fountain of the Four Rivers* play for the
first time in the Piazza Navona, he "became ecstatic"—mute testimony to the
powers of a sculptor who could make a living pope, as well as living stone, take
on the lineaments of gratified desire in public. No wonder that Lambeck, a

Protestant, fell under the spell of the city and the church's charms and became a Catholic.

Yet the Rome of the fifteenth through seventeenth centuries was no city of brotherly love—even if male tourists treated it as a sex capital and turned their carriages into observatories, in Montaigne's words, as they craned their necks to gawk at the courtesans displaying themselves at open windows. The triumphant Rome of Bernini and Borromini sincerely and beautifully embodied the powers of sacred and profane love. But it was also a self-consciously staged and dramatized reply to new forms of secular power that threatened the preeminence of Rome. Catholic and Protestant monarchs had refused to let the pope's ambassadors take part in the negotiations that settled the Thirty Years' War in 1648–49, since the pope no longer commanded substantial military or political resources. The Piazza Navona was, in part, a response to this challenge. Moreover, the larger Baroque city it belonged to was not the first version, or vision, of Rome designed chiefly to serve as a fortress against the enemies of the church.

Nicholas V, the mid-fifteenth-century pope who planned to transform the Borgo into a magnificent new Jerusalem, explained to the cardinals that he hoped both to provide "eternal testimonies" that would win devotion for the church and to protect her "against the foreign enemies and local rebels who continually conspired" against her authority. Nicholas did not succeed in making the Vatican into a new Solomon's Temple, as he had planned. But he did manage to rebuild the Castel S. Angelo, and he had the Roman rebel Stefano Porcari hanged from its battlements as a sign of the fate that awaited those who refused to accept the papacy's newly regained authority. Nicholas—like many of his successors—practiced tough love.

No one has shown more vividly than Rowland herself, in her classic study *The Culture of the High Renaissance*, that the new Rome of the Renaissance and the Baroque was in very large part the product of strife. The popes and the city struggled in each other's grasp like Laocoon and his serpents. Martin V, a pope from the great Roman family of the Colonna, started the city's Renaissance in the 1420s. He revived the ancient office of the *magistri viarum*, appointing members of the city's nobility to a commission and charging them to rid the streets of the "viscera, tripes, heads, feet, bones and skin" with which local fishmongers and butchers regularly filled them. Yet the very terms of this appointment reveal the distance between clean aesthetic ideals and smelly, messy realities. Great families like Martin's own, the Colonna, perpetually refused to play along with papal plans. So, less violently but more persistently, did the local clerics and tradesmen who liked their city as it was, smells and all. From the 1440s onward, popes tried to clear off the piazzas before the old Basilica of St. Peter and the Pantheon in the name of order, good taste, and sanitation. They found themselves balked again and again by the merchants whose livelihoods depended on their ability to flog fish and kitsch in their open markets—as well as by the cathedral canons who depended on the rents they collected from these merchants. It took decades before the narrow, dark streets of the old city, dominated by fortified towers and impossible to police, gave way to broad avenues and bright palaces. The papal reach certainly grew longer, in fits and starts, throughout this period—from the 1450s, when Nicholas V fortified the Capitoline and set the papal arms on its towers, to the 1580s, when the austere Franciscan pope Sixtus V expelled the courtesans, for a time, and made the unruly city a model of Counter-Reformation decorum. But the papal grasp never extended quite as far as Nicholas and Sixtus wished. The famous statue of Pasquino, a battered but handsome figure of Menelaus that the Romans decorated with squibs and satires against the powerful, regularly gave voice to the Romans' resentment of barbarians and Barberini alike. He and other grumpy, articulate sculptures spoke for many of the city's inhabitants, as they still do. Even in modern times, the Borgo—the area nearest to the Vatican—has notoriously colored itself red, not black.

Popes and planners, moreover, confronted more than opposition from the city: they also found themselves stuck with the faits accomplis of their predecessors and the obdurate individuality of their artists. The popes of this period, most of them scions of great families and all of them proud and individualistic, could never confine themselves to working out their predecessors' unfinished plans. Each tried to set his stamp on the city—or at least strategic parts of it. But that meant either leaving earlier projects unfinished, or transforming them in the course of execution—as St. Peter's, to name only the most famous example, changed shape again and again in the decades of its construction. It also meant trying to dominate brilliant painters, architects, and sculptors, few of whom shared Raphael's suave ability to mask his resolute independence from the suspicious glare of those he worked for. Julius II's quarrels with Bramante and Michelangelo are still famous: in their day, they were a more or less normal accompaniment to major artistic and architectural projects.

Rome, finally, was the cynosure of the world, the most vivid and brilliantly illuminated public stage in Europe. It drew talents toward it as a lantern attracts moths on a summer night. But many of the most brilliant men who came to Rome—from Leon Battista Alberti, Flavio Biondo, and Lorenzo Valla to Erasmus and Luther, and from Francesco Guicciardini to Giordano Bruno and Athanasius Kircher—saw visions and dreamed dreams of a very different church and city than the one they found. Alberti and Valla wished for a pre-Constantinian, austere Christian community, its churches pruned of fake antiquities. Bruno and Kircher imagined a magical, Egyptian Kunst- und Wunderkammer, its squares inhabited by talking statues. Through all the decades during which Guicciardini served the church, he hoped for a Hercules— at times, he thought Luther might play this role—who would cleanse its Augean stable of the church. Fast footwork, a grim sense of humor, and a firm mastery of Aesopian language saved most of these men from papal "hand grenades, assault troops, and the Inquisition," to quote Rowland. But nothing could save those who came, as Bruno did, as prisoners, from the death that awaited con- tumacious heretics. The presence of dissenters at every level helped to turn the city into a whispering gallery—an echo chamber in which cardinals sat at spyholes in their own palaces, listening to what their attendants said of them, while satirists, writers of newsletters, and preachers struggled to shape and control the flow of information in one of premodern Europe's liveliest public spheres.

In arguing that Rome was a city of strife, I do not mean to challenge the arguments Rowland puts forward in her wonderful essay but to draw out an implication that may not be obvious to those unfamiliar with the city and the period she describes. Love, in this world—love as imagined, for example, in Francesco Colonna's *Hypnerotomachia*—always came bearing a sword. The very title of Colonna's book—which its first English translator, Richard Dallington, rendered in 1592 as *The Strife of Love in a Dreame*—suggests that Eros could lead his votaries up some steep and rugged paths. Poliphilo, the protagonist, falls in love, or at least in lust, with many women, both of flesh and of stone. Ancient Eros certainly rules. At times, in fact, it seems that the slightest glimpse of Ghirlandaio hair or a pearly white foot in a sandal is enough to make Poliphilo go off like an espresso machine at breakfast time in an Italian city bar. But fulfillment never comes. Ruins remain ruins. Antiquity is always too distant, and too ruinous, to be reanimated. Nymphs of flesh and blood inflame Poliphilo to the brink of apoplexy. Yet even as his arteries snap like pipe stems, they offer him not the solace of their charms but elaborate medicines that will calm him down. Even Polia, the love of his life, disappears from his arms. All lovers, in this story's universe, are Petrarchists, left to rueful contemplation of the refined tortures that Eros inflicts on his votaries. In that sense—and only in that period sense—Rome genuinely was a city that stood for and taught love, both pagan and Christian. With that small clarification, Rowland's portrait stands. Sharp in its outlines and brilliant in its texture as a Renaissance medallion, it celebrates a city that can still inspire love—hopeless, painful, fearful love—in those who are forced to live, unlike her protagonists, in a dull, dead age.

———

READ BY MARK STRAND
AT THE EROTIKON SYMPOSIUM

TO A STRANGER | Walt Whitman

Passing stranger! you do not know how longingly I look upon you,
You must be he I was seeking, or she I was seeking, (it comes to me as of a
    dream,)
I have somewhere surely lived a life of joy with you,
All is recall'd as we flit by each other, fluid, affectionate, chaste, matured,
You grew up with me, were a boy with me or a girl with me,
I ate with you and slept with you, your body has become not yours only nor
    left my body mine only,
You give me the pleasure of your eyes, face, flesh, as we pass, you take of my
    beard, breast, hands, in return,
I am not to speak to you, I am to think of you when I sit alone or wake at
    night alone,
I am to wait, I do not doubt I am to meet you again,
I am to see to it that I do not lose you.

From *Leaves of Grass*, 1860/1867.

LOVE AT FIRST SIGHT / Wislawa Szymborska

They're both convinced
that a sudden passion joined them.
Such certainty is beautiful,
but uncertainty is more beautiful still.

Since they'd never met before, they're sure
that there'd been nothing between them.
But what's the word from the streets, staircases, hallways—
perhaps they've passed by each other a million times?

I want to ask them
if they don't remember—
a moment face to face
in some revolving door?
perhaps a "sorry" muttered in a crowd?
a curt "wrong number" caught in the receiver?
but I know the answer.
No, they don't remember.

They'd be amazed to hear
that Chance has been toying with them
now for years.
Not quite ready yet
to become their Destiny,

it pushed them close, drove them apart,
it barred their path,
stifling a laugh,
and then leaped aside.

There were signs and signals,
even if they couldn't read them yet.
Perhaps three years ago
or just last Tuesday

a certain leaf fluttered
from one shoulder to another?
Something was dropped and then picked up.
Who knows, maybe the ball that vanished
into childhood's thicket?

There were doorknobs and doorbells
where one touch had covered another
beforehand.
Suitcases checked and standing side by side.
One night, perhaps, the same dream,
grown hazy by morning.

Every beginning
is only a sequel, after all,
and the book of events
is always open halfway through.

XX / Mark Strand

Is it you standing among the olive trees
Beyond the courtyard? You in the sunlight
Waving me closer with one hand while the other

Shields your eyes from the brightness that turns
All that is not you dead white? Is it you
Around whom the leaves scatter like foam?

You in the murmuring night that is scented
With mint and lit by the distant wilderness
Of stars? Is it you? Is it really you

Rising from the script of waves, the length
Of your body casting a sudden shadow over my hand
So that I feel how cold it is as it moves

Over the page? You leaning down and putting
Your mouth against mine so I should know
That a kiss is only the beginning

Of what until now we could only imagine?
Is it you or the long compassionate wind
That whispers in my ear: alas, alas?

Reprinted, with permission, from *Dark Harbor* (New York: Knopf, 1993).

XXII | Mark Strand

It happened years ago and in somebody else's
Dining room. Madame X begged to be relieved
Of a sexual pain that had my name

Written all over it. Those were the days
When so many things of a sexual nature seemed to happen,
And my name—I believed—was written on all of them.

Madame X took my hand under the table, placed it
On her thigh, then moved it up. You would never know
What a woman with such blue eyes and blond hair
Was not wearing. Did I suffer,
Knowing that I was wanted for the wrong reasons?
Of course, and it has taken me years to recover.

We don't give parties like that anymore.
These days we sit around and sigh.
We like the sound of it, and it seems to combine

Weariness and judgment, even to suggest
No eggs for the moment, no sausages either,
Just come, take me away, and put me to bed.

Reprinted, with permission, from *Dark Harbor* (New York: Knopf, 1993).

TOUCH ME / Stanley Kunitz

Summer is late, my heart.
Words plucked out of the air
some forty years ago
when I was wild with love
and torn almost in two
scatter like leaves this night
of whistling wind and rain.
It is my heart that's late,
it is my song that's flown.
Outdoors all afternoon
under a gunmetal sky
staking my garden down,
I kneeled to the crickets trilling
underfoot as if about
to burst from their crusty shells;
and like a child again
marveled to hear so clear
and brave a music pour
from such a small machine.
What makes the engine go?
Desire, desire, desire.
The longing for the dance
stirs in the buried life.
One season only, and it's done.
So let the battered old willow
thrash against the windowpanes
and the house timbers creak.
Darling, do you remember
the man you married? Touch me,
remind me who I am.

THE EROTIC NIETZSCHE: PHILOSOPHERS WITHOUT PHILOSOPHY

ROBERT B. PIPPIN

Not ist nötig.

FRIEDRICH NIETZSCHE, «DIE FRÖHLICHE WISSENSCHAFT»

Nietzsche's most comprehensive term for the historical and psychological situation that in the present age requires a "transvaluation of values," is *nihilism*. Or at least that is the term that probably comes most quickly to mind, even though it does not appear much in his published works.[1] *Nihilism* is more properly a term of art in the *Nachlass*, but the problem that it evokes—What is it that provokes or requires a transvaluation of values?—whatever one calls it, is certainly frequently addressed by Nietzsche, often with great literary and rhetorical flourishes: the death of God, the twilight of idols, nausea and a

An earlier version of this essay appeared as "Morality as Psychology, Psychology as Morality: Nietzsche, Eros, and Clumsy Lovers," in *Nietzsche's Postmoralism: Essays on Nietzsche's Prelude to Philosophy's Future*, edited by Richard Schact (New York: Cambridge University Press, 2001); reprinted with the permission of Cambridge University Press.

I am grateful to participants in discussions of this essay at two conferences: "Nietzsche, Value and 'Revaluation'" at the University of Illinois, Urbana-Champaign, in October 2000, organized by Richard Schacht, and "Erotikon" at the University in Chicago in March 2001, organized by Thomas Bartscherer and Katia Mitova. I am especially indebted to my colleague Eric Santner for his very helpful commentary at the latter conference and to Jim Porter for his thoughtful comments on an earlier draft.

1. Apart from a few references in *On the Genealogy of Morals* and *The Antichrist*. I discuss the link between the death of God/nihilism problem and the problem of Nietzschean desire in more detail in "Love and Death in Nietzsche" (which relies on and repeats some of the quotations and analysis presented here).

potentially fatal illness,[2] bows that have lost their tension, human archers who have lost sight of a goal, an enervating contentment, the emergence and dominance of "the last men," a simple fatigue, the "weariness of man,"[3] and so forth. But the surface meanings of these claims about what necessitates a transvaluation have suggested many different sorts of provocations and so raise questions about how Nietzsche wants us to understand at the most general level the conditions possible now for the success of that activity he seemed to treat as identical to a distinctly human living: esteeming, *schätzen*, valuing. ("Man," Zarathustra says, "means esteemer.")[4]

On one hand, the problem of nihilism can look like a problem of knowledge, or at least of reasonable belief. What had once seemed known, or worthy of belief, now seems a lie, unworthy of belief. A typical version of this view of nihilism as a crisis of knowledge or reasonable belief is the following from the *Nachlass*: "What has happened, at bottom? The feeling of valuelessness was reached with the realization that the overall character of existence may not be interpreted by means of the concept of 'aim,' the concept of 'unity,' or the concept of 'truth.' Existence has no goal or end; any comprehensive unity in the plurality of events is lacking; the character of existence is not true, is false. One simply lacks any reason for convincing oneself that there is a true world."[5] Such calmly cognitivist terms suggest an anthropologist watching the disenchanting enlightenment of a primitive tribe and so appeal to such double-edged enlightenment as the best explanation for how we have come to be the first civilization that must live self-consciously without any confidence that we "know" what civilized life is for, without "the truth."[6]

On the other hand, especially when Nietzsche is trying to draw a distinction between what he calls a passive and an active nihilism, what we have come to claim to know or to believe, while important, is not the whole or the chief issue. "Active" nihilism is interpreted as a "sign of increased *power* of spirit"; "passive" nihilism, as "decline and recession of the *power* of spirit."[7] In passages like these, Nietzsche is more likely to say that nihilism results when we are threatened with the impossibility of willing at all, of fulfilling

---

2. Nietzsche, *Will to Power*, 12, 24. 4. Nietzsche, *Zarathustra*, bk. 1, p. 15.

3. Nietzsche, *Genealogy*, bk. 1, p. 12. 5. Nietzsche, *Will to Power*, sec. 12A, p. 13.

6. One reason why Nietzsche's thought has become more and more relevant: "the West" now lives for the first time since the advent of political modernity without either the specter or the beacon (depending on one's point of view) of any revolutionary aspiration.

7. Nietzsche, *Will to Power*, sec. 22, p. 17.

the conditions necessary for decision and commitment, "value." We choose instead to try to regard ourselves as *willing* "nothing," as bravely insisting on such an absence, and so are able to construe the realization as a result of our "active" self-enlightenment, righteousness, and honesty and not as a passive, merely endured fate. Indeed many of the passages that seem to appeal to worthiness of belief alone as the source of the crisis conclude by suggesting instead that nihilism is at bottom a matter of *strength or weakness of will*. The "feeling of valuelessness" passage just quoted concludes by saying that the categories "which we used to project some value into the world, *we* pull out again; so the world looks valueless."[8]

The force of these passages suggests a familiar, skeptical attitude about the practical implications of any such putative intellectual enlightenment. For one thing, the emerging modern consensus in European high culture about the disenchantment of nature, skepticism about teleology, and a spreading atheism are all, on their own, as assertions about the facts, motivationally or practically inert. This is so because, according to Nietzsche, contra the cognitivist formulations, it is extremely unlikely that belief in any such first principle of value or objective moral order originally or subsequently played any decisive role in the commitment to a value or in keeping faith with it. The justifiability of a belief is not, in itself, one of the practically necessary conditions of value (although, as we shall see, in special circumstances it may become so). Nietzsche is quite explicit about this in *The Gay Science*:

> The mistake made by the more refined among them [the modern historians of morality] is that they uncover and criticize the perhaps foolish opinions of a people about morality, or of humanity about all human morality—opinions about its origin, religious sanction, the superstition of free will and things of that sort—and then suppose that they have criticized the morality itself. But the value of a command, "thou shalt" is still fundamentally different from and independent of such opinions about it and the weeds of error that may have overgrown it—just as certainly as the value of a medication for a sick person is completely independent

8. Ibid., 13 (my emphasis). This is like a passage from *The Twilight of the Idols*: "Whoever does not know how to lay his will into things, at least lays some meaning into them: that means that he has faith that they already obey a will" (18). And compare, "That it is the measure of strength to what extent we can admit to ourselves, without perishing, the merely apparent character, the necessity of lies" (Nietzsche, *Will to Power*, 15). Likewise: "It is a measure of the degree of strength of will to what extent one can do without meaning in things, to what extent one can endure to live in a meaningless world because one organizes a small portion of it oneself" (ibid.).

of whether he thinks about medicine scientifically or the way old women do. Even if a morality has grown out of an error, the realization of this fact would not as much as touch the problem of its value. (345)

For another thing, claims about value do not, for Nietzsche, report the discovery of moral facts, but express, enact, and partially realize a commitment. Accounting for, giving a genealogy of, such commitments (and the various conditions necessary for these to serve as ways of life) can never be completed by an inventory of theoretical beliefs; something else must always be added. It has seemed to many modern philosophers that such an addition must be a kind of *subjective* reaction—an outpouring of sympathy, a recoil in pain, the stirring of a passion—and therewith an imposition or projection of a "value" as an embrace or rejection of some situation. This is not Nietzsche's position, but for now we need only note that while we can base reasons to act or to undertake commitments on such beliefs, the strength or weakness of the theoretical claim about "what there is" is not itself an *independent* factor in such commitments, in such acts of valuing. Acting is *negating* what there is and so presumes some sort of experience where some state of affairs becomes unacceptable, not merely noted; it is experienced as something-that-must-be-overcome. Acting in the light of this unacceptability is "acting for a value," and what we are in effect looking for is the source and meaning of such unacceptability in the absence of any notion of a natural completion or telos, natural law, common human nature, or some objective ideal or divine legislator. (This is partly the problem with our pale atheists. They dogmatically believe that the absence of God in itself *matters*; that a "faith" of sorts can be made of this denial. It mattering to them, their *being* atheists, is a reflection of some other lack or need or fear unthought by the atheists.)

Whatever else nihilism and the death of God involve, then, they involve this problem of value. So what *does* "touch the problem" of value? The passages we have been citing suggest strength of will, resolve, power, and courage; they focus on the problem of strong and weak will and have long been part of the canon of quotations cited in "existentialist" readings of Nietzsche (of a Kierkegaardean "leap" or Sartrean "condemned to freedom" variety).[9]

9. Moreover, adding to the plausibility of the "strength of will" interpretation is the fact that for Nietzsche there are no direct practical consequences, and hardly any nihilistic consequences, from any intellectual disillusionment. Anyone who thinks some sort of action would therewith be required or rendered impossible is himself willing that consequence, creating it, not

This duality (treating nihilism as either a problem of belief or of will power) is of a piece with a more familiar, very general tension in interpretations of Nietzsche: that is, the tension between those who focus on a doctrinal Nietzsche, with radically new answers to traditional problems, and those who insist on a wholly rhetorical, much more literary Nietzsche, fiercely resistant to alldoctrine. According to this latter Nietzsche, civilizations should be understood as collectively projected and sustained fantasies of value and importance, fantasies that have an essentially psychological origin and a kind of organic "life" and "death" in unceasing repetitions, requiring periodically some new master rhetorician and fantasy maker.[10] Every so often, as a matter of luck, some such value-legislator, a Sophocles, Socrates, St. Paul, Goethe, or Nietzsche, is found. And so too the familiar dialectic in understanding Nietzsche: the doctrinalists or naturalists or metaphysicians of the will to power look too much like the dogmatists Nietzsche clearly sweepingly rejects (they still evince a naive confidence in the value of truth); the philosopher of will and rhetoric looks like a doctrinalist *malgré lui*, not able to keep from asserting a doctrine about rhetoric and rhetoricality.

Our original question was, What provokes the unsustainability of an interconnected set of values: morality, religion, and faith in the beneficence of enlightenment or the "value of truth"? Why, it might be formulated, did agreement in a form of life fail? Even though the considerations discussed above are sketchy and incomplete, it is already clear that Nietzsche is not likely suggesting as answers that (a) we discovered that our metaphysics and religion were false or that (b) we lost our nerve and could not muster the strength of will to "posit," subjectively, new values.[11]

---

inferring it. As Nietzsche says frequently throughout the published and unpublished works: "One interpretation has collapsed; but because it was considered *the* interpretation it now seems as if there were no meaning at all in existence, as if everything were in vain" (*Will to Power*, sec. 55, p. 35).

10. For a more detailed discussion of the category of "psychology" as employed by Nietzsche, see Pippin, "Morality as Psychology."

11. At this point we could just leave it at that and treat Nietzsche as an interesting example of the still unsolved post-Kantian problem that looms as his greatest legacy to modern philosophy—that is, the great difficulty in thinking together coherently the emerging third-person or naturalist perspectives on morality and all normativity, with any recognizable, apparently irreducible first-person or agent perspective. The "sideways on" perspective was of course developing with very great rapidity in the nineteenth century as the modern social sciences—psychology, sociology, and anthropology—all roared into action. Together with philosophical movements

What I want to suggest at this point is that we treat the phenomenon of nihilism in a way closer to Nietzsche's images and figures and tropes, many of which were cited at the outset of this essay: images of death, decay, and illness, the absence of tension, a "sleep" of the spirit (he sometimes claims that what is needed now is an ability to dream without having to sleep), and, perhaps the most intuitive metonymy of failed desire, boredom. These images suggest that the problem of nihilism does not consist in a failure of knowledge or in a failure of will, but in a *failure of desire*, the flickering out of some erotic flame. Noting how often and with what significance Nietzsche refers to life and the "perspective of life" as the issue of an erotic striving, noting what makes possible the origination of such a wanting, and noting what sustains it and the sacrifices it calls for, and so forth, casts a completely different light on the nature of the nihilism crisis and on what Nietzsche regards as a possible way out of it. This approach frames all the issues differently, especially since the failure of desire can be baffling, quite mysterious, not something that, in some other sense, we ever "want" to happen, as mysterious as the issue of how one might address such a failure.

Some of these erotic images are well known because they occur at the beginnings of his most well known books. "Truth is a woman," and "philosophers are clumsy lovers" (*Beyond Good and Evil*); Zarathustra "goes under" because "he loves man" (*Thus Spoke Zarathustra*); "where your treasure is, there will your heart be also" (the beginning of *On the Genealogy of Morals*). And there are the rich associations of *The Gay Science* (*Die fröhliche Wissenschaft*) itself; *gaya scienza*, with its evocation of the *gai saber*, a troubadour or warrior-poet who produced essentially lyrics or love poems, whose main claim to knowledge was of erotics.[12] (All show that Nietzsche is also inherently claiming as his subject the one thing Socrates ever claimed to know: eros.) In fact *The Gay Science* as a book is so important because it represents Nietsche's first concentrated presentation

---

like naturalism and historicism, and of course Nietzsche himself, these developments threatened the authority of any claim to normative knowledge, or at the very least challenged any easy connection between any such putative knowledge and any motives for action. While one may come to believe that one's post-Christian values are the result of the slavish nature produced by one's slavish culture, in deciding what to do, one cannot "wait" for one's slavish nature to do its thing. One must decide; one cannot somehow let the decision happen. And no rhetorical call to arms, no invocation of the will is of much help and cannot count as the appropriate response to our suddenly valueless world.

12. See Pippin, "Gay Science and Corporeal Knowledge."

of affirmative postphilosophic activity after he had abandoned the so-called romantic fantasy of a Wagnerian revival. There is now to be some new form of reflective engagement with the world and with others. The question at issue in such engagement is always the question of value, but at the heart of that question is the erotic issue, and all of this somehow is what the *gai saber* knows. A gay science, in other words, is a new way of thinking about value, a new kind of thinking activity and therewith valuing, but one intelligible only if we understand its unique goal and why that goal has become important, why we now strive for it.

Some of the erotic images repeat, become like motifs in Nietzsche's work. In *Thus Spoke Zarathustra*, Zarathustra announces the advent of nihilism as an erotic problem: "Alas the time is coming when man will no longer shoot the arrow of his longing beyond man, and the string of his bow will have forgotten how to whir" (17). In the preface to *Beyond Good and Evil*, he notes that our long struggle with, and often opposition to and dissatisfaction with, our own moral tradition, European Christianity, has created a "magnificent tension of the spirit the like of which never yet existed on earth: with so tense a bow we can now shoot for the most distant goals." But, he goes on, the "democratic enlightenment" sought to "unbend" such a bow, "to bring it about that the spirit would no longer experience itself so easily as a 'need'" (3). This latter formulation coincides with a wonderfully lapidary expression in *The Gay Science*. In discussing "the millions of Europeans who cannot endure their boredom and themselves," he notes that they would even welcome "a craving to suffer" and so "to find in their suffering a probable reason for action, for deeds." In sum: "neediness is needed"! (Not ist nötig).[13] (One of Nietzsche's most striking formulations of the death of desire occurs in *Ecce Homo*, when he notes what is happening to us as "one error after another is coolly placed on ice; the ideal is not refuted—it freezes to death.")[14]

Attending to this erotic problem in Nietzsche should also help free us from the grip of the image that has probably the greatest hold on the imagination of Nietzsche's modern readers, that of a world discovered to be intrinsically valueless and thus calling for the spontaneous creation and injection of value by creative subjects, thereby provoking a kind of crisis of conscience (nihilism), a despairing that we, frail, finite creatures that we are, could do that. (This is

13. Nietzsche, *Gay Science*, 117.

14. In Nietzsche, *Genealogy*, 284. Trying to "refute" an ideal is called an "idealism" (a faith in the autonomy of ideals) and is rejected (ibid.).

the most frequent combination of the cognitive and volitional elements previously noted.) But from the "erotic" point of view, all such considerations of what Nietzsche is after start much too far downstream. Rendering a possible state of character or society actually valuable would be being able somehow to render it desirable.[15] It would be to be able to create a longing for such an object or to find others in whom a possible spark of such longing could be found and fanned. Such a possibility is hard to imagine, since no subject, however strong willed, could simply inject such erotic value "into" the world from a position "outside" it like this. Any such desire can only be found and inspired and sustained *in* a certain sort of world, a world where already some intense dissatisfaction can be balanced by an aspiration at home in that very world, a world, in other words, lovable enough to inspire as well as frustrate.[16] Consider this summation of the issue (a passage from *The Gay Science* that also renders pretty irrelevant most of Heidegger's *Auseinandersetzung* with Nietzsche as well as the subjectivist/projection, neo-Humean readings of Nietzsche on value): "The whole pose of 'man *against* the world,' of man as a 'world-negating' principle, of man as the measure of the value of things, as judge of the world who in the end places existence itself upon the scales and finds it wanting—the monstrous insipidity of this pose has finally come home to us and we are sick of it. We laugh as soon as we encounter the juxtaposition of 'man and world,' separated by the sublime presumption of the little word 'and'" (286–87).

Passages about eros and about the worldliness of eros have not of course been wholly ignored, but they are often folded into a general discussion of Nietzsche's views on the body, his naturalism, and what he often refers to as the problem of instincts. And there is no particular reason not to see this emphasis on constant, powerfully motivating, human longing (or the enervating experience of its failure) as an aspect of what Nietzsche talks about elsewhere as instinctual forces (or their absence). He began his career with *The Birth of Tragedy*, apparently positing elemental longings or drives, either for the

---

15. Obviously for a Kantian moral theorist, the assumed premise here—that actions conceived as motivated by "pure practical reason" and in no way responsive to desire are impossible—is a questionable one. And there might be other ways of moderating the strict dualism between impartial rationality and partial desire (as in Schiller's and Hegel's treatments). But for the sake of this discussion I proceed under Nietzsche's assumptions, noting only that his position on the centrality of desire, or some erotic attachment to an ideal, certainly need not be egoistic or, in the conventional sense, a species of ethical "naturalism." He would clearly regard such a limitation as base, venal, low-minded.

16. On this topic, cf. the discussion by Lear, *Love and Its Place in Nature*, 132–55.

destruction of form and individuation and for a self-less, Dionysian indeter-minacy, or for determinacy, form, and clarity. He notes also a longing for an "animal" forgetfulness that required millennia of pain and training to over-come, such that we could have new longings and become animals capable of keeping promises; he describes an unavoidable, instinctual striving to render suffering meaningful, and so forth; not to mention that apparently elemental drive: the will to power.

But a wholly naturalistic account would be much too hasty here. The very multiplicity and range of the different possible drives appealed to, and the fact that Nietzsche's accounts of prevolitional drives and instincts are often as much historical as organic (tied essentially to a specific historical self-understanding), indicate already that the basic question for him has remained interpretive, a question about meaning; the basic response, a matter of Bildung (culture), not causality. (So, any question about some presumed Nietzschean ultimate explainer, like *Macht*, or power, must always leave room open for the prior and decisive question of what counts as having power or exercising it.) For example, Nietzsche notes in *The Gay Science* that all love has to be *learned*: "Even those who love themselves will have learned it in this way; for there is no other way. Love too has to be learned" (sec. 334). He does not mention here what he stresses in "Schopenhauer as Educator," a difficulty that suggests a tragic pathos to this position: "It is hard to create in anyone this condition of intrepid self-knowledge because it is impossible to teach love; for it is love alone that can bestow on the soul, not only a clear, discriminating and self-contemptuous view of itself, but also the desire to look beyond itself and to seek with all its might for a higher self as yet still concealed from it."[17]

The thought beginning to emerge throughout these passages is paradox-ical—that we can desire, long, strive (suffer from some burden of "excess," of too much meaning, too many possibilities) without knowing or ever finding what would satisfy that longing, without the experience of a determinate or natural lack or gap that cries out for satisfaction. We "learn" in some sense to want and feel in some way, but it is forever impossible to formulate what would ultimately satisfy such a polymorphic longing, relieve the distress caused by such a burden. Yet what Nietzsche is getting at is all phenomenologically quite familiar, as familiar as the *essential* ambiguity of the great "quest" objects of modern literature and the irony of those quests, those hopes for resolution and completion and redemption: Quixote's adventure and windmills, Tennyson's

---

17. Nietzsche, *Untimely Meditations*, 163.

Holy Grail, Emma Bovary's desperate romance, the White Whale, the Ring of the Niebelungen, Godot, K's trial, Pynchon's V, and so forth.

But this multiply realizable interpretive activity, I should hasten to add, is not at all a reflective activity directed *at* some brute, somatic event that we can isolate, whose simple causes we can investigate. While there *are* clearly desires provoked exogenously by natural objects, while it is clear that the world in its cold and heat and weather and scarcity provokes a very determinate dissatisfaction with and so a desire to overcome these natural limitations, clear that there are fixed human drives, there is another level, the one Nietzsche is interested in, on which human existence is plagued by a deeper, categorically different dissatisfaction and so a longing that is not just such a *response to a lack.* (In the familiar words of parents everywhere: we "*make ourselves miserable*" and could in a sense, *stop* doing so. But that would be to live like last men. There is no argument in Nietzsche that we should not so live, and Nietzsche seems more interested in the question of "under what conditions" his interlocutors would find such a life shameful rather than successful.) So, at this level, such dissatisfactions cannot be said to have simple causes or determinate objects. Rather we continue to try to express a dissatisfaction we also cannot pin down and so cannot satisfy, even though without this self-induced dissatisfaction, we *would* be last men, for that (that absence of such dissatisfaction or the self-contempt that, according to Nietzsche, springs from "love") is precisely their state. They are, in other words, *happy.* Such dissatisfaction exists then, in a very mediated sense, only "because of us," because of what we will not settle for, not because of our nature or transactions with the world. Such a desire for "more" is nothing but our determinate expression of a dissatisfaction, and yet that determinacy can never be fixed with certainty and can no longer be tied to transcendent aspirations. Thus, from *The Gay Science*, "when a strong stimulus is experienced as pleasure or displeasure, this depends on the interpretation of the intellect which, to be sure, generally does this work without rising to our consciousness" (184). And especially in *Human, All Too Human*: "Since we have for millennia looked upon the world with moral, aesthetic, and religious demands ... the world has gradually *become* so remarkably variegated, terrible, soulful, meaningful, it has acquired color—but we have been the colorists" (20).

There *is* a gap, an experience of not being something or other, but *we* open up that possibility and hold it open by means of these expressions of dissatisfaction, even though we do not do so in some individual, intentional, volitional sense. There *isn't*, say, a legitimate authority or distributive justice problem waiting to be found by philosophers. There is such a problem only if philosophers find a way of picturing "life" such that life is lacking without addressing such problems. They don't impose such a view onto life, because there isn't, properly speaking, a life to lead without such a yearning. In the language of the classical German philosophical tradition, we would call this dissatisfaction and longing a "self-negation," that is, a dissatisfaction *due to us*, a *refusal* on our part ever to rest content, rather than a reaction to a natural lack. (Even righteous subjection to the moral law in Kant, for example, becomes an object of striving, a matter of possible perfectibility, only because, as Kant says, we are the "authors" of such a law; we subject *ourselves* to its constraint.)

I think Nietzsche is trying to suggest with his somatic and erotic images that human experience is, at its core, at a level deeper than everyday dissatisfactions and desires, a great longing, even though not a determinate lack that must be filled. The odd and somewhat mawkish image Nietzsche often uses to make this point is that of a bee or hive overloaded with honey. The image suggests desires well beyond any need, or a surfeit or abundance of desires (one might even say, desires for ever "more," for "excess" meaning) that can be communicated and shared.[18] (In this sense, although Nietzsche would often poke fun at Kant's account of aesthetic pleasure, it could fairly be said that the post-Kantian understanding of aesthetic experience as preconceptual and sensual, but not "interested," desire satisfaction is one source for this image of desire in excess, not responsive to a missing fulfillment or a need, but a surplus outside of any calculability.) The generosity and even potential frivolity in decorating, beautifying, and so forth, even at the expense of prudence and sober self-interest, is, Schiller maintained, the first manifestation of a desire that exceeds any logic of calculation. Consider from Schiller's *Letters*: "Not content with what simply satisfies Nature and meets his need, he demands superfluity; to begin with, certainly, merely a superfluity *of* material, in order to conceal from his desires their boundaries, in order to assure his enjoyment beyond the existing

18. Compare this passage from *Twilight of the Idols*. "The genius in work and deed is necessarily a squanderer (Verschwender): that he squanders himself, that is his greatness. The instinct of self-preservation is suspended, as it were; the overpowering pressure of outpouring forces forbids him any such care and caution. People call this 'self-sacrifice' and praise his 'heroism,' his indifference to his own well-being, his devotion to an idea, a great cause, a fatherland: without exception, misunderstandings. He flows out, he overflows, he uses himself up; he does not spare himself— and this is a calamitous, involuntary fatality, no less than a river's flooding the land. Yet because so much is owed to such explosives, much has also been given them in return: for example a higher kind of morality. After all, that is the way of human gratitude: it *misunderstands* its benefactors" (sec. 9, p. 44).

need, but soon a superfluity *in* the material, an aesthetic supplement, in order to be able to satisfy his formal impulse also, in order to extend his enjoyment beyond every need."[19]

In the *Nachlass*, Nietzsche tries frequently to distinguish his position from what he considers the neediness and nonaesthetic status of "romanticism": "Is art a consequence of dissatisfaction with reality? Or an expression of gratitude for happiness enjoyed? In the former case, romanticism; in the latter, aureole and dithyramb (in short art of apotheosis): Raphael too belongs here; he merely had the falsity to deify what looked like the Christian interpretation of the world. He was grateful for existence when it was not specifically Christian."[20]

And this distinction between romanticism (and romantic pessimism, Schopenhauer, Wagner) and what Nietzsche favors, "art of apotheosis," is said to be based on a "fundamental distinction." "I ask in each individual case 'has hunger or superabundance become creative here,'" and he affirms an art he says is based on "gratitude and love," not hunger. "The full and bestowing" is what he affirms, not "the seeking, desiring."[21] (He makes the same distinction in *The Gay Science*, distinguishing between two kinds of sufferers: those who suffer from "over-fullness of life," and "romantics," who suffer from the "impoverishment of life.")[22]

As noted, part of Nietzsche's "experiment" is to suggest that such an "excess" erotic insistence can come to seem as ennobling as the equally "useless" impulse for aesthetic production; indispensable in a life being human, but which, paradoxically (*the same paradox* we have been encountering all along) cannot be undertaken *for* that reason, because we "need" it "in order to be" human.

This thought—that human nature is such as to deny *itself* satisfaction (in an evolutionary metaphor, human beings have evolved to be beyond any natural niche or function; everything about them that is distinctly human is evolutionary excess, waste)—is a theme that resonates with many philosophers whom Nietzsche would disown, but who form an exclusive club. It is the founding

19. Schiller, *Aesthetic Education*, 132. Cf. especially the insightful use made of Schiller in Gerhardt, "Zu Nietzsches Frühem Programm," especially p. 67.

20. Nietzsche, *Will to Power*, sec. 845, p. 445.

21. Ibid., sec. 846, sec. 843, pp. 445–46.

22. Nietzsche, *Gay Science*, sec. 370, p. 328. See also the preface to the second edition of *Gay Science*, where Nietzsche distinguishes a philosophy based on need from one that understands itself as simply a "beautiful luxury," the "voluptuousness of a triumphant gratitude" (33–34).

thought of a decisive strand of modern philosophy—Rousseau's thought, and thanks to Rousseau it shows up in Kant's account of our "unsocial sociability" (ungesellige Geselligkeit), in Hegel's account of the nonnatural (or "excessive") claim of the other for recognition, and in Marx's famous account of the social (not natural) significance of organized labor. It shows up for different reasons in Freud's account of the harshness of the repression of natural (essentially Oedipal) desire and so our self-division (the self-division that makes us human, allows it to be said that we lead lives, rather than merely exist or suffer our existence). (Hegel also says in his aesthetics lectures that human existence itself is a self-inflicted "wound," but one which we can also "heal" ourselves.)[23]

The somewhat mythic picture here is straightforward: the natural world is a world without genuine individuality (just mere particularity, in Hegel's language); it is formless, brutal, chaotic, and indifferent, and to live a human life is (and essentially is *only*) to *resist* this, to *make* oneself anything other than this, all because we will not accept it and have found a way to provoke such dissatisfaction in others and for posterity. (Individuality is always a kind of fragile, unstable, threatened *achievement*, not an original state of being.)[24] We know, in other words, where we don't want to be, what would be a kind of spiritual death, without knowing in effect where to go. (And again, it all also means we *can* cease to resist, become "last men" because barely human at all once this tension is lost.)

The best example of what I have been talking about occurs in section 300 of *The Gay Science*. Nietzsche first claims that necessary preconditions for modern science were the "magicians, alchemists, astrologers and witches" because their "promises and pretensions" "*had to create* (schaffen mussten) a thirst, a hunger, a taste for hidden and forbidden powers" and that much more had to be promised than could be delivered so that this frustration would sustain the scientific enterprise until, much later, the promise could be fulfilled in the "realm of knowledge" (240). Then, in comments on religion, he goes on (or goes so far as) to say that man had to *learn* even to "experience a hunger and thirst for himself" and so to learn to "find satisfaction and fullness in himself" (ibid.). Religious ways of life, in other words, gave this surfeit of human desire a form and a goal; they did not respond to but rather opened up the

---

23. Hegel, *Aesthetics*, 8.

24. Cf. chapter 6 of Lear, *Love and Its Place in Nature*. I consider this position on individuality (as a social and psychological achievement) an essential theme in post-Kantian German philosophy. See Pippin, "What Is the Question for Which Hegel's 'Theory of Recognition' Is the Answer?"

experience of a gap between me and myself, made it possible for me to experience myself as somehow dissatisfying such that I had to become a self, become who I am. And all this just as astronomy does not do better what astrologers attempted; it realizes a desire to know about the stars that had to be originated and sustained, rather than responded to. His next remark is the most elliptical and, as is usual with Nietzschean imagery like this, it creates the very thing it describes: an aspiration to more meaning: "Did Prometheus have to fancy (wähnen), first that he had stolen the light and then pay for that—before he finally discovered that he had created the light by coveting the light and that not only man but also the god was the work of his own hands and had been mere clay in his hands? All mere images of the maker—no less than fancy, the theft, the Caucasus, the vulture, and the whole tragic *Prometheia* of all seekers after knowledge" (ibid.). *Prometheus created the light by coveting it* is the phrase that says it all; the incapacity to rest content, the impulse to give away, is treated by Nietzsche as a kind of luxurious magnanimity and generosity of spirit. The dissatisfaction Prometheus felt was not the occasion of this generosity but its result, and the determinate meaning of what happened, the injustice of Zeus, the meaning of his suffering represent extensions and consequences of the kind of dissatisfaction that he opened up and held open; the excess meaning he creates by his act and that he promises to be able to explain.

One can easily lose one's hold on these suggestions; looking at things "from the point of view of life" can make what we want, perhaps arbitrarily and accidentally want, look like a condition of what we accept as valuable, and that can seem like wishful thinking. And so we seem to be sliding back to some version of the radical rhetorical reading, with meaning and value originally projected or imposed. Moreover, other philosophers, notably Hegel, also began with the assumption that "the religion of modern times is 'God is dead'" (*Glauben und Wissen*). Hegel was happy enough to concede that modern bourgeois life, with its distributed subjectivity or radically divided labor and mundane preoccupations is *prosaic* (his most frequent characterization in the *Aesthetics* lectures), without any possible heroism, so devoid even of beauty, so "liberated" from natural sensibility as to render art itself marginal, no longer of world-historical significance, and religion a merely civic experience. But one can understand Hegel as having also wagered that the realization of freedom embodied in modern law, and modern social institutions like the family and market economy was, one might say, consolation enough; that allegiance (or erotic attachment) to this ideal was psychologically and socially sufficient to sustain and reproduce a form of life. One way of summarizing what we have been discussing is to note simply that Nietzsche thought that a bad wager; that the evidence was everywhere that the ideal had become a self-serving venality, and illusions about it had helped produce widespread chronic social pathologies. So far though, in the passages we have looked at, he seems simply to be painting an alternative antibourgeois picture (of nobility, hierarchy of rank, courage, and so forth) and assuming that we could "choose" it instead.

But we need to remember that the theme in these passages is eros, not will or spontaneous creativity, and that such attempts to inspire a kind of longing, to break the hold of need and fear and inspire a kind of reckless generosity (e.g., like that of Prometheus), can fail, and that it is very hard to understand what kind of erotic promises will get a grip and why. It is also one of the reasons there is little in the way of a programmatic response to nihilism in Nietzsche's texts. The failure of desire and its experiential manifestations in everyday life—boredom, loneliness, and fatigue—are very hard to diagnosis and extremely hard to respond to. (The pathos of romantic failure, the ever possible sudden disappearance of desire, the role of illusion in sustaining any such romantic desire, and the total impossibility of any rational translation of desire into a calculus of mutual satisfaction are major metaphorical variations on the theme of eros throughout Nietzsche's writings.)[25] And again, sometimes, the extraordinarily enigmatic metaphors and images used by Nietzsche—the eternal return of the same, the spirit of gravity, the pale criminal, a Zoroastrian prophet, a gay science—all seem mostly to provoke what he has said we need: "neediness" itself; the *expectation* of meaning, and therewith alone the sustenance of a "noble" human desire, a new kind of victory led by Nietzsche over our present "weariness with man."

But, in the little space left, it is possible to note several guideposts for any further reflection on Nietzsche and the problem of desire. There is, for example, a strict condition that he places on any such new engagement with the world, one that right away should dampen enthusiasm for a radically aesthetic or rhetorical reading. The second paragraph of *The Gay Science* contains a great contempt for "the majority" who do not have an "intellectual conscience," who "do not consider it contemptible to believe this or that and to live accordingly, without first having given themselves an account of the final and most certain reasons pro and con, and without even troubling themselves about such reasons afterward" (76). He is describing here a historical situation peculiar to "us," an aspect of what we have inherited from the Socratic and modern

25. See Pippin, "Morality as Psychology" and "Deceit, Desire, and Democracy."

Enlightenment, but without which we cannot now live, even though it might have been otherwise. An earlier formulation from *Daybreak* makes the historical point clear while returning directly to the erotic images. Nietzsche notes that "our passion," "the drive to knowledge," "has become too strong for us to be able to want happiness without knowledge or [to be able to want the happiness] of a strong, firmly rooted delusion; even to imagine such a state of things is painful to us! Restless discovering and divining has such an attraction for us, and has grown as indispensable to us as is to the lover his unrequited love, which he would at no price relinquish for a state of indifference—perhaps, indeed, we too are unrequited lovers" (428). In fact, the possibility of such an unrequited love, especially the possibility of sustaining it, turns out to be one of the best images for the question Nietzsche wants to ask about nihilism and our response, although there is space here only for an introduction to these questions.

In his own language, given this unavoidable intellectual conscience and the impossibility of living whatever lie seems most beautiful or pleasing, the question he wants to ask is, What is the alternative to "last man" contentment, itself quite a consistent turn to a "this-worldly" form of life? Here "alternative" means not only an engagement we can care about, but one that also looks like some form of this-worldly dissatisfaction, provoked by some not-being that we strive to cancel, overcome, a form of self-overcoming without asceticism or transcendence. We want a picture of striving without the illusion of a determinate, natural lack that we can fill. To anyone with an intellectual conscience, it will have to feel as though there just can be no human whole, not as proposed by Plato or Aristotle or Christianity or Schiller or Hegel, and so forth, and yet it can't just "not matter" that there can be no such harmony or completion, because all of the ways we have come to think about such desire start out from these assumptions about caused needs or an incompleteness that we strive to complete. The "last men" are atheists, scientific secularists, antimetaphysicians, and naturalists in ethics. (They look, that is, like many of the standard interpretations of Nietzsche.) But they provoke only contempt in Nietzsche. (Contrary to his remarks about the last men, there is always detectable a grudging admiration in Nietzsche for ascetics, priests, Platonists, and so forth. They "made life interesting," made it *life*, inspired and sustained desire.) Is there an *other* way, then, of thinking about this activity?[26]

26. What determines whether this sense of our own eros is dispiriting and enervating and hopeless, simply tiring, or a great field of possibilities, inspiring, or, in one of his favorite terms for it, "innocent" is a central question. (To see being itself as innocent is to see this surfeit and

This is a hard question to pursue, not only because it is so abstract but also because it is the sort of question addressed more regularly by modern romantic and confessional poetry than by philosophy. But I want to conclude by noting two additional guideposts given us by Nietzsche. Predictably, they are images, and just as predictably they only help in framing the question. There is first his own formulation of the problem, and this does have recognizable philosophical cousins. Consider section 11 of *The Gay Science*: "To this day the task of incorporating knowledge and making it instinctive is only beginning to dawn on the human eye and is not yet clearly discernable; it is a task that is seen only by those who have comprehended that so far we have incorporated only our errors and that all our consciousness relates to errors" (85). Also, in section 110, Nietzsche notes that for us knowledge has become "a piece of life itself" because we have made "the impulse for truth" a "life-preserving power," but one that tends also to render suspect, unstable, and ultimately unworthy a wide range of fragile beliefs, expectations, and aspirations that are also "necessary for life" but which cannot withstand such unconditional skeptical scrutiny.[27] The struggle defines our age and "compared to the significance of this fight, everything else is a matter of indifference" and so now "the ultimate question about the conditions of life has been posed here...to what extent can truth endure incorporation (Einverleibung)? That is the question; that is the experiment."

With this formulation, Nietzsche again enters a long, nineteenth-century discussion begun by Rousseau and intensified by German Romanticism and Idealism. When Rousseau's first *Discourse* raised the question of the distinction between progress in the arts and science and progress in moral life, and of the apparent lack of any real connection between the two (that the former could not be said to have become "incorporated" in the life of the latter), he framed the distinction in a way that would recur and resonate again and again without resolution. It is most prominent in Schiller's and Hegel's reaction to Kant's moral theory (their charge of the "positivism" of the moral law and against

---

endlessness not as morally dispiriting, but as *not morally anything*. It would be to be able to think of it as the mere play of an innocent child, Heraclitus's *pais paizon*, such that to "blame" the world would feel like blaming an innocently destructive and disruptive child.)

27. Nietzsche, *Gay Science*, 170. Cf. also Nietzsche, *Human, All Too Human*: "All states and orderings within society—classes, marriage, education, law—all these derive their force and endurance solely from the faith the fettered spirits have in them: that is to say in the absence of reasons, or at least in the warding off of the demands for reasons" (109).

Kant's virtual self-colonization model of rectitude) and in the Left-Hegelian question of alienation, but it is not limited to questions of moral rigorism or moral motivation or social identity, and it should not be construed as a "merely empirical" or sociological question. It goes to the possibility of an ideal itself being an ideal or, in Nietzsche's case, to the possibility of a kind of hopeless desire, not as a belief or probabilistic assessment, but as a new and heretofore unimagined form of life itself, one in which such a hopeless desire, despite being futile, could be incorporated. (The general name for such a heroic futility is often "nobility" in Nietzsche's works, and it of course still resonates with an admiration for the tragic hero.)

When Nietzsche tries to formulate an image of this possible incorporation, he introduces his most famous and mysterious expression of such an embodiment question. Like many other notions associated with the mature Nietzsche, it is introduced first in *The Gay Science*. A prefigurement occurs already in section 1. Man, he says, "has become a fantastic animal" because "he cannot flourish without a periodic trust in life, without faith in reason in life." A rank order of significance, even sacredness, has to be established, and so prohibitions against "laughter" and frivolity need to be instituted.[28] The "sublime unreason" that is also a part of life is designated "the tragic" and is thereby also incorporated. (That is what tragic drama makes possible: incorporation.) But these consolations are described as *essentially* episodic and eventually all are deemed unsatisfying. And our awareness of this ceaseless embodiment and eventual death is treated as a "new law of ebb and flow," and we are asked whether we "understand" it (75–76).

The full dimensions of this question or hypothesis are spelled out in section 341 of part 4, the penultimate paragraph of the first edition of *The Gay Science*. This is the first full expression of the idea of the Eternal Recurrence of the Same, the idea Nietzsche calls the "basic idea" of *Thus Spoke Zarathustra*, the work he considered his most important. The question posed is whether this *absolutely* antiteleological possibility of eternal repetition would be experienced as crushing, nothing but "the greatest weight," or as a divine liberation. And in the light of what we have said heretofore, we should pay special attention to how he poses this latter possibility: "If this thought gained possession of you (über dich Gewalt bekäme), it would change you as you are or perhaps crush you. The question in each and every thing, 'Do you want this once more and innumerable times more (willst du diess noch einmal und noch unzählige

---

28. Nietzsche, *Gay Science*, 75.

Male)?' would lie upon your actions as the greatest weight. Or how well disposed would you have to become to yourself and to life to strive (verlangen)—for nothing more than for this confirmation and seal?" (273). Because this is a question about desire and its possibility, it can, given the mysterious and largely unreachable origins of desire, only remain a question in Nietzsche, whether the endlessness and futility of our desire for more than we need, whether our new sense that a completion and satisfaction of such a desire for significance can never come, would crush (*zermalen*) such a desire or not. As he said: "That is the question; that is the experiment."

Sometimes, lots of times actually, Nietzsche suggests that a good deal of the answer depends on him, on whether he can portray the heroism of such futile attempts well enough, can inspire a sense of nobility not dependent on guarantees, payoffs, benefits, and probabilities. Looked at broadly, though, the historical answer to Nietzsche's question is clearly negative; the experiment with him at the center did not take, his "truth" could not be successfully incorporated. He did not become a new Socrates, and his cultural and historical impact has been much more as a kind of "dissolving fluid," a value debunker, an immoralist, than as any prophet for a new form of life. But something of what Nietzsche is suggesting is still visible, and in a way that testifies to the fruitfulness of his formulations.

That phenomenon is the continuing existence of philosophers, even though there is not, any longer, as a matter of wide and deep historical consensus, any possibility of philosophy, or let's say philosophical hope, as traditionally understood. Kant, as Nietzsche himself frequently noted, put an end to that. As Giorgio Colli expressed it in his afterword to *The Gay Science*, what Nietzsche realized was that "die Philosophie existiert nicht mehr, aber die Philosophen müssen weiter existieren" (philosophy doesn't exist any more, but philosophers must continue to exist).[29] What after all, could be more futile and hopeless than the two-thousand-year tradition of philosophy? What desire less satisfiable, what striving easier to satirize? Can anyone say what philosophers want? Yet, even without any confidence in the possibility of a priori knowledge of substance, or the human good, or the nature of man, or the nature of numbers, the realization of the endless, infinitely repetitive nature of philosophic striving has not "crushed it." (So far, anyway; the jury has been out on this one for a hundred years or so.) Philosophical dissatisfaction is still sustainable, even if now not in the old teleological sense. In what new sense? If we now

29. Nietzsche, *Kritische Studienausgabe*, 3:661.

appreciate that we do not lack anything fundamental, then again the question is, What separates us from the last men, who are happy, content, and who, as in section 125 of *The Gay Science*, also mock the experience of "loss" at the death of God?[30]

We have apparently "learned" another sort of love, the one Nietzsche proposes as the unique accomplishment of his new "philosophers of the future," and as the condition for the continuation of philosophers, without philosophy; lovers of wisdom without the possibility of wisdom. Such a love is not pacific, and its turbulent, potentially violent, uncompromising side is everywhere on view in Nietzsche's work. Moreover, another question about diagnosis and pathology suggests itself. Nietzsche may have avoided the melancholy of someone interminably mourning the death of God, only to retreat into a hysterical fantasy, convinced that all life is Tantalus-like or, to use his earlier term of art, simply tragic.[31] But its positive, erotic side is also on view. This is the last "guidepost" I want to mention, and it can only be mentioned here. As in section 276 of *The Gay Science*,

> I, too, shall say what it is that I wish from myself today, and what was the first thought to run across my heart this year—what thought shall be for me the reason, warranty and sweetness of my life henceforth. I want to learn more and more to see as beautiful what is necessary in things; then I shall be one of those who makes things beautiful. *Amor fati*: let that be my love henceforth. I do not want to wage war against what is ugly. I do not want to accuse; I do not even want to accuse those who accuse. Looking away shall be my only negation. And all in all, and on the whole: some day I wish to be only a yes-sayer. (223)

30. The death of God should neither be experienced as an enlightening liberation nor as a weighty, nearly unbearable catastrophe. Nietzsche himself treats both as pathologies. See Pippin, "Nietzsche and the Melancholy of Modernity." The issue here is like the one that comes up in trying to understand Kafka or Rothko: how a kind of absence or frustration of determinate meaning is experienced as a kind of determinate presence, a persistent intimation of possibility that cannot be definitively closed off or redeemed.

31. This possibility was suggested to me by Eric Santner in his commentary on this essay, also in this volume. Santner quotes from Juan-David Nasio: "the hysteric unconsciously invents a fantasy scenario designed to prove to himself and the world that there is no pleasure except the kind that is unfulfilled" (*Hysteria from Freud to Lacan*, 5). I would want ultimately to be able to show that the situation Nietzsche describes is more fruitfully understood as much more like Schiller's picture of "useless" and "excess" aesthetic experience than Freud on hysterics, but that must remain a promissory note.

WAS WILL DER PHILOSOPH?

ERIC L. SANTNER

In my response to Robert Pippin's essay, I will first try to summarize his argument very briefly and then suggest some paths of further inquiry. I begin with his account of the limits of the canonical ways of understanding Nietzsche's diagnosis of nihilism and move on from there.

According to Pippin, the cognitivist position misses the performative dimension of valuations, the fact that speech acts asserting the value of something are not merely constative but rather in some fashion produce the value in question. Any disturbance in the capacity for establishing values cannot, then, simply be a matter of a disenchantment of belief, a realization that we don't really have secure knowledge of what had been presupposed as a firm, epistemological basis for our commitments to this or that value. To put it simply, God doesn't die simply because man comes to realize that his grounds for believing in God have been proven to be susceptible to doubt, that some bit of knowledge that supports belief is discovered to be flawed. Though historical scholarship on the composition of the Bible or the life of Jesus may complicate one's relation to the Judeo-Christian tradition, it would be a mistake to see such scholarship as the root cause of the illness of concern to Nietzsche. For Nietzsche, historicism would no doubt count among the symptoms rather than the causes of nihilism.

The seeming alternative to the cognitivist position, call it the claim of radical performativity, would have it that values are created and sustained by rhetorical capacities backed by strength of will, by a capacity to project values into the world beyond what could be grounded in some sort of positive knowledge. Nihilism would thereby be reduced to an exhaustion of such capacities and will, the drying up of the pool of robust value-legislators who could do what Socrates, Paul, Goethe, or even Nietzsche managed to do. We might put it this way: When we identify ourselves with a set of commitments linked to a name—when we say, "I am a Marxist" or "I am a Freudian"—we are never merely asserting our endorsement of a set of views propounded by the thinker in question (that would be an example of the cognitivist position); we are also establishing our subordination to the *name* and *person* of the thinker, to the force exerted by a symbolic identification beyond the framework of agreement or disagreement. To put it simply, if you are really a Freudian and have difficulty understanding one of Freud's texts, it is *your fault*, not his. This second view of how values come into the world involves, then, the dimension of *transference*. Transference is not an impersonal relation of knowledge but rather an affectively charged relation to, as Lacan put it, *the one supposed to know*. Nihilism, according to this view, would mean a generalized incapacity to establish and sustain such transferential relations with a value-legislator, a producer of master signifiers. Within the framework of this view, the totalitarian leader could be understood as the one who rushes into this vacuum, providing not so much an opportunity for filling it as for disavowing it or blaming others for it.

According to Pippin, both of these positions are examples of metaphysical thinking, thinking that seeks some sort of direct "contact" with what ultimately provides human life with meaning and direction. (Nihilism would thus follow from a *loss* of such presumed contact.) In the cognitivist view, this contact typically takes the form of knowledge of a final "why," a final ground that makes human life rationally satisfying—we have contact with what ultimately guides and constrains our specifically human existence, our life in the space of reason. In the volitionist view, we have contact not with a source of knowledge but with the force of a creative will that both opens and delimits a horizon of possibilities. In the course of his essay, Pippin argues that for Nietzsche, the emergence of nihilism cannot be fully accounted for by either of these positions; the etiology of nihilism can only be properly understood, he suggests, if we shift our focus to the place of *desire* in Nietzsche's thought. For desire gives us the chance to think about absence without having to conceive it as the loss or lack of a determinate something, a loss or lack of contact with something that was or could be present.

Just as important as the positive elaboration of Nietzschean desire is Pippin's characterization of how such desire ought not be understood. The misunderstanding often encountered in the literature is a form of naturalism whereby desire is linked to a multiplicity of somatic instincts, to a discord pertaining to the body that only subsequently comes to be endowed with meaning, an act that must itself in turn be traced to bodily exigencies. For Nietzsche the discord at the core of human desire pertains not to the biological body but rather, if I might put it this way, to the "surplus body" we acquire by way of our life within the space of meaning. Pippin suggests that this is at least in part what Nietzsche means when he says that love must be learned, that Eros is not simply an unfolding of natural capacities. But he also argues that desire comes from within, that it is never simply a reaction to determinate objects in the world but rather an inwardly generated excess of tension that can never be alleviated by any determinate "satisfaction." We have, then, something of a paradox here. Desire emerges only on the basis of our life in culture, in historical time, but desire is also always internally generated and sustained. The *cause* of our desire is, to use a Lacanian formulation, not intimate but rather *extimate*: outside and inside at the same time, an alterity located in the most intimate recesses of our subjectivity. (This paradoxical topography is, I think, what stands behind Lacan's famous pronouncement that the unconscious is the discourse of the Other.) But this also means that the *cause* of our desire can never be simply equated with the *object* of our desire. The objects we seek in the pursuit of our desire are never "it." Indeed, we might say that for the so-called last man, the cause of desire finally does coincide with a determinate object. Put somewhat differently, the last man lives fully within the pleasure principle but has become numb to what is "beyond the pleasure principle." (Several recent American films—one thinks of *Happiness* or *American Beauty*—seem to argue that the violence in contemporary suburbia is an attempt to shatter this numbness, to perform a kind of autotraumatization.)

Pippin ends his remarks with the suggestion that the persistence of philosophy as a form of unrequited love, as a desire that *cannot cease not to be satisfied*, may be an example of a form of life that fully endorses the absence of transcendence—that there is nothing beyond or higher than life in relation to which human life could be found to be wanting—but that nonetheless avoids collapsing into the flat contentment of the "last man." Philosophy would thereby exemplify a life sensitive to what is overwhelming within human life, to an immanent excess, a surplus animation, that makes human life what it is.

One question that comes to mind here is whether this final vision is not one of philosophy as a certain form of hysteria. As Juan-David Nasio has put it, "the hysteric unconsciously invents a fantasy scenario designed to prove to himself and to the world that there is no pleasure except the kind that is unfulfilled."[1] The connection between hysteria and philosophy appears, indeed, to be underlined by the question Pippin raises in his concluding remarks: "Can

---

1. Nasio, *Hysteria from Freud to Lacan*, 5.

anyone say what philosophers want?" I take this to be an allusion to Freud's famous question apropos of femininity and its apparent link to hysteria: *Was will das Weib?* What does woman want? Is Pippin suggesting that Nietzsche's ultimate legacy to philosophy is in some sense to have taught it how to inhabit this hysteria, to love its symptom (rather than, as in metaphysical thinking, to act it out)? That the symptom is the portal, as it were, through which we truly enter the midst of life, infinitely agitated by "some not-being that we strive to cancel, overcome...[but] without asceticism or transcendence"?

My own way of formulating this thought would be to suggest—and I admit that this is a wild suggestion—that the understanding of love that Pippin gleans from Nietzsche's text paradoxically returns us to the very Judeo-Christian legacy that Nietzsche takes such pains to dismantle in his work. What I mean is that the infinitization of desire that Pippin identifies as specifically Nietzschean can perhaps best be understood on the basis of a certain understanding of the I-Thou relation, the relation to one's neighbor. In his *Project for a Scientific Psychology*, Freud distinguished two aspects of the neighbor, or *Nebenmensch*: "And so the complex of the neighbor divides into two constituent parts the first of which *impresses* (imponiert) through the constancy of its composition (durch konstantes Gefüge), its persistence as a *Thing* (Ding), while the other is *understood* by means of memory-work."[2] What I am suggesting is that the surfeit of restless desire that keeps one from becoming a "last man," as it were, is ultimately generated by our proximity to this neighbor-Thing, the opaque, enigmatic density of the Other that we can never fully integrate into our symbolic universe. In his case study of the Ratman, Freud captures this dimension of the Other by noting that his patient's face manifested a "*horror at pleasure of his own of which he himself was unaware.*" Love of neighbor in a Nietzschean vein—would it not mean a yes-saying, a turn toward *this* face of the Other?

2. Freud, *Gesammelte Werke, Nachtragsband*, 426–27; my emphasis.

GIVE DORA A BREAK! A TALE OF EROS AND EMOTIONAL DISRUPTION

JONATHAN LEAR

I

To hear Freud tell it, the psychoanalytic conception of the erotic comes straight from Plato.

> as for the "stretching" of the concept of sexuality... anyone who looks down with contempt upon psycho-analysis from a superior vantage-point should remember how closely the enlarged sexuality of psycho-analysis coincides with the Eros of the divine Plato.[1]

> ...what psychoanalysis calls sexuality was by no means identical with the impulsion towards a union of the two sexes or towards producing a pleasurable sensation in the genitals; it had far more resemblance to the all-inclusive and all-embracing love of Plato's *Symposium*.[2]

> We are of the opinion, then, that language has carried out an entirely justifiable piece of unification in creating the word "love" with its numerous uses, and that we cannot do better than take it as the basis of our scientific discussions and

I first presented these ideas at a seminar I gave at the University of Chicago with the composer Richard Einhorn (who is composing an opera on Dora). I later presented them at a faculty seminar at the Institute for Psychoanalysis, Chicago. I learned enormously from both discussions. I also want to express a more general debt to Irad Kimhi and Hans Loewald for conversations about psychoanalysis, which stretched out over many years.
1. Freud, "Three Essays on the Theory of Sexuality," 134. The quote is from the preface to the fourth edition, published in 1920.
2. Freud, "Resistances to Psychoanalysis," 218.

expositions as well. By coming to this decision, psychoanalysis has let loose a storm of indignation, as though it had been guilty of an act of outrageous innovation. Yet it has done nothing original in taking love in this "wider" sense. In its origin, function, and relation to sexual love, the "Eros" of the philosopher Plato coincides exactly with the love-force, the libido of psycho-analysis.[3]

And so, if we take Freud's word for it, the psychoanalytic conception of Eros stands squarely in the Western philosophical tradition of thinking about the human psyche. But it is also Freud who taught us to be suspicious of any tradition's account of its own development. For while the tradition will present a homogeneous story of inheritance and development, in fact that story will be covering over a series of ruptures, discontinuities, and evasions. There is no reason to think that psychoanalysis should be exempt from this tendency.[4]

If we look to what actually happened, it appears that Freud's invocation of Eros was part of a rather hasty attempt to cover over a trauma to psycho-analytic theory, for it is not an exaggeration to say that the traumas of World War I induced a trauma in psychoanalytic theory. Freud recognized that psychoanalysis—in its then current form—could not account for the so-called dreams of the traumatic neuroses. "Dreams occurring in traumatic neuroses have the characteristic of repeatedly bringing the patient back to the situation of his accident, a situation from which he wakes up in another fright. *This astonishes people far too little.*"[5] What was astonishing to Freud was that there seemed to be no way to account for these dreams as disguised—and perhaps conflicted—expressions of sexuality. They could not be understood in terms of the myriad mental functionings according to the pleasure principle. Each night the traumatized soldier would be brought back to the scene of utter terror, and there was no way to see such a dream as seeking pleasure in any way, however conflicted or inhibited.

But the problem was much graver than the need to extend psychoanalytic thinking to encompass a new area of psychological phenomena. The war neuroses are Freud's epistemic entrée. Once he sees an exception to the functioning of sexuality—according to the pleasure principle—he sees exceptions to it

---

3. Freud, "Group Psychology," 90–92.

4. It is Jean Laplanche who has systematically tried to work out what a distinctively psycho-analytic account of the history of psychoanalysis might look like. See, for example, Laplanche, *Life and Death in Psychoanalysis*, and *Entre séduction et inspiration: L'homme.*

5. Freud, "Beyond the Pleasure Principle," 3; my emphasis.

everywhere. In particular, he sees that these exceptions occur in the heart of the transference in psychoanalytic therapy. "Patients repeat all these unwanted situations and painful emotions in the transference and revive them with the greatest ingenuity. They seek to bring about the interruption of the treatment while it is still incomplete; they contrive once more to feel themselves scorned, they oblige the physician to speak severely to them and treat them coldly; they discover appropriate objects for their jealousy.... *None of these things can have produced pleasure in the past.* ... In spite of that they are repeated under pressure of a compulsion" (21). In effect, Freud admits that his entire theory of the transference neuroses, his theory of psychoanalytic therapy and cure, needs to be revised. And it has to be revised to account for a fundamental force that Freud admits he doesn't fully understand.[6] This is nothing less than a foundational crisis in psychoanalysis, and it would be hard to overestimate the importance of Freud's next theoretical step.

It is at this point that Freud covers over the crucial nugget of his own insight: that the mind can disrupt its own functioning. The reason he misses this is that he succumbs to the temptation of speculative thinking. He seems to assume that if his thinking is bold enough, it can seize fundamental truth. He posits a basic teleological principle—the death drive—running through all of animate nature, which sets "the final goal of all organic striving." "The aim of all life," Freud concludes, "is death" (37–38). His style of thinking here is like that of a pre-Socratic: by reflecting on the phenomena of life, he seeks to grasp the metaphysical principles that will explain it. Indeed, at the end of his career, Freud cites Empedocles with admiration. He takes himself to be repeating, in modern times and in a psychoanalytic context, that basic opposition between love and strife that Empedocles was the first to lay down.[7]

It is as though Kant had never written. Freud here seems oblivious to the modern idea that human thought itself stands in need of a critique. In particular, we need to know how human thought is capable of grasping such truths. I have argued elsewhere that, though Freud was right to see that existing psychoanalytic theory was inadequate to account for important psychological phenomena, and thus right to think that important revision was needed, his argument for the death drive does not succeed.[8] I am not going to repeat the argument here, but the basic idea is that the postulation of the death drive is

6. Ibid., 23.

7. Freud, "Analysis Terminable and Interminable," 245–47.

8. Lear, *Happiness, Death, and the Remainder of Life*, ch. 2.

a much more extravagant conclusion than the phenomena call for. We need to search for a more austere conclusion that nevertheless accounts for these astonishing psychological phenomena.

Before we do that, though, we should note that, when Freud invokes "the death drive," he is attempting an inaugural act of naming, which misfires. He takes himself to be naming a real thing in the world, but he is in fact injecting an enigmatic term into our discourse. There is no naming, for nothing has been genuinely isolated for him to name. His hope is to provide an explanation; in fact, all we get is the illusion of one.

Now what is striking in this context is that Freud introduces Eros not because of a deepening of the concept of sexuality but because he needs an adequate complement to his new principle, Death. Indeed, Freud first introduces the idea of Eros as a drive in *Beyond the Pleasure Principle*:

> Let us make a bold attempt at another step forward. It is generally considered that the union of a number of cells into a vital association—the multicellular character of organisms—has become a means of prolonging their life. . . . Accordingly we might attempt to apply the libido theory which has been arrived at in psycho-analysis to the mutual relationship of the cells. We might suppose that the life instincts or sexual instincts which are active in each cell take the other cells as their object, that they partly neutralize the death instincts . . . in those cells and thus preserve their life; while the other cells do the same for them, and still others sacrifice themselves in the performance of this libidinal function. . . . In this way the libido of our sexual instincts would coincide with the Eros of the poets and philosophers which holds all living things together. (50)

In other words, Eros is hastily invoked to be a suitable complement to Freud's new-found principle, Death. Since next to nothing is known about the death drive, it should not come as too much of a surprise to discover that even *Eros* is functioning mainly as an enigmatic term. The death drive is supposedly an entropic force for decomposition, so it makes sense that Eros should be an opposing force for unification. But, really, virtually nothing is known about it—because there is nothing to know. Freud is not in the process of discovering a new life force, he is in the process of trying to cover over a trauma to psychoanalytic theory. In this way, invoking Plato and the ancients gives a false sense of legitimacy and security. It lulls us into thinking we do know what we are talking about; we've always known.

Insofar as we have been living with the assumption that we do have a psychoanalytic conception of Eros, this psychoanalytically minded reconstruction of the history of Freud's thought should make us suspicious. The point is not to ditch the psychoanalytic conception of the erotic, but to free us up to formulate one. To this end, it helps to recognize that, for all practical purposes, we don't have one. Perhaps hitching ourselves up to Plato will prove fruitful, but it is important to recognize that as yet we have little more than a promissory note.[9]

I I

What did Freud really accomplish? Roughly speaking, I think Freud was right to think that certain phenomena—like traumatic dreams, certain kinds of compulsive repetitions—are exceptions to the workings of the pleasure principle, but that in trying to conceptualize them, he went off the theoretical deep end. Let us simply abandon the assumption that if there are *exceptions* to workings of the pleasure principle, there must be a *"beyond"*—a hidden principle waiting to be discovered. And let us ask instead, how might we characterize austerely the empirical content of Freud's important discovery? It seems to me that what Freud has shown is that, on the broadest possible scale, there are two different types of mental activity. The first comprises the by now familiar workings of the mind according to the loose associations of the pleasure principle, which Freud so brilliantly described in the *Three Essays on the Theory of Sexuality*, *The Interpretation of Dreams*, and *Studies on Hysteria*. Here we have displacement and condensation, as well as various forms of inhibition and repression, which altogether serve to diffuse our associations as well as express them in dreams, bodily expressions, and other symptomatic acts. These are, of course, themselves all sorts of different mental activities, but they can all be summed up under one grand type: the functionings of the mind according to the pleasure principle (and its variant, the reality principle). I call this type of mental functioning *swerve* because it exercises a kind of gravitational pull on the entire field of conscious mental functioning, bending it into idiosyncratic shapes. By way of analogy, we detect the existence of black holes by the way light swerves toward them. We detect this type of unconscious process by the ways our conscious reasoning, our bodily expressions, our acts, and our dreams swerve toward them.

Before 1920, Freud thought he could account for all relevant pathology in terms of psychological conflicts that were themselves all instances of

---

9. I made my own first attempt in *Love and Its Place in Nature*. See also Loewald, *Essential Loewald*. Hans Loewald, I think, is the first psychoanalytic thinker to take Eros seriously.

swerve-like mental phenomena. The kernel of Freud's discovery in *Beyond the Pleasure Principle* is that this is not so. There are significant psychological phenomena that cannot be understood in terms of any type of swerve. We need to recognize a fundamentally different type of mental activity, which is in fact the *disruption* of primary-process mental activity itself. I give the generic name *break* to all types of mental activity that serve to disrupt—or break apart—the ordinary functionings of the mind. So, for instance, the so-called dreams of the traumatic neuroses are instances of break because, as Freud showed, they are not really dreams. That is, they are not an ordinary manifestation of the wish-fulfilling capacity to dream; rather, they are a disruption of that capacity. In traumatic neuroses, the ordinary swerve-like capacities of the mind are repeatedly disrupted, and the mind gets stuck in repeated disruptions.

There are three features of break that need to be emphasized. First, break is a *genus* concept, not a species concept. This is important. In conversation, colleagues have assumed that I am trying to introduce a new mental force, and their natural response is, "Why do we need it? Don't we already have the concept of trauma?" That is like saying, "Why do we need the concept of animal when we already have the concept of human being?" The point of the concept of animal is not to introduce a new species—as though we have humans and chimps and now we also have animals—nor is it to say, now that we have the concept of animal, we no longer need the concept of human being. Rather, the concept of animal allows us to see, at a higher level of generality, that there might be some salient things in common between humans and, say, ant eaters. With the concept of animal we can see a certain unity where before we saw only differences.

Similarly with break. The point is not to introduce it as something at the same level as trauma, nor is the point to replace the concept of trauma with the concept of break. Rather, the point is to divide mental activity into two broad categories: those which manifest the ordinary functionings of the mind, and those which disrupt them. In the broad genus of break, there are myriad species: trauma is the obvious example, but included in this category are also "attacks on linking," projective identification, introjection, and various forms of acute bodily attacks and spasms, as well as certain kinds of moments of dissociation and fugue states. In particular, they are extremely minor, nontraumatic, and difficult to detect.[10] I do not pretend to be able to give a complete

10. These are the sorts of break Paul Gray listens for in his close process attention. See Gray, *Ego and Analysis of Defense*. One of the values of the concept of break is that it encourages us to think about what one of Gray's miniscule breaks and a massive psychotic break might have in

taxonomy of all the kinds of break, but I think that that is a fruitful area for future research.

The second feature of break that needs to be remembered is that breaks can come from inside as well as from outside the individual mind. Another person or an event can inflict a trauma upon us that utterly disrupts mental functioning. But, on Freud's economic model, the human being is a repository of drives and psychic energy that can on occasion overwhelm the mind.

Third, and most important, a person can become active with respect to break. That is, in periods of stress and anxiety, a person can use the heightened psychic energy to disrupt his own mental functioning. In this way, break can become a primitive defense mechanism.[11] It can also be used to provoke more minor disruptions: in this way, small breaks can be incorporated into more sophisticated defenses.

III

I should now like to return to our ordinary, pretheoretical notion of erotic life and ask how the concepts of swerve and break might be useful with respect to it. I am going to focus on two brief moments in the life of an adolescent woman whom Freud came to call Dora.[12] The first moment is when Dora gave her suitor a slap across the face, thus putting an end to an erotic relationship in the making. The second is when she metaphorically repeated that act by abruptly ending her treatment with Freud. One aim is to rethink this clinical rupture in the light of our revised understanding of the theoretical rupture.

By now it is well known that Dora was treated by her adult world as an object of exchange. Her father was having an affair with a family friend, Frau K, and Dora was allowed, even encouraged, to receive the attentions of the husband, Herr K. For a while Dora collaborated with this arrangement, but there came a moment when she broke this social world apart. Herr K propositions her by a lake; she slaps him—and all the adults gang up and insist that Dora has invented this story. She writes a suicide note, faints, and her father brings her to

---

common. There is a tendency to assume that the primitive mental phenomena Melanie Klein describes must be utterly different from the miniscule disruptions Paul Gray describes in his close process monitoring of high-functioning neurotics. The generic concept of break enables us to see something in common.

11. What Bion calls an attack on linking is one such defense mechanism; see Bion, "Attacks on Linking."

12. Freud, "Fragment of an Analysis."

Freud—in the hope that Freud will help restore the early adulterous harmony. What broke up this harmony?

Here is Freud's first account of the moment:

> None of her father's actions seemed to have embittered her so much as his readiness to consider the scene by the lake as a product of her imagination. She was almost beside herself at the idea of its being supposed that she had merely fancied something on that occasion. For a long time I was in perplexity as to what the self-reproach could be which lay behind her passionate repudiation of this explanation of the episode. It was justifiable to suspect that there was something concealed, for a reproach which misses the mark gives no lasting offense. On the other hand, I came to the conclusion that Dora's story must correspond to the facts in every respect. *No sooner had she grasped Herr K's intention than, without letting him finish what he had to say, she had given him a slap in the face and hurried away. Her behavior must have seemed as incomprehensible to the man after she had left him as to us,* for he must long before have gathered from innumerable small signs that he was secure in the girl's affections.[13]

This slap is arguably the decisive moment in Dora's life. Nothing would ever be the same again. Note that, in the moment, Freud insists on an interpretive breakdown: neither the participant in the scene nor Freud himself can make immediate sense of what Dora is doing. But as the analysis progresses, Freud comes to think that, in her slap, Dora is expressing her anger: Dora is angry because she thinks Herr K's approach is *only* a seduction.

Of course, angry outbursts are part of many an erotic relationship. And perhaps anger would have been an appropriate response for Dora in this one, but there is an important sense in which that was not Dora's response. And if Freud had understood that, he might have been able to save the analysis.

I should like to follow the account given by Jacques Lacan, not because I think it is necessarily right about Dora, but because it provides a useful framework in which to investigate her slap.[14] (But the account I offer is compatible with a broad range of interpretations.) According to Lacan, Dora is in the process of becoming a woman, and this process has a significant unconscious dimension. In fantasy, Dora is trying to figure out what the erotic kernel to

13. Ibid., 46, my emphasis.

14. Lacan, "Intervention on Transference" and *Psychoses*. Note: I am only following one thread of Lacan's complex presentation of the Dora case.

being a woman is—and, with fascination, she suspects that Frau K possesses the enigmatic secret. The primordial model Dora used to explore the world was through her older brother. Dora again resorts to that model, exploring Frau K's enigmatic femininity through an identification with Herr K. If this interpretation is correct, then Herr K is doubly mistaken about his relationship with Dora. First, he thinks her interest in him is primarily directed *to* him when in fact she needs him as a vehicle for exploring the sexualized femininity of Frau K. That is, Herr K believes himself to be Dora's erotic object, when he is in fact a vehicle for finding out what Eros is. Second, he assumes she is already a woman when her problem is that she is trying to figure out how to become one. He assumes she already understands erotic life; she is trying to figure out what it is.

In the postscript to the case study, Freud admits that, at the climactic moment of the analysis, he did not notice that Dora was in the process of transferring her feelings for Herr K onto him.[15] But even in retrospect, Freud remains unaware of how much he encouraged such a transference. For in the analysis he makes the same two assumptions about Dora that Herr K did. He assumes that Dora's evident interest in Herr K is really a disguised love for him; and he assumes that the reason she does not express that love openly is because she is neurotic. The idea that she cannot express love because she is not yet ready to be in love is not one that occurs to Freud. In particular, he seems unaware that occupying a sexualized gender role is a developmental achievement that itself requires massive activity in unconscious fantasy. The point here is not to question the overall diagnosis of Dora as hysterical. The point is that Freud, like Herr K, treats her as having more erotic understanding than she does. He assumes that a certain kind of eroticized gender role has already been achieved.

This leads to a significant misinterpretation of Dora's slaps. Freud thinks that Dora slaps Herr K because she is angry, hurt, and jealous. She is in love with Herr K, but when he uses the same words on her that he used on the governess, Dora assumes that he is treating her as a seductive trifle.

It is here that Freud gets misled by the logic of the emotions. He thinks he is making an empirical discovery about the unconscious when in fact he is following out the logic of a concept. For it is constitutive of anger that if someone is angry at X, she must believe that X somehow deserves her anger.[16] Anger makes an implicit claim that it is itself an appropriate response: thus it

---

15. Freud, "Fragment of an Analysis," 118–20.
16. Aristotle *Rhetoric* II.2, 1378a31–80a4. See also, Freud, "Fragment of an Analysis," 47–51.

makes a claim for its own rationality. So if Dora is angry at Herr K, it would seem that she must have a reason for it. And if that reason is not conscious, then there is *conceptual* pressure to assume that it must be unconscious. Since no one lives with a single reason, that unconscious reason must fit in with other unconscious beliefs and desires about Herr K. In this way, the unconscious begins to look as though it has to be the locus of a fair amount of rationality of its own.[17]

It would seem that if irrationality is going to enter at all, it cannot be because of the way unconscious beliefs and desires themselves fit together. Rather, irrationality could only appear in one of two ways. Either the unconscious would have to interact with consciousness in nonrational ways, or the unconscious reasons would have to seem—from a conscious, evaluative perspective—not to be very good reasons.

Now if the unconscious really were like this, then Freud's therapeutic technique would make sense. For if the unconscious were this hive of bad reasons, it would make sense to bring these reasons to conscious awareness: then one could evaluate them and correct them in the light of one's conscious judgment. The discovery of unconscious content would be what it meant to "make the unconscious conscious." It is clear that this is what Freud takes himself to be doing. He acts as though he were a detective cross-examining a somewhat reluctant witness.

A problem arises, though, if Dora's unconscious is not as well organized as Freud takes it to be. For if Freud is not discovering hidden contents, then he is bombarding her with them. It is not just that the contents are sexual, erotic, and aggressive; it is that Freud is making an allegation that these are *her* contents. His interpretations are allegations, and it is easy to imagine Dora experiencing this as an intrusion—for that is what it is. He, like Herr K, is treating her as though she already has these fully formed eroticized thoughts, and thus it is understandable that he should provoke a similar reaction.

But what is this reaction? How should we understand Dora's slaps? If we go back to that moment by the lake, it seems to me clear that Dora provokes a break. If we observe Herr K's pursuit, there is no doubt that the overall erotic tension was rising—and along with it, Dora's anxiety. And due to her own inhibited development, Dora had a limited number of ways of dealing with it. If we add Lacan's hypothesis that, in fantasy, Dora was using Herr K as a vehicle

---

17. See Davidson, "Paradoxes of Irrationality," and Lear, "Restlessness, Phantasy and the Concept of Mind."

for exploring Frau K's femininity, then his remark—"I get nothing from my wife" or "My wife means nothing to me"—was not merely for Dora the repetition of a cynical seductive line that he had already used on the governess. It threatened to disrupt her entire orientation to the world. For if Dora is to discover who she is—or, rather, construct who she is to become—through a fantastic exploration of Herr K's fascination with Frau K, then Herr K's lack of interest in Frau K would threaten the very core of Dora's emerging existential project. It is not because she thinks Herr K is cynical that she slaps him, but because she is threatened by being overwhelmed by his truth.

The suggestion, then, is not that Herr K traumatizes Dora, but that Dora induces a break. That is, Herr K's proposal is threatening, and Dora responds with one of the very few defenses at her disposal: she induces a break. And in this way she disrupts her own world: she avoids *being* overwhelmed by overwhelming *herself*. Break can thus be considered a defense because a person invoking it can avoid the passivity of being overwhelmed. But with this kind of a break, it must be considered a primitive defense because it is literally *self*-defeating: it inhibits psychological growth.[18]

As we shall see, precisely because we are trying to recognize an unfamiliar type of psychic phenomenon, it is necessarily difficult to find the right vocabulary with which to describe it. Still, it seems misleading to say that Dora slaps Herr K out of anger. For Dora is breaking apart a world in which anger might have been the appropriate response. Anger seems to require that one form reasons for one's anger, but Dora is in the process of breaking up any such psychological activity.

Ironically, if this account is correct, then Dora's "hysterical" defense has the same basic structure as the traumatic neuroses that, nineteen years later, Freud would recognize to be beyond the pleasure principle. In both cases there are active attacks on ordinary sexualized mental functioning. And once Freud does discover that there is some kind of mental activity that is "beyond the pleasure principle," there is reason to go back to the earlier cases—before he recognized this—to see if one can find it already there. My suggestion is that Dora was functioning "beyond the pleasure principle," but Freud was not yet ready to see this. And this gives us reason to suspect that *hysterics do not suffer, as Freud put it in "Studies on Hysteria," "mainly from reminiscences," but mainly from primitive*

---

18. As Lacan put it, "And after that what will be for her?: this puppet who has nonetheless just broken the enchantment under which she has been living for years" ("Intervention on Transference," 101).

defense mechanisms. That is, they induce break as a first line of defense then try to heal over the mental wounds with fantasies that are often experienced as reminiscences.

At this point, a moment of conceptual therapy might be in order. This very inquiry occupies some vague borderland between philosophy and psychoanalysis. Psychoanalytic thinking may well seek to introduce new vocabulary or induce a shift in ordinary usage. Philosophical activity, if we follow the example of the later Wittgenstein, does not seek to change our usage, only to describe it. This hybrid inquiry pulls us in both directions. And it seems to me that it is all right to go in either direction, even in both directions—just as long as one remains clear about what one is doing. On one hand, there is good reason not to call Dora's slap an expression of anger. For anger seems to be partially constituted by the belief that the anger is itself directed toward someone who deserves it. Anger makes a rationalizing claim that it is a response that it is merited. Dora's slap, by contrast, is an outburst that lacks this complex structure. Indeed, it is a disruptive gesture that itself inhibits the development of this very structure. Thus it can be wildly misleading to call anger the very activity that prevents the complex emotion of anger from developing.

On the other hand, anger, the full-fledged rationalizing emotion, is a developmental achievement. And it has roots going back to infancy. We say that an infant's outburst is angry even though it does not yet have the capability of thinking that its outburst is warranted. And it is from these angry outbursts that, if psychological life is not too disrupted, the full-fledged emotion of anger develops. There is a tendency in ordinary language to call any outburst along the developmental route an expression of anger. And thus there is a tendency to call a slap like Dora's an expression of anger. And, of course, one could not tell from casual inspection whether that outburst was itself on a developmental route toward the mature expression of anger—or whether it was a disruption of that very developmental process. Certainly, on the basis of the ordinary use of emotion terms, Dora looks angry. And we want our emotion terms like *anger* to be applicable on the basis of relatively casual observation. In an observationally identical moment, Dora could give a slap that was a full-fledged expression of anger. And we don't want to have to go through a whole analysis before we can say whether a slap is angry or not.

The real mistake, it seems to me, is not to opt for one use or the other, but to opt for one use and then to think that one has to find the criteria of the other. So, for example, Freud interprets the slap as an expression of anger—and then thinks he has to find reasons for it. He cannot find conscious ones, so he looks for unconscious ones. Through a misunderstanding of grammar, a misleading picture of the unconscious begins to take shape.

This is a moment in which the psychoanalytic tradition and the philosophical tradition come together in an unfortunate way, for in the philosophical tradition there is a tendency to think that interpretation requires some kind of rationalization. If Dora's slap is to be interpreted as an expression of anger, she has to have a belief that Herr K has offended her and a belief that her anger is a justified response. And if these beliefs are not conscious, they must be unconscious. Thus philosophy itself would seem to dictate how the unconscious must be.

One antidote to this tendency is to pay attention to the phenomenon of break. On my interpretation, Dora's slap does not express her anger so much as it disrupts her life. In particular, it disrupts the development of her capacity to express anger. (Having seen this distinction, if you then want to go ahead and call Dora's slap a slap of anger, that is fine with me.) Whether or not this is right about Dora, we become aware of how easy it is to overrationalize such a moment. The disruption may be *strategic*—it disrupts a world that itself is becoming overwhelming—but it is not *intentional*.[19] That is, it is not caused by Dora's beliefs about Herr K; it is a motivated disruption of the world in which she might form beliefs.

Freud insists on interpreting swerve, and he thereby precipitates a break. He is looking for hidden emotions, and he cannot see that Dora is at the precipice, ready to throw herself "beyond the pleasure principle." In the penultimate session, Freud focuses on an uncanny moment of break-like activity. Dora had had a sharp attack of stomach pains that, at the time, were interpreted as appendicitis. Freud interprets this as an attack Dora herself had induced. And upon learning that the attack came nine months after the catastrophic scene by the lake, Freud told Dora that she had in fact been enacting a fantasy of childbirth.[20]

Now there might be occasions on which interpretive activity such as Freud's might have worked. After all, mental life itself is a symphony of swerves and

19. See Johnston, "Self-Deception." A second antidote is to insist that, insofar as the unconscious does have a content, it is to be interpreted in terms of swerve-like fantasies, and fantasies are not propositional attitudes or objects of propositional attitudes. There should be no conceptual pressure to rationalize these fantasies. See Lear, "Restlessness, Phantasy and the Concept of Mind."

20. Freud, "Fragment of an Analysis," 103–5.

breaks—and we are often trying to recover from disruptions in mental life by dreaming and fantasizing. So, for example, we can easily imagine that some inchoate sense that it was nine months later caused enough anxiety that Dora induced another break. And after that break she constructed swerve-like fantasies around it. As Freud himself would later describe it in his account of traumatic dreams, "These dreams are endeavoring to master the stimulus *retrospectively*, by developing the anxiety whose omission was the cause of the traumatic neurosis."[21] In other words, after a break, the mind tries to get itself back into the swerve-like activity of sexuality, fantasy, dreaming. Had Freud proceeded more gently—or, indeed, if he had left more of the interpretive work to Dora—he might have facilitated Dora's own attempt to provide a swerve-like interpretation to her previous breaks. But his interpretations are too much too soon. Like Herr K's advances, they are genuinely intrusive—and instead of analyzing the previous breaks, they cause another.

It is this moment of break that Freud later sees as transference. Unbeknownst to him at the time, Dora is in the process of transferring her feelings for Herr K onto Freud. The irony is that this transference has been unfolding all along in swerve-like ways. The moment that Freud retrospectively identifies as transference is in fact a moment when transference is *interrupted* by a break.[22] Now, of course, the break is a repetition—and it is a repetition of an act that Dora performed in the presence of Herr K. But I do not think we can understand this act if we think only of the swerve-like connections between Herr K and Freud. For although Dora may well have made certain unconscious connections between Herr K and Freud, a more salient fact is that when she is made anxious she has few psychological defenses. Herr K made her anxious; Freud made her anxious. In each case she defended herself. The repetition, in my opinion, occurred not because she unconsciously connected Herr K and Freud, but because each of them triggered one of her only defense mechanisms. Of course there is a repetition of break: what else is she going to do? (The squid squirts its ink, and it squirts again: not because it has made a deep association between the two moments, nor because it is compelled to repeat, but rather because, when threatened, it has only one defense in its repertoire. There is repetition, there may be compulsion, but there is no compulsion *to* repeat. That is, repetition is not the aim of the compulsion.)

21. Freud, "Beyond the Pleasure Principle," 32.

22. This, I think, is at least one of the things Lacan means when he says that transference is resistance in the analyst; see, e.g., Lacan, "Intervention on Transference," 102.

Break becomes an obstacle to the analysis precisely because Freud cannot recognize it as such. For if one is aware of the phenomenon of break, one will be at least as interested in psychological *activity* as in searching for hidden psychological *content*. And one will help an analysand maintain a comfortable level of anxiety. Freud did not see the break coming—and there has to be a question of whether he didn't want to see it, for Freud says he wrote up the case history in order to validate his theory of dreams and his theory of the role dreams play in hysteria. But those theories fall within the broad domain of the pleasure principle and, as we have seen, one of Dora's favorite psychological activities lies "beyond" it. Was Freud too much caught up in his own wishes to see that, rather than confirming his theory, Dora revealed an important inadequacy in it?

Perhaps that is an unconscious reason why, when Dora returned to Freud for help fifteen months later, he refused to give it. Freud says: "One glance at her face, however, was enough to tell me that she was not in earnest over her request."[23] One glance? Obviously this is a rhetorical expression, but it makes a telling point. By now we take it as obvious that when one is convinced by "one glance"—whatever that might mean precisely—one ought to spend more time thinking about one's own emotional life. Freud continues: "I do not know what kind of help she wanted from me, but I promised to forgive her for having deprived me of the satisfaction of affording her a far more radical cure for her troubles" (122). In my opinion, this is the one and only moment in the analysis in which Freud behaves unconscionably. Freud has been much criticized in recent years over his treatment of Dora, but I think it is also important to recognize that Freud did Dora much good. He was the first adult to accept her account of family events as true; he was the first to ask her to think about what it meant to her; and he was the first to offer her a vocabulary in which she might think about it. He did it flat-footedly and intrusively, to be sure, and Dora took a break! But it is arguable that over the ensuing fifteen months Dora had recognized that Freud had helped her, that she had gathered up some strength and was ready to try again. The idea that Freud can say to himself and to his reader, "I do not know what kind of help she wanted from me" and yet refuse her request out of hand ... well, it at least has to raise the question of whether Freud felt the need to *give himself a break* from this analysis.

And what of those telling words that, more than a century later, still pack an emotional wallop: "I promised to forgive her for having deprived me of the

23. Freud, "Fragment of an Analysis," 120–21.

satisfaction of affording her a far more radical cure for her troubles." Freud is furious with Dora; his pride is wounded, and he is trying to inflict revenge. But isn't the remark also a symptom? It seems to me to betray an inchoate sense on Freud's part that, even if he wanted to, he is not yet in the position to afford her a more radical cure. At some level he grasps that it is not *Dora* who is depriving him of this satisfaction.

IV

This is a moment from a case study that illustrates how erotic life and emotional life can get disrupted. It also shows how those disruptions can recur within a clinical situation. It seems that we need a distinction between those forms of mental activity which express the mind's capacities to make associations, dream, and imagine on one hand and those forms of activity that disrupt those capacities on the other. This is a theoretical difference that can be detected in a clinical setting—and it is important to do so. For overall, it seems to me, psychoanalysis is committed to facilitating the growth of the capacity to dream, to associate, to imagine. Overall, this is a commitment to facilitating erotic life—in some broad and intuitive understanding of that notion. In part, this allows for the development of emotional life. Too often what looks on the surface like the expression of an emotion—say, anger—is at the same time the disruption of the capacity to express that emotion. It is easy to see that Dora's slap is an expression of her anger; it takes psychoanalysis to realize that she is at the same time disrupting the development of her capacity to experience and express anger.

This does not mean that there is only one kind of clinical response to a moment of break, nor does it mean that swerve is "good," break is "bad." Obviously, there cannot be one type of clinical response since the concept of break covers such an extended family of phenomena: we don't treat a psychotic break in the same way as we treat a momentary disruption of conscious thought.

Less obviously: quite apart from the type of break, there is a question of the context in which the break occurs. So, for example, high-functioning neurotics tend to live with repetitive structures of unconscious fantasy that constrict their lives. And every core unconscious fantasy comes with its own implicit metaphysical theory: it sets out a field in which *all* possibilities are supposed to lie. An obsessional patient of mine inhabited a world in which everything that happened was an occasion for guilt. All his possibilities were guilty ones. And, though we don't know Dora well enough to know for sure, we can imagine that she inhabited a world in which she was constantly being disappointed and betrayed—by loved ones, parents, authority figures. Of course, her real-world experience was like that, but there is a further question of whether she got herself trapped in a disappointing world because of those real life experiences. In such contexts, various forms of break can have a liberating effect. For although the capacity to imagine is disrupted, the disruption itself breaks the rigidity of associations. The disappointing world, the guilty world itself breaks open. This provides an occasion for the imaginative capacity itself to develop in more creative and open ways. In this way, a break can facilitate the opening up of erotic life. A break may thus become a possibility for new possibilities.[24]

This is the kind of break Dora needed.

24. I give a clinical example in *Happiness, Death, and the Remainder of Life*, 114–18.

THE SWERVE OF THE REAL

SLAVOJ ŽIŽEK

My starting point is strategically dogmatic, if not strategically essentialist: Jacques Lacan revealed the Truth, and the task is to compare Jonathan Lear's text with Lacan's Teaching. The only decision to reach is *why* Lear's text should be burned. (Recall the old allegedly Muslim reasoning: all books except Kur'an should be burned: if they do not say the same thing as Kur'an, they are sinful and should be burned; if they say the same thing, this thing was already said better in Kur'an, so, again, they should be burned.)

Lear starts with the insight that Freud's "pre-Socratic" turn to Eros and Thanatos as the two basic polar forces of the universe is a false escape, a pseudo-explanation generated by his inability to properly conceptualize the dimension "beyond the pleasure principle" he encountered in his clinics. After establishing the pleasure principle as the "swerve" that defines the functioning of our psychic apparatus, Freud is compelled to take note of the phenomena (primarily repetitions of traumatic experiences) that disrupt this functioning: they form an exception that cannot be accounted for in the terms of the pleasure principle. For Lear, it is "at this point that Freud covers over the crucial nugget of his own insight: that the mind can disrupt its own functioning." Instead of trying to conceptualize this break (negativity) as such in its modalities, he wants to ground it in *another*, "deeper," positivity. In philosophical terms, the mistake here is the same as that of Kant according to Hegel: after Kant discovers the inner inconsistency of our experiential reality, he feels compelled to posit the existence of another, inaccessible, true reality of Things-in-themselves, instead of accepting this inconsistency. According to Lear, "Freud is not in the process of discovering a new life force, he is in the process of trying to cover over a trauma to psychoanalytic theory. In this way, invoking Plato and the ancients gives a false sense of legitimacy and security."

One cannot but fully agree with Lear: far from being the name of an un-bearable traumatic fact unacceptable for most of us (the fact that we "strive towards death"), the introduction of Thanatos as a cosmic principle (and the retroactive elevation of libido into Eros as the other cosmic principle) is *an attempt to cover the true trauma.* The apparent "radicalization" is effectively a philosophical domestication: the break that disrupts the functioning of the universe—its ontological fault, as it were—is transformed into one of the two positive cosmic principles, thus reestablishing the pacifying harmonious vi-sion of the universe as the battlefield of the two opposing principles. (And the theological implications are here also crucial: instead of thinking to the end the subversive deadlock of monotheism, Freud regresses to pagan wisdom.)

Lear introduces here the notion of "enigmatic terms," terms that seem to designate a determinate entity while, effectively, they just stand for the failure of our understanding: according to Lear, when Freud mentions Thanatos he "takes himself to be naming a real thing in the world but he is in fact injecting an enigmatic term into our discourse. There is no naming, for nothing has gen-uinely been isolated for him to name. His hope is to provide an explanation, in fact all we have is the illusion of one." Examples from the history of science abound—from flogiston (a pseudo-concept that betrayed the scientist's igno-rance of how light effectively travels) to Marx's "Asiatic mode of production" (which is a kind of negative container: the only true content of this concept is "all the modes of production that do not fit Marx's standard categorization of the modes of production.") But is Lear not too dismissive of "enigmatic terms"? Are they really just indexes of our failure and ignorance? Do they not play a key structural role? "Enigmatic term" fits exactly what Lacan calls the Master Signifier (phallus as signifier), the "empty" signifier without signified: this sig-nifier (the paternal metaphor) is the substitute for the mother's desire, and the encounter with the mother's desire, with its enigma (*che vuoi?* what does she want?), is the primordial encounter with the opacity of the Other. The fact that phallus is a *signifier*, not the signified, plays a pivotal role here: the phallic signifier does not provide an explanation to the enigma of the mother's desire; it is not its signified (it does not tell us "what mother really wants"), it just designates the impenetrable space of her desire. And, furthermore, as it was developed by Claude Levi-Strauss (on whom Lacan relies here), *every* signifying system necessarily contains such a paradoxical excessive element, the stand-in for the enigma that eludes it.

The homology with Lacan goes even further: in Lacanese, is Lear's point not that the Freudian pleasure principle is "non-All": there is nothing outside it, no external limits, and yet it is not all, it can break down? Why, then, do breaks occur? When does our mind disrupt its own functioning? These breaks simply occur, ungrounded in any deeper principle: as a "blind" destructive *passage à l'acte* when we find ourselves in a deadlock; as a traumatic encounter. Again, what Lear calls the split between the psyche's normal functioning (under the swerve of the pleasure principle) and its break perfectly fits Lacan's coupling of *automaton* and *tyche* (taken from Aristotle, also Lear's great reference); when Lear describes how, "after a break, the mind tries to get itself back into the swerve-like activity of sexuality, fantasy, dreaming," he clearly echoes Lacan's notion of how fantasmatic formations and symbolic fictions endeavor to patch up the intrusions of the Real. And, furthermore, when Lear emphasizes that trauma is just a species, one of the modalities, of the break, is this not strictly homologous to Lacan's thesis that trauma is only one of the modalities of the Real?

Does this mean that Lear's text should be burned since everything it claims is already said in Lacan? Is the misunderstanding between Lacan and Lear purely and simply terminological? In his critique of Freud's treatment of Dora, Lear claims that Freud repeats the mistake of Herr K and "assumes [Dora] is already a woman, when her problem is that she is trying to figure out how to become one. He assumes she already understands erotic life; she is trying to figure out what it is." In short, Freud interprets Dora as a sexually mature woman with clear (although unconscious) desires instead of perceiving her as what she was—a girl still in search of the mystery of feminine desire and projecting the solution of this mystery into Frau K, her "subject supposed to know (how to desire)." But Lear seems to miss the point here, which is that being in search of this mystery is the very definition of a feminine hysterical subject: there is no woman who really knows how to desire—such a woman would be the Lacanian Woman, *the* woman, who doesn't exist, whose existence is a fantasy.

The more general conclusion to be drawn from this concerns the location of Eros with regard to the break. Lear tends to locate Eros within the swerve of the pleasure principle. But is love, the shattering experience of falling in love, not a break par excellence, the mother of all breaks, the opening up of the possibility of new possibilities? Consequently, is love itself not the supreme example of the "enigmatic term"? It refers by definition to an unknowable X, to the je ne sais quoi that makes me fall in love—the moment I can enumerate reasons why I love you, your properties that made me fall in love with you, one can be sure that this is not love. And, mutatis mutandis, does the same not hold also for sexuality? Is, as it was elaborated by Jean Laplanche, the child's shattering encounter of the impenetrable enigma of his or her parents' sexuality not *the* break that disturbs the child's narcissistic closure and compels him or her to confront new possibilities?

The further conclusion to be drawn from this difference is that, perhaps, one cannot oppose swerve and break as simply as Lear tends to do. Here is how Lear defines swerve: "I call this type of mental functioning *swerve* because it exercises a kind of gravitational pull on the entire field of conscious mental functioning, bending it into idiosyncratic shapes. By way of analogy, we detect the existence of black holes by the way light swerves toward them. We detect this type of unconscious process by the ways our conscious reasoning, our bodily expressions, our acts, and our dreams swerve toward them." For Lacan, however, the Real (of a trauma) is also a "swerve," a black hole detectable only through its effects, only in the way it "curves" the mental space, bending the line of mental processes. And is sexuality (this Real of the human animal) also not such a swerve? One should endorse here Freud's fundamental insight, according to which sexuality does *not* follow the pleasure principle: its fundamental mode of appearance is that of a break, of the intrusion of some excessive jouissance that disturbs the "normal" balanced functioning of the psychic apparatus.

Does this mean that Lacan repeats Freud's mistake and again locates the cause of the break into some preexisting positive external entity, like the Thing, *das Ding*, the impenetrable substance of the Real? Since Lear himself alludes to physics (black holes), one should refer here to Einstein's passage from the special to the general theory of relativity. While the special theory already introduces the notion of the curved space, it conceives of this curvature as the effect of matter: it is the presence of matter that curves the space; that is, only an empty space would be noncurved. With the passage to the general theory, the causality is reversed: far from *causing* the curvature of the space, matter is its *effect*. In the same way, the Lacanian Real—the Thing—is not so much the inert presence that "curves" the symbolic space (introducing breaks in it) but, rather, the effect of these breaks. In contrast to Lear, for whom swerve is the swerve of the pleasure principle, acting as the force of stability and occasionally disrupted by the breaks, Lacan views swerve as the destabilizing force whose gravitational pull disrupts the psychic automaton.

Does this mean, then, that Lear's text should be burned because it does *not* say the same thing as Lacan? One should get rid of the structural illusion that all we attributed to Lacan was already there prior to our reading of Lear: the paradox is that it was Lear himself, his perspicuous formulations, that allowed us to trace the difference between him and Lacan, and thus to clearly formulate Lacan's position. The best way to put my admiration for Lear is to say that, even when I do not agree fully with him, I need his text to articulate this very disagreement—so, perhaps, his text should not yet be burned after all.

ON THE WISH TO BURN MY WORK

JONATHAN LEAR

One might suppose that any analyst worth his salt would welcome such a whole-hearted, as it were, expression of ambivalence. Certainly this is less boring than the overblown praise that academic friends (or the stinging critiques that academic enemies) standardly bestow on one another. Still, as I read through Slavoj Žižek's comments, I had an uncomfortable feeling, as on hearing the unfamiliar sounds of a new lover: isn't he *faking* it? Surely he doesn't really want my works consigned to the flames—the wish is uttered as a theatrical gesture—but, then, what is this drama about? Obviously, a real answer to this question would have many layers, but I want to respond by making a point about the reception of French psychoanalytic and philosophical thought in the United States.

Let's first get some preliminaries out of the way. I take Lacan to be one of the most fertile and deep psychoanalytic minds ever; and I take Žižek to be—let's stick with his language of light—a brilliant thinker. And I have, with gratitude, learned much from them both. Still, even the most enthusiastic reader of Lacan or Žižek would admit that austerity is not a characteristic of their work. Žižek expresses confusion about how my work can be distinguished from Lacan's. It is around the concept of austerity that one can make this difference clear.

My hitherto unspoken hero is Hume. Hume's standard technique would be to notice that people would seem to think they have a certain idea—say, an idea of cause—but that there wouldn't seem to be any impression from which that idea could have arisen. He would then ask how we could have acquired this supposed idea—and what would emerge would be a deflationary account. We would come to see that we didn't really have the idea that we thought we had.

Now for years I read and reread *Beyond the Pleasure Principle*, utterly baffled by how Freud could get to the death drive. Yet I also didn't want simply to dismiss Freud's argument impatiently. I finally tried an approach that was broadly Humean in spirit: Freud seems to have an idea of "the death drive," and yet there doesn't seem to be any impression from which that idea could have arisen. As Freud himself says, the death drive works in silence. So, then, how could this supposed idea have arisen?

My original training is in logic and analytical philosophy, so I decided to look at the fine-grained structure of Freud's argument to see whether there might be a step where the argument fails. It seemed to me that I found it in an unnoticed ambiguity in the expressions "repetition compulsion" and "compulsion to repeat." On one hand, there obviously are motivated compulsive repetitions: this is the stuff of psychoanalysis. On the other hand, Freud himself assumed that repetition was *the aim or goal* of the compulsion. This is an additional assumption: that the compulsion to repeat is a compulsion *to* repeat. In my book *Happiness, Death and the Remainder of Life*, I argue that this assumption is not justified. That is, it is not valid to infer that compulsive repetitions are actually aiming at repetition. This is a small point, but it makes a significant difference. Because if repetition is not the aim of the compulsion, one cannot go on to argue, as Freud does, that the drives are inherently conservative; and one cannot go on from there to Freud's conclusion that the aim of life is death. Freud's argument for the death drive is invalid.

Now once one sees that there really isn't anything that corresponds to our supposed idea of "the death drive," there arises the question of what empirical content our idea might actually have. This deflationary question cannot arise until one sees that the argument for the death drive fails. I argued that the empirical content of Freud's insight is that there are two different types of unconscious mental functioning, which I called swerve and break. I don't want to overdo the importance of this result. It is yeoman's work; somebody had to do it. But as far as I know, this result is not to be found in Lacan or anyone else. Of course, anyone who insists on the importance of the drives and of the economic factor, as Freud and Lacan both do, will in some sense be in the same neighborhood of concern, just as Locke and Berkeley's discussions of causation were in a similar neighborhood to Hume's—but without the Humean deflationary argument, you can't get the Humean result.[1]

---

1. The point of the current essay was to go back to one of Freud's earlier case studies—written before *Beyond the Pleasure Principle*—and rethink it in the light of this distinction. It has long puzzled me why Freud did not revisit his case studies in the light of his later theoretical advances.

By contrast, consider this passage from Lacan (one of many that could be used):

> Whatever the significance of the metapsychological imagining of Freud's that is the death drive, *whether or not he was justified in forging it*, the question it raises is articulated in the following form by virtue of the mere fact that it has been raised: How can man, that is to say a living being, have access to knowledge of the death drive, to his own relationship to death?
>
> The answer is, by virtue of the signfier in its most radical form. It is in the signifier and insofar as the subject articulates a signifying chain that he comes up against the fact that he may disappear from the chain of what he is.[2]

Lacan here explicitly wants to ignore whether or not Freud was justified in postulating the death drive. He also wants to ignore the significance of his metapsychological imagining—and yet by the end of that very sentence, he is talking about our access to knowledge of the death drive and equating it with our relationship to death. By the next sentence he is equating it with an awareness of our relationship to a linguistic formation, the signifying chain. Lacan is a suggestive thinker, a pregnant thinker; yet it is also true that the quality of argument here is poor. Should this matter?

The answer must be yes. Žižek asks rhetorically whether I am "too dismissive of enigmatic terms." My complaint is not with the use of enigmatic terms per se, but with a certain defensive and self-misleading use to which they can be put. There are certain terms—say, *happiness* or *freedom*—that are by their nature enigmatic but whose presence has provoked some of the deepest thinking in the philosophical tradition. But that is because the enigmatic nature of these terms is recognized as such—and it is also recognized that it matters whether or not there is something that answers to the call of "freedom." By contrast, the invocation of "the death drive" has had the function of foreclosing questions in the name of answering them. I cannot tell you how many case-study presentations I have heard in which the speaker will say that such-and-such an aggressive act was "a manifestation of the death drive"—without the speaker realizing that with this extra phrase she has added nothing. It is *as-if*

2. Lacan, *Ethics of Psychoanalysis*, 295; my emphasis. I make the slight emendation of everywhere translating "*pulsion de mort*" and "*Todestrieb*" as "death drive" rather than "death instinct."

explanation: it is as if an explanation has been given when in fact only an enigmatic phrase has been invoked.

Now the reason it is worth spelling this out is that something funny has happened in the reception of French philosophical and psychoanalytic thought. If one looks to other disciplines, say, classics or history, one can see an astonishing influence of French thinking. But when it comes to philosophy, there is a kind of institutional splitting. Philosophy departments in America have been dominated by the analytic tradition. And while this tradition has made remarkable contributions to the philosophies of mind, language, action, logic—and while it has raised standards of argument to an impressive level—it has nevertheless proceeded largely in ignorance of the so-called Continental tradition. By and large, analytic philosophers are ignorant of the works of Hegel, Kierkegaard, Heidegger—not to mention all the French thinkers, like Lacan, who have been influenced by them. Similarly, their knowledge of Freud tends to be cursory, to the point of caricature, so there is simply no way they could responsibly interact with a thinker like Lacan. This has created a vacuum—one that has been filled largely by scholars from literature departments. A marvelous body of work has emerged, but it is nevertheless true that there has been less concern with whether an argument actually works than there would be if this had been taken up by analytic philosophers. And when it comes to philosophy, this does matter.

We need to train a generation of scholars who will overcome this split, who will be able to deploy the rigor of argument of analytic philosophy on the texts and problems of Heidegger, Freud, Lacan. One reason I need to respond to Žižek's comments is that he is such a charismatic writer that a graduate student who reads him might think it fashionable to argue, "Either it is in Lacan or it isn't: either way we can burn it." Such an argument spares the writer from doing the work to figure out what is there, what isn't, and why it might matter.[3] The other reason is that even if Žižek's call to burn is a theatrical gesture, the fact is that it is only recently (and, even now, only in a relatively

3. Here I part company with Hume as well. He famously closes the *Inquiry concerning Human Understanding* with this injunction: "If we take in our hand any volume—of divinity or school metaphysics, for instance—let us ask *Does it contain any abstract reasoning concerning quantity or number?* No. *Does it contain any experimental reasoning concerning matter of fact and existence?* No. Commit it then to the flames, for it can contain nothing but sophistry and illusion" (173). Enough with the flames already! Note that he, too, invokes the image as part of a justification for the claim that we don't actually need to look any further to see what is there.

small part of the world) that one can write what one thinks without fear that one's work—or, indeed, oneself—will be burned. This is a precious achievement, and given human nature it will remain to some extent tenuous. Thus I must take explicit exception to the call to burn—even if it is made somewhat in jest. You know what Freud said about jokes.

PEOPLE AS FICTIONS:
PROUST AND THE LADDER OF LOVE

MARTHA C. NUSSBAUM

LOVE AT BALBEC

The band of girls approaches on the beach, their features indistinct. As they grow closer, Marcel's gaze fastens on "a girl with brilliant, laughing eyes and plump, matt cheeks, a black polo-cap crammed on her head, who was pushing a bicycle with ... an uninhibited swing of the hips."[1] Their insolence and daring dazzle him. For a brief moment he sees the dark girl's eyes beneath her cap, sees a "smiling, sidelong glance, aimed from ... an inaccessible, unknown world wherein the idea of what I was could certainly never penetrate" (1:851). It is at this moment that love begins, inspired by the sign of a hidden life:

> If we thought that the eyes of such a girl were merely two glittering sequins of mica, we should not be athirst to know her and to unite her life to ours. But we sense that what shines in those reflecting discs is not due solely to their material composition; that it is, unknown to us, the dark shadows of ideas that that person cherishes about the people and places she knows—the turf of race-courses, the sand of cycling tracks over which, pedalling on past fields and woods, she would have

An earlier version of this essay appeared in *Upheavals of Thought: The Intelligence of Emotions* (New York: Cambridge University Press, 2001); reprinted by permission of Cambridge University Press.

In chapter 10 of *Upheavals of Thought* I compare Proust's account of love's ascent with those of Plato and Spinoza; I retain some of those comparative remarks here. But the focus on Proust gives the argument a different shape and character.

1. Proust, *Remembrance of Things Past*, trans. Moncrieff and Kilmartin, 1:850. Volume and page citations within the text refer to this edition. The translation has many defects, but it is the one that is most available to readers, so I alter it only where there is a defect that makes a significant difference in my argument.

drawn me after her, ... the shadows, too, of the home to which she will presently return, of the plans that she is forming or that others have formed for her; and above all that it is she, with her desires, her sympathies, her revulsions, her obscure and incessant will. I knew that I should never possess this young cyclist if I did not possess also what was in her eyes. And it was consequently her whole life that filled me with desire; a sorrowful desire because I felt that it was not to be fulfilled, but exhilarating because, what had hitherto been my life having ceased of a sudden to be my whole life, being no more now than a small part of the space stretching out before me which I was burning to cover and which was composed of the lives of these girls, it offered me that prolongation, that possible multiplication of oneself which is happiness. (1:851–52)

Albertine stands out from the group not for her beauty—for all the girls seem beautiful; not for her defiance—for they all seem bold and dangerous; it is because he sees the light in her eyes, and this light is a sign of a life unknown, ungoverned, that he yearns to join to his own. For the prospect of happiness is only a brief and momentary aspect of Marcel's passion. Immediately after seeing the girls, he is "sick with despair" (855) at the thought that he may not be able to find them again, and this despair—alternating with stretches of boredom when he feels secure in his possession of Albertine—charts the whole course of his love. Albertine is both outside of him, impossibly distant, unpossessable, and inside of him, an internal object that disturbs what is deepest in his sense of life. When, years later, she leaves the little train near Balbec with an ambiguous remark that awakens his jealousy, his own life seems to be departing with her (2:1153–54). But the presence of such an ungovernable external person in the depths of the heart makes the heart itself unstable and unkind. Marcel, possessed by anxiety and tormented by Albertine's ungovernable will, has no room in his life for either friendship or justice. His life becomes obsessively focused on projects of jealous possession, which aim at putting him back in control of his own existence.

A DISEASE AND ITS CURE

Any investigation of the emotions' contribution to ethics must confront the ambivalence and excess of erotic love. For if, as Proust repeatedly suggests, erotic love lies at the root of all the other emotions and cannot be removed without removing them, then even a limited defense of the contribution of the emotions to the ethical life must ask whether love can be part of a morally acceptable life. And Proust's contention has great force. He goes too far when he suggests that all friendly love is really concealed erotic love; and yet he is probably right to see the two emotions as intertwined in such a way that we cannot count on retaining the energy of a beneficent compassion if we eliminate erotic love as a danger to morality.

In Marcel's story we see many of the features of erotic love that moral thought has traditionally found disturbing, and has wished to cure. First and most obvious is love's partiality, which seems to threaten any ethical approach involving the extension of concern. Intense attachments to particular individuals, especially when the attachments are of an erotic or romantic sort, call attention away from the world of general concern, asking it to rivet itself to a single life that provides in itself no sufficient reason for this special treatment, as it imperiously claims all thoughts, all desires. Erotic love is based on unequal concern, an unequal concern not explained by reasons: Marcel knows that there really is no rational basis for his choice of Albertine above the other cyclists. His choice is explained, if at all, by shadowy images reaching back into some distant past; perhaps it is explained only by the quirk of chance that lets him see her eyes before the eyes of the others. And such love exacts an intensity of focus that makes equal concern impossible. Shreds of gossip about the Dreyfus case appear and disappear—reminding us, by their rapid shifts as years pass, that there is a world of events and people outside of Marcel's love, a world of justice and great injustice, and that he is lost to that world through love.

And if all the emotions raise worries about a possibly excessive neediness and vulnerability, and the ambivalence toward the needed object that is so common a part of that neediness, how much stronger must this ambivalence seem in the case of erotic love, with its wish to abdicate control by putting one's happiness at the mercy of an unknown and ungoverned object, with its paralysis of prudence and choice, with its wish to surrender the inner precincts of the self to an incubus who is determined to create misery and upheaval. If, as Marcel suggests, love involves an *open sesame* that sends the external person down into the depths of the heart (2:1165–66), then passivity and uncontrol are constitutive features of love. A need this deep is rarely free of retributive wishes. The only way Marcel can prevent unbearable pain to himself is to inflict pain on Albertine. He sees his jealous demand that she sever all her other friendships as the only way of "exorcising my hallucinations," "cur[ing] ... the phobia that haunted me" (3:14). In his demand to know everything about her actions, he sees the only hope to "kill the intolerable love" he feels (3:93). But the needs of such a love are so deep that, like and continuous with an infant's need for totality and comfort, they can never be fully or stably satisfied: "Jealousy, which is blindfold, is not merely powerless to discover anything in the darkness that enshrouds it; it is also one of those tortures where the task must be endlessly repeated, like that of the Danaides, or of Ixion" (3:147–48). The life of the lover thus becomes the life of a jailer, who needs the perpetual threat of escape to goad him to new stirrings of love—and of cruelty.

THE PHILOSOPHERS' DILEMMA

For such reasons, philosophers have not often been friends of erotic love. Even philosophers who defend the ethical contribution of some other emotions tend to dislike the impure intensity of the erotic, which seems as subversive of the beneficent social passions as it is of nonpassionate calculation. Schopenhauer, who finds in compassion the root of all morality, notoriously detests women and the desires they inspire. The aim of our lives, properly understood, is freedom from bondage to the will, that is, to erotic striving. Adam Smith, who defends the ethical role not only of compassion but also of certain types of anger and fear and grief, argues that passionate erotic love forms no part at all of the moral equipment of the judicious spectator, his surrogate for moral conscience.[2]

But it is difficult to agree with these thinkers that love is a merely base or undignified passion. Many of us will find in the erotic what Marcel finds there: a sense of mystery and depth, a tremendous power, that can make us wonder, at least, whether a life that forgoes this passion for the sake of acceptable social rationality would be impoverished, a life without radiance, a life possibly lacking in the strongest sources of social beneficence. Accordingly, very few thinkers in the history of the Western tradition have proposed the complete elimination of erotic love. Although it is evidently one of the most dangerous of the emotions, it has also seemed one of the most necessary, even to philosophers who hate the emotions extremely. The Greek Stoics, who propose the complete "extirpation" of anger and grief and fear and hope, and even pity, still wish to preserve for the wise man a certain species of *erōs*, and not a desexualized species either.[3] Following Plato's lead, they held that this reformed passion would provide the basis for a just and reasonable city.

2. For a more extensive analysis of this part of Smith's argument, see Nussbaum, "Steerforth's Arm"; and also "'Mutilated and Deformed': Adam Smith on the Material Basis of Human Dignity," a Tamara Horowitz Memorial Lecture delivered at the University of Pittsburgh, April 2002, and forthcoming as a chapter in Nussbaum, *Cosmopolitan Tradition*.

3. See Nussbaum, "*Erōs* and Ethical Norms."

They were not alone. Repeatedly in the history of Western philosophy and literature, we find attempts to reform or educate erotic love so as to keep its creative energy while purifying it of ambivalence and excess and making it more friendly to general social aims. This tradition centrally uses the metaphor of an "ascent," in which the aspiring lover climbs a ladder from the quotidian love from which she began, with all its difficulties, to an allegedly higher and more truly fulfilling love. In each case, moving the lover up the ladder involves both addition and subtraction; and we must ask whether what is left at the end still contains what was originally valuable and wonderful in love, whether it is still erotic at all and still love at all.

Such ascent projects follow a number of distinct patterns: Christian thought has its own ascent tradition, as does Romanticism. But Proust is in many respects a follower of Plato, and he sets himself within a tradition that I shall call the "contemplative ascent." Articulated first by Plato, the pattern is influentially developed by Plotinus and finds adherents throughout history, from the later Neoplatonists to Augustine's early writings,[4] to Spinoza and his followers, to modern writers such as Proust and Iris Murdoch. Plato gives the pattern its defining features; Spinoza deepens the account of love's necessary ambivalence and of the social benefits of ascent; Proust, alluding directly to the Platonic ladder, places it within a narrative framework, motivating it more explicitly, developing a Spinoza-like account of ambivalence, envy, and jealousy, and making clear what it comes to in a life.

The general idea behind this ascent pattern is that the cure for the vulnerability of passion is the passion for understanding. By focusing on that intellectual goal, and on the goal of creativity that the tradition links with it, one finds oneself able to deal with the very same worldly objects—or so it is claimed—without agonizing dependency, without ambivalence and the desire for revenge, without the self-centered partiality that makes love a threat in the social life.

PROUST: USING INDIVIDUALS AS STEPS

As a boy he longs for his mother's goodnight kiss. There is an aching absence in his soul that he calls love. He wants to be filled up, consoled, comforted; he wants the nullification of the acute pain of feeling and thought. And even though his mother's kiss brings comfort, its effect is so transient that its happy

---

4. I argue in *Upheavals* that there is a major shift in Augustine from the early Platonist writings to a very different, characteristically Christian, understanding of ascent.

imminence is already tainted with the pain of its departure, "so much so that I reached the point of hoping that this good night which I loved so much would come as late as possible, so as to prolong the time of respite during which Mamma would not yet have appeared" (1:13–14). But the price of the absence of pain, that is to say of love, is the extinction of awareness, the absence, one might say, of a life. Habit, that "clever arranger who makes all things habitable," prevents him from truly dwelling in himself. He wishes to possess the entirety of his life, which is to say the story of his longing, without the terrible intermittence of love itself, with a constancy and solidity of consciousness that love does not permit.

Many years later, he tells us in this very passage, waking up in the night, he feels a primitive longing for comfort that is the legacy of these childhood experiences. He tries to mother himself by pressing his cheeks against his pillow, and he thinks that soon "someone will come to his aid. The hope of being comforted gives him the courage to suffer" (10). He now dreams of a woman, and feels sexual arousal, as he senses the warmth of his body mingling with hers. He feels his body pressed down by her weight—as if she were, indeed, a calming and consoling maternal presence, as well as a sexual partner.[5]

We know from this point on that what Marcel will later call the "general form" of his loves points backward toward the past, toward the solitary anxieties of the child who longs passionately for his mother's goodnight kiss and for her reassuring embrace, which blots out alarming stimuli from the world. In his longing for a return to a womblike state of oneness—even in the dream, he wants to "become one with" the woman he sees—he comes to view even his mother's arrival with pain, because he has learned that he is not in the womb, but in a world in which external objects, having arrived, soon depart again (21).

Proust's novel contains traces of many philosophical accounts of love and its therapy. But the Platonist ascent tradition informs the structure of the narrative at a deeper level, I think, than any other. Plato's *Symposium* gives the narrator his definition of love: "Love, in the pain of anxiety as in the bliss of desire, is a demand for the whole.... We love only that which we do not wholly possess" (3:102). And Plato's ladder of love gives the narrator a pivotal image for the trajectory of his thought and desire. In a composite allusion to both the *Symposium* and the *Phaedrus*, placed at the heart of his theoretical account of

---

5. Strictly speaking, the entire narrative is in the *imparfait*, and the experience of waking in the night is said to be followed sometimes by sound sleep, sometimes by nightmares of "childish terrors," and sometimes by this dream of erotic tenderness.

his own literary project and its material in his life, he writes: "Every individual who makes us suffer can be attached by us to a divinity of which he or she is a mere fragmentary reflection, the lowest step in the ascent that leads to it, a divinity or an Idea which, if we turn to contemplate it, immediately gives us joy instead of the pain which we were feeling before—indeed the whole art of living is to make use of the individuals through whom we suffer as a series of steps enabling us to draw nearer to the divine form which they reflect and thus joyously to people our life with divinities" (3:935).[6] Here we see not only the Platonic idea of using individuals as steps on the way to a general form that they imperfectly instantiate, but also the idea, common to both Plato and Spinoza, that an intellectual project addressed to the material of one's life converts life's pain to solid joy. We now need to examine the way in which this idea is worked out in the narrative itself: asking, first, why it is that the love of real people in life yields only agony and instability, and, second, why the ascent of love should take, as it did not for either Plato or Spinoza, the form of narrative art.

Love, in Proust, is a painful awareness of a gap or lack in the self, accompanied by a demand for a restoration of wholeness. It has its roots in the child's unhappy, anxious longing for his mother; and this desire to possess an elusive source of comfort colors every subsequent love. When Albertine appears before him on the beach, in the company of the little band of cyclists, it is the sheer separateness of her will that inspires his desire. His love of her follows the pattern set by its beginning: excruciating longing, issuing in projects of possession and wholeness that can never be fulfilled, punctuated by moments of comfort that are tainted before they arrive either by the pain of jealousy or the deadness of indifference. "We love only that which we do not wholly possess." Agonizing neediness, obsessive partiality of vision, and the evils of jealousy and hate—all three of the Platonic-Spinozistic flaws in love are emphasized here, and traced, through narrative, to the experience of childhood helplessness at which Spinoza only abstractly gestured.

As Marcel repeatedly argues, such a lover cannot but be cruel to the loved one in his attempt to control her every movement and thought. Albertine can

---

6. Where Kilmartin renders *degré* literally, as "step," I have written "series of steps," which conveys more accurately, I think, the distributive meaning of the original. The passage is a fragment in Proust's journals, without a clear placement in the text. It has been inserted by editors into the middle of a discussion of truths derived from reality by the intellect as opposed to impressions of memory. This does not seem quite right, since the passage alludes to the whole work of the artist in basing his narrative on past loves.

escape from his jealousy only when she is unconscious and has ceased, for the time, to be a separate human being:

> When I returned she would be asleep and I saw before me the other woman that she became whenever one saw her full face.... I could take her head, lift it up, press her face to my lips, put her arms round my neck, and she would continue to sleep, like a watch that never stops, like a climbing plant, a convolvulus which continues to thrust out its tendrils whatever support you give it. Only her breathing was altered by each touch of my fingers, as though she were an instrument on which I was playing and from which I extracted modulations by drawing different notes from one after another of its strings. My jealousy subsided, for I felt that Albertine had become a creature that breathes (un être qui respire) and is nothing else besides.... (3:109)
>
> In this way, her sleep realised to a certain extent the possibility of love.... By shutting her eyes, by losing consciousness, Albertine had stripped off, one after another, the different human personalities with which she had deceived me ever since the day when I had first made her acquaintance. She was animated now only by the unconscious life of plants, of trees, a life more different from my own, more alien, and yet one that belonged more to me. Her personality was not constantly escaping, as when we talked, by the outlets of her unacknowledged thoughts and of her eyes. (3:64)

Thus is it only when a human being becomes a plant that she can be loved without hatred.

Proust's novel addresses itself to a reader who is eager for understanding of her own loves and their form, who would like to use the novel as an "optical instrument," so as to see herself more clearly (3:949). So let us imagine a reader named A—distinct from the fictional Albertine, just as (for Proust) any real person is necessarily distinct from any fictional character, a character being always the amalgamation of several different life experiences—reading the novel and applying it to her own life.[7] She will see that the love of ordinary life brings no joy. Even the pleasure she longs for with M is "in fact only experienced inversely," through the anguish of its incompleteness and instability (3:909).

Nor can she, from her position of immersion within her own life, even understand the structures of that life: for the routines of life, together with

7. In *Upheavals*, chaps. 10–12, I imagine the different ways in which the different ascent traditions would educate A.

our vanity, our incessant jealousy, our mechanisms of self-comfort and self-concealment, operate always to conceal from the self the structure of its own love, with its oscillation between anguish and deadness, its repetitious and obsessive pursuit of the impossible. Her ordinary existence exemplifies a process of self-concealment, a process "which, in those everyday lives which we live with our gaze averted from ourself, is at every moment being accomplished by vanity and passion and the intellect, and habit too, when they smother our true impressions, so as entirely to conceal them from us, beneath a whole heap of verbal concepts and practical goals which we falsely call life" (3:932). Moreover, within life itself she can never achieve toward M himself either accurate vision or true altruism: for all her dealings with him are marred by the self-comforting structure of her aims.

The ascent of love is made possible by art—to some extent by the self-scrutinizing work of the reader of fiction, to a far greater extent by the task of writing one's own life story.[8] Unlike Spinoza, who thinks of narration as too mired in emotion to be a vehicle of freedom, Proust plausibly argues that narration is the only true source of freedom, since only through narration do we master the general form of our love, with all its causal connections—at the same time making this mastery a gift to the reader. The task of the ascent is, then, to turn one's own life into a work of literature, using other people as steps on the ladder. The task is a labor more of decipherment than of creation, as one probes one's past for the text "which has been dictated to us by reality, the only one of which the 'impression' has been printed in us by reality itself" (914). Its goal is the discovery "of what, though it ought to be more precious to us than anything in the world, yet remains ordinarily for ever unknown to us, the discovery of our true life, of reality as we have felt it to be" (915). The raw materials of this work are impressions that have been stored up in us by life itself (914); these must be recaptured and then assembled by the work of memory and intellect, until in the end we have recovered our own lost selves (935) and have immobilized by contemplation all that previously eluded us (909). But this task is, then, in effect, the inverse of the usual operations of daily life, in which we

---

8. It is unclear, as also in Plato and Spinoza, whether the ascent is thought to be available to all human beings, or only to those who are specially talented. Proust, like Spinoza, tends to portray the artist's success as depending on a special effort of will and on a renunciation of which few would be capable. It is this mode of life above all that sets the artist apart from the crowd. On 3:931, he writes that all people have the materials of art within them, but most do not seek to shed light on them; therefore their past is "like a photographic dark-room encumbered with innumerable negatives which remain useless because the intellect has not developed them."

live "with our gaze averted from ourselves" (932). For daily life buries the significant beneath habits and jealousies and vanities that mask its significance; art dispels the false covering and reveals the real material of life. It is for this reason that it is only the work of art, and not daily life, that can be called life fully[9] lived (932, 931). "Experience had taught me only too well the impossibility of attaining in the real world to what lay deep within myself" (910).

Before A can attempt this task with any hope of success, she must sever her connection with M, and, indeed, with all the people she intimately loved or has loved, and seek an undisturbed condition within which the internal book of passion may be discovered. "It is our passions which draw the outline of our books, the ensuing intervals of repose which write them" (945). She should not attempt this, if possible, until she has loved a number of different people—for the reality that is characteristic of literary art requires the grasping of general forms, and this, in turn, requires many experiences (945): "The writer, in order to achieve volume and substance, in order to attain to generality and, so far as literature can, to reality, needs to have seen many churches in order to paint one church and for the portrayal of a single sentiment requires many individuals" (945). Indeed, "infidelity toward the individual" is a prerequisite of the appropriate creative posture (945). The artist in her is delighted not by this or that particular love, but by a general form of love and desire that emerges from all the concrete experiences, in the unity of one portion of her past with another: for she "is nourished only by the essences of things"; in these alone she finds her "sustenance and delight" (905).

The material of literary creation will not be only the good and fine in things, as Plato argued. A will find in the painful, the hateful, the despicable, the grotesque rich material for her contemplation. (Here Proust sides with Spinoza and not with Plato.) Calm and happy times, indeed, Proust holds, are the least valuable to her, since they are times of spiritual dullness, in which keen perceptions are not stored up.

Where love is concerned, she will see the unity of one past love with another, and of what she has called love with other pains (for example, the pain of travel) that she has not previously connected with love (911). All such pains and disappointments are simply "the varied aspects which are assumed, according

---

9. On 3:931, Kilmartin translates, "Real life, life at last laid bare and illuminated—the only life in consequence which can be said to be really lived—is literature." But it has recently been recognized that Proust's illegible handwriting actually has *pleinement* ("fully") and not *réellement* ("really") at this point.

to the particular circumstances which bring it into play, by our inherent powerlessness to realise ourselves in material enjoyment or in effective action"
(911). Thus at bottom, for Proust as for Spinoza, love is all about powerlessness
and neediness.

The pain of A's love for M must now "detach itself from individuals so that
[sh]e can comprehend and restore to it its generality" (933–34). M will become
for her an instantiation of a general form of love and desire whose vicissitudes
she endeavors, in general, to comprehend. The remembered pain of their love
will now be surpassed "by [her] curiosity to learn the causes of this calamity"
(433): as in Spinoza, causal understanding quiets pain. Reaching back to their
love in memory, she will now view him as a model who has "quite simply been
posing for the artist at the very moment when, much against [her] will, [he]
made [her] suffer most" (939). And in this way, in the very process of causing
her pain, M has brought his stone "for the building of the monument" that is
her narrative artwork (941). In fact, she will come to think that he really never
was much more for her than a projective construct of her own imagining and
desire, a fictional character already; and the austere truth of this recognition
will itself console her for the fact that he did not love her enough (932–33).[10]
She will come to understand the truth that art reveals: that we are always
alone, however much we love. "Man is the creature who cannot escape from
himself, who knows other people only in himself, and when he asserts the
contrary, he is lying" (459).

Remembering the pain of love will itself be painful: and A will relive her
suffering with the courage of a doctor who experiments on himself (942). But
the suffering is mitigated by the narrative project in which it is embedded:
"At the same time we have to conceptualise it in a general form which will
in some measure enable us to escape from its embrace, which will turn all
mankind into sharers in our pain, and which is even able to yield us a certain
joy" (942–43).

For the life of art is a life of joy, a joy closely related to Spinoza's intellectual
joy, and connected by Proust with a kind of immortality and life beyond the
world. The raw material of self-knowledge and artistic expression is pain. But to

10. See the title essay in Nussbaum, *Love's Knowledge*, for a discussion of the relationship
between skepticism and consolation. I argue that Marcel's adoption of criteria for knowledge of
the other that are impossible to satisfy is a stratagem connected with fear of openness toward
the other, and that it prepares the way for a skeptical conclusion that is welcome more than
painful.

use this pain *as* raw material for a work of universal communicative power and formal beauty is a profound delight (935) and a consolation. It not only supplies the artist with an endlessly fascinating active task, subject to no circumstantial vicissitudes and managed by her alone; it also enables her to escape her own bondage to the present moment and to possess the form of her life as a whole, thus defeating time and moving as close to immortality as any human being can (905–6).

One might suppose that the good of other human beings does not figure in this life at all. This is in a way true, since M has ceased to exist for her as a real person with real needs. On the other hand, the work of the artist gives readers a powerful tool of self-understanding that they may use to uncover the reality of their own selves, and thus progress toward their own immortality. Indeed, Proust instructs A at this point that, earthly relationships being marred as they are by jealousy and personal longing, it is only in the act of creating a work of art, in the artist's sense of obligation to her theme and to her audience, that true giving to others may take place.

In an important passage in which Marcel describes his thoughts on the death of Bergotte, the novelist, he turns to Plato's theory of recollection, announcing that the novelist bears into this world trace memories of moral obligations contracted in another world—and, seeing that he cannot fulfill these obligations in ordinary human relations, he realizes them through his art. "All that we can say is that everything is arranged in this life as though we entered it carrying a burden of obligations contracted in a former life; there is no reason inherent in the conditions of life on this earth that can make us consider ourselves obliged to do good, to be kind and thoughtful, even to be polite. . . . All these obligations, which have no sanction in our present life, seem to belong to a different world, a world based on kindness, scrupulousness, self-sacrifice, a world entirely different from this one and which we leave in order to be born on this earth, before perhaps returning there to live once again beneath the sway of those unknown laws which we obeyed because we bore their precepts in our hearts" (3:186).

Proust is making more than one claim here. One claim is that the artist's pure dedication to art is the only example of pure dedication we have in this world. But he also says that this dedication is an example of "kindness" and "self-sacrifice"—because he thinks of the novel as a gift to readers. Only in this act do we see selfless giving to others—every face-to-face human relationship being marred by jealousy and possessive desire. The relationship between author and reader is free from excessive crippling dependency, free from ambivalence, even free, in a necessary way, from partiality—for the work addresses itself to all alike. It does not know where it is placed in the lives it addresses.

Nor is this the end of the artist's gift: for the gift also creates for the reader a possibility of unselfish and undemanding love, therefore of knowledge of another's mind.[11] All our attempts to know the mind of another real person are doomed by our jealous projects: we are always seeing some aspect of our own needs and wishes. Before the work of art, by contrast, these obstacles fall away and true knowledge can take place.[12] An artist's style: "is the revelation, which by direct and conscious methods would be impossible, of the qualitative difference, the uniqueness of the fashion in which the world appears to each one of us, a difference which, if there were no art, would remain for ever the secret of every individual. Through art alone are we able to emerge from ourselves, to know what another person sees of a universe which is not the same as our own and of which, without art, the landscapes would remain as unknown to us as those that may exist on the moon" (931–32). And this means that art offers us the only possibility of genuine human contact, and therefore the only possibility of a love that is reciprocal rather than solipsistic.

THE PURSUIT OF WHOLENESS

We have an account of a love that has love's energy, beauty, and wonder without crippling passivity, without distraction, without ambivalence—a love that supports reflection rather than seeking its extinction, a love that embraces the entire world with evenhanded joy. If in Plato's version of the tradition the lover confines her attentions to the fine and good, Proust (like Spinoza) shows that this need not be the case: contemplation can also find joy in the ugly and the grotesque, and even, and above all, in the lover's own history of pain. Thus love is purified of the obstacles that stand between it and a beneficent concern for all humanity.

11. This claim would appear to be in some tension with the claim that the artist offers the reader a set of optical instruments through which to view herself and her own love. I think it need not be. As Proust says, so it is: when we read his novel, we are made more keenly aware of the structure of our own love and its particularity, and, at the same time, we encounter another mind, the mind of a distinctive being who animates the text as a whole. In part we discover ourselves through our likeness to this being, but in part, too, through our unlikeness.

12. A significant corollary of this is that the artist, being the only type of human who can be known by another, is also the only sort who can be immortal. Thus "the idea that Bergotte was not permanently dead is by no means improbable." His books "kept vigil like angels with outspread wings and seemed, for him who was no more, the symbol of his resurrection" (3:186).

But anyone who is really concerned with beneficence and justice should pause. For there are three serious concerns we might raise about Proust's account (as about its Platonic and Spinozistic relatives): a worry about compassion, a worry about reciprocity, and a worry about the individual.

1. *Compassion.* According to the Platonic critique of tragedy that influences this entire tradition, no truly tragic emotion—no emotion implying that a good person can come to grief through no fault of his or her own—should remain in the good life. Tragic compassion must depart as surely as anger, grief, and fear, since in our compassion we acknowledge that the misfortune befalling another has deep importance for the self. In the process we set ourselves up for fear at our own uncertain prospects, and even for anger at the cause of our suffering. Spinoza consequently repudiates pity as a painful acknowledgment of human weakness and an inappropriate response to the necessary and determined suffering we see.

Proust is more complex: for he insists that his novel itself is a work of compassion, in which the artist has sacrificed his ease for needy humanity. He portrays his work as the emissary of a world of true altruism and sympathy beyond the ravages of jealousy and human love. There is much that seems compassionate in the work—with its searching portrayal of grief and mourning, its tenderness to the vicissitudes of human suffering. At one point the narrator even states that the compassion for suffering is stronger, even, than the pleasures of love (3:435).

And yet there is reason to feel that the initial compassion is negated by the austerity of the novel's ending, in which we understand all human relationship to be fictitious, all loss therefore as loss merely in fiction. The corollary of loneliness is self-sufficiency. The artist's primary aim has become her own immortality, something that has only a tangential connection with the happiness of the reader. Nor does he seem to be alive to general social concerns. The political events of Proust's time appear through the narrative at a great distance, as so many signs of human folly and inconstancy; and we see why this must be so. No person who follows Proust's advice about love would take a risk for Dreyfus—even an intellectual risk—or get enmeshed in class struggle. Those things are mere distractions from the all-consuming project of self-contemplation. In the end, then, just as the novel adopts a view about the object of sexual love that implies that all sex acts are essentially masturbatory, so too it adopts a view of sympathy and altruism—even, I think in the end, the altruism of the artist—that implies that all such altruism is at bottom egoistic self-gratification. This happens, as in Plato, out of the search for self-sufficiency.

Is there compassion at least for the beloved? M remains important to A in two ways: as a vehicle for creation, and as a part of the reality that contemplation studies with joy. In Plato, he turns out to be a relatively insignificant vehicle for creative thought and speech, since, like any real person, he evidently contains so much less goodness than other objects she can contemplate, and his goodness is so mixed up with bad and neutral properties. In Spinoza's view, he fares somewhat better, since she may study the whole of him and not simply his goodness, and since the understanding of her own history is permitted to play a particular role in transcending her pain. And in Proust's he fares best of all, since he will be a major source for the work of art she will create. Nonetheless, we have to say that M himself, and the happiness of M, vanish from view. He is, to use Proust's image, just an artist's model, just an occasion for a creation that transcends and leaves behind his reality. If she acts beneficently for his sake, it is only insofar as he is a part of the whole world to which her creative activity is addressed. If he really needed her, she could not see it.

In short, the boundaries of the lover's world, while appearing to expand, through love's embrace of the universe, have actually contracted, through the lover's repudiation of the human meanings of events and people in that world. To love human beings as fictional personae is to push them away, not to embrace them.

2. *Reciprocity.* The love depicted in Plato's *Symposium*, though unselfish and creative, appears to lack respect for the lover's separate agency and for reciprocal elements in the love, treating the beloved object simply as a seat of desirable properties. What do we find in Proust? As the lover progresses there is certainly less and less desire to possess or control individual people, less jealousy, less selfishness in the usual sense. But is there any sense of respect for the other person's choices? For Proust, the agency of the beloved object is central—but as a primary cause of the artist's past suffering. In her cured artistic condition, A will regard M only as a model, the origin of a literary character; and the freedom to manipulate that character belongs entirely to her.

3. *Individuality.* Proust, like Spinoza, considers separateness in the object to be a source of pain, something to be defeated rather than respected and loved. The fact that the people we love have their own lives to live is precisely the problem. As for qualitative particularity, this also plays an ever-diminishing role in the increasingly abstract contemplative concern of these followers of Plato. Unlike Plato, Spinoza and Proust do not restrict A's view to what is fine and good in the object—so their views might seem to promise a richer grasp of particularity. But how far do they take us? Proust's narrator does continue

to see the particular loves of his past—but only as so many signs of general essences, and of the general form of his love. It is for this reason that when A writes her Proustian artwork, the man she will portray there will not be M in all of his concreteness. It will be a rather abstract composite of several parts of her history.[13] It will not be surprising if the resulting literary character is as lacking in particularity as Albertine—whose individuating traits fluctuate inconstantly through the novel, and consist in great measure of her tendency to recall to the narrator childhood feelings of pain.

Again, as with Plato, these points about separateness and particularity are not simple. For by removing jealousy and insecurity, Proust has also gotten rid of some of the most powerful impediments to individual love—as he records by emphasizing that ethical relations from the "other world" of kindness are possible *only* in the relationship between artist and reader. Lovers ascend beyond the obstacles imposed by the insecure ego—but only by leaving behind the sight of the real-life individual in all his or her erotic complexity. This seems tolerable to Proust because on his account the individual as such never has been the object of love. The people we love, he concludes, are the ones we see least clearly of all: they are merely "a vast, vague arena in which to exteriorise our thoughts.... And it was perhaps my fault that I did not make a greater effort to know Albertine in herself."

Thus the ascent succeeds only by getting so high above real people that the specificity of their human existence cannot be seen. Like Plato and Spinoza, Proust seems to believe that only in this way can the terrible excessiveness and ambivalence of love be cured. What should we say to A about this? If we agree with the diagnosis but remain discontent with the conclusion, we face, it seems, a difficult choice, especially where social life is concerned: either no hope of overcoming hate, or an overcoming that also wipes out compassion, reciprocity, and particularity, except in the contemplative relationship between philosopher and God, or between reader and text.

The diagnosis of our therapists can now, however, be questioned. For they all begin with an understanding of love that derives from a picture of infantile helplessness and the infantile wish for omnipotence—that sees the wish of love in terms of the restoration of totality and a state without deep need. We might say that they express a kind of pathological narcissism: for they long

---

13. See 3:876: "In this book in which there is not a single incident which is not fictitious, not a single character who is a real person in disguise, in which everything has been invented by me in accordance with the requirements of my theme ... "

for complete control over the world, and they refuse to abandon that wish in favor of more realistic human wishes for interchange and interdependence.[14] Their characterizations of what human life is like are distorted by their wish, for they see only agony and misery wherever there is incompleteness and a lack of dictatorial control, only the threatening wherever there is a body going its own way. Rather than learning to live in a world in which every lover must be finite and mortal, the contemplative lover finds marvelously ingenious devices to satisfy the desires of infancy—deploying, to remarkable effect, the wonder and curiosity that are so prominent in a human infant's initial makeup. Rather than renouncing the wish for totality in favor of a more appropriate human wish, this lover has continued to be motivated by infantile omnipotence and has for this very reason had to depart from a world in which the infant's wishes can never be satisfied.

None of our three worries can be well addressed, so long as the ascending lover continues to hold on to omnipotence, or complete control of the good, as a goal. Reciprocity requires a willingness to live alongside others who are equals, and this means a willingness to admit limits on one's own control of good things. One cannot hate the very fact of another person's uncontrolled existence and still live with others on terms of reciprocity and justice. Compassion typically involves seeing oneself as one among others, similarly vulnerable, with similar possibilities for worldly misfortune. One cannot have compassion for others if one is unwilling to acknowledge the reality and the salience of another human life alongside one's own. And, as Proust admits, seeing the particularity of another truly and clearly requires a stance that does not try to incorporate or swallow that other particular, the stance of one who is willing to live in a world where there are agencies external to the self that go on being the way they are. In that sense he is absolutely correct: it *was* his fault that he did not get to know Albertine as she was in herself. But it was his fault not (as he thinks) because he fell in love with her, but on account of the specific goal he set for himself in love, and the account of love he adopts, so well suited to that underlying goal.

Why is this aim chosen? Why, to put it differently, is the Platonic ascent so attractive? Why has it had such appeal throughout the history of thought? Proust's diagnosis can stand for all three: it is because of shame. Proust depicts our condition as one of unendurable weakness and need, and he depicts us as riven not only by pain but also by shame about this condition of need. One

14. This is a major theme in Nussbaum, *Upheavals* and *Hiding from Humanity*.

day, recognizing that in kissing Albertine he is really embracing and trying to possess the image of his mother, the narrator acknowledges this limitation. People like him, he says, "know that their emotions and actions are not in a close and necessary relation to the loved woman, but pass by her side, brush up against her, surround her like the tide that crashes along the rocks—and this awareness of their own instability increases still further their conviction that this woman, whose love they so much desire, does not love them.... This fear, this shame, bring about the counter-rhythm, the ebb-tide, the need ... to take back the offensive and to regain esteem and control."[15] It is this starting point that dooms his project to ethical inadequacy. Each of these three visions of a complete love is marred by the particular narcissistic stance of its author toward the world of value.[16]

So too A, cycling along the beach, is self-sufficient. She has had a philosophical education that lifts her beyond shame, beyond revenge, beyond instability—but also beyond politics, friendship, and human love.

15. Kilmartin 2:857–58, my translation of the French. Shame is a theme of long-standing in the novel. Consider, among others, the scene at Balbec where the young Marcel, annoyed that Charlus speaks in a vulgar way about his grandmother, frankly says, "What, Monsieur! I adore her!"—and is promptly told by Charlus that it is shameful to acknowledge one's sentiments openly, just as ridiculous as to have anchors embroidered on one's bathing-dress (1:823). In the Raoul Ruiz film *Time Regained*, this moment is especially well rendered.

16. In Proust there is most room to doubt: for after all, Marcel is not Proust. But the text creates no space in which Marcel's distinctive vision of the world may be criticized from within.

PROUST'S EPISTEMOPHILIA

PETER BROOKS

"Ideas are substitutes for sorrows," Marcel tells us at the moment of discovery of his vocation: they are replacements and successors, *succédanés*.[1] When sorrows and pains are transformed into ideas, they lose some of their harmful effect on us; they indeed create a moment of joy. And in fact, ideas perhaps substitute for sorrows only in a temporal sense, since the Idea (Proust's capital I) was there first, and sorrow was simply the mode in which certain Ideas first entered into us. This comment from *Le temps retrouvé* lends credence to Martha Nussbaum's eloquent and finely textured reading of Proust within the Platonic tradition of "contemplative ascent" from erotic passion to a higher plane of understanding. "The general idea behind this ascent pattern," she writes, "is that the cure for the vulnerability of passion is the passion for understanding."

The ascent claimed by Marcel here is perhaps all too vertiginous in the heights it seeks. As Nussbaum notes with acuity in detailing her three "serious concerns" about Proust's account, it implies self-sufficiency and the negation of our relation to other people. "The fact that the people we love have their own lives to live is precisely the problem": Nussbaum's summary is exactly on target, and the ascent at the end of *Recherche* appears to give up on the problem. It is a world-consuming kind of ascent: everyone he has known, all his loves and sufferings, are sublated in the joy of creation. If Proust is a Platonist, it is not in the tradition of Dante or Renaissance Platonism, where love of the lady, properly disciplined, leads the soul of the lover upward, toward perfection. He stands more in the late-Romantic version of the tradition, as in Wagner's *Tristan und Isolde*: a world-annihilating love.

---

1. Proust, *À la recherche*, ed. Clarac and Ferré, 3:106. I use the "old" three-volume Pléiade edition, which, though imperfect, is more user-friendly than the new four-volume edition, with all its variant texts, edited by Jean-Yves Tadié. Translations are my own.

Love is moreover tainted at the root in Marcel's experience. He first witnesses the erotic at work through the open window at Montjouvain, where Mlle Vinteuil and her unnamed woman lover sadistically profane the portrait of Mlle Vinteuil's father as part of their erotic foreplay. Erotic love comes bound up with pain. It was not, the narrator tells us, that evil seemed to Mlle Vinteuil erotic, pleasurable, but rather that erotic pleasure seemed to her evil, diabolical (1:164). And from this moment—in the first volume—onward, the erotic always seems to be in alloy with pain. *Swann in Love*, which follows closely on the boyhood experience of *Combray*, gives an initial model of love as a consuming jealousy to know and to possess another life, with the concomitant knowledge that in the act of so-called sexual possession, one possesses nothing. *Swann* reveals also the uses of jealousy as a principle of knowing and creating. The jealous lover, constantly anxious about the hidden life of the absent beloved, can make of that most prosaic document, the railway timetable, "the most intoxicating of love novels" (1:293). The jealous desire to know—and the impossibility of its fulfillment—leads to a warped but creative epistemology that is at the inception of fictionmaking, creativity. Marcel's experience with Albertine, whom he must imprison in his effort to possess, recapitulates Swann's with Odette, though even more somberly. The torture of trying to know Albertine endures after her death: he interrogates her friends on the meaning of past incidents, words, and the structure of Albertine's lies. It is all ostensibly an effort to know if she has had lesbian loves. Indeed, the eroticism Proust regularly calls "inversion" matters in the novel partly because it provides an intensification and exemplification of the intransience and instability of the love-object, as opposed to what Marcel sees as the "idealism" of love itself—precisely because it is an idea that creatures of flesh and blood never satisfy.[2]

Proust's scenario of erotic passion triggering the passion for understanding is close to Freud's description of the drive for knowledge, *Wisstrieb*, which James Strachey translates (felicitously, I think) as the "epistemophilic instinct." The core Freudian instance of this "epistemophilia" comes in his essay on Leonardo da Vinci, whose infantile sexual curiosity is focused on looking, and particularly on looking for the mother's absent penis—the search for an imaginary object that becomes the model for Leonardo's subsequent restless investigative energy and creativity. Freud pursues the *Wisstrieb* in his case of the "Rat-Man" ("Notes upon a Case of Obsessional Neurosis"), where he notes that obsessional

---

2. See in particular 3:910, where it is claimed that "sexual inversion" simply magnifies the instructive lesson of love.

patients often have a high intellectual capacity along with a tendency toward neurotic brooding: "The thought-process itself becomes sexualised, for the sexual pleasure which is normally attached to the content of thought becomes shifted on to the act of thinking itself."[3] The joy that Marcel discovers with his vocation sounds very much like the sexualization of thinking. Other people cease to be other, to become what we want to make of them. "Where life walls up, the intellect pierces through a way out" (3:905).

Marcel famously claims for his work to come an optical instrumentality: it should allow his reader to see more penetratingly into her own life. For "each reader is, when reading, the reader of himself" (3:911). And in this manner he suggests how the wastage of life—time wasted—can be redeemed through the intelligence of art. But turning fiction into this sort of cognitive instrument does not solve the ethical problems that Nussbaum identifies. She concludes by noting that Proust's initial view of love as needy and shameful (I would even say sadistic, allied to evil) "dooms his project to ethical inadequacy." But here I want to argue that the cognitive instrument Proust provides also should teach us about the difference between moral philosophy and narrative fiction. Proust's stance toward what Nussbaum calls "the world of value" cannot be measured in the language of ethical reasoning. For all its discursiveness, *Recherche* offers no precepts. Rather, it tells the story of an experience leading to a vocation. Despite the self-preoccupation, indeed the narcissism, of the narrator, it is a book of "negative capability," the work of the "chameleon poet" rather than the "virtuous philosopher," to use Keats's famous distinction.

Another way to put this would be to insist that the book that Marcel at the end promises to write is not the *Recherche* we have just finished. There is an irreducible gap between the two. Marcel's book to come promises to be that of revelation, of the truth about the laws of human existence found and expounded. Whereas the novel we have finished is the book of error, of wandering and searching for the truth in signs that point to the revelation to come but remain obscure, not quite decipherable. It is a book of pathos, of "cette perpetuelle erreur qu'on appelle la vie," of mistakes to be overcome. With some exaggeration, one could say that the book to come will be something like Dante's *Paradiso*, whereas the narrator has led us step by step through the *Inferno* and the *Purgatorio*. And at the heart of the *Paradiso*, the pilgrim is simply struck dumb by the revelation of God. It is not a narratable experience.

---

3. Freud, "Obsessional Neurosis" (1909), *SE*, 10:245. On Leonardo, see "Leonardo da Vinci" (1910), *SE*, 11:96.

Narrative has to do with finding the way, and its ethics lie along the way. It may be true that Proust's project is doomed to "ethical inadequacy" if your measure is how it stands toward "the world of value." But I don't think one can put to Proust's novel—or most novels—the question of what makes up "the morally acceptable life," to use another of Nussbaum's phrases. Proust, like all the greatest novelists, is very much concerned with the morally acceptable life. But I would not look for the adequacy or inadequacy of his treatment of it—even of the place of love in it—only in the narrator's overt pronouncements or in the novel's explicit point of arrival. It must lie along the way, in the error-prone wandering of the text. Compassion? It's not in the ascent pattern that enables Marcel to become the artist of his life but in the creation of such suffering creatures as Swann, Gilberte, Saint-Loup, Charlus, even the awful Madame Verdurin. That's the chameleon poet at work.

ALL LOVE TOLD: BARTHES AND THE NOVEL

PHILIPPE ROGER

Translated from French by Sharon Bowman and the author

Roland Barthes's name won't surprise in a book devoted to Eros. When Sigmund Freud, fleeing Vienna in 1938, arrived in France on his way to America, he was greeted by a French magazine as "Le maître de l'amour," his bald and bearded head appearing on the cover page surrounded by a constellation of half-naked female silhouettes. Some forty years later, Barthes, without the psychoanalytic profession's privileged relationship to sex as an excuse, would suddenly be declared another "maître de l'amour." In the wake of the popular success of *Fragments of a Lover's Discourse*, a then famous television program devoted to literature organized a memorable confrontation between an uncomfortable Barthes, a shyly blushing Françoise Sagan, and the impassible author-publisher of a Harlequin-like French series of sentimental novelettes. Meanwhile, the French edition of *Playboy* scrambled to secure an interview with Barthes, which appeared as the lead article of its September 1977 issue. To many, the great semiologist had turned palm reader, in spite of his insistent (albeit largely unconvincing) caveats on the strictly discursive and thoroughly "reconstructed" nature of the Love he had decided to put forth in his book and, by his own account, to "defend." While seasoned Barthesians denounced the spate of naive readings coming from the media's co-opting of Barthes, new readers flocked around the delightful "figures" gathered in his book, eager to look, to listen, and to repeat after him, "That's it, that's exactly It!"

Part of this essay appeared as "Caritas Incarnate: A Tale of Love and Loss," in *Yale Journal of Criticism* 14, no. 2 (Fall 2001): 527–33; © Yale University and The Johns Hopkins University Press, reprinted with permission of The Johns Hopkins University Press.

In 1977, I for one had divided my loyalties between a "scholarly reading" of *Fragments* (published in *Critique*)[1] and a playful interview with the author (for *Playboy*)[2] without fully realizing that what I considered an acrobatic and professionally dangerous leap between highbrow chic and mass-circulation trash was a pure reproduction of Barthes's strategic move in *Fragments of a Lover's Discourse*. Despite the delicious shiver of rebellious insolence I felt, I was only following Barthes's lead. I came to fully realize this some time later, when I came across a passage in Balzac that provided me with the missing piece to the puzzle: the ironic source of the much-commented-upon "objet aimé" (loved object), an expression Barthes uses systematically in *Fragments* and which has been interpreted by many commentators as either an antisubjective statement or a rhetorical ruse to avoid the gender mark. Plausible as they may be, those learned interpretations should keep in mind a phrase from Balzac's *Beatrix*, a favorite novel of Barthes's: "the *loved object*, as fortune-tellers say."[3] Back to the palm and tarot readers . . .

But the thrust of my argument is not aimed at *Fragments of a Lover's Discourse*, that canonical Barthesian *summum* on Love. Nor will I address the topic (often presented as eminently Barthesian) of the text as eroticized object, as an erogenous zone of writing and reading, a "fetish that desires me" (a formulation that appears in *The Pleasure of the Text* in 1973).[4] As stimulating as the topic has been, and as seductive as *Fragments* remains—a subtle book, in fact, in which a lover's confidings hide behind the analytical simulation of a lover's discourse—it is elsewhere that I intend to situate my inquiry. Plainly put, my intent is to interrogate in Barthes's very last texts the simultaneous return of Love as supreme value and of the Novel as most desirable literary practice. These texts, posterior to *Fragments*, were written between 1977 and Barthes's death in 1980. They propose a radical reevaluation of Love, which, as I would like to show, is inseparable from a reorientation of the literary project—a double movement for which Barthes had found a code name that gives a literary weight, mythical as well as existential, to his final project. The code name, borrowed from Michelet (who had borrowed it from Giambattista Vico, etc.), is *Vita Nova*. *Vita Nova* is thus both the title of Barthes's last literary project (of which only working notes remain); and, explicitly (Barthes says as much in a lecture

---

1. Roger, "C'est donc un amoureux."
2. Barthes, "Le plus grand décrypteur," in *Œuvres complètes*, 3:780–90.
3. "*L'objet aimé*, comme disent les tireuses de cartes" (121).
4. Barthes, *Le plaisir du texte*, in *Œuvres complètes*, 3:1507.

on Proust from 1977), "the discovery of a new writing practice."[5] Last, but not least, Barthes explicitly linked the new project to a "withdrawal." What Barthes calls, not without solemnity, the "decision of April 15, 1978," can be thus summarized: "I withdraw [je me retire] to start working on a great work [grande œuvre, probably referring more to its planned magnitude than to its hoped-for "greatness"] where Love would be told."[6] A withdrawal from scientificity, to be sure; from mondanity, in the Proustian sense of the word, certainly. But the ambiguous French verb, se retirer, with its strong sexual implication when used absolutely, may suggest another withdrawal: not from Desire as such, but from the possessive drive inherent in sexual desire.

A "new life," then—but new in relation to what past? The quick response would be, new in relation to a writing past concerned with "metalanguage," with "discourse on"—be it on literature or on oneself, as in Roland Barthes on Roland Barthes and even in Fragments, where an evocation of lived experience is once more poured into the scholarly mold—here, both pretext and protection (literary quotations, commentaries, marginalia, interpretations, and authorized references to psychoanalysis or philosophy); but let us also add: which is new in relation to the figure of Eros, which had thus far dominated Barthes's conception of the world.

Barthes thus overturns a traditional schema (almost as old as Love itself, as developed in Western literature): the schema that shows an old-fashioned Love, draped in all of the Golden Age virtues, suddenly being supplanted by Eros—a modern rogue, a heartless, immoral libertine. Among the innumerable recastings of this myth, I have a preference for Marivaux's in his 1731 one-act play, "La réunion des Amours," in which the insolent Cupid (a modern and saucy Eros) humiliates Gallic Love, his sentimental, outmoded rival: "In your day, lovers were only simpletons; they only knew how to languish, to give their 'alas'es, and to recount their sufferings to echoes all around. Oh! but of course, it is no longer so. I have suppressed the echoes."[7] Marivaux craftily depicts the defeat of old-fashioned Love, of courtly Love, of the Love found in old novels but also Platonic, ideal Love. In short, the unseating of selfless, disembodied Love at the hands of an emancipated, practical, and very realistic Cupid, who is enterprising and shows a penchant for "real" gratification. Barthes's Vita Nova proclaims the inverse: a romantic revolution or, to borrow Marivaux's choice

5. Barthes, "Longtemps je me suis couché de bonne heure" (1978), in Œuvres complètes, 3:833.

6. Barthes, transcription of the Vita Nova manuscript, in Œuvres complètes, 3:1304.

7. Marivaux, La réunion des Amours, act 1, sc. 1, in Théâtre complet, 2:4.

image, a restoration of the echoes of yore. Love avenges itself on Desire; the Novel is recalled (as from exile), reestablished in its dignity and even, as we shall see, in its "mission."

This is more than a palace revolution. Until the end of the 1970s, modern Love (to use Marivaux's term) was lord and master over Barthes's writings, taking counsel only from Desire. Eros-Cupid was without rival—to such an extent that in order to create some dialogue, to find an interlocutor, Barthes had to split in two, cleaving himself into Pleasure and Jouissance (an exploration of this coupling is at the heart of *The Pleasure of the Text*). In this sense, Barthes's writings are both of their time (that of Freudo-Reichism and Deleuzian *désirants*) and perfectly faithful to a very French intellectual tradition: voluntaristically nonreligious (even while plunging roots into religious soil) and hedonistic as much by conviction as by predisposition ("lest we ever forget Brecht's and Marx's cigars," Barthes repeats, castigating the Left's own fear of pleasure). Barthes circulates with ease amid a culture characterized by an eroticized intellectualism that aspires to reconcile Rabelais's truculent libertarianism and the modern antinaturalist transgressions of Sade, Gide, or Genet.

"Pleasure" then, and "jouissance," "desire," "Eros," "erotic" (which Barthes often makes into a noun, a calque on "rhetoric": "traditional erotics")—such are the key words or, to use his terms, *les mots-mana*, the magic words weighted with charms and powers, which spur on Barthesian thought through the mid-1970s. It is rarely a question of Love. "Undoubtedly, desire prowls in all literature," writes Barthes in 1964.[8] And the critic prowls around this desire. Barthes analyzes it in Sade, sniffs it out in Fourier, hunts it down even in Ignatius of Loyola; he describes it in Bataille as a "forced syntagma"[9] and in Racine as the very palpitation of alienation; in Loti, he must unmask it: one eroticism can hide another, and the heterosexual longings of the harem can be the fig leaf covering more "pale" and troubling debauches between men. He dissects it in Balzac's "Sarrazine"; he tastes it in Renaud Camus's *Tricks*; he makes it blush (to the university's great scandal) even in the irreproachable Michelet, whom he depicts as fascinated by conjugal menses. Everyone is involved: Marxists and mystics, the Ancients and the Moderns, writers, philosophers, and even critics. Let us not forget, however, that Barthes, beginning in 1954 with his first book, *Writing Degree Zero*, has depicted himself quite differently: as the Blanchotian lover, swooning for and transfixed by a Literature-Eurydice; but over

8. "F.B." (1964), in *Œuvres complètes*, 1:1442.
9. "La métaphore de l'œil" (1961), in *Œuvres complètes*, 1:1351.

the course of two long decades, it is always at the service of Eros Pantocrator that he portrays himself.

Let us come now to the intertwined questions of love and the novel in Barthes's final writings. Paradoxically (if we consider all that has been written on Barthes's reversals and recanting), it seems to me that little of the strangeness and radicalism of his last articles and talks (1977–1980) on the "desire for a novel" has been noticed. Or that if they have been noticed, it has been through the wrong end of the telescope, a telescope pointed at a theatrical, vaguely ridiculous Barthes announcing that he's going to "go there," like opera choruses repeating "onward, onward" while remaining noisily stationary.

It seems to me that this final space—fixed by his death as a kind of destination—does act as a point of arrival. In these texts (and I will concentrate on "Longtemps je me suis couché de bonne heure"), Barthes goes beyond simply breaking the taboo weighing on that obsolete form known as the novel; he goes beyond professing to be in its thrall. He does not even recoil from the difficult avowal of his own "desire for a novel." Instead, he assigns to this refound novel a solemn "mission," and to that character still recently considered "a little ridiculous, the writer," a singularly serious role. The writer, the novelist, is no longer the naive or duplicitous officiant of the impossible cult of an already-lost Literature; he becomes the indispensable depositary of all the world's losses, and their scribe. But not only in the sense meant by Henry James when he wished the novice novelist to be "one of the people on whom nothing is lost"; also, and more surprisingly, coming from Barthes, in the sense that the novelist is the one by whom loss will be redeemed.

It is a veritable conversion to the novel—or reconversion, inasmuch as Barthes had always been a fervent and secret lover of the Novel. (For those wary of the religious connotations, I should add that *conversion*, at least in French, can mean the operation by which novice skiers, uncomfortable on a slippery slope, turn their skis, one after the other, in the desired direction.)

I should also add: Barthes is not converted to the novel at the expense of decryption, of analysis, interpretation, and so on. For him, "going toward the novel" doesn't imply renouncing anything or making some "leap of intellection." His "desire" remains profoundly heuristic. The last lines of "Longtemps" leave little doubt about that: "I postulate a novel to be written, whereby I can expect to learn more about the novel than by merely considering it as an object already written by others" (835–36). [Je postule un roman à faire, et de la sorte je peux espérer en apprendre plus sur le roman qu'en le considérant seulement comme un objet déjà fait par les autres.] Would Barthes himself, time allowing, have struck out on the path of the novel? "How should I know?" says Barthes; so ... how should *I*? What is clear, however, is that this "novel"—dreamed or desired—would have looked very little like the sketches and scribblings of "Notations" and "Incidents," which appeared posthumously; what is clear is that by means of this fantasy or project, Barthes reorganized his world and, singularly, his *amorous world*. In this reorganization, in his breaking away from the temptation or fascination of the fragmentary form, Barthes will find an intercessor and a guide: Proust himself, who not only revisits, revises, and revivifies the Hugolian metaphor of the novel as cathedral but directly addresses the question of the "notation" when he writes in *Time Regained*: "How could a literature of notations have any worth at all, given that it is underneath the little things such as those we note that reality is contained?" (Comment la littérature de notations aurait-elle une valeur quelconque, puisque c'est sous de petites choses comme celles qu'on note que la réalité est contenue).[10] "Underneath" or beyond? That will be the question. There is little doubt, however, that Barthes's last project of a "grande œuvre," explicitly associated with Proust's own masterpiece, implies a repudiation of the forms that had previously intrigued and attracted him—and of his former dreams of a literature of notations, in particular.

Leaving Proust aside only for the moment, a simple question that has been deferred until now, for fear of a misunderstanding, should be posited. Why does the Novel (as in "question of the novel," but also "desire for the novel") reappear at the center of Barthes's later articles, those written between 1977 and 1980—not to mention in *Camera Lucida*, which is also a book convexly about novelistic writing as love's legitimate shrine?

The answer to this question can be found in the new formula (the term here referring to the "chemistry" of the novel, to its molecular nature, not to its proceedings or procedures) that Barthes came to describe and defend. With an insistence that at the time was often little understood or ill regarded, Barthes attempted to delineate the novel after his own heart, to say what it looked like. Pause a second on the image of the desired novel, which Barthes sketched out by combining traits from several novels he loved, particularly *The Remembrance of Things Past* and *War and Peace*.

The idealized novel contrasts interestingly with those that came before it in Barthes's career: worlds away from the purified antinovel, spare and unsparing,

10. Proust, *À la recherche*, ed. Clarac and Ferré, 3:894–95.

which he stridently championed in the 1950s, ratifying for Alain Robbe-Grillet's benefit the law of the New Novel "as it ought to be"; far, too, from the unclassifiable writing he bid for as "forbidden" out of solidarity in the 1970s—that of Sollers in *Drama* and *Paradise*, for example. But just as far from the hedonistic fragmentation and "incidental" writing to which the final Barthes has often been reduced, unhappily booked (as can be said of misdemeanors) as "late" Barthes.

The "desire for the novel" of the final Barthes is worlds away from all that. Far from the dream of purity or avant-gardist "oscillation," Barthes assumed a new value, heavy and cloying, which he called *pathos*. As far from fleetingness as from egotistical frivolity, the novel whose lesson—and perhaps intercession—Barthes solicits is a *gesture of selfless love*, a reversal of a lifelong suspicion toward "oblation," a poignant and lucid apology of *caritas*.

First of all, pathos. Writing in the vein of Proustian marginalia, Barthes rehabilitates in "Longtemps" the idea of "*pathos* in the simple, non-pejorative sense of the term," "as a force of our reading" (834). Why must we "recognize" pathos, to use Barthes's expression? Because the novel, as he has come to desire it, is most important for its "moments of truth," which "are the *plus-value* points of the anecdote": the "vital, concerned reading," Barthes advances, is a walk from one peak of pathos to the next (ibid.). By way of a geographic, geological metaphor, the great novel becomes an enormous rubble heap, a magic mountain forced by our reading into a "'deterioration'(un délabrement) that leaves only certain moments standing, moments that are strictly speaking its summits" (ibid.). The novel, the real novel (which is also the "great" novel), used to be a "cathedral" (the very word used by Barthes when commenting on Hugo: "la cathédrale du roman"); here it is a block that offers itself to the crumbling (*émiettement*) of its "whole" by our reading of it. It is the immense enterprise by which the reader can see a skyline: the earth pillars of his own emotions. Through this rich and surprising imagery, not only is the whole question of the fragment overturned; the novel as a "whole"—a "whole" to be "crumbled" by and for pathos—is affirmed.

Rather than Blanchot's impossible literature, or the eluded, trumped, or vanished literature of Robbe-Grillet, Queneau, or Perec, Barthes in extremis substitutes the idea of a dilapidated literature, which, contrary to the New Novel still vulnerable at its "points of overripeness,"[11] draws its strength of pathos from the very fact that it is degradable. On one hand, Barthes reaffirms

---

11. Barthes, "Littérature littérale" (1955), in *Œuvres complètes*, 3:1214.

the unimportance of the "anecdote," of storytelling—only the "punctum" or the *plus-value* of the "moment of truth" matters; on the other, he gives the novel back its volume and its mass, no longer as an architectonic "monument" (the Hugolian "cathedral"), but as a mountain whose "essence is not in its structure" but in the "skyline" of moments of pathos traced by an astounded reading.

Why astounded? The scenes Barthes cites to back up his argument speak for themselves: the grandmother's death in Proust, or rather, the reappearance of her death in the narrator's grieving memory; the death of Prince Bolkonsky in *War and Peace* and the brutal revelation by which Princess Maria, his daughter, comes to understand that she was loved and not scorned by her father. Two scenes of mourning, then, but in which the scandal of death reveals a dazzling love; two scenes where, for Barthes, it is the evidence of love that (too late?) overcomes the subject. Henry James created from this heartrending tangle an entire narrative, *The Beast in the Jungle*, which I am not sure if Barthes ever read. I have a hunch, though, that he would not have guessed its author, precisely because James constructs the whole tale's suspense around a misunderstanding, rather than having its pain emerge in a "moment of truth" that might have been written, as in Proust and Tolstoy, in letters of tears on the walls of the narration.

We see, then, that the novel in Barthes's conception is the depositary less of death, less of mourning, than of love.

It is destined to "say whom we love." This is, Barthes adds—conscious of the word's weightiness—its "mission." I had to "acknowledge," Barthes writes (and it wasn't a given), that "the work to be written...actively represents, *without saying so*, a sentiment of which I was sure, but which I now have great difficulty naming." (Note the change of tense.) "This sentiment which must animate the work has something to do with love." But this something is neither Eros nor agape. "What then—kindness? generosity? charity? Perhaps simply because Rousseau has given it the dignity of a 'philosophème': pity (or compassion)."[12]

What are we to make of this final secular prudishness, by means of which Barthes hides under the wing of Rousseau and his "pity"—a less compromising notion inasmuch as it is endowed with a philosophical "dignity"? Is Barthes mocking himself and his avowed anxiety, which leads him to run for cover under the wing of any "great system" at hand? Or might he also be suggesting

---

12. "Longtemps je me suis couché de bonne heure," 3:834.

the long-awaited reconciliation, within himself, of the "philosophème" and the emotion—a reconciliation that, he notes, has been attempted, in Western history, by only a few mystical thinkers? Those questions, however answered, leave no doubt as to Barthes's focus: it is in fact *pietas* Barthes is talking about. *Pietas* and—I'll use Latin again to break away from the "circle of worn-out words," as he does—*caritas*, a pity that has nothing to do with the general disposition toward humans and even animal species described by Rousseau, but with the specific distress and irrepressible revolt the horrible oxymoron of love and death calls forth in men and women—"What Lucifer," Barthes suddenly asks (himself), "created *at the same time* love and death?" Two years later, in one of the handwritten fragments of the *Vita Nova*, dated December 12, 1979, Barthes would give up his last resistance, abandon all prudishness, and list explicitly *charité* among his hypotheses for a new life—and a new kind of writing.

What is the novel for? The Barthesian response is simple and strong. It makes "pathos speakable." It "permits me to *say* whom I love." It "testif[ies] that they [the loved ones] have not lived (and frequently suffered) 'for nothing.'" It allows "these lives, these sufferings, [to be] gathered up, pondered, justified" (834). The most valuable aspect of such narratives is their obliqueness: the novel can speak of love and loss directly and indirectly at the same time; it is discreet, in the strongest sense of the word. It can point to emotions and suffering without pointing at them. The new novelist praised by Barthes is therefore the perfect antagonist to the voyeur. He is not—cannot be—a narcissist. He is not—cannot be—a predator of others' lives. He is the one who indicates what should not be looked at—out of respect and caring, rather than shyness or disgust.

An ineffable goodness is required of the novelist—a goodness that, nevertheless, does not exclude the possibility of a deep-seated wickedness. How could we find a cooler, crueler look at men and women, and entire worlds, than Flaubert's? And how could we find a more delicate, sensitive, tactful, and loving presentation of loss and solitude than in his portrait of Félicité in the short story "A Simple Soul"? A character very similar to Félicité appears briefly in *Madame Bovary*, during the famous scene of the agricultural fair: an elderly maid is awarded a medal for her many years of "servitude"; to the eyes of the "well-fed bourgeois" on the town council, she appears a deaf, credulous, and stupid brute. But to the novelist's caring eyes, her double, Félicité, becomes a shrine of naive, uncorrupted sublimity.

The novel cannot be true to its "mission," according to Barthes, by forging the lies of a gentler, kinder fictional universe, but rather by setting on our imperfect, violent world the eyes of Love and *Pietas*. Denouncing the cold and selfish gaze of the bourgeois set upon the misery of their social inferiors (in *Madame Bovary*) and revealing the fragile and sublime selflessness of the servant Félicité (in "A Simple Soul") are two sides of the same golden coin—the only medal worth melting down, for the novelist.

But examples of the novel according to Barthes—of the novel as the vehicle of oblative Love—need not be taken from the misty past of the genre. We see the same novelistic *telos* in a recent novel by Don DeLillo, *Underworld*. We also find in this work a fictional parable of what could be called the pious vision required of the novelist. An old Italian-born superintendent's comments on an eviction thus become a shorthand *Ars Poetica* of the novelist: "Someone was evicted, put out on the street, chairs, table, bed, right around the corner—the bed, John said, the super. Frame, springs, mattress, pillows, out on the sidewalk. *Porca miseria*. What a wretchedness it was, what a complete humiliation of the spirit. You're like a museum of poverty. People walk by and look. The bed, the plates and glasses, the suitcase with your clothes, a pair of old shoes in a paper bag. Imagine shoes. And they walk and look. Who says this, who says that, who sits in a chair, who points from a car. They should be ashamed to look. A man's shoes on the sidewalk" (768).

DeLillo's novel is also a quest for a secular *Caritas*, culminating in a wistful miracle: the supernatural apparition, every night, of a raped and murdered teenage girl, whose face shines for the "faithful" on a giant billboard over the nearby expressway—until finally even that mirage fades away, as the dwindling number of witnesses sends Esmeralda—a very Hugolian name—back to noth-ingness: "How do things end, finally, things such as this—peter out to some forgotten core of weary faithful huddled in the rain?" (803).

It is, we come to see, not lightly that Barthes chooses and repeats the word "mission"; nor is it blindly that he evokes, quoting Michelet, the "resurrection in History." The novel (the novel after his heart) is written under the double invocation of *Pietas* and *Caritas*, the accomplishment of rites owed the dead, and the "transcendence of egotism." The line of this reevaluation is so clear, it's surprising to see how little understood it has been: doubtless it seemed too contradictory in the face of the cliché Barthes, sparkling with bantering hedonism.

Barthes, between 1977 and his death, rebaptized the novel. He made its genre out to be that of an antilyric enunciation: "saying whom one loves" is opposed to "saying to them that I love them (which would be a strictly lyri-cal project)" (835). Teleologically, he assigns it the "mission" of "transcending egotism," and in this light, it is thus surprising that the coherence unifying

"Longtemps, je me suis couché de bonne heure" and "One Always Fails in Speaking of What One Loves" has been ignored. The latter text illustrates, by way of Stendhal, the transcendence of egotism (for lack of which Stendhal's *Journal* fails, in Barthes's opinion) through the great achievements of *The Charterhouse of Parma* or *Lucien Leuwen*, the fusion of History and story into the novel. This is clearly the same argument as the one on Proust, and if the article's title has troubled critics, it is only because of its pronoun: the one who fails is the one attempting to tell what he loves (or likes, or enjoys); the novelist does not fail, because he says *whom* he loves: the loved ones. And in both cases, Barthes is trying to thwart the "fiasco stalking lyric desire" as well as a more prosaic failure, the "fiasco du style," which "bears the name of platitude."[13]

In *saying* whom he loves, the novelist saves them (from forgetfulness, from indifference, from inanity), but he also *incarnates* them, as opposed to the essay, even a largely autobiographical essay like *Fragments of a Lover's Discourse*. *Fragments* borrowed from Barthes-as-subject almost all of the figures that Barthes-as-essayist sewed together into the well-ordered folds of a cultural curtain, stopping short of a gesture of incarnation. Despite all of its personal material and intimate echoes, *Fragments* is still a book of "figures," constructed around characters—including that of Barthes in the role of suffering subject. "One of the greatest tragedies of my life," wrote Oscar Wilde, "is the death of Lucien de Rubempré."[14] Then, comments Barthes, came the day he discovered Reading Gaol. Such a day comes for everyone: the day when death is no longer only that of Lucien de Rubempré and when "heartrending love" is no longer only the love brought to lost Literature; the day when Eurydice's loss stops being an elegant allegory.

It is not the least astounding aspect of Barthes's career, in my view, that whereas so many other critics consumed their days with finding, behind every tale of death, the dreadfully dull allegory of the death of Literature, he preferred, as a carrier of his own pain, to consecrate his final literary reflections, not to the loss of the novel, but to the novel that could speak the loss, the real loss, of loved ones.

Plato's *Phaedrus* already posited, through narratives and myths, the serious question of the nature of Love and, no less serious, that of what to do when someone else requires love from you. The scene takes place on the banks of

13. Barthes, "On échoue toujours à parler de ce qu'on aime" (1980), in *Œuvres complètes*, 3:1216.
14. "Decay of Lying," 16.

the Illissos, under the shade of a plane tree. Young Phaedrus is transported by Lysias's discourse, which has shown that it is more suitable to give oneself to the desirous lover than to the enamored one. Dared to "do better," Socrates throws himself into an even more convincing apology of non-Love (or Desire without Love). But before he begins, he covers his head: "It is with my head veiled that I will speak."—an unusual oratory posture, to which the fiery Phaedrus gives too little importance: "Just speak! and as for the rest, do as you will."[15] In fact, the veiled head is well and truly part of the discourse. Or rather, it indicates how the discourse should be received. It invites the good listener (which Phaedrus is not) to hear its irony and wait for the palinode—the truthful discourse of "reparation" to the offended Eros that will be later delivered by the same Socrates, now bareheaded.

During the last three years of his life, a bareheaded Barthes (re)turned to Love, not as a topic, but as the very matter of Literature. Love is what makes Literature, and matters about it. True, for a while, he had proceeded masked. In 1969, less than ten years before the *Playboy* interview in which Barthes admits to a personal identification with all of the "figures" of amorous speech scripted in *Fragments*, he responded to another questionnaire, entitled "Ten Reasons for Writing."[16] Of the ten reasons Barthes gave, not one had anything to do with Love. But then, 1969, apart from being the year of the "Summer of Love," was also the apex of Barthes's "dream of scientificity." Eros seemed to be everywhere, except on Barthes's agenda or writing pad. Phaedrus-like disciples applauded the last theoretical performance—*S Z* was the order of the day—and failed to notice the veil. Many complained bitterly (and comically), afterward about not having being "warned." They should have kept in mind the many instances in which Barthes, as early as the 1950s, had praised the Cartesian "larvatus prodeo" and its Brechtian version, adopted by Barthes: that of a masked actor pointing at his mask.

A few years later, Barthes would nevertheless accomplish his coming-out—not, however, the one he was so often reproached for avoiding. He would declare himself for Love and, at the same time, fully reconcile himself with his own love for Literature: the same "heartrending love" that had inspired his early, Blanchotian texts of the 1940s and early 1950s. Fiction writing, along with Love, returns to the forefront of Barthes's interests in the late 1970s—this time as a difficult, painful, mind-boggling challenge. A lifelong process of nostalgia

15. Plato, *Phaedrus*, 237a.

16. Barthes, "Dieci ragioni di scrivere" [1969], *Œuvres complètes*, 2:541.

(the longing for return) and a much less ironic palinode, definitively, than that of Socrates—who already knows, when he gives his first impious discourse, that he will immediately unweave it with his second one. We don't find, in Barthes's itinerary, this premeditation of a palinode. Neither do we find, in fact, its completion—that is, the work announced by the title *Vita Nova*. Interrupted by his death, this search for a new writing of Love remained unfinished and the question of its form, unanswered.

RESPONSE TO PHILIPPE ROGER

ERIC MARTY

Translated from French by Thomas Bartscherer

Dear Philippe,

I read with the greatest care your propositions concerning Barthes and the novel. We two were among the witnesses of those last years and thus, in a certain sense, we were in attendance as this question was formulated in the very mouth of the "Master." I recall quite well the lecture "Longtemps je me suis couché de bonne heure" at the Collège de France. The evening was a bit sad, or sufficiently strange in any case, and it seemed to me that he was practicing solitude, a strange asceticism, in the very act of exercising the magisterial word. I believe you heard this lecture, on which you comment throughout your text, a short while thereafter, when Barthes went at your invitation to New York, but I do not know what accounted for the climate or the atmosphere in which transpired what Mallarmé would have called "a chat" (*causerie*) or "a rambling" (*divagation*). At the time, I was most profoundly gripped by the feeling (I was very young, and when one is so young, one suffers for one's Master) that Barthes was a voice crying out in the desert. He who had hitherto constructed an image of himself as one protected, intimidating, marked by the still vivid recollection of a taste (not so remote at the time) for "terrorism," for the violence and radicalism of "*theoria*"; he who was, as you yourself described him at the beginning of that famous interview for *Playboy* magazine, "the greatest decrypter of contemporary myths" displayed in this lecture—delivered in a lax, very muted, weary voice—nothing but the image of *vulnerability*. I had a sense of disappointment, but a strange disappointment, because this vulnerability did not seem to me at all involuntary but, on the contrary, like the first step of an asceticism, which then took the form of a methodic regression. This word *regression* should certainly be understood not merely in its psychological sense but also with attentiveness to the theme of "return," of "retracing one's steps"—in brief, a slow and thoughtful advance, where it is a matter of recovering something or someone or, in still other words, the movement Orpheus makes in conducting Eurydice. But precisely this regression Barthes could only accomplish *alone*. Just as one can forge ahead only with a cortege (the cortege of friends) or with a troop following behind (readers and disciples), so likewise it seems one cannot retreat except alone: the path of return is always a solitary path.

That is why I was very affected by certain details in your observations—your commentary on the verb *to withdraw* (*se retirer*), for example, which you rightly read in an intransitive and absolute sense; or your remark that in reality the strangeness and the radicalism of Barthes's last articles—those around and accompanying the lecture in question—have not been made the object of a proper analysis. And so it is precisely this analysis that you engage in, very appropriately associating Barthes's long and insistent meditation on "love" with the "desire for the novel." What I referred to with an ambiguous word, *regression*, in the case of Barthes goes beyond merely the question of his person. In suddenly proclaiming the values, the words, and a practice that had been made the object of a spectacular dissection during the twenty preceding years, Barthes made a gesture that could not but have caused a stir, more or less well suppressed. Ultimately—why not say it?—*Fragments of a Lover's Discourse* received practically no attention among Parisian intellectuals, who regarded it as an incomprehensible object. Likewise the "desire for the novel" associated with a pathos of love, thanks to which the work would find its justification; the idea that in saying "whom I love" through the novel, the loved ones would thereby not have lived in vain—all that seemed to most people to be a truly inaudible discourse. It was a discourse of pure subjective conviction, having strangely renounced trying to convince, to persuade, to argue; it was a discourse that placed Barthes outside of all issues of intellectual power, which is to say, outside of every problem proper to the intelligentsia. On account of this, it is perhaps necessary to hear, behind a discourse apparently estranged from all actuality and behind an apparent vulnerability, the subversive power that Barthes really intended to deploy and that he had begun to deploy in *The Pleasure of the Text*, where the critique of the then triumphant Marxism and Freudianism had not been accepted, except thanks to the fragmentary form of the text and to the (at times a bit underhanded) skill with which Barthes made pleasure into a kind of counterterror (*contre-terreur*), something that could be called a counterpower (*contre-pouvoir*).

Love, which it should be noted does not have the same meaning in *Fragments of a Lover's Discourse* as it does in the project for the Novel, had in the following years (those of which you speak, 1977–1980) a subversive power every bit as important. In making compassion-love the essence of the novel and of his own novelistic project, Barthes was certainly aware of effecting considerable reversals in the modern idiom. And this was not only on account of a distaste for the mimicry of modernity, the arch examples of which he undermined (Freud, Marx, "theory," etc.), but also for more profound reasons. Barthes knew that there was no ethics of language and therefore of writing except on the basis of *positivity*, and it seemed to him that the field of modern theory was at that time incapable of producing positivity. As a discourse, this theoretical field seemed capable of postulating only critical, negative, reductionist, or purely analytical positions . . . and this negativity could not be ethical because it was unproductive; it did not engage at all with the visible world. To write a novel in which love would be spoken, then, appeared for Barthes the only gateway—a narrow one—toward an ethical language and writing, the only access route to "the open" of a visibility, a presence, and a light for which the "camera lucida"— *photography*—would finally be the ultimate form. This "final" work attests to the fact that his quest, deliberately subjective, solitary, and apparently sterile (because no novel, not even the beginning of a novel, ever saw the light of day), had not been undertaken in vain.

You conclude, dear Philippe, with an evocation of the *Vita Nova* that death interrupted, leaving the question of Love in the incomplete state of an interrogation that had nullified every other preoccupation—political, aesthetic, ideological—and that, in the strange silence Barthes henceforth inhabited, remained in fact infinitely open like the pages of a book still to come. It is not forbidden to think that this book still to come was, for Barthes, in a certain sense the surest trace he as a writer intended to leave behind; this bequest is all the more precious because no last will and testament preceded it.

THE DESIRE AND PURSUIT OF THE HOLE:
CINEMA'S OBSCURE OBJECT OF DESIRE

TOM GUNNING

It is the image of the ungraspable phantom of life; and this is the key to it all.
HERMAN MELVILLE, «MOBY DICK»

PROLOGUE: CLOSE ENCOUNTERS IN DARKENED ROOMS

In the Western tradition, two seemingly antithetical images of love intertwine, perhaps complementing each other, perhaps contradicting each other. One is the view of Love as an overflowing abundance, the divine source of existence and creation. As expressed by the philosopher most devoted to this view, the nineteenth-century German Romantic Franz von Baader, creation resulted from God's love, which he describes as "his absolute Overflow into the Overflowing" (seinen unbedingten Überfluss ins Überflussige hinein).[1] Baader rooted existence in this free-flowing love of God, reworking Descartes' "Cogito ergo sum" into "I am loved, therefore I am" (112). In an impulse uniquely Christian, Baader distinguished this overabundant Love from its opposite, desire, which signifies lack, declaring: "Only the rich soul loves, only the poor soul desires" (120).

But it is difficult to conceive of eros in Western art and literature only in terms of such tautological abundance, without the lack that inscribes desire and that, according to many theories of narratology, also kicks off most stories.[2] There is, in fact, a primal story that narrates the relation between these two views of love, as wholeness and as lack: the tale Plato puts in Aristophanes'

---

1. Betanzos, *Von Baader's Philosophy of Love*, 120.

2. See, for instance, Tzvetan Todorov's statement, "An 'ideal' narrative begins with a stable situation which is disturbed by some power or force" (*Introduction to Poetics*, 51). Many structuralist theorists of narrative point to the kidnapping of the princess in Vladimar Propp's *Morphology of the Folktale* as an exemplar of the sort of lack or disequilibrium that incites a narrative.

mouth in the *Symposium*. According to this rather satirical fable, human beings once existed in three sexes—male, female, and hermaphrodite—and possessed spherical bodies with four legs and arms, two heads, and two sets of genitals. Fearing the strength of this powerfully endowed mankind, Zeus divided them in two, weakening their strength by half. However, each separate being now yearned for its complement: those carved out from men desired other men; those from women, other women; and, in the case of hermaphrodites, the now separate men and women longed for each other. Aristophanes proposed love as the result of—and compensation for—this primal separation, declaring: *Tou holou oun tei epithumia kai dioxei eros onoma.*[3] The elegant British novelist known as Baron Corvo used this Greek phrase as both title and motto of his "Romance of Modern Venice," following Benjamin Jowett's classic translation, "The desire and pursuit of the whole is called love."[4] I would like to stress two things about this founding Western myth of Love. First, most obviously, it reconciles lack and fullness through a quest to recover a lost whole. Less obviously, but perhaps even more significantly, it founds this quest on both a primordial unity and an almost primordial tragedy of division. The quest therefore always refers backward to primal states and primeval events.

As the major twentieth-century inheritor of the task of telling stories, the cinema has shouldered the burden of portraying both images of eros, the overflowing and the agonistically divided. But it should not surprise us that, as the medium in which words and pictures intertwine—in which stories are visualized and pictures move through time—cinema plays it own games with eros. Cinema does not simply carry the old myths and stories as inert freight but gives them a new twist, imbuing them, as it were, with aspects of the nature of film itself. Passionate devotion to the medium of film has its own name, a term without a parallel for devotees of art or literature: *cinephilia*. The term evokes a connotation of fetishistic perversion and was coined by the culture most devoted (in the West at least) to speaking of both cinema and love, the French. What is it about the filmic image, the moving shadow projected by electric light onto a screen surrounded by darkness, that—in itself—evokes the erotic? Just as the act of reading provides one enduring image in the West of generating erotic fantasy, going to the movies has accumulated its own eroticism.

3. Plato, *Symposium*, trans. Joyce, 542–46 (189–93 in the standard Greek edition).

4. Corvo, *Desire and Pursuit of the Whole*; Plato, *Dialogues of Plato*, trans. Jowett, 1:509. Joyce's more colloquial translation runs: "when we are longing for and following after that primeval wholeness, we say we are in love" (545).

For many, the environment of projection itself, the darkness of the film theater, becomes a sort of erogenous zone. Roland Barthes has described the darkness of the cinema as "the 'color' of a diffused eroticism," the definition and condition for modern urban erotics.[5] At the dawn of cinema, in an era when legitimate theaters still maintained a certain level of house lights to enable spectators to see each other and their surroundings, only the cinema and the Wagnerian rituals of Bayreuth plunged spectators into obscurity as they gazed fascinated at spectacle and filled their ears with music. The technical requirement of darkness for clear film projection constituted a scandal. In fact, in 1908 the mayor of New York City ordered the closing of film theaters citywide, claiming that these unlit rooms enabled a new form of degeneracy as acts of darkness reputedly took place under the cloak of an artificial cinematic night.[6] Undeterred, the newly emerging institution of the cinema accepted and standardized its erotic role, focusing the attention of its eroticized audience (already dwelling, Barthes claims, in a hypnotic state, immersed in the shadows)[7] onto the incandescent illumination of the cinematic star as image of the perfect erotic body.

From the beginning, cinema had been associated with erotic and often disreputable environments. Maxim Gorky saw the first Lumière projections in Russia in 1896 at Aumont's, an attraction at the Nizhni Novgorod Fair that promised all the delights of Paris for a few rubles. One could even watch the latest Parisian novelty of moving pictures seated next to an imported French chorus girl, who might even be persuaded to accompany one upstairs after the show for a few rubles more. Gorky noted the contrast between the wholesome scenes of family life that made up the Lumière films and the environment in which they were shown but predicted that soon the screen itself would show films with such titles as *Madam at her Bath* or *As She Undresses*.[8] Pornography had already become a staple of still and stereoscope photography, and *scènes grivoises et piquantes* soon found their way into early film catalogues with almost exactly the titles Gorky had predicted.[9] As a device invented (by scientists and photographers like Eadweard Muybridge and Etienne-Jules Marey) partly in

5. Barthes, "On Leaving the Movie Theater," 346.

6. Gunning, *D. W. Griffith*, 151–55.

7. Barthes, "On Leaving the Movie Theater," 345.

8. Maxim Gorky, in Leyda, *Kino*, 407–9, trans. "Leda Swan." A detailed analysis of the three texts Gorky wrote about this early encounter with the cinema can be found in Tsivian, *Early Cinema in Russia*, 36–37.

9. This phrase covers a category of films in the Pathé catalogue from 1907.

order to record the motion of bodies with a greater precision than previously possible, the cinema, as Linda Williams has shown, seemed destined for an encounter with pornography.[10]

But does cinema's portrayal of Love's promise of fullness really reside in this sort of fidelity and accuracy, extending to the climax of pornography, which Williams tells us is known in the cinematic skin trade as the "money shot"?[11] Pornography would seem rather to derive primarily from what Barthes describes as "the school boy's dream," the desire to denude, to know, founded more in *curiositas* than eros.[12] The body of the movie star excludes the possibility of pornography by promising more and delivering less, withholding visual demonstration in favor of the always-deferred promise. This promise of fantasized physical presence, pleasure, and fulfillment can be expressed, I think, not only by the icons of screen romance—say, Dietrich, Garbo, Valentino, or Brando—but by the erotically polymorphic bodies of the silent comedians Buster Keaton and Charles Chaplin. Keaton's perfect athleticism in pursuit of desire, as when he swings at the end of the rope in *Our Hospitality* to rescue his beloved, portrays a fulfillment of the erotic through a pure physical grace before which any pornographic image must confess impotence.[13]

But it is perhaps Chaplin who truly embodies the God Eros in the twentieth century, displaying a body that proclaims nothing but love to the camera.[14] Late in his career, when reactionary and paranoid American politics, Hollywood scandals, and a growing old age seemed to steal from Chaplin the love of audiences that had been his sustenance, he put his cinematic philosophy (which had remained ineffable for so long) into words. In 1952, in his last screen masterpiece, *Limelight*, Chaplin, playing the aging music hall clown Calvaro, sings a song that turns Baader's vision of the "absolute Overflow into the Overflowing" into an unforgettable musical hall turn:

What is this thing?
Of which I sing
That comes in spring?

10. Williams, "Film Body" and *Hard Core*.
11. Williams, *Hard Core*, 8 and passim.
12. Barthes, *Pleasure of the Text*, 10.
13. For a description of this scene, see Gunning, "Buster Keaton."
14. One example of the identification of Chaplin with Love would be the early surrealist editorial entitled "Hands off Love," which protests the criticism, coming from his divorce trial, of Chaplin's sexual mores. See Nadeau, *History of Surrealism*, 151.

Oh it's love, it's love, and it's love, love, love, love, love, and love!
Love, Love, Love, Love, Love, Love, Love, Love, Love, Love, Love, Love, Love
Love, Love, Love, Love, Love, Love, Love, Love, Love, Love, Love,
Love, Love, Love, Love, Love, Love, Love, Love, Love, Love, Love
Love, Love, Love, Love, Love, Love, Love, Love, Love, Love, Love, Love!

This is accompanied by Chaplin's dance, one of those filmic moments that resist all translation or description, in which the balletic and the vulgar intertwine in a sublimely earthly evocation of the thing that comes in spring.

This pleonastic expression of love in cinema could only be put into words by the man who resisted the talking cinema the longest, and could only be spoken as a sort of farewell to an audience that had broken faith with him. The aging Calvaro's love song recalls Louis XVIII as portrayed in Balzac's *The Lily of the Valley* when he claimed that men only know true passion in the middle age, when impotence plays a part in it.[15] Thus even cinema's finest expression of Love's plenitude unfolds against the screen of its limitation, the knowledge, as Gorky said when he saw the first projected film images, that the cinema provides only a kingdom of shadows, in which human touch remains an impossibility. The human presence on the screen remains a product of technology, impalpable, "the movement of shadows, only of shadows" according to Gorky.[16] Thus, when pioneer Soviet filmmaker Lev Kuleshov used the cinema to create a perfect woman, he used editing to fashion a woman who could only exist on the screen: "By montage alone we were able to depict the girl, just as in nature, but in actuality she did not exist, because we shot the lips of one woman, the legs of another, the back of a third, and the eyes of a fourth. We spliced the pieces together in a predetermined relationship and created a totally new person."[17] If cinema claims the site of the fantasy of fullness and fulfillment, it can do so only by confessing, and ultimately making visible, the process of its own construction and therefore the possibility of its destruction. Kuleshov's perfect woman might seem to be a counter-enchantment to Aristophanes' tale of primal splitting, but in fact, the seemingly perfect body remains an assembly of disparate parts whose wholeness doesn't exist on the screen but rather solely in the viewer's imagination. As film theorist Christian Metz demonstrated, the power of cinema may lie precisely in the way this medium blends a sense of

15. Balzac, *Lily of the Valley*, 212.
16. Gorky, in Leyda, *Kino*, 408.
17. Kuleshov, "Art of the Cinema," 53.

presence with an undeniable absence: "it drums up all perception, but to switch it immediately over into its own absence."[18] The very ontology of the cinematic image partakes of the paradox of the erotic, promising fulfillment only by withdrawing. To appropriate the title of the farewell work of another great cineaste obsessed with the erotics of the cinema, Luis Buñuel, the cinematic image—and the screen and sheltering darkness that render it visible—provides a powerful staging of the obscure image of desire.

TAKING THE PLUNGE

Alfred Hitchcock's 1958 film *Vertigo* provides perhaps cinema's most beautiful and most bitter image of this erotic quest for the object of desire. The film has been described and interpreted as an allegory of the patriarchal power of the male gaze, and as a primer in Freudian and even Lacanian psychology.[19] But it owes its ever increasing reputation, I believe, not only to the image it presents of love under patriarchy, but also to its revelation of both the pathology and the emotional depth of Love as pursued in the Western tradition. A plot that begins as a detective story becomes rerouted as a tale of desire as the detective misses a crime but uncovers within himself a primal loss and searches agonistically to overcome it, reaching the limits of wholeness through an encounter with the uncertain nature of the love object. In a manner of expression perhaps unique to the visual fascination and almost physical effect of cinema, the film figures the power of eros precisely as vertigo, a state defined as dizziness, often brought on by a view from high places, in which it seems the world spins unsteadily around one. More than a simple evocation of the sensation of dizziness (although crucially it is that, too), the circular and spiral forms of *Vertigo* revolve around the promise of fullness and the fear of loss.

One of the most beautiful and disturbing sequences of the film presents cycles as an image of deep time. A man and woman stand before a redwood tree whose towering mass dwarfs them. The woman describes this tree and those surrounding them in the background as "the oldest living things." The man, Scottie, asks her what she is thinking. She responds in a husky voice: "Of all the people who have been born and died while the trees went on living." The

---

18. Metz, *Imaginary Signifier*, 45.

19. Key commentaries on Vertigo include Wood, *Hitchcock's Films Revisited*, 108–30; Mulvey, "Visual Pleasures," 14–26; Modleski, *Women Who Knew Too Much*, 87–100; Rothman, "Vertigo," 152–73; and Trumpner, "Fragments of the Mirror," 175–88. A complete production history of the film can be found in Auiler, *Vertigo*.

couple come to a cross section of one of the redwoods on which a few rings are traced in white and marked with historical events that occurred during the tree's lifetime: 1066, The Battle of Hastings; 1215, Magna Charta signed; 1492, The Discovery of America; 1776, The Declaration of Independence; and at the very rim, 1930, Tree Cut Down. In an extreme close-up of the outer section of the tree, the woman's dark-gloved index finger points out an unmarked ring within a dark space between the last marked ring and the rim. Off screen she intones in a strange voice: "Somewhere in here I was born"—her middle finger now picks out a slightly more outer ring—"and there I died." She adds, "It was only a moment for you—you—you took no notice." As she stutters over this last phrase, the camera pulls back. Her lips now unmoving, almost as if she had not been the source of the voice we heard off frame in the previous shot, and her eyes oddly unfocused, staring into the distance, she moves out of the frame past Scottie, who turns to watch her. A series of shots follows from Scottie's point of view, showing her walking into the forest then disappearing behind a massive trunk. An eerie electronic tremolo is heard on the sound track as Scottie peers into the forest, unable to see her even as he moves to the side, attempting to see around the trunk.

The cross section of the tree encompasses more than a thousand years of time, a thousand cycles of yearly growth. But most significant are the unmarked rings near the edge of the tree, the small space spanned by two fingers, the space of a lifetime, one which passed, we are told, unnoticed. Unnoticed by whom? Who is the "you" the line of dialogue addresses? Although a range of possibilities exists, the most likely would seem to be the tree itself, whose life cycles passed without regard for the human life span that made up such a small section of their expanse. And who is the "I" whose points of birth and death the finger mark? Clearly we are to understand them as the index of the speaker, the woman whose name Scottie believes is Madeleine Elster. But this voice must speak from beyond the grave if it truly marks its point of death somewhere in the past. The eerie quality of its intonation and the fact that it enters from offscreen (we do not see the woman speak), make the voice seem detached from the woman—alien, perhaps channeled. This, of course, fits in with the story that Scottie has been fed, that Madeleine's identity is being overwhelmed by an alien presence, threatened by "someone dead," "someone within her," someone whom Scottie has been cued to identify as the woman's great-grandmother, Carlotta Valdez.

The short span of human life, especially the fact of human mortality, death, is inserted within the great expanse of the tree's growth. The "you" of the addressed tree challenges the frailty of the "I" that seems to speak from beyond the grave. The tree so strangely addressed does not, cannot respond. That, in fact, is precisely what the "I" accuses it of: a form of unresponsive indifference. Its rings can mark the extent of a lifetime, but it can take no notice of them. The "I," in its mortality, even in its verbal uncertainty and nearly disembodied speech, seems to accuse the tree of its self-contained wholeness, berating the almost endless cycle of nature that could never comprehend human limitations. Yet this tree is dead, and this voice seems to have triumphed over death. But has it? As a revenant, Carlotta does not represent a triumph over death as much as an attraction toward it. Carlotta, we grow to understand, wishes Madeleine to join her in death, perhaps as the substitute for the child taken from her, whose loss caused her madness and, later, her suicide. Equally, it would seem that she wants someone to notice her life and death; she desires a witness: Scottie.

Vertigo places the erotic quest within a *mise en abyme* in which identities are manufactured, confused, concealed, lost, and recreated. In the film's first half, Madeleine Elster seems to give way to the alien Carlotta Valdez, who destroys her host personality, leaving Scottie, who has fallen in love with her (with whom?), bereft. The film's second part rehearses a fetishistic drama of recreation as Scottie tries to refashion the woman Judy into the image of his lost love, Madeleine, only to find he is actually retracing a previous drama, a plot precisely designed to ensnare him and allow Gavin Elster to murder his wife. Judy, in fact, *is* Madeleine—or she was; she had played the part for Scottie, masquerading as the possessed and possibly mad wife in order to make Mrs. Elster's death appear a credible suicide, testified to by the reliable detective Scottie, "the made to order witness." At the film's climax, Scottie realizes his lack of control in this drama after the traumatic revelation that he has not refashioned his lost love but rather uncovered her earlier betrayal of him. His act of refashioning Judy into the image of Madeleine was preceded by another act of refashioning ("He made you over just like I made you over, only better"). The passion and terror released by this revelation leads to Judy's death (her accidental fall from the tower repeating and making actual her earlier, faked death) and apparently cures Scottie's vertigo, his fear of heights brought on by the apparently unrelated police-work trauma that opens the film.

Hitchcock alerts us from the film's opening, even before the action begins, that the film is about cycles in motion, specifically spirals. The credits open with a black-and-white image of the face of a woman, the camera moving in first on her lips, then on her eyes as they dart fearfully, finally framing a single eye. The shot turns red, color invading this world, as the eye widens. From the dark depths of the pupil of this eye emerges the film's title and then the first of a series of complex spirals designed by the pioneering avant-garde computer filmmaker John Whitney.[20] As the spirals spin on the screen, enlarging or coming closer, they evoke the sensation of dizziness described by the title. Vertigo is the sensation that comes from Scottie's acrophobia. It is vertigo that keeps him from climbing the tower and preventing, or so he thinks, Madeleine's suicidal plunge. Vertigo was the weakness that Gavin Elster counted on in making Scottie the fall guy in his murder plot, unable to take action, only able to witness an illusion carefully prepared for him.

But clearly vertigo stands for much more in this film. As we contemplate the span of Madeleine's life in the cycles of the tree, the superimposition of a previous life over a present one, however fictitious it turns out to be, evokes a sense of the uncanny. One could perhaps even describe it as an example of Freud's *Unheimlich*: déjà vu.[21] When Scottie sees Judy and recognizes in her features the lineament of his lost love, he also experiences this déjà vu, this uncanny repetition, but in the form of desire, the need to recover what he has lost. It occurs after a series of visits Scottie makes to sites related to his lost love, many of which end with him approaching a woman as if hoping she might be the dead Madeleine, only to find a totally unfamiliar woman there. One senses a process not simply of nostalgia, or memorialization, but of an attempt at invocation, of summoning the lost one. The recognition of Judy, however, provides only the possibility of this invocation. Scottie undertakes a long, even painful process of actual recreation, costuming Judy, dying and rearranging her hair, until she assumes (or, should we say, reassumes) the form he desires. As she emerges in her hotel room, the last detail of the recreation intact (the spiral pattern in her hairdo), she appears bathed in a green fog, produced by a camera filter only slightly realistically motivated by the green neon sign outside the window. ("*Sequoia semper virens*" Scottie had said when standing before the redwoods, giving, then translating, their Latin name: "Always green, ever living." Yet the green filter here makes Madeleine/Judy seem corpse-like.) Appearing like a green glowing phantom, she steps into Scottie's gaze, awaiting his reaction.

20. For the details of Whitney's collaboration with Saul Bass on these credits spirals, see Auiler, *Vertigo*, 153–54.

21. Freud, "The 'Uncanny,'" 245. Freud here is actually speaking of an experience of déjà vu that occurs in dreams.

The embrace and kiss that follow provide the most complex of the cycles in *Vertigo*. As the couple kiss passionately, the camera appears to circle around them, the green walls of the hotel room revolving behind them. The most immediate effect of this shot is that of an overwhelming emotion, something dizzying. However, about eighteen seconds into this pirouette, the background darkens. Out of this darkness, as the camera seems to continue its revolution, an entirely different background emerges, the stable from the San Juan Bautista mission, the place where Scottie last kissed Madeleine, before she ran away from him and seemingly plunged to her death.

We are dealing with more than the euphoria of a lover's kiss; or rather Hitchcock is founding erotic sensation more deeply than a physical sensation of dizziness. The cycle of time seems to have reversed itself (Madeleine's words to Scottie after this previous, last kiss were: "Too late, too late"). Scottie's fetishistic recreation has been successful. He has not only recreated his lost love, he has reversed the flow of time, returned to the moment before her loss and his failure in saving her. As the change in background occurs, Scottie looks up, as if he has noticed it. As he returns to passionately kissing his love, a brief moment of background darkness signals the return of the hotel room decor, which continues to spin behind them until the window, with its glowing neon light appears, evoking in its aquamarine tones an almost oceanic atmosphere in which the lovers bathe, the background becoming merely an immaterial glow as the kiss ends in a fade-out, which, within movie codes, signals physical lovemaking.[22]

Soon after this consummation—this climax not only of passion but also of the reversal of time from which this passion springs, recapturing not only the lost wholeness but the moment before separation—Scottie realizes the trick underlying his seeming miracle. By seeing through the trick, he encounters again his previous failure. But this is no longer a physical failure—his inability to make it up the stairs and save his beloved—but a failure of perception and insight. Scottie discovers his lack of awareness of the framing drama in which he unknowingly played a prescribed part. Seemingly performing as an author-creator as he tyrannically refashioned Judy into Madeleine (acting as the gentleman who "certainly knows what he wants"), Scottie must now ask who implanted this desire in him? The moment of discovery comes through a pair of shots that not only reveal an essential clue to the plot but also evoke again the process of modeling and recreation. Judy (unwittingly? unconsciously?—she

22. The technical process involved in this tour-de-force shot is described in Auiler, *Vertigo*, 118–20.

actually asks Scottie, "Can't you see?") puts on the necklace she wore as Madeleine. Scottie sees and recognizes the necklace through a reflection in a mirror. The camera moves into a close-up then cuts outside the space and time of this hotel room tryst to the identical necklace in the portrait of Carlotta. The camera then tracks out, revealing a brief flashback to a shot of Madeleine sitting before the portrait of Carlotta in the Palace of the Legion of Honor.

These two shots move from reflected mirror image to a portrait to a woman contemplating the portrait, making a round of representations. In the earlier scene, Scottie observed that Madeleine had modeled aspects of herself on this portrait; camera movements compared Madeleine's spiral hairdo and her bouquet of flowers with the identical ones in the painting. The theme of modeling in which the original seems lost in the mirror play of a *mise en abyme* overwhelms Scottie's triumph, as this brief return to the past of the flashback undercuts his recapturing of the moment before he lost Madeleine. The reflection and recall ensnares Scottie in a play of appearances beyond his control. The necklace appears as the mark left by Scottie's predecessor, the master plotter Gavin Elster, who had given Judy this prop as part of his trap.

In the film's final climax, Scottie once more tries to recapture past time and returns to the tower at the San Juan Bautista mission, physically making the journey by car this time rather than being transported by a magical process shot. He declares, "This is my second chance" as he drags Judy up the stairs he previously could not mount because of his acrophobia and vertigo. He berates her for her mistake in keeping the necklace: "You shouldn't keep souvenirs of a killing. You shouldn't have been . . . you shouldn't have been that sentimental." Immediately after this sarcasm, Scottie gasps out, "I loved you so, Madeleine."

This expression of love in the past tense is paradoxical. Scottie has just learned, and made it clear to Judy that he has learned, that he never knew Madeleine; he only knew Judy's masquerade. And here we reach the greatest pain of *Vertigo*: Scottie's great love was not only founded in a trick but exceeded anything Elster's plot could have foreseen or intended. Is Elster, whose brief and unremarkable appearance in the film makes little impression, really to be seen as the source of this agony? Is he truly the demiurge of Scottie's world of desire? One might pause and recall that the necklace is not entirely Elster's invention: it is patterned on the necklace in the portrait of Carlotta and may even be the authentic heirloom. One could see it, therefore, as Carlotta's mark, appearing in the center of Scottie's romance. Whom did Scottie actually love; whose image was he trying to recreate? Scottie's mistake (if it is one) of calling Judy "Madeleine" brings to mind a number of moments in this film where speaker, referent, or addressee is unclear, including the deeply stacked ambiguity surrounding the second-person pronoun in Judy/Madeleine/Carlotta's words at the tree cross section. Does that "you" who was loved refer to Madeleine, whom Judy plays at this moment, or does it refer to Carlotta, whom Judy could also be referred to as playing (unless, of course, Carlotta plays Judy, not as an actress playing a role but as a musician plays her instrument, Carlotta using Judy/Madeleine as a medium for her voice).

The possibility that Scottie not only loves Madeleine through Judy but also loves Carlotta through Madeleine is hinted at more than once in ambiguous exchanges, both verbal and visual. After Midge and Scottie gather the full story of the beautiful, sad, and mad Carlotta from Pop Leibel, Midge expresses amused incredulity about the possibility that Carlotta has come back from the dead and taken possession of Elster's wife. When she realizes that Scottie is somewhat less skeptical, she asks him, "Is she pretty?" Scottie asks, "Carlotta?" and Midge responds, as if correcting a child, "No, not Carlotta, Elster's wife." After the inquest, when the coroner nearly blames Scottie for Madeleine Elster's death, Elster speaks his last line in the film, apparently meant as a comfort to Scottie: "You and I know who killed Madeleine." Again, verbal ambiguities between intended and understood meanings abound. Elster, of course, knows that he himself killed her, but the unspoken name of the culprit here, the lure devised for Scottie, is clearly "Carlotta."

In the elaborate visual tropes that constitute the dream that brings on Scottie's mental breakdown, we return to the framing in which Elster spoke these words, standing with Scottie by a window. This time a figure stands between them, dressed as Carlotta, but it is not Kim Novak, who plays Judy. The name Elster did not dare to speak has become flesh—or at least an image. This heretofore unseen woman, Carlotta's portrait brought to life by Scottie's dream, appears next in a shot imitating the portrait, as Hitchcock's camera tracks in on the fatal necklace. (Significantly, this camera movement is repeated in the mirror sequence in which Scottie awakens from his induced fantasy.) These images indicate that, for Scottie, at least, Carlotta had become a real presence, whether the force that tore away his love or the origin and object of his love.

The succeeding dream images perform even more complex substitutions. Scottie's dream now fashions itself on the dream Madeleine described to him. But now *he* is in the position Madeleine described for herself, walking toward an open grave, the plunging camera seemingly swallowed by this dark abyss. Madeleine had claimed there was no name on the grave, but in Scottie's dream the stone clearly reads "Carlotta Valdez." Even more extreme is the substitution that ends the dream. From above we see the Spanish tiled mission roof onto which Madeleine fell (and onto which Judy will fall at the film's end). But the silhouette we see plummeting in Scottie's dream is clearly his. As he plunges away from the camera, the roof below disappears and Scottie's dark form hurtles into a brilliant, white void. The vertigo that he experiences here not only superimposes Madeleine and Carlotta and (proleptically) Judy but also himself, as his death or madness is figured in his convergence with the three female characters.

If we take *Vertigo* as a tragic gloss on Plato/Aristophanes' satiric yarn, we experience the seeming impossibility of recovery of a lost wholeness, not simply because the two parts never seem to cohere but because the original time, the primordial epoch of union before division, remains unattainable. Not only the body but time is out of joint. Scottie's doomed quest seeks to reproduce an original and, through this perfect representation, to re-found lost time. But, in fact, no original can be found, only a series of copies and counterfeits, which lead back to a portrait, a piece of jewelry, and a yawning grave. The perfect sphere of the human body Aristophanes imagined becomes a vortex of resemblances, a hall of shattered mirrors that invites Scottie to fall—in love?

EPILOGUE: GEOGRAPHIES OF DESIRE

I have tried here simply to describe certain key moments, certain turning points in this rich and complex film rather than offer a reading or an interpretation. I have also tried to indicate the way that cinema's ability to fragment and reassemble space, time, and the human body allows it to articulate the themes of eros through sounds and images. The logic of *Vertigo* is a round of substitutions in which the erotic undermines any stable sense of identity or gender. Yet it remains a story of desire and loss rather than fulfillment. Could one imagine it otherwise? I want to conclude this discussion of eros and the cinema by turning from one of the most famous films in film history, the work of a director and the Hollywood studio system at the height of their creative and technological power, spending millions of dollars on camera tricks, location shooting, and the perfected bodies of stars, to a film nearly unknown, shot with no money, and using only the bodies of a trio of complexly embroiled lovers: *Geography of the Body*, by Willard Maas, his wife, Marie Menken, and his lover, the poet George Barker.[23]

23. Information about the making of Willard Maas's film comes from the filmmaker file at Anthology Film Archive and also makes use of oral traditions within the American avant-garde

The film was shot in 1943 on the occasion of Barker's leaving the United States and, at least according to legend, his ménage à trois. The trio used a 16 mm Bolex, with a strapped-on dime-store magnifying glass for the effect of enlargement, and shot close-ups of the various parts of one another's nude bodies. The enlargement and isolation of the cinematic close-up, when divorced from the spatial logic of a Hollywood narrative film, presents unfamiliar, even unrecognizable fragments of the body. These evocative and ambivalent images underlie Barker's hilariously surreal fantasy travelogue commentary. Although possibly inspired by the abstraction of such close-up photography as Steichen's nude studies of his wife, Georgia O'Keeffe, this film is not only more primitive technically but also less abstractly sublimated and more Rabelaisianly comical. Through these explorations of a Brobdingnagian body, we are invited to play the game of Name That Body Part. Is this a navel or a nostril? This—the fold of flesh at the base of a thumb or the corner of a crotch? Just as one realizes that what looked like a shocking detail of genitals was actually an enlarged tongue or an ear, actual genitals swarm the screen. We feel ourselves disoriented, lost among these defamiliarized orifices that nicely match Barker's phrase on the sound track, "baroque ingresses." As a series of fragments, the whole body appears polymorphically perverse, a varied landscape of desires. As Barker intones near the beginning of the film, "All combinations appear to be possible."

Barker's daffy commentary encourages confusions in scale, describing expanses of skin as geological and geographical features. A close-up of what I take to be a navel is accompanied by: "Oh Ammon, Ammon, what inhabits those mysterious caverns in which a single jewel reminds us that anatomy also has its prizes?" An expanse of ribbed skin, possibly the palm of a hand, flexes on the screen as Barker narrates: "They shall consider themselves fortunate who, traveling over the wastes of Arabia, encounter illusions." Barker invokes the antarctic explorer Shackleton to portray his exploration of the body as a global quest. As the camera seems to tread its way through a head of hair, the narration explains: "Encouraged by the exhortations of Sir Francis [*sic*] Shackleton we drew our furs more tightly about us and trudged up to the 17th parallel. Under the ice, scarcely breathing, the lovers combed their hair." Yet Barker's comments are not always illustrative; they possess an independent sense, or nonsense, which moves in and out of sync with the images, stressing

film community. This film can be rented from either Filmmaker's Co-op in New York City or Canyon Cinema in San Francisco.

the aleatory dimension of these connections and contiguities, the dream-like and contingent nature of this geography of a body of desire.

The synecdoche inherent in the close-up initially encourages spectators to recognize the part as stand-in for the whole, but the editing between parts ultimately confounds any attempt at coherence, at putting it all together. Rather than assembling a familiar body, these parts selected from three different bodies of two different sexes challenge us to imagine a whole like none we have ever known. But we do not discover here Kuleshov's cinematic "perfect woman," assembled from diverse but interlocking parts like a technologically designed body.[24] There is no established gender or recognizable identity to provide a guide for the montage of this film, as they did for Kuleshov; the concept of a single self or a simple duality of genders becomes undermined by film's possibilities of fragmentation and reassembly. The body whose geography we traverse here can only be assembled if we imagine a new sense of unity, an imaginary juxtaposition of fragments of the sort that cinema can cause us to picture more vividly than any other art form. Could this be the filmic image of Aristophanes' primal whole, a possibility the film underscores by having Barker intone, at end of the film, Plato's phrase, "The desire and pursuit of the whole is called love"? At the film's opening, this Greek phrase is spelled out in plastic, dime-store letters arranged on Menken's nude body. At the close, we hear Barker speak it in English as a close-up of an eye appears on-screen. The eye appears to us not simply as another body part but as the organ and embodiment of sight—and therefore, as in the opening of *Vertigo*, of the possibility of cinema itself. We must ask, What does this eye see? Does it imagine the refashioned body of the lover as Scottie did? Or does it see through this illusion of recovered wholeness, reflecting instead a kaleidoscope of bodies and selves, with numerous trajectories and ingresses to be explored?

My purpose here is not simply to praise the carnivalesque celebration of a noncommercial countercultural cinema over the angst of Hitchcock's patriarchal Hollywood opus. That angst, I feel, is too profound, too much a part of our conception of eros to be simply mocked or laughed away. The final and perhaps

---

24. We might recall here that Kuleshov's great rival in the early era of Soviet filmmaking, the documentary filmmaker Dziga Vertov, also dreamed of the montaged body. Accenting its technological nature, Vertov called it the "Electric Young Man": "I am kino-eye, I create a man more perfect than Adam.... From one person I take the hands, the strongest and most dexterous, from another I take the legs, the swiftest and most shapely; from a third, the most beautiful and expressive head—and through montage I create a new, perfect man" ("Kinoks," 17).

most sophomoric of *Geography of the Body*'s puns and jokes actually dishes up the problem once more. As P. Adams Sitney pointed out to me, because Jowett's translation of Plato is spoken on the sound track, rather than appearing as writing, it takes on an ambiguity, and we have to ask whether it is intended as a translation or as a parody of Plato's words.[25] Is Love the pursuit of the *whole*, or is it, as the imagery of this intimate grope-fest seems to indicate, the pursuit of the *hole*? Removed in this instance from simple heterosexual smut (though smut of a broader sort it may well be), Barker's anti-Platonic pun, in spite of its silliness, seems to return us to *Vertigo*—just as the close-up of the eye that begins and ends *Geography of the Body* recalls the eye from which the spirals of desire emerge and return in Hitchcock's film.

The play of doubles, triples, or quadruples that populate *Vertigo*, and come in and out of focus in Scottie's dream, produce a lineage of reproductions with no clear origin, beyond the open grave. As the image that provokes Scottie's fantasy of falling, the empty, dark or light-filled void becomes the image of vertigo itself, the experience of being at the center of a spinning world with the ground cut out from under one's feet. Ultimately the chain Judy-Madeleine-Carlotta not only becomes identified with Scottie himself but also with his primal trauma, the first sequence of the film in which a miscalculated leap left him dangling over an abyss. This incident, which Judy refers to in the climax as "his accident," made Elster pick out Scottie as the dupe in his scheme. In the film's final moments, as Scottie confronts Judy with making use of his weakness, he suddenly realizes that he has succeeded in his "second chance": overcoming that weakness, he has made it to the top of the tower. At the tower's height, after Scottie murmurs, "I loved you so, Madeleine," Judy tries to convince him of the continued possibility of their love, but he now repeats her earlier line, "Too late. It's too late," and adds, "There's no bringing her back." Judy responds with a passionate kiss, which is interrupted by a sound and ghostly presence offscreen, whose terrifying image propels her into a final fall.

The film ends with Scottie looking down into the unimaged depth that must now contain Judy's body as it once had Madeleine's and, in dream at least, his own. Are we to understand that Scottie has been cured of his vertigo, that he can now stand and look into the abyss? And what are we to make of this abyss, this deep hole into which he peers? Is it the open grave, the

25. I draw here on Sitney's lectures at New York University decades ago. I thank him for his insights and inspiration.

darkness at the center of the eye, the realm of absolute lack and death? Or is it what von Baader, following his master, Jacob Boehme, would call the *Ungrund*, the original nothingness, which is not the lack of something but, rather, the unfounded possibility of everything, the dark freedom from which the will to love arises? Does the only way back to the whole lie through this hole?

«VERTIGO»: A RESPONSE TO TOM GUNNING

ROBERT B. PIPPIN

Tom Gunning, in using the traditional notion of a "quest for wholeness" as a frame for understanding Scottie's rather desperate and near obsessive love in *Vertigo*, has suggested a number of ambiguities and tensions. I found much of what he said very illuminating, so I want here only to supplement his remarks by noting four related topics relevant to this unbelievably rich film.

1. One element of *Vertigo* that complicates or even undermines the "quest for wholeness" issue is the odd, constant dialectical tension in the relationship of the two main characters. It is a pronounced and then reversed subject-*object* relationship, never just a subject-subject reciprocal quest in each other for love or wholeness. I mean by this that each character's belief about who is "running the show," about whose will is subject to whose, is often false (they are really being *subjected*, rather than being subjects). Often the obvious alternative, that the other is subject, turns out to be false as well. Of course, as in everything in the movie, there are ironies everywhere in the presentation of this theme. This memory we are left with—Scottie as the subject of power, manipulating and remaking Judy—is itself doubly ironic: In the first part of the movie, he had been maneuvered and staged, had been "object," not subject. In the second part, the more he succeeds, the more he fails, the closer he comes to destroying the illusion of subjectivity and learning of his original and now renewed (effected by him) object status.

This theme occurs in the first part of the movie too, when Scottie thinks he's "helping" Madeleine escape from pursuit by a ghost. Indeed, he is somewhat smug about this after he pulls her out of the water, undresses her, and is in the position of seeing her as "pure" object. He has seen her naked and unconscious, as a mute object (like Albertine in Proust's famous scene); and, creepy as it sounds, we are given to believe that he probably had a good look. She of course had not really been such an object. This too was an illusion; she was not unconscious but rather was manipulating Scottie's eros.

And there is even a deeper illusion. When Scottie succeeds in making Judy over, and she becomes Madeleine, she is then *not* Madeleine because Madeleine, the Madeleine he knew, is a fabrication of the evil Elster. And this reminds us that Judy has just become *another* fabrication. Scottie has become like Elster, a kind of demonic subject.

This is a general issue in erotics: trying to be the beloved is a tricky dialectical game. Trying to become what will be desired, to make yourself desirable, that is, is always tricky. If you succeed, you fail, since *you* are not being loved. But the contrary, romantic-authenticity ideal is naive, as in another great irony in the film when Judy says: "Scottie, can't you just love me *for me*." This means—ironically, has to mean: "Can't you just love the girlfriend of Elster who set you up in the murder plot?" For *that* is "the real Judy," even though that is not, of course, what she means.

2. Consider the film's treatment of fantasy in erotic life as so essential that the idea of treating fantasy philosophically as a kind of "illusion," falseness, or distortion that we might escape becomes ludicrous. This suggests another large theme: fantasy is essential because beauty is essential to eros. If we want to know what eros is, how it is inspired and how it dies, we will have to know what beauty is, and that also means what the beautiful has become in modernity, of perhaps what has happened to the "auratic" quality of the beautiful.

In more concrete terms, it is very important that Kim Novak is so beautiful as the beloved. But it is also important that this beauty is in a certain sense *false*, manufactured first by Elster and then by Scottie. This suggests the "banalization" of beauty in mass consumer society, beauty as a trick, no longer a natural or trustworthy inspiration—the fragility of beauty we might say, to coin a phrase. (After all, Judy works at a cosmetics counter at I. Magnin's.) This air of artificiality, of "putting your face on," as she says, is raised in the beginning of the film in the funniest way by that bizarre reference to the cantilevered brassiere.

Also, the whole notion of the beautiful as false or manufactured or kitsch is supplemented by the suggestion of reification or fetishization in the details. In both parts of the film, Judy becomes almost literally an object, like that fake horse in the stable scene. And this suggests lots of issues in filmmaking that Hitchcock is clearly playing around with, playing with the idea of making everyone, from Kim Novak to Tippi Hedren, look like Grace Kelly. The directorial control of our fantasy world is thereby explicitly thematized. Elster as director is an obvious theme; as are Scottie as director, the unsustainability of desire if the trick is revealed, and so forth. (Note also that the makeover is a *class* makeover for Judy, raising the theme of "passing" in a society with great class mobility and the theme of what constitutes authenticity.)

3. Consider how the film suggests erotic obsession as repetition, either within the psychology of one's own life or within a mythic cycle one cannot break (that eros is the manifestation of mythic time, not progressive, secular, linear time—as Gunning brought out so well with attention to the tree ring scene). This is clearly also connected to the stately, very slow pace of the film, as if an ancient plot unrolling, characters filling repetitive roles. (There is lots of literal repetition too. Bodies fly past this guy over and over and over, almost to the point of the comic.)

4. All of these, I am trying to suggest, are not unfamiliar images of the brute power of erotic longing, and they remind us in *Vertigo* that there is something about eros that cannot be accommodated easily within Christian or liberal-egalitarian humanism. And of course this satirization of attempts to direct one's own fate is a familiar subject in many other Hitchcock films and has sometimes been read as a religious, even a Roman Catholic theme. (As in: the Protestant ideal of an individual, inner relation to God and to conscience is a dangerous conceit. We are far too unreliable, self-deceived, far too much objects of fate ever to pretend that the achievement of such moral subjectivity is possible.) It is also true that sometimes Hitchcock's satirization is used to debunk the stance of all moralistic judgment and its presumed knowingness, as in *Notorious*, or in regard to that extraordinarily cruel moralist in the autopsy scene. Possessed of almost infinite smugness, he knows nothing. People who think they know what's going on and act accordingly are almost always completely wrong in Hitchcock, and very often the point of view of the viewer is equally off base. In *Vertigo*, we share the point of view of Scottie for much of the film and feel as excited as he does when the chance to remake Madeleine arrives. But I would suggest that because we become so enthusiastic, we slide over what would otherwise seem an unbelievably cruel, fetishizing manipulation by the movie star/good guy (usually) Stewart. Seeing the film a second time (another interesting theme—how watching this film is totally different the second time) and watching Scottie fall in love with Madeleine, it is painful to see how she manipulates him, "absorbs" and uses his tenderness. But the first time, you react that way only to him. And of course, we tend to slide over the fact that in the first half, Scottie's relation to Madeleine is itself a lie, maintained with great consistency: *he deceives her* by not telling her who he is

and why he is following her, even though he acts out the "we're falling in love scenario"—all the while the paid employee of the man he believes to be her husband.

These themes—the illusions and dialectical twists of subjectivity, the dependence on fantasy, the fragility of fantasy, the mythic and repetitive nature of erotic time—are summed up in that line Gunning quotes to such effect. All the pathos in the movie is captured when Scottie says (to a woman he now knows is named Judy): "I loved you so, Madeleine." It reminds me of so many similar themes in Proust and also of what I would nominate as the most powerful statement summing up the qualities of modern love and our anxieties about them, Swann's famous remark about Odette near the very end of *Swann's Way*: "'To think that I have wasted years of my life, that I have longed for death, that the greatest love that I have ever known has been for a woman who did not please me, who was not in my style.'"

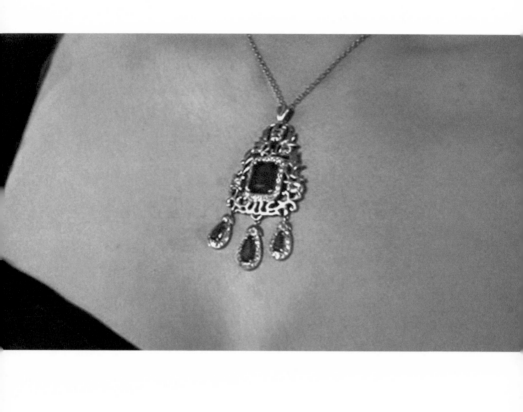

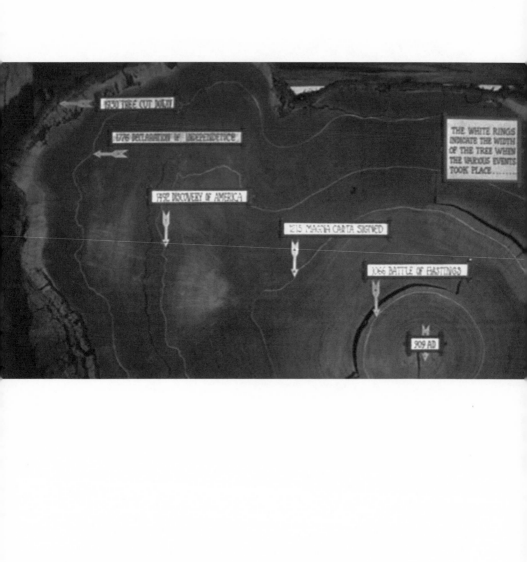

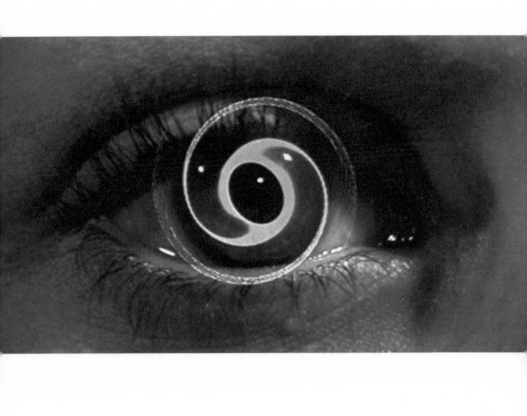

Epilogue

EROS AND PSYCHE

J. M. COETZEE

She met Robert Duncan only once, in 1963, soon after her return from Europe. Duncan and another, less interesting poet named Philip Whalen had been brought out on a tour by the US Information Service: the Cold War was on, there was money for cultural propaganda. Duncan and Whalen gave a reading at the University of Melbourne; after the reading they all went off to a bar, the two poets and the man from the consulate and half a dozen Australian writers of all ages, including herself.

Duncan had read his long "Poem Beginning with a Line by Pindar" that night, and it had impressed her, moved her. She was attracted to Duncan, with his severely handsome Roman profile; she would not have minded having a fling with him, would not even, in the mood she was in those days, have minded having his love child, like one of those mortal women of myth impregnated by a passing god and left to bring up semi-divine offspring.

She is reminded of Duncan because in a book sent by an American friend she has just come across another telling of the Eros and Psyche story, by one Susan Mitchell, whom she has not read before. Why the interest in Psyche among American poets? she wonders. Do they find something American in her, the girl who, not content with the ecstasies provided night after night by the visitor to her bed, must light a lamp, peel back the darkness, gaze on him naked? In her restlessness, her inability to leave well alone, do they see something of themselves?

She too is not without curiosity about the intercourse of gods and mortals, though she has never written about it, not even in her book about Marion Bloom and her god-haunted husband Leopold. What intrigues her is less the meta-physics than the mechanics, the practicalities of congress across a gap in being. Bad enough to have a full-grown male swan jabbing webbed feet into your back-side while he has his way, or a one-ton bull leaning his moaning weight on you; how, when the god does not care to change shape but remains his awesome self, does the human body accommodate itself to the blast of his desire?

Let it be said for Susan Mitchell that she does not shrink from such ques-tions. In her poem, Eros, who seems to have made himself man-sized for the occasion, lies in bed on his back with his wings drooping on either side, the girl (one presumes) on top of him. The seed of gods would seem to gush hugely (this must have been Mary of Nazareth's experience too, waking from her dream still slightly trembly with the issue of the Holy Ghost running down her thighs). When Psyche's lover comes, his wings are left drenched; or perhaps the wings drip seed, perhaps they become organs of consummation themselves. On occa-sions when he and she reach a climax together, he breaks apart like (Mitchell's words, more or less) a bird shot in flight. (*What about the girl*, she wants to ask the poet—*if you can say what it was like for him, why not tell us how it was for her?*)

What she had really wanted to talk about to Robert Duncan, however, that night in Melbourne when he indicated so firmly that whatever she offered did not interest him, was not girls visited by gods but the much rarer phenomenon of men condescended to by goddesses. Anchises, for instance, lover of Aphrodite and father of Aeneas. One would have thought that, after that unforeseen and unforgettable episode in his hut on Mount Ida, Anchises—a good-looking boyo, if one is to believe the *Hymn*, but otherwise just a cattle herder—would have wanted to talk about nothing else, to whoever would listen: how he had fucked a goddess, the most succulent in the whole stable, fucked her all night long, got her pregnant too.

Men and their leering talk. She has no illusions about how mortal beings treat whatever gods, true or feigned, ancient or modern, have the misfortune to fall into their hands. She thinks of a film she saw once, that might have been written by Nathanael West though in fact it wasn't: Jessica Lange playing a Hollywood sex goddess who has a breakdown and ends up in the common ward of a madhouse, drugged, lobotomized, strapped to her bed, while orderlies sell tickets for ten minutes a time with her. "*I wanna fuck a movie star!*" pants one of their customers, shoving his dollars at them. In his voice the ugly underside of idolatry: malice, murderous resentment. Bring an immortal down to earth, show her what life is really like, bang her till she is raw. *Take that! Take that!* A scene they excised from the televised version, so close to the bone of America does it cut.

But in Anchises' case the goddess, when she rose from his bed, warned her sweetheart pretty plainly to keep his mouth shut. So there was nothing left for a prudent fellow to do but lose himself, last thing at night, in drowsy memories: how it had felt, man's flesh lapped in god flesh; or else, when he was in a more sober, more philosophically inclined mood, to wonder: since the physical mingling of two orders of being, and in specific the interplay of human organs with whatever stands in for organs in the biology of gods, is strictly speaking not possible, not while the laws of nature continue to hold, what kind of being, what hybrid of slave body and god soul, must it have been that laughter-loving Aphrodite transformed herself into, for the space of a night, in order to consort with him? Where was the mighty soul when he took in his arms the incomparable body? Tucked away in some out-of-the-way compartment, in a tiny gland in the skull, for instance; or spread harmlessly through the physical whole as a glow, an aura? Yet even if, for his sake, the soul of the goddess was hidden, how could he not, when her limbs gripped him, have felt the fire of godly appetite—felt it and been scorched by it? Why did it have to be spelled out to him, the next morning, what had really happened ("Her head touched the roof-beam, her face shone with immortal beauty, *Wake up*, she said, *behold me, do I look like the one who knocked at your door last night?*")? How could any of it have taken place unless he, the man, was under a spell from beginning to end, a spell like an anaesthetic to blanket the fearful knowledge that the maiden he had disrobed, embraced, parted the thighs of, penetrated, was an immortal, a trance to protect him from the unendurable pleasure of godlike lovemaking, allowing him only the duller sensations of a mortal? Yet why would a god, having chosen for herself a mortal lover, put that same lover under such a spell that for the duration he was not himself?

That is how it would have been for poor bewildered Anchises, one would imagine, for the rest of his life: a whirl of questions, none of which he would dare to air to his fellow cattlemen except in the most general form, for fear of being struck dead in his tracks.

Yet that is not how it was, not according to the poets. If one is to believe the poets, Anchises led a normal life thereafter, a distinguished but normal human life, until the day his city was set ablaze by foreigners and he was plunged into exile. If he did not forget that signal night, he did not think overmuch about it, not as we understand thinking.

That is the main thing she would have liked to ask Robert Duncan about, as an expert on extraordinary intercourse, the thing she fails to understand about the Greeks, or if Anchises and his son were not Greeks but Trojans, foreigners, then about Greeks and Trojans together as archaic eastern Mediterranean peoples and subjects of Hellenic myth-making. She calls it their lack of inwardness. Anchises has been intimate with a divine being, as intimate as intimate can be. Not a common experience. In the whole of Christian mythology, setting aside the Apocrypha, there is only one parallel event, and that in the commoner form, with the male god—rather impersonally, rather distantly, it must be said—impregnating the mortal woman. *Magnificat Dominum anima mea*, Mary is reputed to have said afterwards, perhaps misheard from *Magnam me facit Dominus*. That is pretty much all she says in the Gospels, this maid who is matchless, as though struck dumb for the rest of her life by what befell her. No one around her has the shamelessness to inquire, *What was it like, how did it feel, how did you bear it?* Yet the question must surely have occurred to people, to her girlfriends in Nazareth for instance. *How did she bear it?* they must have whispered amongst themselves. *It must have been like being fucked by a whale. It must have been like being fucked by the Leviathan;* blushing as they spoke the word, those barefoot children of the tribe of Judah, as she, Elizabeth Costello, almost catches herself blushing too, setting it down on paper. Rude enough among Mary's countryfolk; positively indecent in someone two millennia older and wiser.

Psyche, Anchises, Mary: there must be better, less prurient, more philosophical ways of thinking about the whole god-and-man business. But has she the time or the equipment, to say nothing of the inclination, to do so?

Inwardness. Can we *be one with* a god profoundly enough to apprehend, to *get a sense of*, a god's being? A question that no one seems to ask any more, except to an extent her new find Susan Mitchell, who is not a philosopher either; a question that went out of fashion during her lifetime (she remembers it happening, remembers her surprise), just as it came into fashion not too long before her lifetime commenced. *Other modes of being.* That may be a more decent way of phrasing it. Are there other modes of being besides what we call the human into which we can enter; and if there are not, what does that say about us and our limitations? She does not know much about Kant, but it sounds to her a Kantian kind of question. If her ear is right, then inwardness started its run with the man from Königsberg and ended, more or less, with Wittgenstein the Viennese destroyer.

"Gods do exist," writes Friedrich Hölderlin, who had read his Kant, "but they carry on their lives somewhere up above us in another realm, not much interested, it would seem, in whether we exist or not." In bygone times those gods bestrode the earth, walked among men. But to us modern folk it is no longer given to catch a glimpse of them, much less suffer their love. "We come too late."

She reads less and less widely as she grows older. A not uncommon phenomenon. For Hölderlin, however, she always has time. *Great-souled Hölderlin* she would call him if she were Greek. Nevertheless, about Hölderlin on the gods she has her doubts. Too innocent, she thinks, too ready to take things at face value; not alert enough to the cunning of history. Things are rarely as they seem to be, she would like to instruct him. When we are stirred to lament the loss of the gods, it is more than likely the gods who are doing the stirring. The gods have not retreated: they cannot afford to.

Odd that the man who put his finger on the divine *apatheia*, the inability of the gods to feel, and their consequent need to have others do their feeling for them, should have failed to see the effects of *apatheia* on their erotic life.

Love and death. The gods, the immortals, were the inventors of death and corruption; yet with one or two notable exceptions they have lacked the courage to try their invention out on themselves. That is why they are so curious about us, so endlessly inquisitive. We call Psyche a silly, prying girl, but what was a god doing in her bed in the first place? In marking us down for death, the gods gave us an edge over them. Of the two, gods and mortals, it is we who live the more urgently, feel the more intensely. That is why they cannot put us out of their minds, cannot get by without us, ceaselessly watch us and prey on us. That, finally, is why they do not declare a ban on sex with us, merely make up rules about where and in what form and how often. Inventors of death; inventors of sex tourism too. In the sexual ecstasies of mortals, the *frisson* of death, its contortions, its relaxings: they talk about it endlessly when they have had too much to drink—who they first got to experience it with, what it felt like. They wish they had that inimitable little quiver in their own erotic repertoire, to spice up their couplings with each other. But the price is one they are not prepared to pay. Death, annihilation: what if there is no resurrection, they wonder misgivingly?

We think of them as omniscient, these gods, but the truth is they know very little, and what they know know only in the most general of ways. No body of learning they can call their own, no philosophy, properly speaking. Their cosmology an assortment of commonplaces. Their sole expertise in astral flight, their sole homegrown science anthropology. They specialize in humankind because of what we have and they lack; they study us because they are envious.

As for us, do they guess (what irony!) that what makes our embraces so intense, so unforgettable, is the glimpse they give us of a life we imagine as theirs, a life we call (since our language has no word for it) *the beyond*? *I do not like that other world*, writes Martha Clifford to her pen pal Leopold Bloom, but she lies: why would she write at all if she did not want to be swept off to another world by a demon lover?

Leopold, meanwhile, strolls around the Dublin Public Library peeking, when no one is looking, between the legs of the statues of goddesses. If Apollo has a marble cock and balls, does Artemis, he wonders, have an orifice to match? Investigations in aesthetics, that is what he likes to tell himself he is engaged in: how far does the artist's duty to nature extend? What he really wants to know, however, had he only the words for it, is whether congress is possible with the divine.

And she herself? How much has she learned about gods in her wanderings around Dublin with that irremediably ordinary man? Almost like being married to him. Elizabeth Bloom, second and ghostly wife of.

What she knows for certain about the gods is that they peek at us all the time, peek even between our legs, full of curiosity, full of envy; sometimes go so far as to rattle our earthly cage. But how deep, she asks herself today, does that curiosity really run? Aside from our erotic gifts, are they curious about us, their anthropological specimens, to the degree that we in turn are curious about chimps, or about birds, or about flies? Despite some evidence to the contrary, she would like to think, chimps. She would like to think the gods admire, however grudgingly, our energy, the endless ingenuity with which we try to elude our fate. *Fascinating creatures*, she would like to think they remark to each other over their ambrosia; *so like us in many respects; their eyes in particular so expressive; what a pity they lack that je ne sais quoi without which they can never ascend to sit beside us!*

But perhaps she is wrong about their interest in us. Or rather, perhaps she used to be right, but now is wrong. In her heyday, she would like to think, she could have given winged Eros himself cause to pay earth a visit. Not because she was so much of a beauty but because she longed for the god's touch, longed until she ached; because in her longings, so unrequitable and therefore so comical when acted on, she might have promised a genuine taste of what was missing back home on Olympus. But everything seems now to have changed. Where in the world today does one find such immortal longings as hers used to be? Not in the personal columns, for sure. "SWF, 5′8″, thirties, brunette, into astrology, biking, seeks SWM, 35–45 for friendship, fun, adventure." Nowhere: "DWF, 5′8″, sixties, runs to death and death meets her as fast, seeks G, immortal, earthly form immaterial, for ends to which no words suffice." In the editorial office they would frown. Indecent desires, they would say, and toss her in the same basket as the pederasts.

We do not call on the gods because we no longer believe in them. She hates sentences that hinge on *because*. The jaws of the trap snap shut, but the mouse, every time, has escaped. And what an irrelevancy anyway! How misguided! Worse than Hölderlin! Who cares what we believe? The sole question is whether the gods will continue to believe in us, whether we can keep alive the last flicker of the flame that once used to burn in them. "Friendship, fun, adventure": what kind of appeal is that, to a god? More than enough fun where they come from. More than enough beauty too.

Strange how, as desire relaxes its grip on her body, she sees more and more clearly a universe ruled by desire. *Haven't you read your Newton,* she would like to say to the people in the dating agency (would like to say to Nietzsche too if she could get in touch with him)? *Desire runs both ways: A pulls B because B pulls A, and vice versa: that is how you go about building a universe.* Or if *desire* is still too rude a word, then what of *appetency*? Appetency and chance: a powerful duo, more than powerful enough to build a cosmology on, from the atoms and the little things with nonsense names that make up atoms to Alpha Centauri and Cassiopeia and the great dark back of beyond. The gods and ourselves, whirled helplessly around by the winds of chance, yet pulled equally towards each other, towards not only B and C and D but towards X and Y and Z and Omega too. Not the least thing, not the last thing but is called to by love.

A vision, an opening up, as the heavens are opened up by a rainbow when the rain stops falling. Does it suffice, for old folk, to have these visions now and again, these rainbows, as a comfort, before the rain starts pelting down again? Must one be too creaky to join the dance before one can see the pattern?

Acknowledgments

The idea for this volume originated with the Erotikon Symposium held in March 2001 at the University of Chicago, organized by Thomas Bartscherer and Katia Mitova and sponsored by a coalition of groups led by the Committee on Social Thought. It is not, however, a record of that event. The symposium included elements (a concert, poetry readings, a film screening) that cannot be reproduced in print, and the personnel have changed considerably in the move from symposium to book. Fully half of the contributors to this volume were not present at the original event, and several papers presented at the symposium are not included here. We have, however, sought to preserve one crucial element that the symposium setting enabled, namely, dialogue. To that end, we have invited one written response to each of the essays. The book comprises mostly new material. Aside from the poems, all contributions have either been written or (in four cases) revised for *Erotikon*. The poems in the middle of the book were selected by Mark Strand, and J. M. Coetzee accepted the editors' invitation to read and reflect on the volume as a whole and then write an epilogue in response to it.

We would like to extend our heartfelt gratitude to all of the *Erotikon* contributors; to Douglas Mitchell, Timothy McGovern, and their colleagues at the University of Chicago Press; to the two anonymous readers who commented on the manuscript; and to our manuscript editor, Jenni Fry. We would also like to acknowledge the generous support for this volume provided by the office of Richard Saller, provost of the University of Chicago. We acknowledge with sadness the passing of our colleagues Michael Camille, who had been invited to write for this volume before his untimely death, and Richard Wollheim, who died while the book was in production.

Many people contributed in various ways, first to the realization of the Erotikon Symposium and subsequently to the creation of this book. We apologize in advance to anyone whom we fail to acknowledge. To Katia Mitova, partner in the conception and organization of the symposium, and to Robert Pippin, chair of the Committee on Social Thought, whose support, advice, and encouragement made that symposium possible, we offer our deep gratitude.

We also gratefully acknowledge the efforts of the members of the Erotikon Symposium Committee: Aditya Adarkar, Ewa Atanassow, Peter Kanelos, Margaret Litvin, Svetozar Minkov, Dean Moyar, and Gabe Pihas. For contributions of varying kinds, we would like to thank Eva Antonova Atanassova, Rita Bartscherer and family, Joseph Bartscherer, Anne Eaton, Anne Gamboa, Maggie Hivnor, Brett Keyser, David McNeill, Janel Mueller, Naomi Rood, Richard Rosengarten, Diane Shamash, Geoffrey Stone, William Stull, and Ker Wells.

Bibliography

Adams, J. N. *The Latin Sexual Vocabulary*. Baltimore: Johns Hopkins University Press, 1990.

Adkins, Lesley, and Roy Adkins. *The Keys of Egypt: The Obsession to Decipher Egyptian Hieroglyphs*. New York: HarperCollins, 2000.

Angela of Foligno. *Complete Works*. Translated by Paul Lachance. New York: Paulist Press, 1993.

Anselm. *Proslogium*. In *Basic Writings*, translated by S. N. Deane, 6–206. La Salle: University of Southern Illinois Press, 1932.

Anton, John Peter, George L. Kustas, and Anthony Preus. *Essays in Ancient Greek Philosophy*. Albany: State University of New York Press, 1971.

Armisen-Marchetti, Mireille. *Sapientiae facies: Étude sur les images de Sénèque*. Paris: Les Belles Lettres, 1989.

Augustine of Hippo. *Augustine of Hippo, Selected Writings*. Translated by Mary T. Clark. New York: Paulist Press, 1984.

——. *The City of God*. Translated by Henry Bethenson. London: Penguin, 1984.

——. *Confessions*. Translated by Henry Chadwick. Oxford: Oxford University Press, 1991.

——. *Retractiones*. Paris: Corpus Christianorum, 1962.

——. *The Trinity*. Translated by Edmund O. P. Hill. New York: New City Press, 1991.

Auiler, Dan. *Vertigo: The Making of a Hitchcock Classic*. New York: St. Martin's, 2000.

Babut, Daniel. "Les stoïciens et l'amour." *REG* 76 (1963): 55–63.

Balthasar, Hans Urs von. *The Glory of the Lord: A Theological Aesthetics*. San Francisco: Ignatius Press; New York: Crossroad Publications, 1983.

Balzac, Honoré de. *Béatrix*. Paris: Garnier-Flammarion, 1979.

——. *The Lily of the Valley*. Translated by Lucienne Hill. 2nd ed. New York: Carroll and Graf, 1997.

Barthes, Roland. *Œuvres complètes*. Edited by Eric Marty. 3 vols. Paris: Seuil, 1993–1995.

——. "On Leaving the Movie Theater." In *The Rustle of Language*. Berkeley: University of California Press, 1986.

——. *The Pleasure of the Text*. Translated by Richard Miller. New York: Hill and Wang, 1973.

——. "Le plus grand décrypteur de mythes de ce temps nous parle d'amour." *Playboy*, September 1977, French edition.

——. *The Rustle of Language*. Berkeley: University of California Press, 1986.

Bataille, Georges. *Erotism: Death and Sensuality*. San Francisco: City Lights Books, 1986.

——. *The Tears of Eros*. Translated by Peter Connor. San Francisco: City Lights Books, 1989.

Beauvoir, Simone de. *The Second Sex*. Translated by H. M. Parshley. New York: Knopf, 1953.

Benardete, Seth. *On Plato's Symposium*. Edited by Heinrich Meier. Munich: Siemens, 1993.

Berger, Adolf. *Encyclopedic Dictionary of Roman Law, Transactions of the American Philosophical Society*. New ser., vol. 43, pt. 2. Philadelphia: American Philosophical Society, 1953.

Bernard of Clairvaux. *Sancti Bernardi opera*. Edited by Jean LeClerq. Rome: Editions Cisterciennes, 1957–77.

———. *The Works of Bernard of Clairvaux*. Edited by Kilian Walsh. Kalamazoo, MI: Cistercian Publications, 1983.

Betanzos, Ramón J. *Franz Von Baader's Philosophy of Love*. Vienna: Passagen Verlag, 1998.

Bion, W. R. "Attacks on Linking." *International Journal of Psycho-Analysis* 40 (1959).

Bishop, Clifford, and Xenia Osthelder. *Sexualia: From Prehistory to Cyberspace*. Cologne: Könemann, 2001.

Blondel, Éric, ed. *L'amour*. Paris: Flammarion, 1998.

Bonaventure. *Bonaventure: The Soul's Journey into God, the Tree of Life, the Life of St. Francis*. Edited by Ewert H. Cousins. New York: Paulist Press, 1978.

Bonnefoy, Jean Francois. *Le Saint Esprit et ses dons selon Saint Bonaventure*. Paris: Vrin, 1929.

Boothby, Richard. *Death and Desire: Psychoanalytic Theory in Lacan's Return to Freud*. New York: Routledge, 1991.

Bösel, Richard. "Morfologia spaziale." In *Borromini e l'universo barocco*, edited by Richard Bösel and Christoph L. Frommel, 333–45. Milan: Electa, 2000.

Brenk, Frederick. "Plutarch's Erotikos: The Drag Down Pulled Up." *Illinois Classical Studies* 13 (1988): 457–71.

Brennan, Teresa, and Martin Jay. *Vision in Context: Historical and Contemporary Perspectives on Sight*. London: Routledge, 1995.

Brown, Peter Robert Lamont. *Augustine of Hippo: A Biography*. Berkeley: University of California Press, 1967.

Brown, Robert D. *Lucretius on Love and Sex: A Commentary on De Rerum Natura IV 1030–1287, with Prolegomena, Text, and Translation*. Vol. 15 of Columbia Studies in the Classical Tradition. Leiden: E. J. Brill, 1987.

Budick, Sanford, and Wolfgang Iser, eds. *Languages of the Unsayable: The Play of Negativity in Literature and Literary Theory*. Stanford, CA: Stanford University Press, 1987.

Burnaby, John. *Amor Dei: A Study of the Religion of St. Augustine*. London: Hodder and Stoughton, 1938.

Butler, Judith. *Bodies That Matter: On the Discursive Limits of "Sex."* New York: Routledge, 1993.

———. *Gender Trouble: Feminism and the Subversion of Identity*. New York: Routledge, 1990.

Bychkov, Oleg. "A Note on Achilles Tatius 1.9.4–5, 5.13.4." *Classical Quarterly* 49 (1999): 339–41.

Calame, Claude. *The Poetics of Eros in Ancient Greece*. Translated by Janet Lloyd. Princeton, NJ: Princeton University Press, 1999.

Camerota, Filippo. "Architettura obliqua." In *Borromini e l'universo barocco*, edited by Richard Bösel and Christoph L. Frommel. Milan: Electa, 2000.

———. "Geometria." In *Borromini e l'universo barocco*, edited by Richard Bösel and Christoph L. Frommel. Milan: Electa, 2000.

———. "Scienze Naturali." In *Borromini e l'universo barocco*, edited by Richard Bösel and Christoph L. Frommel. Milan: Electa, 2000.

Cantarella, Eva. *Bisexuality in the Ancient World*. New Haven, CT: Yale University Press, 1992.

Carson, Anne. *Eros the Bittersweet: An Essay*. Princeton, NJ: Princeton University Press, 1986.

Chandès, Hervé, ed. *Amours*. Paris: Actes Sud: Fondation Cartier pour l'art contemporain, 1997.

Clarke, John R. *Looking at Lovemaking: Constructions of Sexuality in Roman Art, 100 BC–AD 250*. Berkeley: University of California Press, 1998.

Coetzee, J. M. *Disgrace*. New York: Viking, 1999.

———. *Elizabeth Costello*. New York: Viking, 2003.

Cohen, David. *Law, Sexuality, and Society: The Enforcement of Morals in Classical Athens*. Cambridge: Cambridge University Press, 1991.

Cohen, David, and Richard Saller. "Foucault on Sexuality in Greco-Roman Antiquity." In *Foucault and the Writing of History*, edited by Jan Goldstein, 35–59. Cambridge, MA: Blackwell, 1994.

Combalía, Victoria, and Jean-Jacques Lebel, eds. *Jardín de eros*. Milan: Electa, 1999.

Connors, Joseph. "Palazzo Carpenga." In *Itinerario Borrominiano*, edited by Elizabeth Sladek. Milan: Electa, 1999.

Corvo, Baron [Frederick Rolf]. *The Desire and Pursuit of the Whole: A Romance of Modern Venice*. New York: New Directions, 1953.

Courcelle, Pierre Paul. *Late Latin Writers and Their Greek Sources*. Cambridge, MA: Harvard University Press, 1969.

———. "Plotino e il Neoplatinismo in Oriente e in Occidente." In *Atti del Convegno Internazionale: Plotino e il Neoplatinismo in Oriente e in Occidente: Roma, 5–9 Ottobre 1970*. Rome: Academia nazionale dei Lincei, 1974.

Cousins, Ewert H. *Bonaventure and the Coincidence of Opposites*. Chicago: Franciscan Herald Press, 1978.

Dalla, Danilo. *Ubi Venus Mutatur: Omosessualitáa e diritto nel mondo Romano*. Milan: A. Giuffráe, 1987.

Danto, Arthur. *Playing with the Edge: The Photographic Achievement of Robert Mapplethorpe*. Berkeley: University of California Press, 1986.

Davidson, Arnold Ira. *The Emergence of Sexuality: Historical Epistemology and the Formation of Concepts*. Cambridge, MA: Harvard University Press, 2001.

Davidson, Donald. "Paradoxes of Irrationality." In *Philosophical Essays on Freud*, edited by Richard Wollheim and J. Hopkins. Cambridge: Cambridge University Press, 1982.

DeLillo, Don. *Underworld*. New York, NY: Scribner, 1997.

Diogenes of Oenoanda. *Diogenes of Oinoanda: The Epicurean Inscription*. Edited by Martin Ferguson Smith. Naples: Bibliopolis, 1993.

Dover, Kenneth James. *Greek Homosexuality*. London: Duckworth, 1978.

duBois, Page. "Phallocentrism and Its Subversion in Plato's *Phaedrus*." *Arethusa* 18 (1985): 91–103.

Dufresne, Todd. *Tales from the Freudian Crypt: The Death Drive in Text and Context*. Stanford, CA: Stanford University Press, 2000.

Dupré, Louis K. *Passage to Modernity: An Essay in the Hermeneutics of Nature and Culture*. New Haven, CT: Yale University Press, 1993.

Du Roy, Olivier. *L'intelligence de la foi en la Trinité selon Saint Augustin: Genèse de sa théologie Trinitaire jusqu'en 391*. Paris: Études Augustiniennes, 1966.

Edwards, Catharine. *The Politics of Immorality in Ancient Rome*. Cambridge: Cambridge University Press, 1993.

Erickson, Keith V. *Plato: True and Sophistic Rhetoric, Studies in Classical Antiquity*. Vol. 3. Amsterdam: Rodopi, 1979.

Fagiolo dell'Arco, Maurizio. "Bernini: 'regista' del Barocco." In *Gian Lorenzo Bernini: Regista del Barocco*, edited by Maria Grazia Bernardini and Maurizio Fagiolo dell'Arco. Milan: Skira, 1999.

Fantham, Elaine. "*Stuprum*: Public Attitudes and Penalties for Sexual Offenses in Republican Rome." *Échos du monde classique* 35 (1991): 267–91.

Fedotov, G. P. *The Russian Religious Mind*. Vol. 1. Belmont, MA: Norland, 1975.

Ferrari, G. R. F. "Platonic Love." In *The Cambridge Companion to Plato*, edited by Richard Kraut, 249–75. Cambridge: Cambridge University Press, 1992.

Fiorenza, Elizabeth Schussler. *Jesus: Miriam's Child, Sophia's Prophet: Critical Issues in Feminist Christology*. New York: Continuum, 1984.

Fitzgerald, William. *Catullan Provocations: Lyric Poetry and the Drama of Position, Classics and Contemporary Thought*. Berkeley: University of California Press, 1995.

Florenskii, P. A. *Iconostasis*. Crestwood, NY: St. Vladimir's Seminary Press, 1996.

Foster, Kenelm. *The Two Dantes, and Other Studies*. Berkeley: University of California Press, 1977.

Foucault, Michel. *The History of Sexuality*. Vol. 1, *An Introduction*, translated by Robert Hurley. New York: Vintage, 1990.

——. *The History of Sexuality*. Vol. 2, *The Use of Pleasure*, translated by Robert Hurley. New York: Vintage, 1990.

——. *The History of Sexuality*. Vol 3, *The Care of the Self*, translated by Robert Hurley. New York: Vintage, 1986.

Francis and Clare. *The Complete Works*. Translated by Regis J. Armstrong and Ignatius Brady. New York: Paulist Press, 1982.

Freud, Sigmund. "Analysis Terminable and Interminable." In *The Standard Edition of the Complete Psychological Works of Sigmund Freud*, edited by James Strachey, vol. 23. London: Hogarth Press, 1984.

———. "Beyond the Pleasure Principle." In *The Standard Edition of the Complete Psychological Works of Sigmund Freud*, edited by James Strachey, vol. 18. London: Hogarth Press, 1984.

———. *Briefe, 1873–1939*. Edited by Ernst L. Freud and Lucie Freud. 2nd ed. Frankfurt am Main: S. Fischer, 1960.

———. "Fragment of an Analysis of a Case of Hysteria." In *The Standard Edition of the Complete Psychological Works of Sigmund Freud*, edited by James Strachey, vol. 7. London: Hogarth Press, 1984.

———. *Gesammelte Werke: Chronologisch Geordnet*. London, 1940.

———. *Gesammelte Werke, Nachtragsband: Texte aus den Jahren 1885–1938*. Frankfurt am Main: S. Fischer, 1987.

———. "Group Psychology and the Analysis of the Ego." In *The Standard Edition of the Complete Psychological Works of Sigmund Freud*, edited by James Strachey, vol. 28. London: Hogarth Press, 1984.

———. "Leonardo Da Vinci and a Memory of His Childhood." In *Standard Edition of the Complete Psychological Works of Sigmund Freud*, edited by James Strachey, vol. 11. London: Hogarth Press, 1957.

———. "Notes upon a Case of Obsessional Neurosis." In *Standard Edition of the Complete Psychological Works of Sigmund Freud*, edited by James Strachey, vol. 10. London: Hogarth Press, 1957.

———. "Resistances to Psychoanalysis." In *The Standard Edition of the Complete Psychological Works of Sigmund Freud*, edited by James Strachey, vol. 19. London: Hogarth Press, 1984.

———. *The Standard Edition of the Complete Psychological Works of Sigmund Freud*. Edited by James Strachey. 24 vols. London: Hogarth Press and the Institute of Psycho-analysis, 1953–1974.

———. "Three Essays on the Theory of Sexuality." In *The Standard Edition of the Complete Psychological Works of Sigmund Freud*, edited by James Strachey, vol. 7. London: Hogarth Press, 1984.

———. "The 'Uncanny.'" In *The Standard Edition of the Complete Psychological Works of Sigmund Freud*, edited by James Strachey, vol. 17. London: Hogarth Press, 1957.

Frontisi-Ducroux, Françoise. "Eros, Desire, and the Gaze." Translated by Nancy Kline. In *Sexuality in Anceint Art*, edited by Natalie Kampen and Bettina Ann Bergmann, 81–100. Cambridge: Cambridge University Press, 1996.

Frontisi-Ducroux, Françoise, and Jean Pierre Vernant. *Dans l'oeil du miroir*. Paris: O. Jacob, 1997.

Galilei, Galileo. *Le opere, edizione nationale.* Florence: G. Barbera, 1896.

Gerber, Douglas E., ed. *Greek Poetry and Philosophy: Studies in Honour of Leonard Woodbury,* Homage Series. Chico, CA: Scholars Press, 1984.

Gerhardt, Volker. "Zu Nietzsches Frühem Programm einer Ästhetischen Rechtfertigung der Welt." In *Pathos und Distanz.* Stuggart: Reclam, 1988.

Ghazzali, Abu Hamid Muhammed al-. *The Alchemy of Happiness.* Armonk, NY: M. E. Sharpe, 1991.

Gill, Christopher. *Personality in Greek Epic, Tragedy, and Philosophy: The Self in Dialogue.* Oxford: Clarendon Press, 1996.

Gilson, Etienne. *The Mystical Theology of Saint Bernard.* Translated by Alfred Howard Campbell Downes. New York: Sheed and Ward, 1940.

Gleason, Maud W. *Making Men: Sophists and Self-Presentation in Ancient Rome.* Princeton, NJ: Princeton University Press, 1994.

Goldhill, Simon. *Foucault's Virginity: Ancient Erotic Fiction and the History of Sexuality.* Cambridge: Cambridge University Press, 1995.

———. "Refracting Classical Vision: Changing Cultures of Viewing." In *Vision in Context: Historical and Contemporary Perspectives on Sight,* edited by Teresa Brennan and Martin Jay, 15–28. London: Routledge, 1996.

Goodman, Lenn Evan, ed. *Neoplatonism and Jewish Thought.* Vol. 7 of Studies in Neoplatonism, Ancient and Modern. Albany: State University of New York Press, 1992.

Gould, Thomas. *Platonic Love.* New York: Free Press of Glencoe, 1963.

Gray, Paul. *The Ego and Analysis of Defense.* Northvale, NJ: J. Aronson, 1994.

Greenberg, Clement. "Counter-Avant-Garde." *Art International* 14, no. 5 (1971): 16–19.

Griffin, Miriam T. "Philosophy, Politics, Politicians." In *Philosophia Togata: Essays on Philosophy and Roman Society,* edited by Miriam T. Griffin and Jonathan Barnes. Oxford: Clarendon Press; New York: Oxford University Press, 1989.

Griffith, Michael A. "Left-Hand Horses, Winged Souls, and Plato's *Phaedrus*: Sex and Philosophy." *Midwest Quarterly* 38 (1996–97): 31–40.

Griswold, Charles L. *Self-Knowledge in Plato's "Phaedrus."* New Haven, CT: Yale University Press, 1986.

Gunning, Tom. "Buster Keaton, or the Work of Comedy in the Age of Mechanical Reproduction." *Cineaste* 21.3 (1995).

———. *D. W. Griffith and the Origins of American Narrative Film: The Early Years at Biograph.* Urbana: University of Illinois Press, 1991.

Habinek, Thomas N. "An Aristocracy of Virtue: Seneca on the Beginnings of Wisdom." *Yale Classical Studies* 29 (1992): 187–203.

———. *The Politics of Latin Literature: Writing, Identity, and Empire in Ancient Rome.* Princeton, NJ: Princeton University Press, 1998.

Hallett, Judith P., and Marilyn B. Skinner. *Roman Sexualities.* Princeton, NJ: Princeton University Press, 1997.

Halperin, David M. "Forgetting Foucault: Acts, Identities, and the History of Sexuality." *Representations* 63 (1998): 93–120.

——. "Historicizing the Subject of Desire: Sexual Preferences and Erotic Identities in the Pseudo-Lucianic *Erotes*." In *Foucault and the Writing of History*, edited by Jan Goldstein, 19–34. Cambridge, MA: Blackwell, 1994.

——. *One Hundred Years of Homosexuality, and Other Essays on Greek Love*. New York: Routledge, 1990.

——. "Plato and Erotic Reciprocity." *Classical Antiquity* 5 (1986): 60–80.

——. "Plato and the Erotics of Narrativity." In *Innovations of Antiquity*, edited by Ralph Hexter and Daniel Selden, 95–126. London: Routledge, 1992.

——. "Platonic Eros and What Men Call Love." *Ancient Philosophy* 5 (1985): 161–204.

Halperin, David M., John J. Winkler, and Froma I. Zeitlin. *Before Sexuality: The Construction of Erotic Experience in the Ancient Greek World*. Princeton, NJ: Princeton University Press, 1990.

Hardy, Richard P. *Actualité de la révélation divine: Une étude des Tractatus in Iohannis Evangelium de Saint Augustin*. Paris: Beauchesne, 1974.

Hazlitt, William. "On the Love of Life." In *The Round Table: Characters of Shakespear's Plays*, 1–4. London: J. M. Dent; New York: Dutton, 1962.

Hegel, Georg Wilhelm Friedrich. *Aesthetics: Lectures on Fine Art*. Translated by T. M. Knox. Oxford: Oxford University Press, 1991.

Henderson, John G. "The Pupil as Teacher: Persius' Didactic Satire." *Ramus* 20 (1991): 123–48.

Hill, Charlotte, and William Wallace. *Erotica II: An Illustrated Anthology of Sexual Art and Literature*. New York: Carroll and Graf, 1993.

——. *Erotica III: An Illustrated Anthology of Sexual Art and Literature*. New York: Carroll and Graf, 1996.

Homer. *The Odyssey of Homer*. Translated by T. E. Shaw. Norwood, MA: Plimpton, 1932.

Hume, David. *An Inquiry concerning Human Understanding*. Indianapolis: Bobbs-Merrill, 1975.

Idel, Moshe. *Kabbalah: New Perspectives*. New Haven, CT: Yale University Press, 1988.

Iversen, Erik. *The Myth of Egypt and Its Hieroglyphs in European Tradition*. Princeton, NJ: Princeton University Press, 1993.

James, William. *The Varieties of Religious Experience: A Study in Human Nature*. New York: Random House, 1994.

Johnston, Mark. "Self-Deception and the Nature of Mind." In *Philosophy of Psychology: Debates on Psychological Explanation*, edited by Cynthia Macdonald and Graham Macdonald. Oxford: Blackwell, 1995.

Jones, Ernest. *The Life and Work of Sigmund Freud*. 3 vols. New York: Basic Books, 1957.

Jung, Wolfgang. "Borromini e il 'foror mathematicus' nel disegno dell' architettura." In *Francesco Borromini: Atti del Convegno Internazionale: Roma, 13–15 gennaio 2000* edited by Christoph L. Frommel and Elisabeth Sladek. Milan: Electa, 2000.

Kampen, Natalie, and Bettina Ann Bergmann. *Sexuality in Ancient Art: Near East, Egypt, Greece, and Italy*. Cambridge Studies in New Art History and Criticism. Cambridge: Cambridge University Press, 1996.

Kant, Immanuel. *The Conflict of the Faculties [Der Streit Der Fakultäten]*. Translated by Mary J. Gregor. New York: Abaris Books, 1979.

———. *Practical Philosophy*. Translated by Mary J. Gregor. Cambridge: Cambridge University Press, 1996.

Kastenbaum, Robert. *The Psychology of Death*. 3rd ed. New York: Springer, 2000.

Kaster, Robert. "The Taxonomy of Patience, or When Is Patientia Not a Virtue?" *Classical Philology* 97 (2002): 133–44.

Kern, Stephen. *The Culture of Love: Victorians to Moderns*. Cambridge, MA: Harvard University Press, 1992.

Keshavarz, Fatemeh. *Reading Mystical Lyric: The Case of Jalal Al-Din Rumi*. Columbia: University of South Carolina Press, 1998.

Kinsey, Alfred C. *Sexual Behavior in the Human Female*. New York: Pocket Books, 1953.

Kinsey, Alfred C., Wardell Baxter Pomeroy, and Clyde E. Martin. *Sexual Behavior in the Human Male*. Philadelphia: Saunders, 1948.

Kircher, Athanasius. *Iter Exstaticum Coeleste*. Würzburg: Endter, 1660.

Knuuttila, Simo. "Time and Creation in Augustine." In *The Cambridge Companion to Augustine*, edited by Eleonore Stump, 103–16. Cambridge: Cambridge University Press, 2001.

Kosman, L. A. "Platonic Love." In *Phronesis*. Suppl. vol. 2 of *Facets of Plato's Philosophy*, edited by W. H. Werkmeister, 53–69. Assen: Van Gorcum, 1976.

Kraut, Richard. *The Cambridge Companion to Plato*. Cambridge: Cambridge University Press, 1992.

Kretzmann, Norman, and Eleonore Stump. *The Cambridge Companion to Augustine*. Cambridge: Cambridge University Press, 2001.

Kristeva, Julia. *Tales of Love*. Translated by Leon S. Roudiez. New York: Columbia University Press, 1987.

Kuleshov, L. V. "The Art of the Cinema." Translated by Ronald Levaco. In *Kuleshov on Film: Writings of Lev Kuleshov*, edited by Ronald Levaco. Berkeley: University of California Press, 1974.

Kunitz, Stanley. *Passing Through*. New York: Norton, 1995.

Lacan, Jacques. *The Four Fundamental Concepts of Psycho-Analysis*. Translated by Alan Sheridan. New York: W. W. Norton, 1981.

———. "Intervention on Transference." In *In Dora's Case: Freud—Hysteria—Feminism*, edited by Charles Bernheimer and Claire Kahane, 92–104. New York: Columbia University Press, 1985.

———. *Le séminaire, Livre II: Le moi dans la théorie de Freud et dans la technique de la psychanalyse, 1954–1955*. Edited by Jacques Alain Miller. 1955; Paris: Seuil, 1978.

——. *The Seminar of Jacques Lacan, Book III: The Psychoses 1955–56*. New York: W. W. Norton, 1993.

——. *The Seminar of Jacques Lacan, Book VII: The Ethics of Psychoanalysis, 1959–1960* translated by Dennis Porter and edited by Jacques-Alain Miller. New York: W. W. Norton, 1992.

Laplanche, Jean. *Entre séduction et inspiration: L'homme*. Paris: Presses Universitaires de France, 1999.

——. *Life and Death in Psychoanalysis*. Translated by Jeffrey Mehlman. Baltimore: Johns Hopkins University Press, 1976.

——. *Problématiques IV: L'inconscient et le ça. Suivi de l'inconscient: Une étude psychanalytique par Jean Laplanche et Serge Leclaire*. Paris: Presses Universitaires de France, 1981.

Lavery, G. B. "Metaphors of War and Travel in Seneca's Prose Works." *Greece and Rome* 27 (1980): 147–57.

Lavin, Irving. *Bernini and the Unity of Visual Arts, Franklin Jasper Walls Lectures, 1975*. New York: Oxford University Press / Pierpont Morgan Library, 1980.

Lear, Jonathan. *Happiness, Death, and the Remainder of Life*. Cambridge, MA: Harvard University Press, 2000.

——. *Love and Its Place in Nature: A Philosophical Interpretation of Freudian Psychoanalysis*. New Haven, CT: Yale University Press, 1998.

——. *Love and Its Place in Nature: A Philosophical Interpretation of Freudian Psychoanalysis*. New York: Farrar, Straus and Giroux, 1990.

——. "Restlessness, Phantasy and the Concept of Mind." In *Open Minded: Working Out the Logic of the Soul*, 80–122. Cambridge, MA: Harvard University Press, 1998.

Lebeck, Anne. "The Central Myth of Plato's *Phaedrus*." *Greek, Roman and Byzantine Studies* 13 (1972): 267–90.

Leitao, David D. "Senecan Catoptrics and the Passion of Hostius Quadra (Sen. Nat. 1)." *Materiali e Discussioni* 41 (1998): 127–60.

Levinas, Emmanuel. *Totality and Infinity: An Essay on Exteriority*. Pittsburgh, PA: Duquesne University Press, 1969.

Leyda, Jay. *Kino: A History of the Russian and Soviet Film*. London: George Allen and Unwin, 1960.

Lifton, Robert Jay. *The Life of the Self: Toward a New Psychology*. New York: Simon and Schuster, 1976.

Lilja, Saara. *Homosexuality in Republican and Augustan Rome, Commentationes Humanarum Litterarum, 74*. Helsinki, Finland: Societas Scientiarum Fennica, 1983.

Lobel, Edgar, and Denys Lionel Page, eds. *Poetarum Lesbiorum Fragmenta*. Oxford: Clarendon Press, 1955.

Loewald, Hans. *The Essential Loewald*. Hagerstown, MA: University Publishing Group, 2000.

Loizou, Andros, Harry Lesser, Northern Association for Philosophy (Great Britain), and Society for Greek Political Thought. *Polis and Politics: Essays in Greek Moral and Political*

Philosophy. Avebury Series in Philosophy. Aldershot, Hants, England: Avebury, 1990.

Lonergan, Bernard J. F. *Verbum: Word and Idea in Thomas Aquinas.* Notre Dame, IN: University of Notre Dame Press, 1970.

Long, A. A. *Epictetus: A Stoic and Socratic Guide to Life.* Oxford: Clarendon Press; New York: Oxford University Press, 2002.

———. "Soul and Body in Stoicism." *Phronesis* 27, no. 1 (1982): 34–57.

Lucie-Smith, Edward. *Ars Erotica: An Arousing History of Erotic Art.* New York: Rizzoli, 1997.

Lucretius. *De rerum natura I.* Edited by P. Michael Brown. Bristol: Bristol Classical Press, 1984.

———. *De rerum natura VI.* 3 vols. Edited by Cyril Bailey. Oxford: Clarendon, 1947.

Luhmann, Niklas. *Love as Passion: The Codification of Intimacy.* Translated by Jeremy Gaines and Doris L. Jones. Cambridge, MA: Harvard University Press, 1986.

MacMullen, Ramsay. "Roman Attitudes towards Greek Love." *Historia* 31 (1982): 484–502.

Makowski, John F. "Nisus and Euryalus: A Platonic Relationship." *Classical Journal* 85 (1989–90): 1–15.

Malinowski, Bronislaw. *Sex and Repression in Savage Society.* London: Harcourt Brace, 1927.

Malinowski, Bronislaw, and Havelock Ellis. *The Sexual Life of Savages in North-Western Melanesia: An Ethnographic Account of Courtship, Marriage and Family Life among the Natives of Trobriand Islands, British New Guinea.* New York: Halcyon House, 1929.

Marivaux, Pierre Carlet de Chamblain de. *Théâtre complet, Bibliothèque de la Pléiade.* Paris: Gallimard, Bibliothèque de la Pléiade, 1994.

Markus, R. A. "Augustine, Reason, and Illumination." In *The Cambridge History of Later Greek and Early Medieval Philosophy*, edited by A. H. Armstrong, 362–73. London: Cambridge University Press, 1967.

Masters, William H., Virginia E. Johnson, Bruce R. Voeller, and Reproductive Biology Research Foundation (U.S.). *Human Sexual Response.* Boston: Little Brown, 1966.

McClure, Laura K., ed. *Sexuality and Gender in the Classical World: Readings and Sources.* Oxford: Blackwell, 2002.

McGinn, Bernard. "Love, Knowledge, and *Unio Mystica* in the Western Christian Tradition." In *Mystical Union and Monotheistic Faith: An Ecumenical Dialogue*, 59–86. New York: Macmillan, 1989.

———. *The Mystical Thought of Meister Eckhart: The Man from Whom God Hid Nothing.* New York: Crossroad, 2001.

Mead, Margaret. *Coming of Age in Samoa: A Psychological Study of Primitive Youth for Western Civilisation.* New York: Morrow, 1928.

———. *From the South Seas: Studies of Adolescence and Sex in Primitive Societies.* New York: Morrow, 1939.

Melville, Robert. *Erotic Art of the West.* New York: G. P. Putnam's Sons, 1973.

Metz, Christian. *The Imaginary Signifier: Psychoanalysis and the Cinema.* Translated by Celia

Britton, Annwyl Williams, Ben Brewster, and Alfred Guzzetti. Bloomington: Indiana University Press, 1982.

Meyendorff, John. *Byzantine Theology: Historical Trends and Doctrinal Themes*. New York: Fordham, 1974.

Modleski, Tania. *The Women Who Knew Too Much: Hitchcock and Feminist Theory*. New York: Routledge, 1988.

Morewedge, Parviz. *Neoplatonism and Islamic Thought*. Albany: State University of New York Press, 1992.

———. *Neoplatonism and Jewish Thought*. Albany: State University of New York Press, 1992.

Mulvey, Laura. "Visual Pleasures and Narrative Cinema." In *Visual and Other Pleasures*, 14–26. Bloomington: Indiana University Press, 1989.

Nadeau, Maurice. *The History of Surrealism*. London: Penguin Books, 1973.

Nagel, Thomas. *The View from Nowhere*. New York: Oxford University Press, 1986.

Nasio, Juan-David. *Hysteria from Freud to Lacan: The Splendid Child of Psychoanalysis*. Translated by Susan Fairfield. New York: Other Press, 1998.

———. *Hysteria from Freud to Lacan: The Splendid Child of Psychoanalysis*. Northvale, NJ: J. Aronson, 1997.

Natali, Monica. "Gli Influssi Del Platonismo Sul Neostoicismo Senecano." *Rivista di filosofia neo-scolastica* 84 (1992): 494–514.

Nietzsche, Friedrich Wilhelm. *Beyond Good and Evil: Prelude to a Philosophy of the Future*. Translated by Walter Kaufmann. New York: Vintage Books, 1966.

———. *Daybreak: Thoughts on the Prejudices of Morality*. Translated by R. J. Hollingdale. Cambridge: Cambridge University Press, 1982.

———. *The Gay Science*. Translated by Walter Kaufmann. New York: Vintage, 1974.

———. *Human, All Too Human: A Book for Free Spirits*. Translated by R. J. Hollingdale. Cambridge: Cambridge University Press, 1990.

———. *On the Genealogy of Morals*. Translated by Walter Kaufmann and R. J. Hollingdale. New York: Vintage Books, 1969.

———. *Sämtliche Werke: Kritische Studienausgabe*. Edited by G. Colli and M. Montinari. Munich: DTV; New York: De Gruyter, 1988.

———. *Thus Spoke Zarathustra: A Book for All and None*. Translated by Walter Kaufmann. New York: Viking Press, 1966.

———. *Twilight of the Idols; and, the Anti-Christ*. Translated by R. J. Hollingdale. Baltimore: Penguin, 1968.

———. *Untimely Meditations*. Translated by R. J. Hollingdale. Cambridge: Cambridge University Press, 1990.

———. *The Will to Power*. Translated by Walter Kaufmann and R. J. Hollingdale. New York: Vintage, 1968.

Nussbaum, Martha Craven. *The Cosmopolitan Tradition*. New Haven, CT: Yale University Press, forthcoming.

——. "*Erôs* and Ethical Norms: Philosophers Respond to a Cultural Dilemma." In *The Sleep of Reason: Erotic Experience and Sexual Ethics in Ancient Greece and Rome*, edited by Martha Nussbaum and J. Sihvola, 55–94. Chicago: University of Chicago Press, 2002.

——. "Eros and the Wise: The Stoic Response to a Cultural Dilemma." *Oxford Studies in Ancient Philosophy* 13 (1995): 231–67.

——. *Hiding from Humanity: Disgust, Shame, and the Law*. Princeton, NJ: Princeton University Press, 2004.

——. *Love's Knowledge: Essays on Philosophy and Literature*. New York: Oxford University Press, 1990.

——. "Steerforth's Arm: Love and the Moral Point of View." In *Love's Knowledge: Essays on Philosophy and Literature*, 335–64. New York: Oxford University Press, 1990.

——. *The Therapy of Desire: Theory and Practice in Hellenistic Ethics*. Princeton, NJ: Princeton University Press, 1994.

——. *Upheavals of Thought: The Intelligence of Emotions*. Cambridge: Cambridge University Press, 2001.

Nussbaum, Martha Craven, and Juha Sihvola, eds. *The Sleep of Reason: Erotic Experience and Sexual Ethics in Ancient Greece and Rome*. Chicago: University of Chicago Press, 2002.

Nye, Robert A., ed. *Sexuality*, Oxford Readers. Oxford: Oxford University Press, 1999.

Nygren, Anders. *Agape and Eros*. Translated by Philip S. Watson. New York: Harper and Row, 1969.

Ober, J., and B. Strauss. "Drama, Political Rhetoric, and the Discourse of Athenian Democracy." In *Nothing to Do with Dionysus?* edited by J. J. Winkler and F. I. Zeitlin, 237–70. Princeton, NJ: Princeton University Press, 1990.

O'Daly, Gerard J. P. *Augustine's Philosophy of Mind*. Berkeley: University of California Press, 1987.

Oliensis, Ellen. "The Erotics of *Amicitia*: Readings in Tibullus, Propertius, and Horace." In *Roman Sexualities*, ed. Judith P. Hallett and Marilyn B. Skinner, 151–71. Princeton, NJ: Princeton University Press, 1997.

Osborne, Catherine. *Eros Unveiled: Plato and the God of Love*. Oxford: Clarendon Press, 1994.

Ostwald, Martin, Ralph Mark Rosen, and Joseph Farrell. *Nomodeiktes: Greek Studies in Honor of Martin Ostwald*. Ann Arbor: University of Michigan Press, 1993.

Parker, Holt. "The Observed of All Observers: Spectacle, Applause, and Cultural Poetics in the Roman Theater Audience." In *The Art of Ancient Spectacle*, edited by Bettina Ann Bergmann and Christine Kondoleon, 163–80. Washington: National Gallery of Art, 1999. Distributed by Yale University Press.

——. "The Teratogenic Grid." In *Roman Sexualities*, edited by Judith P. Hallett and Marilyn B. Skinner, 47–65. Princeton, NJ: Princeton University Press, 1997.

Paz, Octavio. *The Double Flame: Love and Eroticism*. Translated by Helen Lane. New York: Harcourt Brace, 1995.

——. *An Erotic Beyond: Sade*. New York: Harcourt Brace, 1998.

——. *Marcel Duchamp, Appearance Stripped Bare*. New York: Arcade, 1990.

Pelikan, Jaroslav Jan. *What Has Athens to Do with Jerusalem? Timaeus and Genesis in Counterpoint.* Ann Arbor: University of Michigan Press, 1997.

Percy, William A. *Pederasty and Pedagogy in Archaic Greece.* Urbana: University of Illinois Press, 1996.

Perlove, Shelley Karen. *Bernini and the Idealization of Death: The Blessed Ludovica Albertoni and the Altieri Chapel.* University Park: Pennsylvania State University Press, 1990.

Phillips, Adam. *Darwin's Worms.* New York: Basic Books, 2000.

Pippin, Robert B. "Deceit, Desire, and Democracy: Nietzsche on Modern Eros." *International Studies in Philosophy* 32, no. 3 (2000): 63–70.

———. "Gay Science and Corporeal Knowledge." *Nietzsche-Studien* 29 (2000).

———. "Love and Death in Nietzsche." In *Religion after Metaphysics*, edited by Mark Wrathall. New York: Cambridge University Press, 2003.

———. "Morality as Psychology; Psychology as Morality: Nietzsche, Eros, and Clumsy Lovers." In *Nietzche's Postmoralism: Essays on Nietzche's Prelude to Philosophy's Future*, edited by Richard Schacht, 79–99. Cambridge: Cambridge University Press, 2001.

———. "Nietzsche and the Melancholy of Modernity." *Social Research* 66, no. 2 (1999): 495–519.

———. "What Is the Question for Which Hegel's 'Theory of Recognition' Is the Answer?" *The European Journal of Philosophy* 8, no. 2 (2000): 155–72.

Plato. *The Dialogues of Plato.* Translated by Benjamin Jowett. Oxford: Clarendon Press, 1876.

———. *Platonis opera.* Edited by John Burnet. 5 vols. Scriptorum Classicorum Bibliotheca Oxoniensis. Oxonii: E typographeo Clarendoniano, 1902.

———. *Plato's Phaedrus.* Translated by R. Hackforth. Cambridge: Cambridge University Press, 1972.

———. *The Symposium of Plato.* Edited by Robert Gregg Bury. 2nd ed. Cambridge: W. Heffer and Sons, 1932.

———. *Symposium.* Edited by Kenneth James Dover. Cambridge: Cambridge University Press, 1980.

———. *Symposium.* Translated by Michael Joyce. In *Collected Dialogues of Plato*, edited by Edith Hamilton and Huntington Cairns, 526–74. Princeton, NJ: Princeton University Press, 1961.

———. *Symposium.* Translated by Alexander Nehamas and Paul Woodruff. Indianapolis: Hackett, 1989.

———. *Symposium.* Translated by Alexander Nehamas and Paul Woodruff. In *Plato: Complete Works*, edited by John M. Cooper, 458–505. Indianapolis: Hackett, 1997.

———. *Symposium.* In *Lysis, Symposium, Gorgias*, edited by W. R. M. Lamb. Vol. 3 of *Plato in Twelve Volumes*. London: Heinemann, 1925.

Pope, Marvin H. *Song of Songs: A New Translation with Introduction and Commentary.* Vol. 7 of *The Anchor Bible.* Garden City, NY: Doubleday, 1977.

Porter, James I. "Epicurean Attachments: Life, Pleasure, Beauty, Friendship, and Piety." *Cronache Ercolanesi* 33 (2003): 129–51.

———. "Lucretius and the Poetics of Void." In *Le jardin Romain: Épicurisme et poésie à Rome*, edited by Annick Monet, 197–226. Villeneuve d'Ascq: Université de Charles-de-Gaulle-Lille 3, 2003.

Portoghesi, Paolo. *Roma Del Rinascimento*. Milan: Electa, 1971.

———. *Rome of the Renaissance*. London: Phaidon, 1972.

Price, A. W. *Love and Friendship in Plato and Aristotle*. Oxford: Clarendon Press; New York: Oxford University Press, 1989.

Proust, Marcel. *Du côté de chez Swann*. Vol. 1 of *À la recherche du temps perdu*. Edited by Jean-Yves Tadié. Paris: Gallimard, 1987.

———. *À la recherche du temps perdu*. Edited by Pierre Clarac and André Ferré. 3 vols. Bibliothèque de la Pléiade. Paris: Gallimard, 1954.

———. *Remembrance of Things Past*. Translated by C. K. Scott Moncrieff and Terence Kilmartin. New York: Random House, 1981.

———. *Swann's Way*. Vol. 1 of *In Seach of Lost Time*. Translated by C. K. Moncrieff, Terence Kilmartin, and D. J. Enright (revis.). New York: Modern Library, 1992.

Ragland-Sullivan, Ellie. *Essays on the Pleasures of Death: From Freud to Lacan*. New York: Routledge, 1995.

Rahner, Karl. "Thomas Aquinas on the Incomprehensibility of God." In *Celebrating the Medieval Heritage: A Colloquy on the Thought of Aquinas and Bonaventure*, edited by David Tracy, 107–25. Chicago: University of Chicago Press, 1978.

———. "Thomas Aquinas on the Incomprehensibility of God." *The Journal of Religion* Suppl. 58, no. 5 (1978): 107–25.

Raubicheck, Walter, and Walter Srebnick. *Hitchcock's Rereleased Films: From "Rope" to "Vertigo."* Contemporary Film and Television Series. Detroit: Wayne State University Press, 1991.

Rice, Louise. "The Pentecostal Meaning of Borromini's Sant' Ivo Alla Sapienza." In *Francesco Borromini: Atti del Convegno Internazionale, Roma, 13–15 Gennaio 2000*, edited by Christoph L. Frommel and Elisabeth Sladek, 259–70. Milan: Electa, 2000.

Richlin, Amy. *The Garden of Priapus: Sexuality and Aggression in Roman Humor*. 2nd ed. New York: Oxford University Press, 1992.

———. "Not before Homosexuality: The Materiality of the *Cinaedus* and the Roman Law against Love between Men." *Journal of the History of Sexuality* 3 (1993): 523–73.

———. ed. *Pornography and Representation in Greece and Rome*. New York: Oxford University Press, 1992.

Rist, John M. *Augustine: Ancient Thought Baptized*. Cambridge: Cambridge University Press, 1994.

———. *Stoic Philosophy*. London: Cambridge University Press, 1969.

Roger, Philippe. "C'est donc un amoureux qui parle et qui dit . . ." *Critique* 361–62 (June–July) (1977).

———. ed. *Éros 2000—Critique (June–July 2000)*. Paris: Critique, 2000.

Roller, Matthew B. *Constructing Autocracy: Aristocrats and Emperors in Julio-Claudian Rome*. Princeton, NJ: Princeton University Press, 2001.

Rosen, Stanley. *Plato's Symposium*. 2nd ed. New Haven, CT: Yale University Press, 1987.

Rothman, William. "*Vertigo*: The Unknown Woman in Hitchcock." In *The "I" of the Camera: Essays in Film Criticism, History, and Aesthetics*. Cambridge: Cambridge University Press, 1988.

Rougemont, Denis de. *Love in the Western World*. Translated by Montgomery Belgion. New York: Harcourt, Brace, 1940.

Rowe, C. J. *Plato's Phaedrus*. Wiltshire, England: Warmister, 1986.

Rowland, Ingrid D. *The Culture of the High Renaissance: Ancients and Moderns in Sixteenth-Century Rome*. Cambridge: Cambridge University Press, 1998.

Sandbach, F. H. *The Stoics*. New York: W. W. Norton, 1975.

Santas, Gerasimos Xenophon. *Plato and Freud: Two Theories of Love*. Oxford:Blackwell, 1988.

Scarry, Elaine. *On Beauty and Being Just*. Princeton, NJ: Princeton University Press, 1999.

Schiller, Friedrich. *On the Aesthetic Education of Man in a Series of Letters*. Translated by Reginald Snell. New York: F. Ungar, 1965.

Schütze, Sebastian. "L'architettura come esercizio morale: Letture Senechiane Di Borromini." In *Francesco Borromini: Atti del Convegno Internazionale, Roma, 13–15 Gennaio 2000*, edited by Christoph Luitpold Frommel and Elisabeth Sladek, 483. Milano: Electa, 2000.

Scott, John Beldon. "S. Ivo Alla Sapienza and Borromini's Symbolic Language." *Journal of the Society of Architectural Historians* 41 (1982): 302–3.

Scotti, Aurora, and Nicola Soldini. "Borromini milanese." In *Il giovane Borromini: Dagli Esordi a San Carlo Alle Quattro Fontane*, edited by Manuela Kahn-Rossi and Marco Franciolli. Lugano: Museo cantonale d'arte and Skira, 1999.

Scruton, Roger. *Sexual Desire: A Moral Philosophy of the Erotic*. New York: Free Press, 1986.

Sells, Michael Anthony. *Mystical Languages of Unsaying*. Chicago: University of Chicago Press, 1994.

Silverman, Hugh, ed. *Philosophy and Desire*. London: Routledge, 2000.

Simona, Michea. "Le geometrie del Borromini." In *Il giovane Borromini: Dagli Esordi a San Carlo Alle Quattro Fontane*, edited by Manuela Kahn-Rossi and Marco Franciolli. Milan: Skira, 1999.

Singer, Irving. *Meaning in Life: The Creation of Value*. New York: Free Press, 1992.

———. *The Nature of Love*. 3 vols. Chicago: University of Chicago Press, 1987.

Singer, Peter. *Rethinking Life and Death: The Collapse of Our Traditional Ethics*. New York: St. Martin's, 1994.

Soble, Alan. *The Philosophies of Sex and Love: An Introduction*. St. Paul: Paragon House, 1986.

———. *The Structure of Love*. New Haven, CT: Yale University Press, 1990.

Solomon, Robert C., and Kathleen Marie Higgins. *The Philosophy of (Erotic) Love*. Lawrence: University Press of Kansas, 1991.

Spinoza, Benedictus de. *Ethics*. Translated by G. H. R. Parkinson. Oxford: Oxford University Press, 2000.

Steinberg, Leo. *Borromini's San Carlo alle Quattro Fontane: A Study in Multiple Form and Architectural Symbolism, Outstanding Dissertations in the Fine Arts*. New York: Garland, 1977.

Stinger, Charles L. *The Renaissance in Rome*. Bloomington: Indiana University Press, 1998.

Stokes, Michael C. *Plato's Socratic Conversations: Drama and Dialectic in Three Dialogues*. Baltimore: Johns Hopkins University Press, 1986.

Strand, Mark. *Dark Harbor*. New York: Knopf, 1993.

Strauss, Leo. *Leo Strauss on Plato's Symposium*. Edited by Seth Benardete. Chicago: University of Chicago Press, 2001.

Szymborska, Wislawa. *View with a Grain of Sand*. Translated by Stanislaw Baranczak and Clare Cavanagh. New York: Harcourt, Brace, 1995.

Taylor, Rabun. "Two Pathic Subcultures in Ancient Rome." *Journal of the History of Sexuality* 7 (1996–97): 319–71.

Tillich, Paul. *Systematic Theology*. Chicago: University of Chicago Press, 1967.

Tobin, Frank J. *Meister Eckhart, Thought and Language*. Philadelphia: University of Pennsylvania Press, 1986.

Todorov, Tzvetan. *Introduction to Poetics*. Translated by Richard Howard. Minneapolis: University of Minnesota Press, 1981.

Tomkins, Calvin. *Duchamp: A Biography*. New York: H. Holt, 1996.

Torre, Chiara. "Il cavallo immagine del Sapiens in Seneca." *Maia* 47 (1995): 371–78.

Tracy, David. *Plurality and Ambiguity: Hermeneutics, Religion, Hope*. Chicago: University of Chicago Press, 1987.

Tracy, Valerie A. "Roman Dandies and Transvestites." *Échos du monde classique* 20 (1976): 60–63.

Trapp, M. B. "Plato's *Phaedrus* in Second-Century Greek Literature." In *Antonine Literature*, edited by D. A. Russell, 141–73. Oxford: Clarendon Press; New York: Oxford University Press, 1990.

Trimingham, J. Spencer. *The Sufi Orders in Islam*. Oxford: Clarendon Press, 1971.

Trumpner, Katie. "Fragments of the Mirror: Self Reference, Mise en Abyme, *Vertigo*." In *Hitchcock's Rereleased Films: From "Rope" to "Vertigo,"* edited by Walter Raubicheck and Walter Srebnick, 157–88. Detroit: Wayne State University Press, 1991.

Tsivian, Yuri. *Early Cinema in Russia and Its Cultural Reception*. Translated by Alan Bodger. London: Routledge, 1994.

Van Sickle, John. "Plat. Phaedr. 255d, 3–6." *Museum Criticum* 8/9 (1973–74): 198–99.

Verstraete, Beert Christian. "Slavery and the Social Dynamics of Male Homosexual Relations in Ancient Rome." *Journal of the History of Sexuality* 5 (1979–80): 227–36.

——. *Homosexuality in Ancient Greek and Roman Civilization: A Critical Bibliography with Supplement*. Toronto: Canadian Gay Archives, 1982.

Vertov, Dziga. "Kinoks: A Revolution." Translated by Kevin O'Brien. In *Kino-Eye: The Writings of Dziga Vertov*, edited by Annette Michelson, 17. Berkeley: University of California Press, 1984.

Veyne, Paul. "L'homosexualité à Rome." *L'Histoire* 30 (1981): 76–78.

Vlastos, Gregory. *Platonic Studies*. Princeton, NJ: Princeton University Press, 1973.

Vries, Gerrit Jacob de. *A Commentary on the "Phaedrus" of Plato*. Amsterdam: Adolf M. Hakkert, 1969.

Walker, Andrew. "Eros and the Eye in the Love-Letters of Philostratus." *Proceedings of the Cambridge Philological Society* 38 (1992): 132–48.

Walters, Jonathan. "Invading the Roman Body: Manliness and Impenetrability in Roman Thought." In *Roman Sexualities*, edited by Judith P. Hallett and Marilyn B. Skinner, 23–43. Princeton, NJ: Princeton University Press, 1997.

———. "Making a Spectacle: Deviant Men, Invective, and Pleasure." *Arethusa* 31, no. 355–68 (1998).

Ward, Graham. *The Postmodern God: A Theological Reader, Blackwell Readings in Modern Theology*. Malden, MA: Blackwell, 1997.

Warren, James. "Epicurean Immortality." *Oxford Studies in Ancient Philosophy* 18 (2000): 231–61.

White, F. C. "Love and the Individual in Plato's *Phaedrus*." *Classical Quarterly* 40 (1990): 396–406.

Whitman, Walt. *Leaves of Grass*. Edited by Harold W. Blodgett and Sculley Bradley. New York: W. W. Norton.

Wilde, Oscar. "The Decay of Lying." In *Intentions*. London: Methuen, 1913.

Williams, Bernard. "The Markopulos Case: Reflections on the Tedium of Immortality." In *Problems of the Self: Philosophical Papers 1956–1972*, 82–100. Cambridge: Cambridge University Press, 1973.

Williams, Craig A. *Roman Homosexuality: Ideologies of Masculinity in Classical Antiquity, Ideologies of Desire*. Oxford: Oxford University Press, 1999.

Williams, Linda. "Film Body: An Implantation of Perversions." In *Narrative, Apparatus, Ideology: A Film Theory Reader*, edited by Philip Rosen, 507–34. New York: Columbia University Press, 1986.

———. *Hard Core: Power, Pleasure, and the "Frenzy of the Visible."* Berkeley: University of California Press, 1989.

Winkler, John J. *The Constraints of Desire: The Anthropology of Sex and Gender in Ancient Greece*. New York: Routledge, 1990.

Wollheim, Richard. *The Thread of Life*. Cambridge, MA: Harvard University Press, 1984.

Wood, Robin. *Hitchcock's Films Revisited*. New York: Columbia University Press, 1989.

Zeitlin, Froma I. Foreword to *The Poetics of Eros in Ancient Greece* by Claude Calame. Translated by Janet Lloyd. Princeton, NJ: Princeton University Press, 1999.

Žižek, Slavoj. *The Ticklish Subject: The Absent Centre of Political Ontology*. London: Verso, 1999.

Zupančič, Alenka. *Ethics of the Real: Kant, Lacan*. London: Verso, 2000.

Contributors

SHADI BARTSCH is a professor of classics and in the Committee on the History of Culture and the Committee on the Ancient Mediterranean World at the University of Chicago.

THOMAS BARTSCHERER is a doctoral candidate in the Committee on Social Thought at the University of Chicago.

PETER BROOKS is a university professor of English at the University of Virginia.

J. M. COETZEE is the Distinguished Service Professor in the Committee on Social Thought at the University of Chicago and an honorary research fellow in the Department of English at the University of Adelaide.

CATHARINE EDWARDS is a senior lecturer in the School of History, Classics, and Archaeology at Birkbeck College, the University of London.

ANTHONY GRAFTON is the Henry Putnam Professor of History at Princeton University.

TOM GUNNING is a professor of art history and in the Committee on Cinema and Media Studies at the University of Chicago.

DAVID M. HALPERIN is the W. H. Auden Collegiate Professor of English Language and Literature at the University of Michigan.

VALENTINA IZMIRLIEVA is an assistant professor of Slavic languages and literatures at Columbia University.

JONATHAN LEAR is the John U. Nef Distinguished Service Professor in the Committee on Social Thought and of Philosophy at the University of Chicago.

ERIC MARTY is a professor of literature at the Université Paris 7.

SUSAN MITCHELL is the Mary Blossom Lee Professor in Creative Writing at Florida Atlantic University.

GLENN W. MOST is a professor in the Committee on Social Thought at the University of Chicago and a professor of Greek philology at the Scuola Normale Superiore di Pisa.

MARTHA C. NUSSBAUM is the Ernst Freund Distinguished Service Professor of Law and Ethics, of Philosophy, and of Divinity at the University of Chicago.

ROBERT B. PIPPIN is the Raymond W. and Martha Hilpert Gruner Distinguished Service Professor in the Committee on Social Thought and a professor of philosophy at the University of Chicago.

JAMES I. PORTER is a professor of classical studies and of comparative literature at the University of Michigan.

PHILIPPE ROGER is a researcher with the French National Center for Scientific Research and professor of literature at the École des Hautes Études en Sciences Sociales, Paris, and the University of Virginia, Charlottesville.

INGRID ROWLAND is the Andrew W. Mellon Professor in the Humanities at the American Academy in Rome.

ERIC SANTNER is the Philip and Ida Romberg Professor of Germanic Studies and a professor in the Committee on Jewish Studies at the University of Chicago.

MARK STRAND is the Andrew MacLeish Distinguished Service Professor in the Committee on Social Thought at the University of Chicago.

DAVID TRACY is the Andrew Greeley and Grace McNichols Greeley Distinguished Service Professor in the Divinity School, in the Committee on

Social Thought, and in the Committee on the Analysis of Ideas and Study of Methods at the University of Chicago.

RICHARD WOLLHEIM was, at the time of his death in 2003, a professor of philosophy at the University of California, Berkeley.

SLAVOJ ŽIŽEK is a researcher at the University of Ljubljana.

Index